Charlotte Ford's
Book of

Modern Manners

CHARLOTTE FORD

A FIRESIDE BOOK

Published by Simon and Schuster

NEW YORK

First Fireside Edition, 1982

Published by Simon and Schuster
A Division of Gulf & Western Corporation
Simon & Schuster Building
Rockefeller Center
1230 Avenue of the Americas
New York, New York 10020

FIRESIDE and colophon are trademarks of Simon & Schuster

Designed by Eve Metz

Manufactured in the United States of America

10 9 8 7 6 5 4 3 2 1
10 9 8 7 6 5 4 3 2 1 Pbk.

Library of Congress Cataloging in Publication Data

Ford, Charlotte, date.
  Charlotte Ford's Book of Modern Manners.

  Includes index.
  1. Etiquette. I. Title. II. Title: Book of
Modern Manners.
BJ1853.F68   1979   395   79-22251

ISBN 0-671-24268-7
ISBN 0-671-45769-1 Pbk.

TO ELENA WITH LOVE

ACKNOWLEDGMENTS

This book is the result of the efforts of many people.

John Balan, Edward Bleier, Janet Brown, Catheryn Cheal, William Clark, Bonnie Dahan, David Faulkner, Penny Feinberg, Dierdre Francis, Pamela Barkentin Goldstein, Martha Grossman, George Harpootlian, Michael Naté, the National Gay Task Force, Bridget Potter, Tanya Priber, Judith Sachs, Lynn Schneider, Elsie Stern, Brita Stone, Marvin B. Sussman, Ph.D., Helen Terplak, Sheldon Wachler, Catherine Wyler, Huibert Zuur and especially *Bride's Magazine* all contributed their expertise in specific areas.

Carol Baum, Thomas Baum, Barbara Held, Venable Herndon, Cora Marcus, Patricia Meehan, Honor Moore, Carolyn Parqueth, Vera Schneider and Adrienne Starkman offered valuable suggestions and support.

Berenice Hoffman, Emily Levine, Cheryl Merser, Charlotte Sheedy, Bennett Sims and Nan Talese were cheerful and enthusiastic participants throughout. Their time and their excellent advice were most important.

Finally, I want particularly to thank Claudia Stern, whose constant participation helped me so much to make this book a reality.

CONTENTS

8 CONTENTS

THE WEDDING TAKES PLACE, 249
Seating • The Processional • The Ceremony (The New Wedding) • Old Problems at New Weddings • The Recessional

THE RECEPTION, 256
The Responsibilities of Bride and Groom at the Reception • The Receiving Line • Special Problems • Throwing the Bouquet • A Do-It-Yourself At-Home Reception • A Reception at a Friend's House

MARRYING AGAIN, 262
Telling the Children • Getting to Know Future Stepchildren • Telling Your Ex • Invitations • What to Wear • The Ceremony • Your Children and Your Wedding • Thank-You Notes

8 • MARRIAGE   269

BEGINNINGS, 269
Changing Your Name—Or Not • Sharing Bed and Board • Decorating: Starting from Scratch • What's Mine Is Yours • The Second Time Around: Redecorating • Sharing Closets • Sharing a Bathroom • Sharing a Bed

FINANCES, 275
Managing Money Jointly • Investments and Savings • Two-Career Families: Keeping Your Money Separately • When a Woman Supports a Man

MARRIAGE CONTRACTS, 279
What Does a Marriage Contract Contain? • Names • Careers • Finances • Children • Divorce • Care of the Household • Other Items to Include in a Marriage Contract

CHILDLESS OR CHILD-FREE, 285

9 • LIVING TOGETHER   286

MOVING IN TOGETHER, 287
My Place or Yours • A Living-Together Announcement and Change-of-Address Card • Telephone and Mailbox Listings • Moving into a New Apartment Together • Establishing Yourself in the Community • A Housewarming

DEALING WITH FAMILY, 291
Telling Them the News • Family Telling Others in the Family • Winning Over Unaccepting Parents

WHEN TO BE SPECIFIC ABOUT YOUR RELATIONSHIP, 294

LIVING TOGETHER AND YOUR PROFESSIONAL LIFE, 295

WHEN ONE OF YOU IS A PARENT, 296
"Stepchildren" • "Stepparent" • Introductions

INTRODUCTION

As a child, I lived in a house with a large staff of servants and many rules. My sister, my brother and I were not allowed to answer the telephone (that was the butler's job) or go into the kitchen (we might disrupt the kitchen staff) or make our own beds!

Today very few families have the kind of household my parents maintained, but we all still live in a world of certain social traditions. Even in a country where the frontier expansion and the assumption of class mobility blurred the lines of rigid class distinctions, manners, particularly in the cities, were considered important. Learning the code that "Society" had established gave so-called plain folk the means of acquiring the symbols of status. The popularity of etiquette books throughout most of our history is proof enough that proper behavior has always been a foremost concern.

Inevitably, the notion of what's proper has changed over two centuries, but never so rapidly as it is changing today. Automation has produced a do-it-yourself way of life which has changed the old conventions. Louis Sullivan, an architect working in Chicago at the turn of the century, declared that the design of a building must follow the function of the building. Sullivan coined a sensible slogan for modern times: "Form follows function." This can be used to characterize the way our social forms follow the style in which we live. Our style of life has no room for the baroque touches of an era past, an era where the word "etiquette" conjured up visions of drawing rooms, silver services, straight backs aligned in straight chairs and servants summoned silently by the pull of a velvet cord. We are no longer faced with endless rules governing propriety. Just as our art and design have become minimal in style, so the frills of our manners and protocol have been stripped away —shirt sleeves have taken the place of vest, jacket and tie, and the barbecue the place of the seated formal dinner—until we are left the core of what is etiquette today. That core is graciousness; the way in which we make other people feel at home and comfortable in any situation is the essence of today's etiquette. But it would be a mistake to confuse flexibility with a lack of structure.

At this time in the twentieth century we are less concerned with doing something in a certain way "because it is done" than we are with expressing our own individuality. But while expressing ourselves it is important to maintain peaceful coexistence with family, business associates, friends and, yes, enemies.

In many ways, we pride ourselves on living in the do-your-own-thing era. Individuality is fine, but we are all social beings, and, after all, no man is an island. We rely, most of all, on the courtesy of those we come in contact with; we all value the person who is polite, and who simply knows how to make others feel good. This is really what etiquette is all about—it's the graciousness to coexist peacefully and productively in the lives that we, as individuals, have set up for ourselves. A large part of graciousness comes from the heart and cannot be learned from any book, but there are certain foundations that we have set up in our society, customs that make coexisting pleasurable—and, for that matter, civilized. Whether you wear white gloves (I don't) is entirely a matter of choice; when courtesy requires a thank-you note is not. Certainly we must be true to ourselves, but being true to others is just as important—and just as satisfying.

I still set a fairly formal table, which I prefer and which is also for me a matter of habit. This, of course, is not everyone's preference, and strict formality seems to be disappearing rapidly. But even in informal settings, etiquette is important. There is a solid foundation on which the varying rules of etiquette must be built for manners to have meaning in our lives, and the keystone to that foundation is graciousness—a graciousness that makes people feel at ease with themselves, with you, with the situation, whatever it may be.

We live in a world where social patterns are no longer fixed or even stable. Your social position doesn't make your behavior acceptable; gracious behavior speaks for itself. As we travel farther and faster between different worlds with their differing cultural demands, we must become ever more flexible and adaptable. Today I might spend the afternoon in a designer's loft in SoHo and the evening dancing at a formal charity ball. The next morning will find me in my office offering coffee in a Styrofoam cup to a buyer from Duluth. The variety in our lives demands that our behavior be flexible, but the basic concept underlying our behavior remains the same. Now that the rules are not so set, we're freer to think of good manners in the most basic sense: consideration for others and respect to them.

Because behavior has become more flexible, I have set about writing a new book on etiquette. The chapters that follow do advise which fork to use and what present is appropriate for the second wedding—I think knowing these distinctions makes us all more secure—but my real intention is to help answer the whys and hows of situations for which there are no longer exact standards of proper behavior. Even though we live in a world of rapid change, we're still living in a society of standards and expectations.

Interestingly, you'll find books of etiquette in the library catalogued just next to the folklore section—a significant placement. Etiquette is, in large part, folklore, and like folklore it has entered the fabric of our lives. The reasons for some of our prescribed actions have worn away with time. The rituals, however, remain. And every family has its rituals: Aunt Netta always gets the drumstick at Christmas dinner; when the Cousins Club meets every Fourth of July, Uncle Samson remembers to tease the children and give them candy and the children remember to set up elaborate plans to tease him back. Such ceremonies weld the family together; even years later when one member of the family is practicing medicine in the Congo and another is playing the conga drums in a jazz band, when it seems, in fact, as if they no longer have anything in common, a family gathering can be eased and the sense of family strengthened by common remembrance and observance of its acknowledged customs.

In China, the ideograph for tradition is the same as the one for good manners. The two are inevitably linked. In exactly the same way, etiquette, in the sense that it is folklore and tradition, plays the same role: etiquette exists because people feel comfortable when they understand and operate within certain forms, set patterns in which people can find their way and feel secure. I may give a dinner party for forty people in different walks of life. Etiquette is the tie that binds. When all the guests share the same understanding of what constitutes a gracious introduction and which fork to use for the salad, each person feels more secure within himself and with others.

It is far easier for us to adapt to technological innovations than it is for us to change our social values; we learn to say "Please" and

"Thank you" when we respond to recorded messages on tele-phone-answering machines. We use new inventions with old social conventions. In the same way it is far easier to toss out old tradi-tions than to construct workable new ones. Today, for example, the traditional roles assumed by men and women no longer hold true. We have no third-person pronoun which is not gender spe-cific, and the masculine "he" used exclusively is no longer appro-priate. To break through this literary restriction, I've used "he" and "she" indiscriminately throughout this book. Our times have taught us that what we need now is no longer a codified set of rules, but a flexible set of suggestions—no longer a code of good manners, but rather a mode of good manners.

When we can no longer rely on folklore and tradition to provide meaningful standards of behavior, we ourselves must develop a system, a method, to provide those most essential courtesies. I have tried in this book to pare the etiquette for today down to the essence of what etiquette is really about: logical, sensible patterns of behavior we can all follow in order to make our relationships with others pleasant, courteous—and gracious. What follows, therefore, is a reexamination of those customs (certainly including the most usable of folklore and tradition) that can provide us with a flexible, living etiquette for today.

Tradition is a guide and not a jailor.
—W. SOMERSET MAUGHAM

1 EVERYDAY MANNERS IN PUBLIC PLACES

GREETINGS

Simple Introductions

Traditionally a man has always been presented to a woman: "May I present Basil Prout." Or, more informally, "May I introduce Basil Prout. Basil, this is Eden Collinsworth." Or you can travel the shortest distance between two points, which is always appropriate in an informal introduction: "Basil Prout—Eden Collinsworth." Today, who is introduced to whom is considered by many to be of little consequence, but when you're with someone who is older it is polite to remember the custom and introduce the man to the woman. Include both first and last names of those whom you are introducing, even if one is a vice-president and the other is just climbing out of the mailroom. During introductions, at least, all people are equal. Don't invoke the social hierarchy by calling the vice-president "Mr. Janis" and the less exalted mailroom person "Tom." An introduction serves to bring people together and not to put them in their place. The only people I introduce using only their first names are children.

A married woman who has retained her maiden name is introduced when she is with her husband in this way: "This is Edna Klepper and her husband, Lance Loomer," unless she has made it known that she prefers to use her maiden name only in business, in which case you say, "This is Edna Loomer and Lance Loomer."

At a formal occasion when people are addressed by their title and last name a married woman with a professional title should be introduced by her title. Dr. Madora Waxley does not become Mrs. Waxley after office hours. Similarly if Dr. Waxley is known professionally by her maiden name and she is married to Mr. Clay the couple is introduced thus: "This is Dr. Waxley and her husband, Mr. Clay."

Let me interject here that when someone is speaking of his or her spouse, the spouse is referred to as "Mary" or, more specifically, "My wife, Mary," but never as "Mrs. Crouch."

When introducing women who insist on Ms. in place of Miss or Mrs., abide by their preference. Some who are slow to adapt to changing social forms still insist that Ms. works very well in print but remains unpronounceable. Ms. (pronounced Miz), though a recent addition to the language, should not be shunted aside. It's deprecatory to use one form of address when you know that the woman you are introducing would prefer you to use another.

When making an introduction, you may want to add a bit about the person you are introducing—it's an ideal conversation starter. You might, after the name, mention that Eden's children go to the same school as Basil's or that Eden works in public relations.

Do not, however, turn the introduction into a sales pitch. Never say, "This is Mr. Mariano, vice-president of Robbins and Company, who also keeps a string of polo ponies." You don't have to sell one guest to another, nor do you have to trumpet the grandness of your friends. Instead, keep Thoreau's words in mind: "I do not judge men by anything they can do. Their greatest deed is the impression they made on me." If it's appropriate, add something about the person you're introducing, but you needn't qualify each introduction.

Men should always stand, and most women prefer to, when being introduced to older people or to high officials. A man always stands when being introduced to another man or a woman, and today at small gatherings more and more women feel comfortable standing when the men stand to be introduced to a newcomer. I think it shows both consideration and a special interest to stand and devote your full attention to someone new. It is not out of place for a woman in a group of women to stand when introduced to someone new.

When two people are introduced by their titles and last names the person who leads the relationship to the more intimate one of first names is the one who is older or in a more celebrated position. Between a man and a woman of equal age it is the woman who suggests using first names, though in today's relaxed society a man would not be considered out of place if he made the suggestion.

Introducing Couples Who Live Together

That the relationship which exists between an unmarried couple lacks social definition becomes glaringly clear when one is faced with the problem of introductions. Although the relationship is certainly important enough to deserve a name, the phenomenon is as yet too new and unspecific for an identifiable term to be adopted easily into the language. Consequently, many people, faced with introducing a couple who live together, pass them off as married, replacing the woman's last name with that of the man's. This may be an attempt to clarify the relationship for social purposes, but it puts both the woman and the man in an uncomfortable position later on when she may be asked about her husband or he about his wife. When introducing an unmarried couple, no matter how married they seem to you, give both of their full names. You need not comment on their relationship. Your task in an introduction is not to bring to light their shared history.

To leave out last names entirely also makes for a poor introduction, I think, even today among young people who are immediately on a first-name basis. The mother of a man I know always introduced the woman he was living with by saying, "This is Janice." I guess she hoped that Janice, with only half a name, would not stand out so inexorably as a non-bona-fide member of the family. I think this is a poor and an obvious way of glossing over the facts. When a couple are left to introduce themselves it's best if they do so by name only. We're still wrestling with terms which don't fully describe the circumstances. Most feel that "girl friend" or "boy friend" diminishes their relationship as giddy or childish. To say "my lover" sounds as though you've left your spouse at home. "We share the rent," is misleading and too cute. To say, "This is Dorothy Winette, the woman I live with," may be interpreted as presumptuous—it does sound a bit as if you're trying to make points for your lack of convention—or simply too pompous. We are left with the simple and unenlightening "This is Dorothy Winette." Her relationship to you will have to remain something of a mystery until you are better acquainted with the people you've just met. Similarly when introducing a homosexual couple, simply introduce them by their full names.

(For children introducing parents to their friends and for children saying hello to adults, see Chapter 10, "Children." For children introducing an adult who lives with their parent in the household, see Chapter 9, "Living Together.")

Official Introductions

Both men and women are presented to the President: "Mr. President, may I present Mr. Prout."

When presenting someone to a king, a queen or a member of a reigning family, only the person being presented is mentioned by name, just as with the President. As a rule, men bow and women curtsy to royalty. At court, women make a deep curtsy, and at a private home a simple bob. In the United States, women instead of curtsying incline their heads in a slight bow. A king or queen is addressed in the third person, as "Your Majesty," which may be varied with "Sir" or "Ma'am" during a conversation.

One is presented to the Pope, "Your Holiness, may I present Mr. Collingsworth." To a cardinal, "Your Eminence, may I present Mr. Prout." Catholics kneel by dropping one knee almost to the ground while taking the extended hand of the Pope or the cardinal and almost touching their lips to his ring in a kiss. Non-Catholics bow.

If you're in doubt as to the proper form of address for an official, it is always correct to address a man as "sir" or a woman as "madam," though "madam" is a bit jarring to the ear as we in the United States don't hear the term often.

(For more on proper forms of address, see Chapter 6, "Correspondence.")

Forgetting a Name

It has happened to all of us that in the middle of making an introduction we forget a name. Don't stand there struggling at an attempted cover-up. Admit your memory lapse and say, "I am terribly sorry, but I've forgotten your name." A sensitive and polite person whose name you've forgotten will generally recognize your predicament and will introduce him- or herself even before you have time to make your apologies.

Shaking Hands

In the Middle Ages when armed men approached each other they extended empty hands to show they were advancing in peace. The extended hand and the handclasp have remained as a sign of friendship.

Men always shake hands with each other when being introduced. Traditionally, when a man and a woman met, the man waited for the woman to offer her hand. Nowadays a man need no longer wait. If a woman doesn't extend her hand immediately, a man may offer his. Shake hands firmly, but without bone-crushing enthusiasm. When meeting outdoors, shake hands with gloves on. If you hesitate and attempt to pull off your glove, you may leave someone in the awkward position of standing with an outstretched empty hand.

Men have devised so many intricate handshakes within the past few years—slapping palms, interlocking thumbs, grasping wrists —that a man extending his hand to a stranger can no longer be sure that it will be clasped in an old-fashioned shake. A disconcerting prospect, bungling such a familiar and dependable ritual. Unless one man knows the other and the two have customarily engaged in one of the various handshakes described, it's best when meeting someone new to extend your hand in the traditional manner to avoid any awkwardness or confusion which might result if you deliver a surprise shake with which the other person is unfamiliar or is simply not expecting.

(For more on introductions, see Chapter 2, "Entertaining.")

Social Kissing

Kissing has become almost *de rigueur* when greeting friends and even acquaintances. A handshake seems too formal in our informal world, and the social kiss has taken its place. Social kissing has many styles, from two women who peck at the air in a simulation of a kiss, leaving each other's cheeks lipstick-free, to the far from dainty wet-mouth kisser who more often than not leaves his quarry the worse for wear. The former is a symbol of a warm hello; to avoid the latter turn your cheek so that the offender will at least miss the direct target. Although a social kiss is a gesture of a warm and friendly hello, if you'd prefer to reserve your kisses for special friends you can take a nonkissing stand. Because touching is expected as part of a greeting or a leavetaking, a variation of the handshake will suffice to avoid the kiss and include the touch. To complete a kissless greeting or farewell, take your friend's hand in yours and cup it with your other hand. The gesture demonstrates your warmth and at the same time allows you to keep your distance without appearing standoffish.

Though European men have pecked each other on the cheek for generations, in America a kiss among men has until recently been identified with Judas and was limited to certain members of the underworld. The kiss was bestowed upon a marked man—it was "the kiss of death." Today, however, it's common to see two men greet each other with a hug rather than a handshake, and some even accompany the hug with a kiss. Because men are relaxing some of the restrictive rules that contained the masculine world, they are now unashamed to demonstrate to one another feelings of physical affection.

Chance Meetings

When meeting a friend or acquaintance by chance on the street, if you stop and chat even for a moment, introduce the person you're with. Just the name is sufficient. Then you may speak to the person you've just met. Though you needn't try to include a third person in your short conversation, the third person should always be acknowledged by being introduced.

If you're met on the street by a friend when you're with someone you shouldn't be with or don't want anyone to know you are with, it is doubly incriminating and makes the situation much more awkward to leave that person by your side unacknowledged. Do introduce the person you are with. No further explanation is needed.

Sometimes we all have trouble placing faces with names when the face is out of its usual context. If the face of a person on the movie line is familiar but you can't place it and that person seems to know you, don't attempt to bluff your way through a conversation. If after the first couple of sentences you still don't know to whom you are speaking, say, "I'm sorry, I know we've met, but I can't remember where."

When you say hello to someone and you see a blank look on his or her face, help that person by introducing yourself and adding a word or two about where the two of you have met. Don't ask someone to play guessing games. If you ask, "Don't you remember me?" be prepared for a rude "No."

CONVERSATION

Conversation is like a dance, in that one partner leads and the other follows, the difference being that the roles of leader and follower shift continuously. Therefore, conversation involves an effort—pleasurable, to be sure, but an effort nonetheless for all concerned. A good conversationalist is above everything else a good listener. Your curiosity in what another is saying breeds good conversation. Don't be self-involved; it inhibits conversation because it prevents spontaneity. Concentrate fully on the conversation, and look directly at the person with whom you are speaking.

It's disconcerting, to say the least, to speak with someone who is surveying the room and who is glancing at everyone who walks by. A woman who met Jackie Onassis at a large cocktail party reported that while they talked Mrs. Onassis acted as if there were no one else in the room. Mrs. Onassis was right in making the person she was talking with at the moment feel important and interesting.

When someone gives a strong point of view on a subject, don't adopt the opposing philosophy as a clever way to begin a conversation. Such a contrived and hostile approach will at best cut down on the natural flow of a discussion; at worst it will lead what began as an attempt at lively controversy to end in a bitter argument. Responding honestly to someone's feelings will spark a sincere and therefore more interesting debate. Too often all of us have been in a conversation and become aware that one of the other participants isn't listening but is merely waiting for a lull so that he can jump in with an anecdote or comment of his own. This attitude turns a conversation into a series of monologues and prevents real communication. Wait until the other person has finished the thought and respond to what has been said. If you don't know the subject under discussion, don't pretend to know—it's far more effective to admit ignorance and show your interest by asking questions. Most people are flattered by your interest and are very willing to elaborate.

Although the days of demurring from discussion about sex, religion and politics are, thank heavens, past, you must still think before you speak. There are, of course, certain topics that aren't suitable in certain situations (discussing an X-rated movie with someone older, for example). Get to know your audience by listening. One must also be aware of peculiarities in regional topics. For instance, nowhere but in New York City, where apartments are at a premium and their specific virtues or drawbacks a common topic of conversation, can one virtual stranger ask another, "How much rent do you pay?" without being considered offensive.

Beginning a Conversation

There are a lucky few who can walk into a room full of strangers and effortlessly engage one person after another, delighting everyone they meet with their lighthearted and amusing conversation. Those people are an enigma to most of us. When asked, "How do you do it?" they are for once left speechless. "Do what?" is their genuine reply. Easy conversation is so natural to them that it remains as undefinable as any other talent. Those who aren't so blessed might do well to keep on hand some conversational openers which, though they may seem contrived or clichéd, serve their purpose and get a conversation started.

It is commonplace today to open a conversation with the question "What do you do?" This approach may be perceived as too direct for most of us; a more gracious way to begin might be "I work in the clothing industry. We are really beginning to notice the energy shortage. Does it affect your business?" In the past, when people spent their lives in the same community, the question "Who are you?" precipitated the answer "I'm a Greenwald" or "I'm a Meeker." This simple answer revealed a whole history. Today, most of us settle down in new communities once we are adults. And this has opened the way for judging each other as individuals with specific interests. Learning about these interests—mountain climbing, the PTA or professional concerns—is the contemporary way to start an acquaintance.

Another icebreaker: compliment the person on something he or she is wearing. Follow up your remark with a comment on current fashion, pro or con—what you'd like to see come back into style or go out of style.

Making a comment relating to any consumer subject is always effective. No matter whom you're talking to—the president of a corporation or an aspiring assistant—everyone has to live with utility companies, car repairs and food prices, and I haven't yet met someone who would hesitate to share his own story with someone new.

Evading Personal Questions

The definition of what constitutes a personal question varies with each of us. Some may be willing to discuss their most intimate lives quite openly, while others don't feel comfortable divulging the slightest personal detail. If someone asks you a question which to your questioner appears insignificant but is nonetheless a question you'd rather not answer (such as "How much did it cost?" whether "it" is a dress, a car or a yacht), an evasive but polite answer is the best reply: "I don't remember," or "It was a present." There's no need to become huffy or indignant when inquisitiveness triumphs momentarily over tact. To potentially hazardous questions asked in ignorance, I suggest a partial answer. For instance, a friend who had just come from a visit with her lawyer about her separation agreement was confronted at a cocktail party by a curious, well-meaning acquaintance with "How do you keep your marriage happy?" She replied, "I think being friends in a marriage is very important," which satisfied the questioner without giving away any secrets.

Those who ask obviously tactless and implicitly antagonistic questions meant to put you on the defensive are best answered with another question which throws the original questioner off guard—and gets him off your back. "How come you're not married?," a question which is often put to single people by the smugly married, may be countered with "Are you about to propose?" or, less coyly, "I'm flattered by your personal interest and curious as to why you're so curious about me." When asked "Are you seeing a therapist?," one woman asked in turn, "Are you recommending yours?" A smart-aleck question deserves a smart-aleck reply—if you can think of one. If you can't, the best solution (and defense) is to take the question absolutely seriously and answer as truthfully as you can, or refuse politely to answer at all.

Compliments

Some find a compliment one of the most difficult things to accept. There are those who insist that the beautiful dress is really just an old thing that has been hanging in the back of the closet for months, the superb *crème brûlée* was thrown together and not nearly as good as Mother always makes it, or the lovely new upholstery on the couch doesn't really go with the curtains. While these protestations are generally made out of embarrassment, they also embarrass the person making the compliment and leave doubt as to his or her taste. When you are given a compliment, learn to accept it with grace and a thank-you.

Conversation Problems

A host* must at times act as conversation referee, moderator and rescuer. An alert host can separate guests who are showing the first signs of antagonism, thereby preventing a confrontation before it begins, and can rescue someone who is obviously being bored by a discussion. In either case, break into the discussion to suggest that there is someone whom you've been wanting the person to meet. A bored listener will go with you willingly; a bull pawing the ground in anticipation of a fight will need a bit more coaxing.

One certain way to ease tension or boredom is for the host to intervene and say to the bore or the bull, "May I borrow Caruthers for a minute? Antonia has been asking to meet him." Take the guest by the elbow and away from the trouble spot. When separating potential adversaries, it's safest to rescue the one on the defensive and not the aggressor, who may turn the aggression on you.

If you're too late and a fight is already in progress, it's best to let it run its course. Though a deft host may be able to break in and quell the argument, you may be left with hot tempers which will simmer all evening, affecting the other guests. Depend on the

---

* Throughout this book I am using the word "host" rather than "host and hostess," because "host" defines a role and because the similarities of graciousness and consideration required of both men and women in this role override any gender differences.

good sense and courtesy of the opponents, and if that evaporates in the heat of argument, the best you can do is try to patch things up after the worst is over, when both participants have come back to their senses, at least partially.

Don't try to introduce a newcomer to everyone in the room. Accompany your guest to one group of people and make the introductions. Similarly, if you see a guest struggling alone, introduce him to an already established conversation group. To do this effectively, attract the attention of one of the group by saying his or her name first, or your introduction may get lost in the ongoing conversation.

When guests are enjoying their conversation, don't interfere. Even though you are sure Talbot and Solange would adore each other, if Solange is already conversing with a group of guests don't interrupt her in order to introduce her to Talbot. Trying to improve on a guest's pleasure is generally counterproductive.

Changing the Subject

Every host has been in the dilemma of having to divert a conversation which has gotten off on the wrong foot. One of the most harrowing stories I've heard comes from Antoinette, who had just seated her eight guests at dinner. Antoinette's party took place a few years ago when both Betty Ford and Happy Rockefeller had had mastectomies, and two guests brought to the table a discussion about the women's operations (a subject which, in the first place, should have been changed before dinner). Only Antoinette knew that one of her other guests had recently had a mastectomy. After a moment of blind panic, during which Antoinette considered sweeping a serving dish off the table to distract her guests from the current topic, she resorted to less drastic methods and simply asked the group at large, in a loud and rather domineering-schoolteacher voice, "Did you know Cecily Margolis is getting braces, along with her oldest, Agatha? She says people are mistaking her for a teenager!" Any fairly well-known bit of gossip is permissible in this situation; just don't resort to heralding news you've promised never to tell.

Though Antoinette's statement at the time seemed a bit silly, it did the trick and steered the conversation in an alternate direction. As a host, your actions in time of stress may seem inexplicable to most and a bit foolish to some, but if an innocuous sentence or two accomplishes your mission don't be afraid to act. To change the subject, ask whatever springs into your mind about current events, the weather, a recent movie, even though it may be inappropriate to the discussion. Asking a question is more effective than delivering a pronouncement, which can be overlooked. The most persuasive element of your question is not what you ask but how you ask it. Use a tone loud enough for guests to hear and with enough conviction so that your question demands an answer and cannot be ignored.

Yawning

George Washington, in his "Rules of Civility and Decent Behavior," gave what is still the best advice on yawning: "If you yawn, do it not loud but privately and speak not in your yawning but put your handkerchief or your hand before your face and turn aside." If your yawn interrupts a conversation, apologize by blaming your yawn on lack of sleep, even when boredom is its cause. If indeed unexciting conversation is the problem, an obvious yawn won't extricate you from that conversation, nor will it make the person speaking a more interesting conversationalist. So there is nothing to be gained by yawning to make a point.

When caught with a bore, try to corral passersby to join your group. Hope that they will take over the conversational reins. Then you can try for a quick getaway and paraphrase Robert Browning, who said, possibly in similar circumstances, "But, my dear fellow, this is too bad. I am monopolizing you."

When You Speak a Second Language

When Americans who speak a second language are part of a larger gathering, it's pure affectation not to speak English if the company is primarily Americans. Speaking a language that isn't understood by everyone present limits the flow of conversation and serves to isolate members of the gathering.

A host of someone from abroad speaks English in an American gathering. A foreign guest can be included if the host takes the opportunity during a pause in the conversation to turn to the guest and translate the gist of the discussion.

(For more on conversation, see Chapter 2, "Entertaining.")

THEATER, OPERA, CONCERTS

When going to the theater, an opera, a ballet or a concert, be considerate to others in the audience as well as to the performers on the stage. To let people pass easily to seats in the middle of a row, stand and lean against the back of your folded seat. You may remain seated and move your legs to one side if the space is wide enough to let people pass without stepping over your legs. Don't take it out on those passing by that the architect of the theater must not have had full-grown adults in mind when planning the seating. Remain seated and move your legs to one side to accommodate latecomers if the performance has started.

Europeans walk through the row facing those already seated, which I think is more polite than to slide past those already seated, giving them your back. This approach also has a more utilitarian purpose: you are able to see where legs and pocketbooks are placed and will be aware if there is an elderly person who has not risen and of whom you must be especially careful.

Don't try to avoid the crush by leaving before the performance is finished. It's distracting to the performers and to the audience as well.

Applause

People today tend to applaud as a kind of audience participation, which has developed, I think, from televised sports events at which the audience is cheering—or booing—almost continually. In the theater the audience often applauds at the entrance of the main characters, when the curtain is raised, and they even sometimes applaud the set.

Although every performer wants to hear the audience's appreciation, during an opera, a ballet or a concert it's best to check your enthusiasm rather than take a chance of breaking the rhythm continuity of the program with your applause.

At the opera the audience claps when the conductor takes his place at the podium. Applause is generally expected after an aria, but be sure the aria is finished before you begin your applause. Sometimes there are curtain calls between acts, in which case it's better to save your applause for that time.

At the ballet the audience applauds when the conductor makes his entrance and sometimes after solos and pas de deux.

At a concert applaud when the conductor takes his place at the podium and when the concert is completed. Applause is also expected after each work listed on the program is completed. Applause between movements of a symphony or after a concerto solo breaks the flow of the music, although exuberant audiences have been known not to hold back their applause. If you aren't familiar with the music being played, it's better to wait and see if others begin to applaud or yours may be the sound of one pair of hands clapping. Take the time in between movements to clear your throat if you must and to shift your position. Have cough drops or hard candy on hand to alleviate a tickle in your throat. Noise from the audience is frowned upon. I once attended a concert during which the harpsichord soloist took his time between movements to admonish a snoring man sitting in one of the first few rows. If you don't know the music well, take your cue from the conductor as to when the concert is finished or when it's time for intermission. When he leaves the podium it is always appropriate to applaud.

Boxes at the Opera and Concerts

The woman host sits in the front row of the box in the seat farthest from the stage. Older women in the party sit in the front row with the host. In the second row sit the younger women and the most prominent or older men. Younger men and the host sit in the last row. If a group of friends subscribe to a box, they alternate the seats during the season.

On Monday night at the opera it is traditional to dress formally if you'll be sitting in a box. Those sitting in the orchestra sometimes wear evening clothes, too.

MUSEUMS

Ivory-tower reverence of art is a thing of the past. Attendance figures at American art museums go up every year, which attests to the fact that the enjoyment of art is for everyone and not for only a few. Special exhibits which now travel throughout the country are in great demand and consequently are very crowded. The

Tutankhamen Exhibition's arrival in New York City at the Metropolitan Museum is a perfect example: the exhibition itself was glorious, but in order to see it one had to wait in line and then view the works under crowded conditions. When you are in similar circumstances remember that consideration is catching—and so is boorishness. Be patient and courteous while waiting in line in order that viewing the exhibit will be enjoyable for all who are present. Speak softly and don't walk in front of others viewing a work of art, thereby obstructing their vision; wait until they move on if they are obstructing yours. A general rule for conduct in museums is to be as considerate of the rights of others as you are of the works of art.

THE DISABLED

Disabled people want to live independent lives with dignity. You can help by treating them as individuals. Remember that a person with a disability is just like anyone else, except for the special limitations of his or her disability.

The National Easter Seal Society for Crippled Children and Adults makes these suggestions for when you meet a handicapped person:

Ask if he wants help before you rush in with assistance. If help is wanted, the person will tell you how best to assist.

When speaking with someone in a wheelchair, take a seat, if possible, instead of towering over her.

Be patient. Let the disabled person set his pace in walking or talking.

When dining with a person who is disabled, don't offer to help cut his food. He will ask you or the waiter for help if it is needed.

Don't ask embarrassing questions. If someone wants to tell you about his disability he will bring up the subject.

A disability needs to be accepted or taken for granted between friends.

Children and the Disabled

Children too young to have discovered the subtlety of tact may stop and stare at a disabled person or ask embarrassing questions.

It's natural for a child to be curious, but a child must learn to be considerate of others' feelings. Consideration in this case does not mean that one ignores the person who is disabled. To pretend that a disability is being overlooked is to make the person separate from the rest of society, something all disabled people want to avoid.

The Hearing Impaired

The National Association for the Deaf in Silver Spring, Maryland, and the Lexington School for the Deaf in New York City have some suggestions on how to best communicate with and treat someone with a hearing loss.

It's important to remember to be patient when speaking with someone whose hearing is impaired. Often it takes extra time to communicate successfully. You might have to repeat what you're saying in order to be understood. Don't be impatient. Someone who is deaf is particularly perceptive visually and reacts quickly to your signs of frustration and impatience. You must also take the time to properly understand someone who is deaf until you become accustomed to his or her speech, which may sound strange at first, due to the hearing loss. In no way has this to do with intelligence. The degree of hearing loss and the age of the person affect the way in which he or she communicates. If you don't understand, don't hesitate to ask a deaf person to slow down or to repeat what he has just said.

The sign language of the deaf is the third-largest language used in the United States today. Nevertheless, many people who are partially or almost completely deaf use speech when conversing with those of normal hearing. When speaking to someone who is deaf, remember to talk directly to the person so that she can *see* you speak at all times. If you don't understand a person, say, "I don't understand you. Please say it again." Speak in a normal voice, without shouting and without exaggeration, but a little more deliberately and with more gestures than usual. Since deaf people will watch your lips particularly closely, be careful not to obscure your face with your hands.

The Blind

The Lighthouse of the New York Association for the Blind has some suggestions on how to best treat someone who is blind.

When you want to help a blind person on the street, ask if assistance would be helpful. Sometimes a blind person prefers to get along unaided. If she does want your help don't grab her arm. Offer your elbow. You will then be walking a half-step ahead, and the movements of your body will indicate she should change direction, stop and start and step up or down a curbside as you cross the street.

When dining out with a blind person, again offer your elbow and guide the person to your table and place his or her hand on the back of the chair she will be sitting in. Blind people know how to seat themselves. Outline the table setting briefly. When the food arrives, describe where the different items are placed on the plate and the side dishes.

Talk with a blind person as you would with a person who can see. If you enter a room in which a blind person is alone, make your presence known by speaking or introducing yourself. In a group, address a blind person by name. Excuse yourself when you are about to leave.

If a blind person has a Seeing Eye dog, don't pet or distract the dog in any way—he is working and needs all his concentration to do a good job.

RESTAURANT DINING

Who's Who in the Cast

The maître d'hôtel (maître d'), or headwaiter, stands at the entrance to the dining room. He shows you to your table and seats you and is the man to talk to about any special service you require. He can be identified easily because he wears a tuxedo. He acts as a captain in a smaller restaurant. Food prepared at the table, such as Steak Diane, is cooked by the captain (or maître d').

The captain takes your order and sees that it is prepared correctly and served properly. In restaurants which have no maître d' the captain takes on those responsibilities. He also dresses in a tuxedo.

Waiters pick up your order from the kitchen, the bar or the dessert area and serve the food.

Busboys are responsible for cleaning your table and for such jobs as filling water glasses and providing clean ashtrays.

The wine steward, or sommelier, presents the wine list to the host. You may ask him to make suggestions.

The Menu

An à la carte menu means that each item on the menu is priced separately. Often the entrée on an à la carte menu will include potatoes or rice; the vegetable will be additional. On a table d'hôte or prix fixe menu the price fixed beside the entrée includes an entire dinner with appetizer, salad and dessert as well as the entrée.

Giving Your Order

The captain does not defer to the woman at the table by taking all orders directly from the man. He first asks each woman separately for her order and then asks the men. The host's order is taken last. When the party is large, the captain asks each person in turn for his order. If the menu is in a foreign language, tell the captain or the waiter that you need some help—that's what he's there for—and he'll translate the menu for you. Even English menus often need interpretation for those items named for the chef or the proprietor's Great Aunt Mim.

Serving Yourself

When you are served your vegetable or potato in a side dish, you may, if you prefer, transfer the food onto your plate by serving yourself with a large spoon.

You may also wish to share some of your meal with your dinner partner, in which case you would serve her a portion of your food with a serving spoon before you begin eating. Similarly, if two people order different entrées with the intent of sharing them, divide the portions, serving each other with a serving spoon before you begin to eat.

If you can't finish what is on your plate and you're dining with someone who has a large appetite, serve that person the untouched portion of your meal with a clean serving spoon.

The Wine List

The wine steward (sommelier) or, if there is none, the captain, will show the host the wine list. The host may defer to someone more knowledgeable about wines. If no one at the table is a wine connoisseur, ask the wine steward what he would suggest. His expertise will help you put the proper wine (not the most expensive) together with the food you've ordered, but don't be ashamed to limit his suggestion to a modestly priced wine. If some at your table order meat and others fish you may all agree to drink either a red, a white or a rosé with your meal, or half bottles of red and white may be ordered.

When the wine is served, the bottle is shown to the host so that he can read the label to be sure it is the wine that was ordered. After the bottle has been opened, the cork may be handed to the host in order for him or her to be able to feel that the cork is strong; the host may sniff the cork to be sure it is free from any musty smell. About an inch of wine is then poured into the host's glass. The host tastes the wine and may smell its bouquet to be sure it's good. Another reason for pouring the wine first into the host's glass is so that the host will receive any bits of cork which may have been floating at the top of the bottle. If the host is still sipping a cocktail when the wine is brought to the table, he may ask someone else at the table to taste the wine, so that the waiter won't have to stand and wait and so that guests may begin to drink their wine without waiting for the host. During the meal the waiter refills the wineglasses. Guests should not have to pour the wine themselves. Glasses are filled only halfway.

(For more on wines, see Chapter 2, "Entertaining.")

Your Relationship with the Staff

Address the maître d' as "sir" and the captain by his title. When addressing a waiter or a busboy I think the most courteous address is "sir" and not "waiter" or "busboy" (never address a busboy as "boy"). People like to be shown respect, and "sir" shows more respect than "waiter."

If a woman is serving you, "waitress" is not correct. "Miss" is inappropriate if the woman is not young. I think "ma'am," although the term is used primarily in the South, is the most respectful address.

Some feel it necessary to strike up a conversation with the waiter. Remember that to engage someone in conversation when he is working may distract that person from doing his job.

On the other hand, if you're inclined to halt your conversation each time a waiter approaches, for fear that the waiter will overhear you, Rosina Harrison, Lady Astor's personal maid for many years, will put your mind at ease. In her book *Rose: My Life in Service*, she advises us: "It's difficult if you start getting interested in what's being said among the guests because if you do your concentration goes." In other words, no one has time to listen.

How to Complain

When being seated, if the table you are offered is unsatisfactory —because it is too close to a noisy kitchen or too near a drafty door, or for any valid reason—say so immediately. If any other tables are available you'll be shown to another.

If you are not happy with the service you are receiving during the meal, let your feelings be known. Complain to the captain or the maître d'. You're entitled to your money's worth. Tell him politely that you are dissatisfied, and make your complaints specific. Don't wait until after your meal to say that you'd have liked to see the waiter more often or that some part of your meal was not to your liking. If your food comes to the table improperly prepared or not the way you ordered it, tell the captain the specific problem and ask that the food be replaced. Don't make a scene— you needn't be loud or abusive—but firmness is important and will be respected.

Entertaining in a Restaurant

When you plan to entertain in a restaurant, telephone to make reservations and ask to speak with the maître d'. Tell him how many people will be in your party and specify that you are the host. Now is the time to let him know of any special requests you may have. One New York restaurateur says that the most-often-requested special service—requested mainly by women—is that the bill not be brought to the table. In such cases, the host, man or woman, tells the maître d' that he or she will leave a credit card with him at the beginning of the evening and will sign for the meal in the front of the restaurant away from the guests.

Some restaurants stock unpriced menus which you may request for your guests.

When entertaining a fairly large group of people, eight or ten, for instance, you may wish to call up the restaurant beforehand and order the entire meal. I've found that when I entertain groups of people in a restaurant, they would much rather that everything be taken care of just as it would be if I were entertaining them at home. Ordering ahead makes the dinner more relaxed and pleasant.

(For business entertaining in a restaurant, see Chapter 5, "The Business World.")

"No Host" Parties

When a group gathers together in a restaurant or a club for some special occasion—to entertain an out-of-town friend or relative, for instance—the person who is organizing the evening will send a written invitation. In order that those who are receiving the invitation should not begin to assume that the person responsible for the party's organization has shouldered the financial responsibility as well, a follow-up telephone call is necessary. Explain that George and Martha can be entertained on such a lavish scale only because everyone has agreed to pay his or her share of the entertainment.

Dining in a Restaurant Alone

Single diners are very often given steerage-class treatment in even the most elegant restaurants. The staff isn't pleased to see a table for two taken by one—a single guest means a smaller bill and therefore a smaller tip. (I'm only giving reasons for shoddy treatment that many single diners experience; I'm certainly not giving excuses for such treatment.) A person dining alone has the right to expect the same service and courtesy accorded other customers. Insist on it. Refuse the table hidden in the back. Don't let insecurity or self-consciousness rob you of a pleasant meal. There is no need to apologize for being alone. Reading a book or a magazine during your meal won't contribute to the convivial atmosphere that restaurants want to establish, but if it makes you more comfortable to read while you eat alone, do so. A single diner may allay his or her self-consciousness by concentrating on making the meal a personal extravagance. Now's the time to become a gourmet and a wine connoisseur. Spend extra time studying the menu and the wine list, since there is no one to hurry you. Ask questions about both. Here is your chance to savor your meal without conversational interruptions. As Robert Morley once said, "No man is lonely while eating spaghetti; it requires so much attention." You'll find that dining out can be a pleasurable experience in itself and doesn't necessarily require social intercourse to be a success.

Doggie Bags

Some restaurants serve enormous portions which their customers can't possibly finish. When this happens it is appropriate to ask the waiter to have uneaten portions wrapped for you to take home. I think it shows prudence and foresight to take food home rather than to allow perfectly good food to be thrown out in the restaurant kitchen.

What to Do with Paper Wrappers at the Table

The convenience of pre-packaging has brought to the table paper wrappers for sugar and butter, and cardboard and plastic containers for jams. A sugar wrapper may be placed in the ashtray at the table of nonsmokers or crumpled and tucked under your saucer or left flat lying next to your plate. If you find the discarded paper a form of littering, call over the busboy or the waiter and ask that the paper be taken away. Leave butter wrappers on your butter plate; jelly containers may be left either on the side of your plate or on the table.

Table Hopping

When someone comes over to your table to say hello, keep the visit to a greeting. Someone standing in the aisle may obstruct a busy restaurant staff. If you want to chat with a visitor, pull up an extra chair to your table. Introduce the table hopper to others in your party if you'd like him or her to stay and chat. To refrain from introductions is a way of saying this isn't the right time to visit.

If you see friends in a restaurant to whom you would like to say hello, don't table-hop while they are still eating. Wait until they have finished their meal, when it will be convenient for them to greet a friend.

When a Man Should Stand

When a woman returns to the table, men generally stand. If standing is inconvenient, a man will rise partially in his chair to acknowledge the courtesy. If your group is a fairly large one, only the men sitting on either side of the woman partially rise when she returns to the table. The other men at the table do not disrupt the flow of conversation and the course of the meal to rise.

In our modern age of equality some men and women may object to a man rising when a woman returns to the table (though in many restaurants tables are packed so closely together that both men and women may have to rise to make room for a dinner partner to sit down). I think if a man stands in a smooth, natural gesture, there should be no objection. Some men have that Fred Astaire touch of effortless grace in their courtesy. If a woman says, "Please do sit down," a man may take the remark as a cue and need not rise again the next time she returns to the table.

When a table hopper is introduced, men seated at the table rise to say hello. If a man is sitting at a banquette it is almost a contortionist's feat to stand, so in that case he may just nod his head to acknowledge the greeting.

Dress Requirements for Men

Even in today's informal world many restaurants still turn away men whom they consider to be inappropriately dressed. Jackets and ties are *de rigueur* in some restaurants. It's worth phoning ahead or asking about dress requirements when you make your reservation. Most men feel silly wearing a waiter's bow tie and a lost-and-found jacket that almost fits, even if the restaurant will supply such pieces of the required uniform for guests.

Checking Coats

Men check their coats. A woman may check her coat or, if she prefers, she may wear it to the table and drape it over the back of her chair. It's wise for men or women to check umbrellas or parcels. To leave them leaning against the leg of the table or chair might obstruct the restaurant staff.

Splitting the Check

The person who asks for the check is the one to receive it. When dining with friends, instead of asking for separate checks divide the check evenly by the number of people at the table. Unless one person ate only a salad and the rest enjoyed a three-course meal, don't take an accounting of each shrimp cocktail and piece of pecan pie. If you prefer, one person may pay in the restaurant and the rest may settle up after the meal. In our society handling money in public is looked upon with a certain amount of embarrassment. This cultural prejudice may one day evolve into a taboo as credit cards become more prevalent and cash is scarcely seen! I see nothing unseemly, however, for friends to settle while still at the table. If two people would like to pay by credit card, the bill may be divided in half and each would put his or her share on the credit card. Or one person may pay by credit card and is then reimbursed by others in cash.

I know one advertising executive with whom the credit card has fallen into disrepute. He mistrusts those colleagues who pay for the entire meal with their card and then accept fellow diners' cash. He grumbles that they are crediting the meal to their expense accounts and making a profit at his expense. I believe that the use of a credit card has nothing necessarily to do with an expense account, and that the advertising VP is overly suspicious. Those who break bread together should trust one another.

Tipping

The gratuity originated as an expression of thanks. The word itself is derived from the Medieval Latin *gratuitas*, which means a present or a gift. The original meaning has changed, as a gratuity is expected nowadays. In Europe it is a fixed part of the bill. In America the amount of the gratuity is usually decided upon by the customer.

A tip is a gesture of appreciation for service; the percentage of the tip isn't an absolute, so consider the quality of the service before deciding on the amount you will leave.

Though your tip should in part reflect your gratitude or your lack of it in regard to service and courtesy, a tip of some sort is mandatory. To leave no tip at all is a vengeful gesture. Since waiters and captains make their living from tips, I think it is unduly harsh to omit a tip completely.

If you are unhappy with the service or lack of courtesy, give the waiter a chance to improve by complaining early in the meal, and if you see no results a ten percent tip will make your point. In fact, if you leave a smaller tip than is generally expected the maître d' or captain may approach your table and inquire if there was something wrong with your meal.

How Much to Tip

A waiter is tipped between fifteen and twenty percent of the bill, including drinks, before taxes. (In New York City, where the sales tax is eight percent, an easy way to determine the amount of the tip is simply to make it double the amount of the tax.) The wine steward is tipped ten percent of the wine check and not less than one dollar. The captain receives a tip of five to seven percent of the check; the tip may be included on the bill if you're paying by credit card, or it may be given to him directly. The maître d' is tipped personally. Those who frequent a certain restaurant on a regular basis usually give the maître d' five dollars every four or five times they eat at the restaurant. If you're a newcomer, a five-dollar tip to the maître d' in advance of your dinner may well get for you the table by the window or will do much in the way of providing special service should you request it. If you were sitting at the bar, tip the bartender fifteen percent of your drink bill. The tip for your coat is fifty cents.

In fact, the word "tip" was originally an acronym standing for "to insure promptness." Tips in advance, however, are often chancy, since it's possible you might undertip. Giving money to the maître d' is something of an art. Hand it to him quietly, but not secretly; there's no reason to be embarrassed about something which is so very welcome. As you hand him the money, thank him, which is courteous and also serves to take away from the focus of the monetary transaction.

Those Few Whom You Don't Tip

The busboys are tipped by the waiters. Chefs are never tipped; however, they may be complimented personally if the kitchen isn't too busy. Owners and managers are not tipped, though of course they may be thanked. An owner or manager may be distinguished by the clothes he is wearing: he will be the man who looks as though he is in charge; however, instead of wearing a tuxedo, he will be dressed like a customer. If you offer a tip and it is refused, instead of being embarrassed, think of the money you've saved.

If a musician has played your request you may buy him or her a drink in thanks. You may, of course, tip a musician, but anything under five dollars looks a bit meager, so unless you're extravagant, buying a drink is the best solution.

TIPPING IN A BEAUTY SALON

In a beauty salon there are sometimes so many people to tip that it can become a bit overwhelming. Here is a brief breakdown of whom to tip and how much to tip them:

If you spend about twenty dollars for a haircut, tip the stylist who cut your hair and combed it out four dollars if you're delighted with the results, three dollars if you're not overjoyed but still look good. Tip the stylist's assistant one or two dollars, depending how attentive he has been. The person who shampooed your hair should receive one dollar; the coatroom attendant, twenty-five or fifty cents.

For a permanent or a hair coloring your tip should not be under five dollars. Again, tip a bit more if you look wonderful.

For a manicure costing five or six dollars, your tip should be one dollar. The tip for a pedicure costing about twelve dollars should be roughly two dollars.

The guideline for beauty-parlor tipping is fifteen to twenty percent for any service they provide.

Whether or not you visit the salon only a few times a year or you have a standing weekly appointment, your tips should remain consistent. Don't pay less if you visit less often. They are still putting out the same quality work for you.

It's most courteous to give the tip personally, especially to those who have spent a considerable amount of time with you. The staff in a beauty salon provides a very personal service—after all, they are working on your body—and generally while they work they strike up a verbal relationship with the client; some stylists know the most intimate details of their regular clients' lives. If the salon is very busy and you have a handful of people to tip, most salons provide envelopes at the front desk for that purpose. If you're a regular customer it's a more personal thank-you to tip your stylist or manicurist personally and leave the other tips at the desk.

If the owner of the shop has cut your hair, he or she doesn't receive a tip. Often the owner charges more for a cut, so there is no reason to tip, though on your way out show your appreciation with a thank-you. If you didn't know the owner was cutting your hair and you do offer a tip, he or she will probably say, "It's not necessary," in which case don't force the issue; a smile and a thank-you are sufficient.

If you're miserable with the result, instead of not tipping and leaving unhappily, complain to the manager or owner of the shop and ask that they redo the job or at least try to repair the damage. Though you are not obligated to tip, I think that if they tried their best to satisfy your demands you should tip modestly. The owner or manager of the shop is the one responsible for the work performed there. Everyone makes mistakes, and the staff in a salon depends on tips. So unless most of your hair falls out or the result is equally calamitous, tip at least the minimum.

Nowadays men frequent hairdressing salons and their hair is cut as carefully and stylishly as women's hair. Men too must tip accordingly. The day of a shave and a haircut for two bits is past.

At Christmas regular customers often give presents to their stylist, colorist, manicurist and whoever works on them on a consistent basis. You may give money, around twenty dollars for a steady customer, or, if you can't afford such an extravagance, a small present. All Christmas gifts should be given in person.

IN PUBLIC PLACES

Traditional Male Courtesies

There are certain small amenities which until fairly recently were reserved exclusively for men to perform when in the presence of women, but which today have also been taken up by women—opening doors, for instance, and lighting cigarettes. A woman may light her own cigarette and open her own door without waiting for male assistance; she needn't hesitate to light a man's cigarette and open the door for him as well.

Men who have been brought up to extend small courtesies to women may be abashed when instead of being rewarded for their behavior they are admonished. Some women today see men's small courtesies as preserving the inequities between the sexes. As one woman who insists on opening her own doors these days has remarked, "My husband always stood aside to let me go first through the door, but I stood aside and let him go first to graduate school while I worked to support us both. I didn't receive my college degree until after my children were grown." To avoid a possible confrontation over behavior which has until recently been unequivocally the right thing to do but may now be considered by some as the wrong thing, a man may ask a woman he's with, "May I light your cigarette?" or "May I help you with your coat?" Asking first will circumvent any possible embarrassment.

Small courtesies are always correct if they are done naturally in the course of events. Helping someone next to you with a coat or offering to carry someone's packages if the person is weighed down with bundles is a gesture of consideration. Regardless of sex, we should be responsive to the needs of others. When a man holds a door for a woman or lights her cigarette a woman need not interpret the gesture as a chauvinistic one, but rather as polite and caring. If someone, man or woman, does pay you special attention, always repay that person with a thank-you.

Because a woman can no longer take such gestures for granted, it's best for her to wait and see if a man is going to let her pass through the door first. A woman who barges ahead may very likely end up in a collision. It is also presumptuous for a woman to signal a man for a match by wagging an unlit cigarette between her fingers. If her cigarette is not lit for her immediately, she lights it herself, which means she should always carry matches or a lighter with her.

TAXIS

Courtesy

When hailing a taxi, don't cross the street to get to the taxi first when you are aware that someone has been waiting for one before you. Wait your turn. In bad weather one person may offer to share a taxi with a stranger, in which case each person pays the driver for his or her share.

If friends who are going in the same direction agree to share a metered taxi, the one who is let off first offers the passenger remaining what he or she calculates will be half of the full fare plus tip. Don't try to play the big spender by paying for your two-dollar ride with a five-dollar bill. The passenger who is continuing should accept the money. Refusing it at the last minute, though seemingly altruistic, creates a sense of obligation and may make the person getting out feel beholden. The agreement to share should be honored by both partners. In it is a recognition of joint responsibility; friends are treating each other as equals and neither is imposing on the other's hospitality. If you'd like to treat a friend to a taxi, let the person know beforehand by saying, "Can I drop you?" In that case the other passenger is dropped off first and the person who has offered to pay the fare does so at the final destination.

When a man and a woman travel by taxi together, the man, if he reaches the taxi before the woman, opens the door for her.

Though the woman generally precedes the man and gets into the taxi or the back seat of a car first, if she is wearing a long skirt or clothes which are difficult to maneuver in she should get into the car last so that she doesn't have to slide across the seat. A man customarily gives the direction to the driver, but if the woman is the one who knows the address she tells the driver directly.

The Taxi Driver

If the taxi driver wants to converse and you don't, just say, "I'd rather not talk now." If you find yourself in a taxi with a driver delivering a tirade against the government, the weather or the passenger who got out just before you, you may have to use a more persuasive tone and add, "I'm taking this taxi so that I can have a little quiet time to relax."

A taxi driver who plays the radio at high decibels may be asked politely to turn it down, not off. The taxi is his place of business, his office, and if he enjoys music playing in his office, so be it.

A taxi driver is tipped between fifteen and twenty percent. If your driver becomes argumentative or refuses to travel along the route you suggest, I don't think he deserves a tip at all, which is your only recourse since you are trapped in the cab and have no one of higher authority to complain to, as you do with a waiter, for instance.

AUTOMOBILES

A woman is not expected to wait for a man to get out of the car and trot around to open her door for her while she sits there like some delicate hothouse flower. Women no longer need to appear helpless, just as men no longer need to act on that assumption. A woman opens her own car door. If he is dropping her off, a man does not have to reach awkwardly across her to pull the handle of the door for her.

GIVING UP YOUR SEAT ON PUBLIC TRANSPORTATION

On a crowded bus or train one gives up one's seat to someone elderly, someone weighted down with packages or someone who is carrying a small child. Today a woman also shows this consideration to a man. Now that both men and women lead busy active lives and the myth of the weaker sex has been shattered, men are no longer expected to jump up and offer their seat to a standing woman. Small children, especially those small enough to ride for free, should either sit in the accompanying adult's lap or stand if the bus or train is crowded.

ELEVATORS

In an elevator, conversations stop or are conducted in a whisper, as no one wants to be overheard by fellow travelers who may or may not be anonymous. The woman next to you may be your boss's second cousin. People are self-conscious in such close encounters and try to remain as inconspicuous as such proximity will allow. When the elevator stops, whoever is closest to the door gets out first. Neither the elevator doors nor the people in back who want to get out have the patience to wait for a man in front to step back in order to let a woman out first. A man may, after preceding a woman out of an elevator, stand aside and let her pass first. A woman must not charge forward from the back of the elevator assuming that the man will step aside to let her off first. She waits her turn. A man removes his hat in an elevator in a residential building, though he should keep it on if the elevator is crowded. Hats need not be removed in uncrowded public elevators. Even in places where it is still legal to smoke in an elevator, common sense and courtesy dictate that you put your cigarette out before you step into the elevator and wait until after your elevator ride to light your pipe or cigar.

If there is more than one elevator, it's rude to shout to passengers to hold the elevator door open for you or to attempt to do so yourself by thrusting the tip of your umbrella or your arm in between the closing doors. Someone once remarked that this compunction—almost a reflex with some—is the mark of the overachiever who can't wait to get to the top. So don't give yourself away. Be patient, you'll be delayed only thirty seconds or so until the next elevator arrives.

REVOLVING DOORS AND ESCALATORS

Traditionally, a man preceded a woman through a revolving door in order to push the door for her. He was also the first one on the escalator, to be in a position to help the woman on and off. This ritual may still be practiced for form's sake, but if a woman reaches the conveyance first she needn't stand and wait unless she is elderly or is carrying packages and does in fact need help.

WALKING ON THE SIDEWALK

When a man and a woman strolled down the avenue in the days of unpaved and muddy streets the man always walked on the outside of the sidewalk to protect the woman from splashing buggies. Once street conditions were made less primitive, the woman always walked on the man's right. Today, strolling on the sidewalk is so casual a pastime that no specific rules need be followed. For those sticklers of form, it is always correct for the woman to walk on the man's right. A group of friends should always walk no more than two abreast, in order not to obstruct other passersby.

MEETING SOMEONE NEW IN A PUBLIC PLACE

It's always permissible to try to make the acquaintance of an appealing stranger in a public place, as long as you do so politely and desist if your attempts at self-introduction are not reciprocated. Making overtures to a stranger has always been the province of men, but today women are becoming bolder. Courageous women who begin a conversation with a male stranger must also adhere to the rule that if little interest is shown they excuse themselves politely. Man or woman, only a little sensitivity is needed in order to tell if someone is open to an approach. Never be insistent if your first approach is not encouraged.

Start up a conversation with your seat mate on a plane or train, or the person next to you, only if he or she seems agreeable to conversation. A traveling companion is a captive audience and should not be subjected to a fellow passenger's insistence on making conversation.

When dining or having a drink alone, you may, whether you are male or female, suggest to someone of the opposite sex who is also alone that he or she join you. You may also ask two people who you think—or hope—may be agreeable to making a new acquaintance, if you may join them. However, if you have misjudged the situation and they are engrossed in conversation and don't seem too happy at the prospect, excuse yourself and withdraw promptly.

If you do meet a stranger it's best to become better acquainted in a public place. First impressions aren't always accurate.

THE DATE

Women Telephoning Men for Dates

Although in theory women today now have the option to ask men out on dates, in practice I find that only the most courageously assertive among us actually attempt to do so. Men seem to shy away from a woman's direct approach—evidently still trying to retain their exclusive control of selection. After a few discouraging attempts most women go back to the waiting game. I do think a woman who wants to ask a man out should definitely do so. After all, men can't say no forever.

(For more on women asking out men, see Chapter 10, "Children.")

Sharing Expenses

Women speak of the freedom that paying for themselves gives them. With some women the decision to pay their own way is not based on whether the man is rich or poor. When she pays for herself, a woman is asserting her equality; she may then share the decision of what to do on a date and she need not feel guilty if she wants to go home early and alone. A woman who pays for herself may also feel more free to call and ask a man for a date, thereby becoming his partner for the evening instead of always his guest.

Though some women may want to share the economies of a relationship, and pay their share of expenses, if they earn less than men (and usually they do) they very often simply can't afford to. Fifty dollars for an evening may mean almost nothing to a man but may be a sizable chunk of a woman's weekly salary. Some women believe that sharing expenses has to come first before equal pay will follow. Others argue that as long as women are paid less they shouldn't be expected to share expenses with a man. Many women don't want to give up that very special feeling they have when they are taken out. They shouldn't have to. If a woman would like to contribute financially to a relationship, instead of splitting the check she may occasionally treat a man to an evening out which will make her (and him!) feel just as special in a different way. If there is a great disparity in the earnings of a couple, the one earning less shouldn't try to match the other who is making much more money. Instead, expenses may be paid according to the percentage differences between the two salaries. A woman who makes much less than a man she often goes out with may treat him when she has the desire to do so, thereby balancing somewhat the economic scales of the relationship.

A man who doesn't know a woman well may be embarrassed by her suggestion to share expenses. Possibly a woman may want to pay for herself only when and if she gets to know the man better. To let a man know you're amenable to sharing expenses, treat him to after-dinner drinks if he has given you dinner or a movie. You might also invite him to a dinner party at your house or to visit friends with you. If you can afford it, take him out to dinner or to the theater. Theater tickets bought in advance will circumvent any possible protestations. Any or all of these actions will demonstrate that you are willing to share expenses as well as the responsibility of making plans for the evening. After the two of you have become better acquainted, you might just tell him you'd feel more comfortable splitting expenses when you're out together.

A man who would like to suggest that a woman share expenses will do best if he waits until he has taken her out a few times and knows her well enough to anticipate her reaction to his suggestion. Then he may say that it bothers him to carry all the responsibility for the date and that he would like it if the relationship were on a more equal basis. If he's on a tight budget he may mention that they could afford to have more extravagant evenings if expenses were shared. Most women will not be offended by such a sensible proposal. A man shouldn't hesitate to bring up the subject; a woman may not have offered to pay simply because the idea hasn't occurred to her.

Acting as Host

When a man has asked a woman out for the evening, although she is obviously perfectly capable of hailing a taxi or choosing a table in a restaurant by herself, she is now a guest of the man she is with and therefore should let him perform the duties of host. So it follows that when a woman is host such small courtesies are her responsibility. These acts of graciousness have nothing to do with sexual roles, but are inherent in the guest–host relationship.

Taking a Date Home

Today the decision of whether a man should take a woman home at the end of an evening often depends on practical considerations instead of being the inevitable conclusion of the evening. If a woman lives in an unsafe neighborhood a man would of course see her safely to her door. When a man does see a woman home and a doorman opens the door for her, the man needn't get out of the car to see her inside the building. If there is a great deal of traffic on the street and nowhere to park, it is more thoughtful for a man to drop the woman off and remain in the car rather than block traffic still further by seeing her to her door.

If a man and a woman live at the opposite ends of a city, making it extremely difficult for him to see her home, a woman may take a taxi home alone. If the man has paid the expenses for the evening, he may offer the woman the money for cab fare or give the money directly to the taxi driver. Though such a gesture may appear gracious to some, other women may take offense at not being consulted. A man who would like to treat a woman to a taxi may say, "I'm sorry I can't see you home personally, but I'd like to pay for your taxi." Whether or not she accepts depends on the state of her own finances and her feelings regarding such a gesture.

When a man does see a woman home he walks her to her door. A woman who wants to end the evening promptly may suggest to the man, "Why not hold the taxi, it's more convenient for you," in which case the man asks the taxi driver to wait until the woman is safely inside her door.

(See the "Sharing Expenses" section in this chapter for more on the subject.)

Saying Good Night and Meaning It

I remember that as a teenager in the summer I found that the most effective method of saying a pleasant but firm good night to a date was to say it after stepping safely inside the screen door. Because the weather isn't always warm and adults cannot behave in such naïve fashion, it's best to say good night downstairs in the lobby of an apartment building or, if you are standing outside your front door, to complete your thank-you's and good night before you make any attempt to open your door. Though there may be some awkward silences, this strategy will at least prevent any misunderstanding from occurring once the door is ajar.

Breaking Dates

When I was growing up, a date with a boy took precedence over any other social occasion. Though I was never allowed to, girl friends often broke dates with one another if "something better" came up. Women should not adhere to the priorities of their teens. The first responsibility of a woman—or a man—is to honor commitments. If you make an appointment, no matter what it is, never break it because something or someone holding the possibility of more excitement comes along. Don't sacrifice one friendship for the hopes you may have for another.

If you do have to break a date, however, do so as soon as you know—don't wait until the last minute.

LANGUAGE

Even the most circumspect among us are somewhat reconciled to four-letter words today, as they seem to be more and more a part of everyday language. The dialogue in almost every film and even many television shows includes language that only a few years ago would have brought gasps from the public. An occasional swear word used for emphasis by some may add color, as opposed to vulgarity, to their speech. Both men and women at times resort to expletives to make their point. But people who cannot utter a sentence without including in it at least one four-letter word are monotonous to their listeners.

For a man to primly "watch his language" and to chastise other men for their speech because "there is a lady present" is patronizing the woman and also excludes women from the mainstream of men's conversation. It's also unlikely that a woman today would be shocked by the use of an occasional curse word. If a man tells a "dirty joke" the context of which is insulting to women, a woman listener may tell the man she is offended and why. She is not expected to laugh along with the men at a joke which is demeaning to her sex.

"HONEY" AND "DEAR"

Address people by their names, or, if you don't know their names, say "Excuse me" and if necessary get their attention by moving in front of them so that they will be able to see who is speaking to them. It's rude for a man—or a woman—to call a woman "honey," "baby," "sweetie," etc., just as it's rude to address a man as "Mac," "buddy," or "ace." Women, I think, resent being addressed as confections because at times it seems as though many men assume that all women are "honeys" and make few other distinctions. Though many men use such terms out of habit and do not mean to be insulting, a "honey" may reply in a neutral tone, "Please call me Janet" or "Please call me Ms. Schneider." A polite response will bring you the best results.

TELEPHONE MANNERS

When telephoning, it's most polite to ask, "Is Genevieve there?" and then immediately identify yourself, "This is Fenwick Sutch." The person answering the phone then says, "Just a minute, please," if the call is not for him, or "Genevieve isn't home. May I take a message?" If the caller does not identify himself and the person being called cannot come to the phone, the person who answers the phone should say so *before* asking who the caller is. If the person who answers asks first who is calling and then says that Genevieve is unavailable, it seems as though Genevieve is taking calls only from a select group or in any case is avoiding Fenwick. If, in fact, you don't want to take certain calls, ask the person who is answering the phone to tell callers you can't come to the phone at the moment and you'll return their call at a later time. In this way you won't antagonize friends who, having been told you are busy after being asked their name, may jump to the conclusion that they are not on your A list.

The phone should be answered at home with a cheerful "Hello." When the call is for another member of the household, don't ask immediately who is calling. Although it is polite for the caller to state her name, if she does not it is rude to ask who is calling if the call is made to a private house. In a business the secretary or assistant who answers the phone certainly asks who is calling, since she may well be in a position to help the caller. In a household, asking a caller to identify himself may seem as though the caller must pass a test of exclusivity. It is helpful to the caller, if the person he is trying to reach is out, to ask if you can take a message.

When someone calls and begins talking immediately without giving her name, instead of trying to decipher the voice, speak up and ask "Who is this calling, please?" The caller then identifies herself and refrains from beginning a guessing game.

When calling a friend, keep in mind that the telephone is a marvelous instrument for conveying information but dropping in by phone can be a nuisance. If your call will take more than just a few moments, don't take it for granted that the person you are calling will have the time free to talk. Ask first, "Am I calling at a convenient moment?" or "Is this a good time for you to talk?" If your call will, in fact, take only a few moments, alert the person you're calling: "Do you have a moment to answer a quick question?"

If you've dialed the wrong number, don't blame the person who answers the phone. Simply ask "Is this 972-4138?" If not, say, "I'm sorry to have bothered you, I have the wrong number," and hang up. Similarly, if a stranger calls you by mistake, don't be surly. The more helpful you are, the less likely you are to be bothered again by the same caller.

Answering Machines

Though many complain that with the advent of the telephone-answering machine even their friends have become automated, the machine is a necessary evil for many who work at home or who are at home infrequently. The machine is for the caller's convenience as well, since he need call only once and leave a message and not be bothered with the necessity of making frequent calls.

When confronted with a machine, leave a simple message. Don't just hang up. Though I'm a firm believer in the philosophy of "if it was important they'll call back," I know that many people suffer overwhelming curiosity when their machines play back long silences in place of messages.

For those plagued with hang-ups on their machines, possibly the fault may lie with the recorded message. Keep your message short. Though one friend begins his recording by quoting a different statistic from *The Guinness Book of World Records* each day, most callers haven't the patience to wait out a long preamble before the beep. Don't apologize that you're not home, and stay away from cute remarks about the machine. The most persuasive monologue I've heard is one which begins: "This is Cinderella Small" (pause), then, just as the caller may be inclined to hang up, "Please don't hang up. Leave your message and I'll get back to you shortly." Cinderella reports that her hang-up rate is almost nil.

(For teenagers' telephone manners, see Chapter 10, "Children.")

SMOKING

Today health warnings regarding smoking not only have brought heightened awareness of the problems caused by tobacco but have also brought about a change in our social attitudes about cigarettes. The once rhetorical question "Do you mind if I smoke?" has taken on new meaning in these days when "Yes, I do mind" isn't an impolite response. Because smoke may be irritating or even harmful to others, it is thoughtful to ask if you may smoke instead of making the assumption that you may.

Smoking is out of fashion—so much so, in fact, that smokers are legally as well as socially discouraged from pursuing their habit.

Many states have legislation against smoking in public places. In some parts of the country a smoker can be jailed or fined up to five hundred dollars if he lights up where the law says he shouldn't. Some restaurants have smoking and nonsmoking sections. Smokers must always abide by the rules of equal but separate when there are specific rules; when there aren't, a smoker must take care to offend as few as possible.

Smoking today is socially only quasi-acceptable. Before lighting a cigarette in between courses, ask those on either side of you if they mind if you smoke. After dinner, if your dinner partners object to your smoking, rearrange seats to form your own smoking section. In fact, some hosts plan seating arrangements to take smokers and nonsmokers into consideration. Whether it's legal or not, don't smoke in a confined space such as an elevator or a crowded car.

Smokers' Rights

Smokers are also entitled to consideration and should not be treated as pariahs. A nonsmoker must realize the misery a veteran smoker feels when deprived of a cigarette. Though nonsmokers have the right to speak up firmly but politely when a smoker causes them discomfort, a smoker should not have to submit to a righteous harangue by a smugly superior nonsmoker. A nonsmoker keeps the peace by moving to a different location.

(For more on smoking, see Chapter 5, "The Business World," and Chapter 10, "Children.")

HOSPITAL VISITORS

Although I'm sure every hospital visitor has the best of intentions to bring warmth, good cheer and support to the patient, someone sick enough to be hospitalized may cause friends and relatives to act awkwardly; visitors sometimes feel helpless in the face of the patient's illness. The patient is indeed the one who is helpless. Here are a few points to remember to keep what is by its nature a serious situation from becoming a difficult one:

In the majority of cases, your visit shouldn't extend beyond a half hour. When the patient already has lots of visitors, stay only ten or fifteen minutes so as not to tire the patient or perpetuate a cocktail-party atmosphere. If you're the only visitor and the patient is inordinately glad to see you and if your presence has brought the patient out of the doldrums, stay all afternoon if visiting hours and your schedule permit.

One is often warned about not discussing the patient's illness with the patient. Most patients are absorbed by their illness and wish to talk of little else. Try "How are you feeling?" or something equally general. If the patient skirts the question or answers with a succinct "Fine" or "Terrible," bring up the movie you both saw last night on the late show, or something just as far removed from illness. Most patients, at the drop of a "How are you feeling?," will be happy for the chance to tell it all over again.

Commiserate positively. Keep your negative feelings to yourself. If your cousin Lou had the same operation but the story doesn't have a happy ending, don't tell it. Don't make a diagnosis or suggest that the doctor's diagnosis is wrong, no matter what old Dr. Abrams told Mrs. Fairweather when she was plagued with a similar problem. Doctors differ in opinion as to what is the best way back to health. No matter how gray the patient looks, don't burst out with your surprise that he looks so awful.

Try not to bring up unpleasant topics that may cause the patient to worry. If something unfavorable is brewing at the office, wait until the patient is feeling a bit better before he has to face the discordant music. Be careful not to go too much in the other direction and be falsely jovial.

Always ask if you may smoke. In a semiprivate room or a ward there may be others who can't tolerate smoke. Even if the patient is in a private room and is a smoker, possibly illness has made the patient temporarily sensitive to smoke.

I tend to become a patient myself when I'm confronted with someone connected to tubes or just someone who is obviously sick. My visit doesn't help either of us. Instead of visiting, I call and ask how I can be of help. If you're like me you might offer to feed the cat, postpone appointments or bring drugstore items to the hospital.

Maternity Patients

I think the most obvious and frequent cases of blindness to a patient's condition involve the visitors to a maternity ward. Pregnancy is not a pathology and is one time when it is truly joyful to be in a hospital. Having a baby is, however, very hard work and requires a few days' rest afterward. It may also be the last time in months that the patient will have the opportunity to rest. A maternity patient should be treated with the same consideration as any other patient in the hospital.

Psychiatric Patients

Treat a psychiatric patient just as you would any other patient. Don't make the mistake of pretending that everything is all right. Instead, ask, "How are you feeling?" It is helpful to the patient to acknowledge his illness and to accept it. To deny the reality of a mental illness is, in fact, to deny the importance of the patient's feelings. Mental illness is no longer discussed in whispers. In our society, which is often accused of creating mental illness, there is now room for open acknowledgment of its existence.

Flowers

If you send or bring flowers, be sure they are already in a container. Hospitals don't always provide vases, and if flowers are not already arranged the nurses have to do the extra work.

Before you send flowers, it is a good idea to phone the patient to ask if there is anything he would like or needs, a gourmet delicacy perhaps, or some fruit, if his diet permits. So many people send flowers that patients' rooms are sometimes overflowing with them. One friend who after a car accident needed many blood transfusions asked her friends to donate a pint of blood instead of sending flowers, since in many hospitals there is a continuous shortage of blood.

When You Are the Patient

Hospital patients find themselves caught in the mainstream of a brave new world. People who lead active, productive lives are suddenly quite helpless in an institutional world which whirls—not always pleasantly—around them. Their condition has rendered them passive, and the often dehumanizing aspects of hospital life can be difficult to adjust to, even temporarily. To make a hospital stay more pleasant, in New York State the Patient's Bill of Rights, which has been made part of the New York State Hospital Code, promises to insure that the patient is treated considerately and courteously, that the patient is to have access to hospital information about his or her care and that the patient has the right to privacy. In New York a patient may ask for a copy of the Patient's Bill of Rights. Possibly your state has drafted a similar document.

Because the workings of a hospital are new and strange to the patient, it may be helpful to point out a few rules to make the role of the patient clearer.

Visiting Hours: There are certain times when one's obligations as host are suspended. You do not have to be sure everyone is having a good time. In fact, visitors are supposed to see that you are the one who, if you're not up to a good time, are at least having a better time or a more cheerful time than you were having without them. If anyone is going to worry whether visiting hours were a social success, let it be the visitors.

A hospital patient is exempt from many social rules. For instance, a patient may certainly eat his or her lunch or dinner while there are visitors present. If even as a patient you can't shake off all your hesitation about eating a meal while others just look on, offer the visitor your celery or roll if it will put you at your ease.

If you're in a semiprivate room or a ward you might introduce your visitor to the person in the next bed. After the introduction and possibly a few words, you and your visitor may hold a private conversation.

When leaving the hospital, it's thoughtful to leave your flowers, books and magazines with the nurses to be passed on to other patients. Don't tip the nurses. Gratuities are forbidden, and since the nurses are professional, tipping them is insulting. You may tip the attendants who cleaned your room if you had a private or a semiprivate room. The tip should be about three dollars for a one-week stay. If you'd like, you may leave the nurses candy with a note thanking them for being so nice, or, if you have one or two favorites, you may give them a small present when you leave.

When you are feeling well enough, write thank-you notes to those well-wishers who sent you something while you were in the hospital and haven't seen to thank them in person.

An especially thoughtful friend sent short thank-you notes to those who visited her when she was in the hospital. A note might read: "Dear Cindy, Thank you so much for taking the time to visit me in the hospital. Seeing your cheerful face gave me quite a lift. I appreciate your thoughtfulness."

If a patient is very sick, a friend or relative may write thank-you notes for the patient, such as: "Dear Ms. Friedman, Anne Marie McPhillips has asked me to write and thank you for the two mysteries. Josephine Tey is very much a favorite and she has enjoyed them immensely."

CLUBS—CITY AND COUNTRY

Joining

Many clubs and organizations are founded around similar interests such as professions and hobbies, and one need only take the trouble and apply to be accepted. Private clubs, however, are formed primarily for social reasons, and therefore a certain exclusivity is characteristic. Common interest is not enough to give a person entry into a private club; new members must be accepted into the club by all existing members. Generally two members are needed to sponsor a membership application: a sponsor and a seconder. Sometimes members of the board of the club will interview the prospective member as well. Then the membership at large votes on the application. Before the vote, the sponsor of the new member may inquire discreetly among the membership to be sure there is no hesitation among any of the members about the new application. This is to circumvent the possibility of the prospective new member being blackballed, a disheartening experience that can befall a prospective member even if only one member has any doubts about him or her.

If you'd like to join a private club, it's best to wait for a friend to suggest that he be your sponsor. If this is not forthcoming or your patience is no substitute for your eagerness, drop a hint that you'd like to join. However, if your friend does have reservations about sponsoring your membership, refusing you will almost surely weaken the friendship; no one likes to discover that a friend isn't as true as one hoped, so it's best to beat around the bush a little first, to give your friend the opportunity to let you know where you stand before you ask the question. In this instance, think like a trial lawyer—he is taught in law school never to ask a witness a question to which he doesn't know the answer.

If you do apply and are turned down, be resolute. Wait a couple of years until you've come to know a few more members and try again with a different sponsor and seconder.

Sponsor's letter of recommendation:

> Board of Governors
> Athletic Club
>
> Gentlemen:
>   I'm writing with pleasure to propose Mr. John Paul Nickerson for membership in the Athletic Club. Mr. Nickerson is a graduate of the University of Michigan and the University of Michigan Law School, from which he received his degree in 1962.
>   Mr. Nickerson is married to Lola Pederson and lives at 20 Lakeshore Drive. He is a partner in Pedersen, Nickerson & Nickerson Co., and he is an avid and excellent tennis player. I think he would be a most worthy addition to the club.
>
> Sincerely,

New Members

A new member must walk softly in the club. The club is not yet your second home; you're open to judgment from all the more established members. Your character and behavior were evaluated before you joined, and members will continue to scrutinize you. Although you are a member, wait for established members to introduce themselves to you. Your sponsor and seconder should also make introductions for you to help pave your way.

Club Payments

In most clubs chits are signed in place of cash payments, and bills are sent out at the end of the month. In some clubs a service charge is added to each monthly bill, so tips are not expected.

There is also a Christmas fund to which all members contribute. Be sure to know your club's policies.

Guests

A guest at a club behaves as she would if she were a guest in someone's home. When in doubt about procedure, wait and see what your host does. Remember, your host holds responsibility for you, so obey all the club's rules. If you're an overnight guest at a residential club, your host may have obtained for you a temporary membership card or a guest card, in which case you sign your name to every chit and pay your bill at the end of your stay. Tip those who have been of service to you just as you would in a hotel. If you have stayed without a guest card and you have never received a bill, your host has, so remember to reimburse him.

If you are a guest for only a few days or a week, sign your host's name along with your name in parenthesis. When you order something to eat or to drink keep track of what you spend, since the bill will be sent to your host and it's up to you to repay the money.

If you've been invited by a member to spend the afternoon at his country club, you need worry only about incidentals, as you are clearly a guest. A guest does tip those who provide special services, such as a locker-room attendant (one or two dollars). A golf-playing guest should make every effort to pay the greens fee and the caddie's fee (for himself and his host); it's good form and a thoughtful way to say "Thank you."

Weekends are the busiest time at a country club. Although members may certainly entertain guests at their club, they shouldn't make it too frequent a practice, as other members will begin to grumble if a constant succession of nonmembers is taking their place on the tennis courts and on the golf links.

Club Meetings

If you aren't familiar with the procedures of the conduct of meetings, look them up in *Robert's Rules of Order*. Though many meetings aren't conducted along the most rigid and formal lines, all meetings follow the *Rules of Order*, however loosely.

Resigning

When you resign from a club write a letter to the president or to the members of the board.

> Dear Mr. Ordway:
> I'm sorry that I must resign from the Metropolitan Club. My firm has transferred me to Nashville and I'll be leaving in September. I would like you to know how much I've enjoyed the time I spent at the Club. I shall miss it.
>
> Sincerely,
> Geoffrey Wasply

A CONVERSATION WITH SOMEONE OLDER

It's unfortunate that in our culture older people must often live with age discrimination. Younger people often find it difficult to converse with someone generations removed from them; they may be uncertain of how to initiate a conversation or they may fear that an older person would not be interested in what they have to say. Because extended families are virtually nonexistent in the United States today, and children no longer live in close communities with their grandparents, aunts and uncles, young people may be unaccustomed to spending time with people in their seventies and eighties.

Younger people often lack the social expertise to do much conversational hurdling, and older people, simply because of their seniority, should be accorded special consideration: one who is younger must make every effort to be courteous and at the same time must be careful not to go overboard in his eagerness and become patronizing while merely trying to be respectful. To begin a conversation, you might ask about grandchildren, where the person is living, his interests and hobbies. Once a conversation gets going, an older person loves nothing more than to relay anecdotes from his life (more often than not a younger person will find himself fascinated). In addition, a younger person should remember to speak clearly and audibly in case the older person has trouble hearing.

When you are introduced to someone who is older, stand to shake hands. A young woman who may prefer to remain seated when introduced to a slightly older man would rise when introduced to a much older man, much as she would stand aside and let an older man go through a door or into an elevator before she does.

2 ENTERTAINING

What makes a good party? Think about those evenings you really had a good time. What accounted for it? The most memorable good times happen spontaneously: the conversation is interesting and the atmosphere relaxed. When inviting guests, whether it's the neighbors in for afternoon coffee or the boss for dinner, remember that the most important ingredient for a good party is lively, easygoing, free-flowing conversation. This sounds easy; but everyone who has ever given a party realizes that all the planning and organization that go into entertaining are done to promote the relaxed atmosphere that encourages this kind of conversation—the most difficult thing to accomplish.

How can you plan a successful party? There are certainly no guarantees to party-giving success, but there's a lot that a host *can* do to steer the evening in the right direction. To begin with, there is the guest list.

THE GUEST LIST

Whom to Invite with Whom

The guest list is very important. After all, the guests determine the flow and content of the conversation. Whom you invite with whom takes some basic psychology and also depends on the kind of party you're planning. It's a good idea to invite one person who loves to talk—not only about himself but about a variety of subjects. This person can act as a kind of centerpiece for a relatively small (six to ten) gathering. The centerpiece should not be the I-love-to-hear-myself-talk-about-myself bore, but rather the I-love-to-hear-myself-talk-and-so-does-everyone-else delight. There are certain people who have an amazing ability to act as the spark that sets off conversation. If your party is a large cocktail or buffet and you're lucky enough to have more than one of these conversation catalysts as friends, things are already off to a good start.

If you're planning a small party in order to introduce some new, interesting friends to a few of your regular circle, the Conversation Starter—either someone from your new circle or one of your reg-ulars—is almost a must. It can easily happen that old friends who have a shared history of experience will huddle together, making it almost impossible for new people to join in. The Conversation Starter has no trouble in this kind of situation. In fact, he or she will probably enjoy the challenge of integrating both groups of people.

Often, parties are inspired by a combination of what, for lack of a better word, I'll call motives. For instance, sometimes you "owe" a dinner invitation to a couple whom you don't know very well, so you include them in a dinner party otherwise composed of old friends. Before you repay their hospitality in this way, make sure your new guests have *some* interests in common with your closer friends.

And, more important, when inviting new people to a party, make sure that they will know at least one other guest there. For instance, when you invite people you've met recently at the house of friends, include the hosts of that party. Not only is it politic in order to avoid accusations of snubbery and general bad feeling, but, because you as host will be busy overseeing the event, the new friends will naturally gravitate to the guest they know and will therefore be able to find their own ground.

It's flattering to turn a party to which you have invited new people into an Occasion. My friend Katherine recently met a woman she liked enormously. Both women are great cooks and had studied at the Cordon Bleu in Paris. Katherine decided to give a party for her new friend. She must have cooked for days, and she presented us a six-course dinner—a masterpiece which in turn inspired a new friendship.

I do think it's a mistake to throw an odd couple or two into an otherwise harmonious guest list just because you owe them dinner. If you feel your other guests won't hit it off with your new acquain-tances, save your pay-back dinners for another occasion when you can ask one couple at a time to your house for a quiet meal. In a cozy atmosphere, people you were reluctant to invite may turn out to be easier guests than you had expected.

It may happen that you find yourself entertaining business friends or others—such as members of a community organization in which you are involved—who you feel would fit in only with a certain group of people. If, in this situation, you think it best not to invite friends whom you'd ordinarily ask to a party, make your explanation to them *before* you issue your invitations. If uninvited friends learn of your plans from other sources, they may feel slighted.

On the other hand, if you tell friends that you're planning a party that is more a business gathering than a social one, no one will be hurt. Many Wall Street men, for example, are immersed in the Land of the Ticker Tape, and when more than two or three of them get together they don't seem particularly interested in talking to anyone else. I don't give this kind of one-note party very often, but all of us—businessmen, businesswomen, wives of businessmen —have had to give such parties. If shop talk is inevitably going to predominate, then it may be best to invite only those who can participate in it avidly, along with those who are resigned to it (wives or husbands of the business guests).

Single Men and Single Women

If you're giving an elegant sit-down dinner party, you may feel that it is only right and proper to have an equal number of men and women (although this tradition is fast disappearing). If you're uncomfortable unless there is a perfect balance of men and women —and today you needn't be—then a necessary ingredient to your dinner party may be the extra man.

Single men, often as hard to find as the kiwi bird, can be invited just to even out the numbers or, more specifically, to be the dinner partner of a single woman. Is it really worth going to all the trouble it sometimes takes to solve the mathematical problem of equal numbers of the sexes? Sometimes the energy and worry expended on details like this become so overwhelming you forget the object of the party is to have a good time. (Remember Billie Burke in *Dinner at Eight?* All her maneuvering and intrigue over her guest list brought her to the brink of a breakdown—very funny in the movie, but not so amusing in real life.)

When I do even out the numbers with an extra man, I don't try to make a match. It's rare that strangers take one look at each other and begin humming "Some Enchanted Evening." I don't seat single guests together and I don't expect them to leave together. It's best to let attractions develop naturally. An extra man I often ask has his radar operating in all directions. If he finds he's interested in a woman, he won't interrupt the flow of the party to concentrate on her but he'll ask for her phone number.

If you want to balance the sexes, be careful about inviting a person who was unattached the last time you looked, but whom you haven't seen for a while. The last time I took this chance, the man I was inviting informed me he was involved with someone. I couldn't very well say, "Stay home, we don't want you!" I had to ask them both. My guest list increased by two and I still didn't have an extra man. Luckily, my newly invited couple offered to bring along a single male friend, so everything worked out with a minimum of difficulty.

You're attempting the Impossible Dream if you ask single people who have been separated or divorced too recently and try to pair them off. A man I know—you probably know one, too—went through a very anxious separation. He would call and talk to me for hours on end a couple of times a week about how unhappy he was, how he'd do anything to stay with his wife, and how he missed his children. After a few months, he calmed down and I invited him to be the dinner partner of an acquaintance who was newly separated. The party was fairly large, so I didn't have much time to see how my matchmaking was working out. But I was hopeful —the couple seemed engrossed in conversation. I called my friend the next day and asked him how his evening had been. He told me: Awful! All his dinner partner had talked about was how unhappy she was, how she hated being separated, how tough it was for the children and so forth.

On the other hand, the time when a person is at his loneliest— after a separation, a divorce or the death of a spouse—may be the time when he needs invitations the most. In our imperfect society, women in particular are socially penalized when they are without a man. If your woman friend was interesting when her husband was around, why shouldn't she be just as interesting now—maybe more so? Anyhow, if your friend needs and wants company, do make her a part of your guest list, even if it means an extra woman.

A case in point is my friend Emily, who complains (quite correctly, I'm afraid) that since her divorce she's been asked to very few dinner parties. She's become what she terms a "kitchen friend." When she's invited for dinner, she is always the only guest and eats in the kitchen with her hosts. "Cinderella" is rarely asked to her friends' parties, and yet Emily's exuberance would add to the gaiety of any party.

Men's stag parties have been around since King Arthur and his Round Table. A few years ago, that table began to turn—"spin" might be a more accurate term. It is no longer unheard of to give a dinner party for women only. One quick look at the climbing divorce rates tells us that women have discovered they don't need men every moment of the day and night. Maxine, a divorced woman, sometimes gives parties just for women; husbands are not invited. The women all have careers of their own and are interesting and stimulating conversationalists. Maxine doesn't always exclude men, but invites *people* whom she finds interesting and who she feels have allied interests and will get along well together. Maxine has found that when men are present at her parties, these days it's often the women who spark the conversation. In fact, one night after dinner the men ended up sitting in a corner by themselves while the women held forth around the dining table. One man, upon leaving, told Maxine that he finally understood what it was like to be a woman because he'd felt totally excluded from the central core of the party.

Last-Minute Additions

We've probably all received that last-minute phone call from a friend who wants to bring a friend. Quite frankly, if you've planned a sit-down dinner, this is an imposition and you need not rise gallantly to the occasion. I have a friend who takes her dinner-party giving very seriously. She told me, at the risk of sounding compulsive, that she has a beautiful dinner service for only six (her ex has the other half), her table seats six most comfortably and she likes everything to be perfect. Even if she does have enough food for an extra guest, she doesn't reshuffle everything at the last minute and mix her stainless with her silver—all for someone she doesn't know. I agree with her. It's fine to give a flat but polite "No" in instances when you cannot accommodate a last-minute addition.

The Special Guest

We've all had the added pleasure (and sometimes added problems) of "the special guest." Sometimes you haven't previously met your guest and therefore have almost no idea of what to expect. If, for instance, a business associate is passing through town, you might decide to have a small dinner for her. Entertaining a stranger need not be a problem. Why not ask a few friends whom you work with or who work in related fields? Prepare your guests by telling them what little you know about the special guest: where she lives and the kind of work she does. Then no one will walk into the party cold. They'll all know a bit about your guest of honor and will be able to direct their conversation easily because the preliminaries have already been established.

Another special guest could be someone in your community—a local politician, the dean of your community college or some other type of celebrity—whom you've always wanted to meet but haven't, for one reason or another. In that case it's up to you to set the time and the place. When issuing your invitation to this august individual, throw your shyness and reticence to the winds if you hope for an acceptance. Helen Lawrenson, in her book A *Stranger at the Party*, tells how Clare Boothe Luce made certain she'd get an acceptance when she issued such an invitation. If she wanted to invite the Duchess of Windsor and Sir Laurence Olivier to a party, she'd call Sir Laurence and mention that the Duchess of Windsor had asked especially that he be invited. Then she would call the Duchess and say that Olivier asked that *she* be invited!

Clare Boothe Luce's way may not be your way, but *do* use everything you can think of. For instance, mention to your prospective guest that you belong to the same country club or that your husband plays golf with his brother and has heard such nice things about him that you'd both love to have him for dinner. Or mention that you and some of your other guests are very involved in the new school-board elections and you think he might be interested in helping to organize your campaign.

If your prayers are answered and the celebrity accepts, your guest list should include friends and acquaintances who either know your special guest or have, like you, admired him from afar and are excited by or involved in his causes.

When I gave a party for good friends of mine who were visiting from Europe, I wanted to make the party special and decided to take my chances and invite some new faces, faces my friends didn't know but I was sure they'd like.

I started by taking a deep breath and inviting the Duchess of Windsor. I've known the Duchess since I was a baby. My mother and father know her very well. But, after all, she *is* a duchess and therefore was very much in demand before poor health curtailed her social life. Though not the easiest person to get, she was worth the effort; she added glamour to any party. At that time the Duchess was in New York City only about six weeks out of the year, and luckily her visit coincided with the date of my party. My secretary called to invite her—for three days running. The Duchess apparently couldn't make up her mind whether she wanted to come or not. Instead of getting myself into a pickle over her indecision, I began to get the machinery around her in working order. I invited a good friend of hers, and the next day the Duchess accepted my invitation, but asked that a car be sent for her. My secretary was quick enough to suggest that she come with her good friend, arranged it for her, and I had one worry taken care of.

Then I did something that took more courage than inviting the Duchess. I called a perfect stranger, Jim Jensen, the charming anchor man on the *CBS Evening News*. We don't know each other, but I wanted interesting people, so I just took the plunge. I tried to reach him for days. There's nothing more frustrating than calling a busy newsroom and never speaking to the same person twice. Finally the message was conveyed to Mr. Jensen, and he sent me a very nice note saying he'd be busy on that date but would love a rain check. Next time I invite him, I'll send a written invitation.

I admit, it's a little scary inviting someone whom you haven't even met; but if you attempt this kind of social feat, you'll be pleased with the results. People are always flattered to be asked, and you might even make a new friend.

INVITATIONS

Issuing an Invitation

Invitations to friends can be issued by phone or mail, though phoning is by far the simpler. If you've asked guests far in advance, the U.S. mail can help people remember where or when, since few of us are used to keeping social calendars filled in more than a week or so ahead.

As a guest, when you receive a written invitation, reply immediately. Don't embarrass your host by appearing when you haven't bothered to answer the invitation. Remember, whether you accept or decline an invitation, you should do it promptly so that the host can plan properly.

I usually invite people at least two weeks in advance. For a large party or a special occasion, I start calling a month ahead. I used to send out invitations first, then wait for a reply. That reply sometimes took forever, so I've devised a scheme to end my waiting. I now call first to get a yes or no as soon as possible. Then I send the invitation, giving the date, the place and the address and put "To Remind" at the top.

Because I'm very insistent about when I eat, I often write on the invitation, "8 o'clock cocktails, 8:45 dinner." If anybody wants to show up at eight-forty, that's fine with me; but we're going to sit down to dinner at a quarter to nine. The written invitation also specifies whether the party is black tie or not.

On occasion, when inviting a couple, a host will discover that only one half of the couple is accepting. When confronted with "I'd love to come, but Paul will be in Minneapolis over the weekend of the twenty-seventh," a host never says, "Oh, in that case, maybe you'll both be able to come next time," but instead must accept one half of the couple without the other, even though it may make the seating plans uneven.

A sensitive guest phrases her response thusly, in such circumstances: "I'm sorry, Paul will be in Minneapolis, so we can't make it," and then waits for the sensitive host to reply, "But *you* must come." A guest who will feel uncomfortable without his or her spouse may certainly decline the invitation.

When issuing an invitation by phone, how much information do you have to give a guest about your party plans? Though you needn't volunteer any more information than the time and the place, I think there are instances when it is courteous to divulge a bit more of your plans. If you're inviting someone who is new to your acquaintance, it's thoughtful to tell that person of one or two other invited guests whom he or she may know or have at least heard about. Or if a friend has mentioned in the past that she wanted to meet someone special whom you've invited, tell her.

To invited guests: you must give your answer as to whether you'll be at the party or not immediately upon being invited. Your answer cannot be predicated on your host's guest list. Though a host may offer such additional information, a prospective guest is never to inquire. To do so would be presumptuous and is also a way of telling your host that her company and entertainment are not sufficient to command your presence.

When inviting a single person, be sure to let him or her know beforehand whether you expect that person to bring a friend. Despite the fact that in many circles it is perfectly acceptable to come to a party alone, some single people are shy about appearing unescorted in married circles and may even think they are unwelcome without a date. You might make them less shy if you include in your invitation that it is perfectly acceptable for them to come alone. You may say, "Please come to dinner the 24th. You certainly may bring a friend if you'd like, but it's not necessary, we'd love to have just you." If you do have a preference, make it clear: "We'd like you to come to dinner on the 24th," or "We'd like you and a guest to come to dinner . . ." Written invitations should read: "Ms. Velvet Cunningham and guest."

(For more on written invitations, see Chapter 6, "Correspondence.")

Extending a Last-Minute Dinner Invitation

It may happen that on the day of your carefully planned sit-down dinner for twelve a guest calls to say she can't make it. When faced with extending a last-minute invitation, extend it to only a good friend or to a party lover who will be so glad to be asked he or she won't consider the last-minute invitation a slight. And tell the truth so that your new guest will be happy to be invited and won't be indignant at being on the stand-by list. Explain the situation: "I'm having a party this evening for the Piccolis, friends of Ricardo's who are visiting over the weekend. Ricardo's sister just called to say she has the flu. I hope you can come. We'd just love to have you and now I have the room."

WHAT TO WEAR

I don't have formal dinners as much these days as I used to. Private parties, even the most important ones, seem to be listing toward informal. I find that women usually dress up for parties anyway, but the party uniform for the men in my circle—if the party is in New York City—is dark business suits, unless black tie is specified. People do tend to dress much more formally when they receive a written invitation to a dinner. If you want your guests to dress casually, say so on the invitation.

If the party is informal, what you wear depends on what you think your host expects. When I'm at my summer house on Long Island or skiing in the mountains, I often go to parties where the men are wearing turtlenecks and sometimes even blue jeans. Most people I know don't give private black-tie dinners. Many men don't own a dinner jacket.

It has happened at my house that almost everyone was in business suits and long dresses and in walked a guest in blue jeans. His jeans must have had a couple of hundred dollars' worth of embroidered sunbursts on them, and he outsparkled all the men (and most of the women) in the room. I wish more men had secret ambitions to be rock stars. I think he made a festive addition to the party; however, he may have felt uncomfortable.

If you don't know your host well, it's best to play it safe. A man wears a suit or a sports jacket and tie. If he arrives and finds all the other men in turtlenecks, he can always take off the tie and the jacket. A woman dressed for dinner in a long dress or a pair of evening pants need never feel out of place.

(For more on what the guest wears, see Chapter 16, "Fashion.")

MENUS AND MEALS

The Host Sets the Tone

The most effective entertaining is that which reflects the personal style of the host. Working people can throw together a casual supper, for example, and some people like to have dinner parties where the guests do their share—chopping food to stir-fry in a wok. Many people love to congregate in a warm kitchen where the host presides over a simmering pot. The host should be able to have as much fun as the guests.

The kitchen is no longer only the woman's domain. More and more men are taking up cooking—and I don't mean just barbecuing steaks. Many men are proficient enough to prepare an entire party menu, or at least a part of it. The old-style division of labor is no more.

In homes where both husband and wife work, party giving has become a joint venture. As a guest, you can no longer assume that your male host will be the one to get you a drink. He may be in the kitchen slicing mushrooms while his wife is tending bar. If the woman is still the sole cook in the house, the man may help clear the table and clean up the kitchen.

If you are a single, working host with little extra time, it's important to structure that time efficiently when preparing for a party. If you're a "morning" person, why not set the table and arrange the bar before you leave for work? If you usually stay up late, do your table setting the night before. And don't worry if you haven't the time to add those little extras you think are so necessary. Your guests will understand that you're a person with a full schedule, a schedule that prohibits extra hours in the kitchen.

Simplicity Is the Key

Every host worries about what to serve; food is very important, even for a cozy dinner of four or six. After all, you're giving a *dinner* party. If you have no help in the kitchen, simply serve what you feel comfortable making. Even if you're giving a "special-guest" party and want to wow your friends with your culinary expertise, it can be dangerous to attempt a gourmet recipe above and beyond your kitchen prowess.

I've found that what works best is simple, good food; food which is easily prepared.

When you're giving a party with no help, it works best to streamline dinner as much as possible so that you can sit down and be part of the conversation. In fact, the more you can prepare before your guests arrive, the better. It's very disconcerting for the guests if the host is constantly hopping up and down during dinner, orchestrating an extravaganza.

If your dining-room or buffet table is set with tender loving care and you've organized your party work in advance so that you have time to spend with your guests, don't think you have to serve a French tour de force. The most important thing for a host is to be relaxed enough to see to the needs of the guests. A preoccupied host running in and out of the kitchen checking on an overly complicated recipe bodes ill for the evening.

Instead of attempting to serve a variety of elaborate and difficult-to-prepare foods, why not concentrate on one special dish? If you make great salads or desserts, spend time on your specialty. A friend of mine serves a delicious dinner of boiled French sausages and boiled potatoes, with a beautiful salad. She doesn't have to worry about meat getting overdone, sauces curdling or soufflés falling.

Appropriate Menus

It's not important how fancy the menu is, but rather how good it is and how easily it's served. I once went to a Fourth of July lunch held outdoors at which we were given exquisite Chinese food elaborately prepared by the proud host's Chinese cook. The food was served with all the ceremony that was its due. This food would certainly have been welcome at a more formal evening party. To me, "Fourth of July" is automatically followed by "picnic." If it's Independence Day and your guests are swimming and sunbathing, why not serve the traditional New England salmon and new peas, or simply a hot-dog-and-hamburger barbecue? Our masterly prepared sit-down (in wet bathing suits) Chinese dinner put a damper on the gathering. Admittedly, the food was delicious; but I think it was served at the wrong time and the wrong place.

I dislike going to friends' houses where each dish is served up with such pomp that I feel I'm expected to comment on the food throughout the meal. A bit of oohing and aahing is always nice, but a complete dissection of every truffle is boring and makes me want to go home early. I love good food, whether it's a cheeseburger or beef Wellington. The food you serve should be a pleasant enhancement to your party, but it need not be the stage show everyone has come to review.

Choosing Your Courses

Your hors d'oeuvres may be simple: *crudités*, which is the French word for cut-up fresh vegetables, usually served with a dip, or pâté are excellent choices. There are certain easy supermarket foods which are among my favorites. For instance, my *pièce de résistance* is peanut butter and bacon on toast, and my friends seem to love my enhanced peanut butter as much as I do.

In today's entertaining, the hors d'oeuvres course may substitute for the appetizer. Substantial—and even quite elegant—fare can be served in the living room with cocktails: shrimp, possibly, or a hot puff pastry with cheese. And if you serve a wide variety of hors d'oeuvres, your guests may not have the appetite for a formal first course. But remember to be careful about choosing what to serve the guests before they are seated; food that is complicated to eat may be awkward (not to mention messy) in the living room. Anything that requires more manipulation than spearing with a toothpick or spreading with a knife cannot be eaten comfortably in the living room. Prosciutto and melon, for instance, unless cut into bite-size pieces, should be served at the dining-room table.

For your main course, choose a casserole or a baked ham which can be prepared before guests arrive (steak and roast beef which should be cooked to order, may dry out if not eaten immediately). Most of us aren't gourmet cooks, and we needn't be. Perfect two or three dishes and they will become your specialties. You'll develop a reputation for making delicious beef Stroganoff or Hungarian goulash. (Frequent guests will be delighted to eat them again at your house, and they may even mention when receiving your invitations that they adore your goulash, hinting that they'd love it if you made it for this party too.) And when planning food quantities it's much better to go overboard than to leave your guests hungry. Leftovers make delicious family meals.

A host need not worry about serving a dish which is obviously not expensive. For instance, I don't serve steak, and I rarely serve roast beef. Fine cuts of beef are often less interesting or spectacular than an excellent stuffed cabbage or chicken paprika. No one is interested in your butcher bill, but rather in the character of the dishes you serve.

I love dessert—it's my favorite part of the meal. After a heavier main dish, I usually serve a chocolate or a fruit mousse; a lighter main course calls for my favorite, vanilla ice cream inside pastry with a chocolate sauce.* Even though thin is in and more than half the people I know—including me—are on constant diets, I've noticed that those diets are quickly forgotten at a party.

When a Guest Doesn't Eat the Food You're Serving

One friend was planning a light summer meal of *moules ma-rinière* when, in the middle of checking her guest list, she realized that one of her guests was Jewish, kept a kosher home and couldn't eat shellfish. She switched to poached salmon in the knick of time. Another friend who makes a wonderful kidney dish always keeps a small steak on hand for kidney night in case an occasional guest doesn't eat organ meat. I think it's very thoughtful—in fact, beyond the call of duty—to give a squeamish guest a choice of menus. If a guest is excessively finicky, don't feel you have to become a short-order cook.

If you'd like to serve an exotic dish, make it when you're having a small party, and ask when you invite your guests, "Do you like lamb curry?" They won't feel shy about saying no before you've cooked it, and it shows your concern toward the comfort of your guests to ask in advance.

For Guests on a Special Diet

If you are under doctor's orders not to eat certain foods, if you keep a kosher home or don't eat meat, tell your host when you're invited. It's most irritating for a host to spend time on a dish that one guest won't touch. If you don't like what's being served, as long as it's not the main dish, don't take it. It's wasteful and con-spicuous to put something on your plate and just play with it with

* Many people prefer to serve fresh fruit with an appropriate variety of cheeses; this is a classic dessert.

your fork. Children do that kind of thing with the school-cafeteria food.

A host with one guest on a special diet has the option of making that guest something special, or she may increase the amount of a side dish so that the guest won't be staring at an empty plate while the others eat. In a more complicated situation—when there are more than six dinner guests and taking individual orders is impossible—it's up to you as a guest to fend for yourself.

HIRING HELP FOR YOUR PARTY

One Person to Lighten the Host's Duties

Katie, a stockbroker, tells tales about how years ago when she was involved in an all-absorbing career she still had time to entertain in style.

She had a couple of favorite restaurants, one Indonesian and one French, which prepared party specialties for her. The day of her party, she would pick up the dinner on her way home from the office and serve it as though it were her own fabulous creation. Even amid all the compliments (especially for her Indonesian delights), she never told. When one impressed guest asked her for her recipe for an elaborate crab-and-ginger dish, Katie blushed and stammered, seemingly sensitive to the compliment. Katie got herself out of the corner by saying the dish was too intricate to divulge at the moment but she'd send it along, which of course she never did. The impressed guest probably assumed that Katie wanted to keep her culinary secrets and troubled her no more. After that close call, Katie served more accessible cuisine, reasoning that she could always divulge a recipe for duck à l'orange and that if it turned out differently than Katie's exquisite masterpiece, well, it must have been because the ingredients were in the hands of a lesser creator. Katie wonders today how she got away with it. Can you imagine walking into somebody's house for dinner, being served a superb meal with no mouth-watering smells from the kitchen, and the kitchen itself, if you should by chance stumble upon it, in search of some ice or a corkscrew, is spotless with nary a pot bubbling on the stove? Of course, if you were to glance at the garbage, you'd be surprised to find it piled high with cardboard cartons—but perhaps your host is not fastidious and hasn't removed the boxes from last night's Chinese takeout. But in those days, Katie reminds us, it was unthinkable that a woman would desert her own kitchen for her own office.

Today, a working woman with no household help does not need to pretend to be superwoman. You may not have a restaurant prepare your dinners as Katie did, if you don't want to miss the fun of entertaining but can't make the time for all the extras a party demands of your time. You might want to hire a cook. One woman —a modern-day Katie—used to feel she had to do everything, work, care for her children, cook and entertain, all this and all by herself. Today when she entertains she hires an aspiring actress who moonlights as a superb cook. The menu is discussed and agreed upon beforehand, and the young woman does all the shopping and cooking. The host prefers to serve and wash up herself. You may prefer to cook yourself but hire someone to serve and clean up at your party. The choice is yours; however, there is no reason to feel guilty because you can't (or simply don't want to) do everything. Ask around in your area. Today there are many young men and women who are excellent cooks and are happy to make the extra money, and they might not charge as much as you'd expected. Or if you know of a superb amateur cook, why not inquire as to whether he or she would like to cook for your party? You might get a positive answer to such a flattering question.

If you are looking for outside help, there are many part-time professional household workers, butlers, waiters (both male and female) and bartenders (both male and female) who work on a free-lance basis. Your neighbor's college-age son or daughter may moonlight as a bartender or dishwasher; your part-time household worker may be able to help you in the evening when you're having a party. Extra help these days is wherever you find it.

Part-time bonded household workers can be hired through agencies. (Bonded means that the insurance company which furnishes the bond will pay for a missing item—provided you can prove it was stolen.) People hired through an agency cost a bit more because the agency takes a fee. When hiring through an agency, either you'll pay the entire cost to the agency, which in turn will pay the household worker, or you'll pay the worker, who will then pay a percentage to the agency. You needn't tip those who work through an agency, as the price is so high it makes tipping prohibitive. You also do not tip someone who works independently and is therefore his own boss. Always remember to discuss payment when you hire somebody, so that neither of you is surprised at the end of the evening. If someone you hire breaks something precious, you don't have to grin, but you do have to bear it. Mistakes do happen and you must make allowances for them. Maybe next time you'll hire someone with less slippery fingers. Breakage is not taken out of wages, and reprimands after the fact won't bring the hollow crystal wine goblet back.

If you do plan on outside help, before you invite your first guest make sure you reserve the help for the date and time of your party. If you begin to cast about for people to help you put your party together after guests have been invited, you may well find yourself going it alone, especially during busy party seasons.

If you've never actually had someone help you at your parties before, here is a general breakdown of the responsibility you can delegate: The person who is helping you can take coats (although you should be at the door as well, to greet the guests), make drinks, serve hors d'oeuvres and serve dinner, clear the table and clean up in the kitchen. If you're lucky and he is a good cook he may also have prepared dinner. If you'd rather greet guests yourself or make drinks, your party helper may be in the kitchen mashing the potatoes or heating up the Bourguignon. Decide on what you do and what your helper will do by thinking about how you run your household and what you like to do or feel most comfortable doing yourself. And be sure to have your help arrive before the guests, so that you can explain what his responsibilities are and show him where to find anything he may need during the evening.

If you would like a household worker to serve at your party, the proper uniform for a woman is a black dress with below-the-elbow sleeves, white collars and cuffs, over which is tied a white apron, which may or may not have over-the-shoulder straps. A blue or beige short-sleeved uniform with a white tie-around apron is less formal (and less expensive). Although in the past women who worked at parties did not wear white, they now may do so, as many women who work as free-lance helpers at parties have only a white uniform to wear. A teenager may wear a dark-colored dress or skirt and blouse. A young man or teenage boy wears dark pants, a light shirt and a tie.

Another source of plate and glass removers and ashtray emptiers is your children, if you have them. Not only are they cheap labor but, because it's their house, they know where everything is kept. This cuts down on the after-the-party search for serving spoons, bottle openers, etc., which well-meaning guests have filed in the wrong drawers. By being present at your party, they will also learn how to be at ease with adults. Such early training will give them poise that will be most helpful to them as they get older. And do pay them for their work.

Caterers

For a large party a caterer can provide you with the perfect event at home, in the back yard, at the beach, on a boat, wherever you fancy. A caterer's fees depend on how much you demand. Food and drink will depend on the elaborateness of your menu and how many people are to be served. If you buy your own liquor, wine and champagne you'll save money even if the caterer serves the liquor for you. Another money saver: use as much of your own equipment as you can. If you'll be using the caterer's equipment, ask to see it first—your taste may not be similar to his.

A caterer charges you on the basis of the type of help and the hour (expect to pay more at night). You may be asked to pay an advance deposit as high as fifty percent of the food costs as a commitment from you that there will be no last-minute cancellation.

Caterers' employees are tipped. Ask friends who have used caterers how much the tip is or ask the caterer, as the amount of the tip varies in different parts of the country. You may tip personally or ask the caterer whether he adds it to the bill.

WINES

When choosing a wine, keep in mind that there are many American wines whose names don't roll Gallically off the tongue, but which are excellent. You needn't buy the most expensive French Bordeaux to keep your guests happy. To make your wine selection you might ask the advice of the manager of the store in which you purchase your wines. In a liquor store that carries a fairly wide selection of wines the salespeople are generally knowledgeable on the subject if you aren't. (And ask your liquor-store manager what the discount is for buying wine by the case.)

Many people have stopped drinking liquor and are drinking only wine before dinner as well as during dinner. To be on the safe side, if yours is a wine-drinking crowd, plan on one bottle of wine per person when you plan your party. If you'll be serving wine at dinner only, figure on one bottle of wine for every two diners.

Serving the Wine

Red wine is served at room temperature. Some say it's important when serving red wine to let the wine "breathe" before it is poured. They believe that the exposure to the air will develop the bouquet of the wine and enhance the flavor, and therefore they open the wine about half an hour before they will be drinking it. Others argue that the theory is false because the tiny opening of the bottle doesn't let in enough air to make the slightest difference in the taste of the wine. Whether or not you open the bottle beforehand depends on which theory you subscribe to.

Chill white wines and rosés about two hours before drinking. When you've forgotten to put the wine in the refrigerator or when there is no room in the refrigerator for the wine, you can chill it quickly by putting a couple of trays of ice cubes and cold water into a large cooking pot in which you then immerse the wine bottle up to its neck. The wine will be cool in about fifteen minutes. Don't use an ice bucket to chill wine, as the bottle is much too big for the bucket and you'll be chilling only the bottom half of the bottle.

If the cork breaks when you are opening the bottle, reinsert the corkscrew at an angle and try to retrieve the remaining piece of cork that is stuck in the bottle. If the cork crumbles, strain the wine into another container. To tell if a wine has been "corked" (spoiled), smell the wet end of the cork. If it smells of fresh and good wine the wine is most likely good. If the cork smells musty, the wine may be spoiled.

To Serve Red and White

The rule of thumb is to serve a light wine with a light dish and a heavier wine with heavier food. A white wine would be served with poached fish, for example, and a full red Burgundy with beef stew. If you'd like to serve more than one wine at the meal, you'd probably serve white wine first, since your appetizer will be lighter than your main dish. Wine is not served with the salad course, as vinegar dressing brings out the vinegar taste in the wine. Wine does have a few other enemies: any kind of citric acid—lemon, grapefruit, orange—often covers up the taste of wine.

Though the general rule is to serve white wine with fish and chicken, red wine with red meat, this rule is by no means inflexible. Many chicken dishes such as *coq au vin* are made with red wine, in which case a red wine (ideally the wine in which the chicken was cooked) is served with the dish. And many people simply prefer one wine to another in spite of what is being served. A pretty addition to your table might be a carafe of red wine and a carafe of white wine so that guests can make their own choice.

Pouring the Wine

The host, just as the meal begins, will rise and walk around the table filling each wineglass. In a more informal meal, the host may first offer wine to those guests who are sitting closest, who will pass those glasses to other guests in their turn. No guest should be sitting at the table with an empty wineglass during the meal, and the host has the responsibility of keeping glasses replenished. Guests will not help themselves to wine, nor will they ask for more. The host may offer the wine bottle to a guest with an empty glass and say, "Please, help yourself."

Wineglasses

There are variously shaped wineglasses for various wines, some with elaborate decorations, but a clear tulip-shaped wineglass with a bowl of about five ounces is ideal for all types of wine. If you're serving two wines at your meal, white wine is poured into a smaller glass and red wine (because of the bouquet) into a larger glass. Inhaling the bouquet is one of the delights of drinking wine; therefore, a large glass which allows more surface for evaporation is best. The glass should be filled only about half full so that the empty half can help channel the bouquet, and so that one will be able to swirl the wine in the glass. This exposes it to the air and furthers the evaporation process, releasing the bouquet. The empty top half of the glass also serves to channel the bouquet; if the glass is filled to the brim, the bouquet will be lost. If your glasses hold less than five ounces, leave at least one inch empty at the top.

Decanting Wine

Older red wines are decanted in order to rid them of sediment. The sediment is harmless and means only that the wine has been left to mature naturally. Generally only red wine has sediment, though some white wines do, too. All wines, however, look lovely sparkling in decanters. Trust that your guests' palates will know that the wine is good; you needn't give them the label to read. Don't hesitate to decant wine if you have a decanter, since it looks so pretty. If you're very proud of the bottle you've decanted you may put the empty bottle next to the decanter on the table so that guests will know what they are being treated to.

To decant a wine with sediment, first let the bottle remain upright for a few hours. Pour it out slowly before dinner, taking care that no sediment escapes from the bottom of the bottle. While you're pouring, hold a light under the neck of the bottle so that you'll know to stop pouring when you see the sediment has reached the neck.

A Wine Cradle

A wine cradle is necessary only if you're serving a bottle of older red wine which you haven't had time to stand upright and decant. Take such a bottle from the rack, carry it gently to the cradle, open it carefully in the cradle and pour from the cradle. The cradle keeps the wine in place so that the sediment won't churn about in the bottle. Otherwise, a cradle isn't necessary.

When serving wine from a bottle, never wrap the bottle in a linen napkin. Guests should be able to read the label on the bottle of wine you are serving. Wrapping the bottle makes it look as though you have something to hide.

THE COCKTAIL HOUR

Being on Time

I'm usually on time for movies, hairdresser appointments and parties. On time for a party often means being the first to arrive. Why do people feel they must apologize for arriving promptly? Quite honestly, I'd much rather have my guests come at the time I invited them than sit and wait for them to straggle in fashionably late. On time means different things, depending on where you live. In some European countries, it means anything from half an hour to an hour after the announced time. In Washington, D.C., at official functions, on time means exactly that. (This goes back to the regal tradition when everyone was in the room waiting for the King or Queen to arrive and no one left until after His or Her Majesty had departed.) It gets a little crowded around the cloak-room, but protocol is maintained. I find that most people arrive at parties about fifteen minutes after the appointed hour.

The Length of the Cocktail Hour

The cocktail hour should ideally run no more than one hour, time enough for all guests, even stragglers, to arrive and for everyone to have two drinks and to find his or her niche in a new place. My cocktail hours run a bit shorter than one hour; guests are invited for eight o'clock, and we sit down to dinner at a quarter to nine. I think there's nothing worse than arriving at somebody's house at eight and having dinner two hours later; I don't think anybody really likes it. People tend to become restive if, after an hour of drinks and chatting, there's no sign of dinner. Most people, myself included, eat light lunches, and my stomach will complain if I neglect it. My guests are delighted when they discover they won't have to nibble celery into the night and are only too glad to put down their drinks and begin eating at a reasonable hour. In any case, if you've invited people to dinner and care at all about the meal you're serving them, extending the cocktail hour defeats your purpose. Too much alcohol dulls the palate; by the time your guests have finished their two hours of drinking, you might as well be serving them bologna sandwiches.

I don't mean to negate the value of a cocktail hour. The cocktail hour serves an important purpose. It's the first act of your party and it can often be the deciding factor as to whether the evening will run smoothly and your party will be successful.

Setting Up the Bar

Your bar need not be elaborate. You might offer gin, bourbon, scotch, soda or mineral water, wine, dry sherry and soft drinks. You don't have to offer anything fancier for mixed drinks unless they are your specialty. Hosts with no help, and especially a single host, should take care to set up the bar for self-service, which will free you for other duties.

Serving Drinks

I find that most people are drinking less now than they used to. More and more often, people will choose wine before dinner instead of hard liquor. This is becoming so prevalent that in some houses only wine is offered.

If the host isn't an expert bartender and isn't used to mixing Daiquiris and other such specialty cocktails, guests will happily make do with what is offered. I know someone who simply tells her guests what's available at the bar—scotch, bourbon, vodka and gin, along with tonic, soda or mineral water, dry vermouth, sherry and white wine, or whatever. That way, she avoids the embarrassment of being asked for something she isn't serving. She also always remembers to have soft drinks available.

During the cocktail hour it's a good idea to keep the room well lit. Though during dinner and after dinner you might prefer a more subdued mood, at the beginning of a party brightness will encourage guests to get to know each other, as it will help them to see each other clearly and to navigate from one group to another. Leave the subtlety of shadows for later in the evening.

Furniture Groupings

For a dinner party of about eight to sixteen, conversations between guests begin naturally if your furniture is arranged in small groupings. If your living room is arranged around a large central table there is a danger that all guests may take their places around that table and the conversation will be dominated by one or two extroverts who will see their chance to hold a gathered audience. In order to avoid this and to break up conversation into small groups, move the furniture so that the seats are not close enough to the table for easy reach. Although reaching for shrimp dip, wine and ashtrays will be a bit of a nuisance, this tactic will also divide people into conversation groups: and once the table has ceased being a focal point, people will have to rely on themselves and each other and not on a piece of furniture.

Greeting the Guests

The beginning of a party is the time when a host should be most available to the guests. Each new arrival must be looked after properly. If you are relaxed and looking forward to an evening of entertaining, this pleasant atmosphere is contagious and the arriving guests will be put at ease.

When a couple is hosting, either the man or the woman greets guests at the door, depending on the division of responsibility for duties at the party. In other words, if the man is making drinks or is busy in the kitchen with last-minute dinner preparations, or making a newly arrived guest feel at home, the woman will, of course, answer the door. Many parties today are so informal that one friend who lives in the suburbs complained, "I find guests answering my front door while other newly arrived guests find their own way in through the kitchen door." If you have hired help for the evening, one of the hosts would still greet guests, as the person who is helping you is most likely busy in the kitchen or serving drinks. I also think that unless your party is enormous or you are a single host with lots to do, it's more welcoming and friendlier for newly arriving guests to be greeted by their host.

Don't rush your guests. When they first arrive, take their coats or let them know where to put them, get them a drink and then introduce the newcomers to earlier arrivals and make sure they are well into conversation and mingling successfully before leaving them.

Don't make the mistake of thinking that all a guest needs is a drink to send him on his way to a good time; drinks are irrelevant as a social crutch. How many times have you witnessed a forlorn stranger standing in the corner of a crowded room watching his ice melt? How many times have you yourself been that "forlorn stranger"? Wouldn't you have welcomed the attention of *your* host?

Sometimes many people arrive at once (if they're following the fifteen-minutes-late rule) and it's impossible to include anything more than names in your introductions.

As a guest, if you've arrived at a large party and your host is very busy or not to be found immediately, I do think you should use your initiative and introduce yourself. I know that breaking into an ongoing conversation can be awkward, but remember, other strangers may feel as awkward and out of place as you do. When you're engaged in discussion and notice a stranger seeking a port in the party storm, you'll be helping the host as well as the stranger by bringing him into your conversation. One way to add a new-comer to your group is through body language: stand aside and put out your arm in a welcoming gesture. This gets the point across without disturbing the conversation. Once the outsiders have joined the huddle, you can recap succinctly what is being discussed to bring new members up to date.

(For more on introductions, see Chapter 1, "Everyday Manners in Public Places.")

Going In to Dinner

Breaking up the cocktail hour and drawing guests to their seats at the table can be a bit of a problem. The time dinner is announced is usually the time that every storyteller is going into the punch line, groups of people are chatting happily—and everyone feels reluctant to move first. Announce in a clear voice that dinner is indeed ready. Then take one or two guests by the arm and gently lead them to the dining room. For some reason, husbands, if they haven't helped with preparing dinner, are the worst offenders and just don't choose to hear the good news about dinner. Once you've begun the procession, retreat to the rear and suggest, firmly, to your spouse that he round up the stragglers and advance. This quasi-military technique, though trying, brings forth effective results. And don't be hesitant to break up conversation; the announcement of dinner is always a welcome interruption.

When called in to dinner, guests leave unfinished drinks in the cocktail area. A guest who is drinking wine may bring an unfinished glass to the table at an informal party.

AT THE TABLE

Place Cards

For a seated dinner of more than eight it's a good idea to have place cards at the table. Simply write guests' first names on the cards for a party of close friends, or first and last names if there are older or distinguished people or acquaintances present. (For proper use of officials' names on place cards, see Chapter 20, "Official Protocol.")

Even for a party of fairly good friends it's best not to leave seating to chance. Work out an arrangement in advance. Especially when you know everyone so well, here's your chance to orchestrate familiar music. Also, don't rely on a written list which you then read to guests just as they sit down to dinner. You certainly may want to have your list handy as guests take their seats to help them find their places—I always hold the list in my hand at the dining-room door so that I can point guests in the right direction as they pass —but relying on the list only and omitting the cards will slow down the seating considerably.

At a very large dinner, place cards are doubly important, as they provide a special seat for everybody, even those guests who may not be familiar with others present. I know I always feel protected at a very large party when I know there is a place setting for me; I know I won't have to make my way to a table among strangers and feel as though I'm intruding.

(For more about table settings, a buffet and the formal dinner, see Chapter 3, "Table Manners.")

The Seating Plan

Seating plans must be given considerable thought. To create a successful plan—to prejudge who will get on with whom—you need to be a psychologist with a Ouija board. There are, however, some guidelines a host can follow to help in the nimble dance of seating. Always separate husbands and wives and couples who are involved in relationships. At big parties I put couples at different tables. This rule can be overlooked in the case of newlyweds or a new love affair when two people are so enraptured with each other they'll only pine if separated and won't make an effort at conversation with anyone else.

A few people, the ideal guests, love to talk about *anything*. Take the various conversational types into account when planning your seating arrangements. It's best to intersperse some listeners among the me-myself-and-I's. Place your ideal guests, the general conversationalists, in spots where you think the waters may be too still or the currents too strong.

If you're able, it's thoughtful to seat each guest next to at least one familiar face. At a party with no specified guest of honor, seat the person who is at your house for the first time next to you. (Take the guest who you think is just a bit dull at parties and seat him next to you, too). When making your seating plan, also think in terms of guests talking across the table. When seating four, eight or twelve people, the host (man or woman) who serves the meal sits at one end and the guest of honor of the same sex sits at the other end of the table. This is done so that two women and two men won't be seated next to each other. It is perfectly all right to alter the plan and seat one host at each end of the table, with the men and the women sitting beside each other.

Another seating suggestion: from experience, I've learned to seat at a table only eight people who know each other well. If your guests are not all good friends, it's best to ask two more people and to serve a buffet which allows for guests to switch conversation groups freely throughout the meal, and your dinner won't get bogged down with a dialogue in which only a couple of people at the table are interested.

Conversation

It's up to the host to begin conversation, if it doesn't begin automatically, when she first sits down at the table. Most people love to talk about themselves and will jump at the chance to expound on even the most rudimentary question about their lives. Others are slow to divulge the broadest detail about themselves. The latter group can be great conversationalists and can bring out interesting aspects of others.

This was proved at one party of mine by a friend who I knew has a knack for bringing out the personal, unexpected side of any dinner partner. I seated him next to Barbara Walters, whose *business* is asking questions, and he turned the tables on her and said, "Barbara, let's not talk about me. We've done that a thousand times. Let's talk about you." He was a disarming interviewer, and Barbara gave him an exclusive to some very personal questions. She was probably relieved that someone else was doing the asking for once.

Dinner Music

My father has always said that dinner music prohibits conversation. Even if he is giving a dinner dance, the music does not begin until after the meal. It's one of those childhood rules that I have grown used to and haven't broken. Nevertheless, many find it a pleasure, even an aid to digestion, to listen to music during a meal. This is certainly not a contemporary phenomenon. Mozart wrote divertimentos for his friends' garden parties, and Haydn wrote music specifically to be played during meals. If you do like your party meals to be accompanied with music, select something not too loud or raucous or dramatic, which would inhibit conversation. A light sound, tuned to a low volume, is most enjoyable.

Latecomers

If one or two guests will be late, begin dinner on schedule. They'll understand that you went ahead without them, whereas the guests already present and accounted for may not understand if you wait. If people arrive late, in the middle of dinner for instance, I don't start them at the top with the first course, but begin serving them at the point to which dinner has progressed. If they arrive during the salad course, they are served salad. If they appear during dessert, they'd better take a big helping. The first time I invited Van Cliburn to my house, he called at eight to apologize; he'd be a bit late for dinner. This was certainly understandable; but meanwhile I was without a dinner partner. Luckily, the pianist I had hired to play after dinner had arrived early. I invited him to have dinner with us and put him in Van's seat. When Van appeared in the middle of the meal, I just squeezed him in on my other side and nestled cozily between the two pianists.

GUESTS HELPING THE HOST

Female hosts who give parties alone cannot expect a male guest to take over the host's chores of pouring drinks or carving meat, just as single male hosts cannot expect a female guest to provide cooking or serving expertise. Guests are coming to your house to relax, not to be recruited. However, a male guest who is a good friend will most likely lend a hand if he sees you busy greeting new arrivals and unable to fill drink orders. A host who appears rushed is all the prodding that's usually needed for a friend to lend a helping hand. If no one comes to your rescue, you may ask, "Do you mind getting Edmund and Alicia their drinks?," but don't assume that your friend will turn into the bartender; your request must end with Edmund and Alicia's order and not extend into the evening.

Hosts are of two schools of thought when it comes to guests helping with the dishes. Some expect it, and others simply will not allow it. I come from the first school. When I go skiing I entertain with no help and I expect my guests to help me. If they don't offer, I suggest. At other people's houses I pride myself in being not only a good conversationalist and a good listener (often a difficult to find commodity) but also first rate at table clearing and dishwasher loading. I think a guest at a party where there is no help should always volunteer to help clear the table and perhaps to help carry dishes to the table and to help clear away the dishes in the kitchen or to load the dishwasher. There is one rule about clearing the table: dishes should not be stacked at the table, but rather carried two at a time, one in each hand. Guests, however, usually take the initiative and stack a couple of plates in order to hurry the task. Guests who are inclined to stack should acknowledge it by apologizing. And a host must not make remarks—a favor can be refused but not criticized.

There are certain guests whose very precision and diligence will impede the table-clearing process. Guests who tend to make more work for the host instead of making things easier can be stopped from helping. In a friendly but firm voice a host may say, "Please do sit down. I have a certain system in the kitchen and it's faster and easier for me to do it myself. Thanks so much for offering to help."

A helping guest should never put away clean dishes. What seems the logical place for the salad bowl may take your host an hour's search to relocate it the next time it is needed.

Now for those hosts who die a little each time a guest cheerfully puts a crystal wineglass into the dishwasher. A host who considers the helping guests a sheer nuisance and an obstruction may simply tell volunteers that they are not needed, that in fact any guest who helps only causes anxiety. For those guests who simply can't seem to leave well enough alone (and there are such guests who are compulsive helpers and organizers), try to keep them busy with a simple unbreakable chore—chopping parsley, perhaps, or emptying unbreakable ashtrays. (Be sensitive to shy guests who feel more comfortable if they are helping.) Then both guests and host should remain satisfied.

LIQUEURS

When liquor changes to liqueur, taste tells. Since after-dinner drinks are consumed in moderation, one bottle goes a long way—and the extra expense of a really good liqueur is worthwhile and a compliment to your guests.

After-dinner drinks are a good way to experiment with unusual liqueurs (and get a reputation for being a truly sophisticated host). Justin, a good friend, was once mistakenly given a bottle of an obscure Spanish brandy called Quarenta y Tres (because it's a blend of forty-three flavors) by a harried liquor-store clerk. Justin tried it, loved it and now recommends it to his friends. Everyone thinks he discovered it somewhere in Spain and is quite a connoisseur; but he's never been to Spain and found his expertise on Eighty-sixth Street in Manhattan. After-dinner drinks often come in small bottles—perfect for sampling.

AFTER-DINNER COFFEE AND CONVERSATION

After dinner I usually serve coffee in the library. Especially if conversation at the table is waning, it's revitalizing to get all the

guests up and rearranged in different groups. If everything is running smoothly at table (discussions animated and going strong),
we'll have coffee in the dining room.

After dinner is that hazardous time when guests may feel a bit
disoriented while conversation groups are reorganized in the living
room. This disorientation can lead to the men seeking security and
conversation only with the men and the women talking only to the
women. As the host, I always make an effort to talk to the men,
who are usually discussing business or politics. If I find myself less
informed than I'd like to be on a topic under discussion, I ask
questions. People in the know are always happy to give their egos
a boost and explain the basic points of an issue. Female guests
often take my lead and prove themselves to be extremely knowledgeable on subjects that not so long ago were considered only
male issues. If the sexes begin to segregate and a man wanders
over to the women in hopes of discussing the merits of the wire
whisk (a new piece of expertise learned in his cooking class), he
may be disappointed to find the women in heated political controversy.

It is extremely rare nowadays for the sexes to occupy separate
rooms after dinner. This can be accomplished only if one has a
house with sufficient space. Few people live in houses so equipped,
except in Washington, D.C., where segregation of the sexes is
definitely *de rigueur*. After dinner, the men seclude themselves in
the library with their cigars and brandy. The women sit in the
living room, left presumably to wait until the men have finished
discussing their serious matters. It's all too Jane Austen for words.
One couple I know tried to break up this ritual by using *de facto*
tactics. The couple stood in the hall, halfway between the living
room and the library, in full view of both groups. Lo and behold,
the mountain came to Mohammed. Some of the men, after much
harrumphing, picked up their brandies and courage and joined the
couple. The living-room contingent soon followed, and after a
minute or so of hesitation the party was going strong in the hall.

This couple managed a tremendous social coup. Washington is
a factory town, and the factory is government. There are structured pecking orders. You're immediately defined by your rank.
There are lists of protocol and Cabinet ranks and civil-service
ranks. And everybody is promoting something. The main objective
of every cocktail party, every dinner party, is commerce. Everyone
is bargaining his or her own political wares. Because of the concen-

trated power in the city—and power is indeed an attractive commodity—there are more groupies in Washington than at a Rolling Stones concert. Senators and the like don't wield guitars; they wield their constituents instead, a far more audible instrument. The people on the staffs of senators and congressmen often come to their jobs from the legislators' home states. They've been transplanted from America's heartland, and they bring with them their own morality and life style. There is no social structure that is inherent in Washington. The Washington style could best be termed "mannerly aggression," quintessentially American—coming out of the country's regional suburbs. It's a tough social nut to crack, and the daring couple in the hall probably set a precedent in the rigid social totem.

GUESTS TAKING THEIR LEAVE

No matter how successful your party is and how flattering it is when guests stay late, it's always somewhat of a relief when people begin going home. Preferably, this will be before dawn. If the party is on a week night, it's safe to say that guests will begin asking for their coats by eleven-thirty or twelve. After all, tomorrow is a work day. The end of the party, when most people have already left and the host can finally take a deep breath and sit down without worry about overflowing ashtrays or not enough flowing brandy, can be the most relaxed part of the evening. It's pleasant to sit up late and do a postmortem on the party. All those times when you were one of the first to leave and you worried that the late stayers were talking about you weren't entirely paranoia—they may indeed have been talking about you. But that doesn't mean they all agreed that you had on too much green eye shadow or too much décolletage, or that your brown shoes and gray suit were certainly indicative of your overall lack of taste. They could also be agreeing what a terrific person you are and how you proved it again this evening.

The Host Calling It a Night

If the host is really tired, and it's really late, it's perfectly acceptable and not a bit rude for him to tell the stragglers he's exhausted and has a busy day ahead, so please can they all call it a night.

For those who leave a party early, say a quiet goodbye to your host. Leave with as little fanfare as possible, as you don't want to be responsible for breaking up the party early, just when your host has cleared away dinner and now has a chance to relax with the guests.

If your host encourages you to stay on, you may surely do so if he has succeeded in changing your mind, or, if not, just smile, look tired and say thank you and good night. When leaving a large party (over forty or so) it's not rude to do so unobtrusively without saying good night to your host if he is not easily available. Do remember to call in the morning or to write a note to thank your host for the evening.

A Woman Leaving Alone

The male host or a male friend may want to escort a woman leaving a party alone to her car or to a taxi. Nevertheless, carrying out this once common courtesy depends on the safety of the neighborhood and the politics of the woman as well. A young woman used to getting about on her own may take it as a slight to her capability if a man accompanies her to her car or a taxi in a neighborhood that is safe after dark. An older woman who is used to such treatment will take it as a slight if the courtesy is not offered.

THANK-YOU'S

I think if someone has been nice enough to ask you to dinner, it is thoughtful to phone the next day or send a short thank-you note within a few days. Though some people enjoy thanking their host with a present, a sincere verbal thank-you is all that is expected. Some guests bring a bottle of wine or flowers when they arrive.

(Note: If guests do bring wine, do not feel compelled to serve it the evening of your party if you've already made plans to serve another wine. Simply thank them for their present and tell them you're looking forward to tasting the wine soon.)

A man I know who just recently married maintains that a single man—if he can afford it—needs a florist. For instance, if my friend was asked to a party, he had his florist send flowers ahead (nothing Hollywood, just a simple arrangement: it's the thought that counts) with a note saying how much he was looking forward to the evening. His host was delighted by the flowers and also delighted that this thoughtful guest was so pleased to be asked.

WHEN TO REPORT YOUR PARTIES TO THE NEWSPAPER

Most society news is handled over the telephone. Publicity agents handle party news for organizations, businesses and celebrities and active society women. They send a release about the party, written in the third person, which includes a date on which the story may appear in the paper and gives the name, address and phone number of the person to contact for more information. Ordinarily, though, one would not have a private party announced in a large city newspaper unless it were a benefit for a hospital or some other charity.

You may, however, want to have your party reported in your town newspaper, and in that case you would not write a release but would simply write a brief letter to the society editor:

> Dear Ms. Warrington,
>
> My husband and I are giving a dinner dance which I thought might interest you for your society page.
>
> The party is on Saturday, the twenty-fifth of September, at the Black Rock Country Club. The guest of honor is Marie Thérèse Duprée, who is visiting from New Orleans.
>
> If you would like more information, my telephone number is 827-7913. I will call you the day of the party to give you the final details.
>
> Sincerely,

When you call, tell the editor about your flowers and decorations, your guest list and the theme of the party, if any.

If you submit a photograph after the party, attach it to a sheet of paper and identify everyone from left to right. Do not write on the back of the photo.

VARIATIONS ON PARTY THEMES

The scope and the styles of home entertaining are many and varied. Sometimes you'll want to structure your party a little differently from the usual cocktail party, buffet or seated dinner. If you're giving a very large party for a special occasion you may want a caterer, or you may find that your budget will stretch only enough to hire one person for the occasion, either to tend bar or to heat and help serve food and clean up. A simple Sunday brunch—good fresh bread and "deli"—can be as festive as a more elaborate party. Part of the fun of entertaining is the many possibilities the word "entertainment" implies. As always, the important thing is to assess what you're capable of doing, given the realities of budget, space and the function being served by having guests, and to entertain accordingly. Be realistic and relax.

Cocktail Parties

When I go to cocktail parties, I'm always out of sorts. Everybody else seems to be engrossed in the most interesting and witty conversations. I guess I'm too busy concentrating on my tired feet rather than on the people around me—there's liquor, liquor everywhere but not a seat in sight.

Most people tell me how much they really abhor cocktail parties. So who's rushing to all these parties like lemmings into the sea? We all are, worst luck, because this kind of gathering is extremely valuable for business reasons as well as social ones. Cocktail parties are essential because they get a lot of people together for a short period of time. Everyone can say a superficial hello and get caught up with others he hasn't seen in a while but would like to keep in contact with.

Cocktail parties make it possible for people who don't entertain often to reciprocate social and/or business obligations on a large scale. This sounds a bit cynical, but let's face it, it's a fairly simple and effective method of returning invitations.

Another reason for giving this type of party (the only party that seems to need a *raison d'être*) is to meet new people—whether you're single, have just moved into a new community, or just want to see some new faces. If this is the purpose of your party, it's worth considering giving it jointly with one or two friends. In this relaxed structure, friends of friends will bring their friends, and your circle of acquaintances will have a chance to grow. Also, joint parties help cut down on expenses and the hard work of preparation.

When inviting people to your cocktail party, whether over the phone or by mail, specify not only what time the party begins but what time it ends as well. Otherwise party lovers may linger till midnight. Not everyone who receives an invitation to a cocktail party will come, so if you want a fairly accurate estimate of how many guests to expect, include on the written invitation an R.S.V.P. for "regrets only."

Your bar should be set up in an open area, since it often becomes a focal point around which guests tend to gather. At a large party, you may want to set up two bars. You need not have a bar with every obscure kind of liquor; just the basics will do. Talk to your liquor-store manager about just how much vodka, scotch, bourbon, gin and wine to order, based on the number of people you anticipate will attend. Some people prefer to just serve a punch, and the idea of serving only wine is becoming more acceptable in most circles. In any case, have plenty of soft drinks, as at cocktail parties there are many closet nondrinkers.

It is expected that you will serve something for the guests to nibble on; particularly during a cocktail party can the hours between lunch and dinner grow interminable. Simple fare can do nicely: platters of cheese and a variety of crackers; baskets of vegetables with a dip; big bowls of shrimp. Do space nicely what you decide to serve; all the food should not be in one section of the room, as you want your guests to mingle freely. And serve plenty of food.

Hot hors d'oeuvres are not necessary, and they can often be a real nuisance if your party isn't catered or at least attended by a few waiters. For all the guests to become aware that hot food is available may take a long time if a room is crowded, and those farthest from the kitchen will feel cheated.

Whatever you serve, make sure that it requires nothing more than a toothpick and a cocktail napkin. A guest moving around a room with a glass, a plate, a fork (and a cigarette or a pocketbook) is a hazard, not only to your furniture but also to your party. Guests who have so much to concentrate upon have no time to converse!

If you do want to serve hot food and are without help, plan a table with several chafing dishes and lots of toothpicks.

Whether the cocktail party is a business function or purely social, it is a situation where guests will have to work hard if they are going to enjoy themselves. You can't rely completely on the host of a large cocktail party to do your leg work for you. You have to sell yourself, and shopping around for buyers is a difficult thing to do. How many times have you been talking to someone at a cocktail party only to watch the other person's eyes dart about trying to pick out someone more socially profitable than yourself? Unless you're an awfully good storyteller or a woman going topless, it's difficult to hold someone's attention—or keep your own steady— in this garden where all fruits are meant to be tasted.

A good way to insure that your stay will be a pleasant one is to concentrate on one conversation at a time. Don't try to carry on a conversation with one person and simultaneously eavesdrop on the discussion going on to your left. Try not to get caught up in the dismaying Johnny Appleseed syndrome of scattering your conversation and attention in many directions at once. You don't have to talk to everyone at the party. If you're not gregarious by nature, it can be most enjoyable to talk in some depth with just a few people at the party instead of flitting from flower to flower when you find it difficult to make small talk.

If you do get stuck with someone who is boring you, the transient aspect of a cocktail party makes the route for escape quite simple. "I must get another drink" and "Excuse me, I see an old friend" are both acceptable getaway lines.

The frenetic high-energy atmosphere of a large party puts up a screen between any two people. Old friends find they have nothing to say to each other when they meet in the midst of a big party. I defy a stranger observing two people in conversation to tell if those people are good friends, husband and wife, or strangers who have just met.

Everyone treats everyone else the same—with a certain blasé cheerfulness, the universal cocktail-party armor. This phenomenon can work for you. Since everyone appears to know everyone else equally well, you needn't continually cast about for new faces. As a defense against silence, husbands and wives often find themselves in conversation with each other. These conversations can develop into interesting dialogues. At one large cocktail party one wife learned from her husband how to handicap the horses—a subject which she'd never bother to listen to at home and which he'd never bother to explain—and she's been winning at the track ever since.

There's an art to giving a cocktail party just as there is an art to having a good time at one. It's important to plan your party according to the occasion and what you have available. It's easier to have a cocktail party in a contained space where people are automatically thrown together. Don't *jam* them together. If you haven't the space for sixty people, don't invite that many. An overly populated living room makes for an uncomfortable, crushed discotheque scene. Make sure guests have enough room to circulate freely and easily. If your living space is large, contain the party in one or two rooms. The best way to accomplish this is to put the bar and the food where you want your guests to stay. It's doubtful that people will wander upstairs to the library and leave the refreshments so far behind.

Move any large pieces of furniture, large tables, bulky chairs, etc., which you think might get in the way. Put ashtrays in every conceivable place where you think someone might be tempted to put out a cigarette, or your potted plants will suffer. If you're planning a buffet dinner, make sure that there are enough chairs so that everyone can sit down when it's time to eat.

These kinds of mass-market parties sometimes bring out the worst in people—or maybe just bring the worst people to your door. My mother once gave a big cocktail party, very unusual for her. She wanted to give a party for a friend, and cocktail party is what her friend wanted. My mother has a fine collection of Fabergé boxes, and during the party two of these boxes disappeared. It has happened at my house, during dinner parties, that cloth cocktail napkins vanish. Men absent-mindedly put them in their pockets, thinking they're handkerchiefs, hardly a premeditated or criminal offense.

Because cocktail parties inspire more fear and trembling than they do good times, a new, very informal quasi-cocktail/dinner party has evolved. Forty, fifty or even more guests are invited for six-o'clock cocktails. Usually, just wine is served. At about eight-thirty, there is an informal one-dish buffet dinner: ham, turkey, chili or moussaka and a salad—something simple. It's up to each guest to decide if he or she wants to stay on till dinner. So you can come early just for drinks and conversation. If you're having a good time, stay for dinner. The meal is very informal. I have a friend who was appalled when she was handed wine in a plastic glass. Not only did she find this socially unacceptable, but, she said, the plastic makes the liquor taste "funny." Not being much of a drinker, I had to take her word for it. My friend must have risen above the plastic and enjoyed herself, because she stayed on to dinner. When the host heaped (excellent) chili on her paper plate and handed her plastic eating utensils, she positively shuddered. In order to shame the host, my friend lifted her plate and in mock imitation looked at the bottom, presumably to see if her plate was genuine Limoges china. My friend believes that paper and plastic belong only at children's parties. I think that if someone is giving a large party with no help paper is a godsend.

Excellent paper plates, shiny and coated to hold warm food, and attractive clear plastic drinking glasses that don't taste "plasticky" are available. They do save wear and tear, and for this kind of cocktail party *cum* buffet most people don't object.

Sunday Brunch

What do you generally do for Sunday lunch? Family dinners after church are becoming rare in some circles. Sunday lunch (or brunch, which means beginning earlier, say at eleven instead of twelve or one) has taken the place of those dinners, and, I'm afraid, in some cases taken the place of church.

Brunch can be very simple. You can serve bread and cold meats and cold smoked fish, a truly wonderful meal and so simple to organize. All you have to do is remove the wrappings and arrange the food on platters. A few sprigs of parsley and some lemon wedges, and lunch is served. If the weather is cold and you're worried that the cold food won't help your guests' circulation, a warm rum grog after lunch will do wonders to warm stomachs. Another menu for Sunday brunch would be fettucini Alfredo, a salad and white wine. Eggs Benedict or eggs Florentine or quiche and a salad are by now traditional brunch specialties, as is a soufflé for those hosts blessed with impeccable timing or help in the kitchen.

Brunch is a simple way to entertain because it is limited and contained in regard to time. After brunch (or lunch), if the weather is good, guests may decide to go for a walk or a drive. Sunday is a good day to invite family and close friends; and Sunday brunch or an early informal dinner may be an excellent opportunity to invite people you don't know too well and want to get to know better without a "best-behavior" or more formal atmosphere and without a large number of people to distract you.

Having the Boss to Dinner

Having the boss to dinner, or the equivalent—giving a dinner purely for the sake of furthering your own career or your husband's —can be scary. It reminds me of *I Love Lucy*—anything can go wrong and too often does. It's a situation where you're pretty much on your own, perhaps with people who are almost complete strangers. If you spill wine on the senior vice-president, will he laugh it off the same way your next-door neighbor probably would?

If you find yourself faced with having the boss to dinner, don't feel that you must impress this esteemed man or woman and his or her spouse with your style of living. If you never hire anyone to help serve your dinner, now is not the time to start. Plan your evening with the boss just as you would plan any other home entertainment. Don't try to show off. The more at ease you are, the more at ease your guests will be. Do, of course, use your best silver, etc., and, if your budget can afford it, an extra-special bottle of wine will show your guests that you think they are special people. Your menu should be something that can be prepared in advance; this, of all evenings, is no time for a kitchen experiment. Once again, I want to stress the importance of fairly simple, easy-to-prepare food, if that's what you're used to making. The boss will be much more impressed with a pleasant and easygoing atmosphere than he will be by a gourmet dinner which, no matter how good, has taken his host into the kitchen and away from the gathering. No one likes to be upstaged, especially by food. Don't give the impression that dinner is more important than the guest(s). Your party will be most successful if you devote yourself to the company. Make sure they are relaxed, participating in the conversation and comfortable in their surroundings. Being gracious and available to your guests can be much more difficult than preparing a gourmet meal. But your graciousness will give you the reward of knowing that your guests have had as good a time as you.

If you're entertaining your husband's boss and the boss is a woman, there's no reason to be intimidated. You don't have to talk only business with her. If your work is mainly taking care of a family, you'd be surprised how much you can learn and how much you have in common with a woman who spends her days in completely different surroundings than your own. And if your work is in the same field—or even different fields—you might try dropping shop talk for a change and discover where you agree and disagree on movies, books, politics, etc.

If you know that your boss (or client) has a drinking problem, schedule dinner early, about half an hour after he arrives. Of course, you can't refuse the boss if he asks for a drink at any time during the evening.

If the boss arrives having had too much to drink, or manages to get drunk or drunker at your house despite your precautions, you'll have to tolerate it and suffer silently. Even if he does something embarrassing, he has the excuse of being drunk and so can choose not to remember it the next day when you see him in the office. So don't bother to be embarrassed for him and don't bother to read the want ads.

(For more on business entertaining, see Chapter 5, "The Business World.")

SPECIAL PROBLEMS

The Problem Party: Some Consoling Words

A friend told me of one calamitous dinner during the difficult days of Watergate, the days when arguments broke out and politics were aired in lines at the neighborhood deli. At dinner my friend was seated next to a rabbi who had just been quoted in *The New York Times* in support of Nixon. My friend's feelings about Nixon were not fit to print. Before her napkin was on her lap, she attacked. The rabbi, exasperated, then furious, told my friend that she was ruining his Shabbas (it was a Friday night). He went on to say that she must not talk to him like that and that he not only would stop talking to her but would turn his back on her. With that, he picked up his chair and turned it so that his back was to my friend. My friend turned her chair. The rabbi spoke to his side of the table, my friend to hers. Everyone, including the host, pretended that nothing had happened. In a situation like this one the host is as helpless as her guests.

There is always an element of chance in the success of a party no matter how much forethought and planning a host has given the event. Sometimes the evening doesn't jell: those you counted on to be lively and witty just aren't. Maybe they are simply tired or just don't feel like performing. Or maybe guests who you thought would get along beautifully take an instant dislike to one another. Whatever surprises occur, console yourself in the fact that they have all happened before and to the most experienced hosts. Though the evening may seem never-ending, you and your guests will live through it. And don't blame yourself, you did what you could.

When to Intervene

What to do when you see a guest unintentionally burning a hole in your carpet or putting a glass down on your prized Queen Anne table? In the first instance, call your guest's attention to the impending disaster immediately. In fact, you probably won't be able to stop yourself from calling out, "There's a live spark on the rug!" It certainly isn't bad manners to prevent a fire. In the second instance, simply hand your guest a coaster or say, "Here is a coaster."

The Problem Drinkers

One of the most problematical situations for a host is dealing with the determined drunk. All drunks are determined—determined to stay where the liquor is. They seem to have taken to heart what F. Scott Fitzgerald once said: "Everybody is one drink away from his true self." If you have someone who has gotten drunk at your house, man or woman, try to ease him or her out the door and into a waiting car (that someone else is driving!). You might ask someone to help you; drunks are unsteady, and if you're not strong you'll list with the ship—and might even sink with it.

Heavy drinking is unfortunately condoned in many social groups. A man who falls off his chair is laughed at, not chastised, possibly because those who applaud him are overcoming their embarrassment. Women, however, are considered "unfeminine" if they *act* drunk, so most women are pretty cool about their drinking. By "cool" I don't mean they don't drink as much, just that they don't show it as much. In any case, mean drunks, affectionate drunks, maudlin drunks can be a problem. Unfortunately, it's very difficult to try to *stop* someone from getting drunk. Even a slight mention of "maybe you've had enough to drink" is like waving a red cape in front of a bull. The receiver of this well-intentioned advice takes it as a call to arms. I guess the only thing you can do is wait until someone is drunk enough to give you reason to lead him out the door—and to safe passage home.

My friend Anya, cleaning up after a party, discovered one of her guests sleeping on her couch in the den. The guest had had too much to drink and had done a wise and safe thing: he had found a quiet corner to crawl into and sleep it off. So Anya covered the guest with a quilt and placed a note by his side with instructions regarding breakfast. When Anya awoke the next morning she found an immaculate kitchen with a note of apology and thanks tucked under the one coffee cup on the counter. I think Anya did the most hospitable thing one can do in such a situation. As long as an invited guest is under your roof, you must treat him as a guest and not as a problem.

Those Who Don't Drink

This leads us to a paradox. Though no one likes someone who drinks too much, there is tremendous social pressure on us all to join the crowd and to have a drink. Those who don't drink at all are looked upon as people trying to upset the social norm. I suggest that nondrinkers hold a glass of soda water or a soft drink to demonstrate that they are willing to share in the social ritual.

When a guest is a member of Alcoholics Anonymous and is not drinking at all, a host need not worry about serving liquor to other guests, but must never encourage someone who is on the wagon to have "just a little one." Some members of AA prefer to keep their membership a secret. However, I think that to tell your host privately, if you would prefer, that you are indeed an AA member is a mark of pride, as it shows your determination and self-control. Also, a host who knows that a guest is a member of AA will try to help instead of hinder and may step in and save the nondrinker from encouragement to drink by a fellow guest.

Marijuana at Parties

Liquor is expected at parties, and it's difficult to protect yourself from the person who drinks too much, either occasionally or habitually. But what about drugs? Most of my friends don't use any kind of illegal drugs, so it has never been a problem in my house.

Of course, it's true that for some party-givers, drugs are not a problem at all. Marijuana, at least, is often dispensed much the same way liquor is by a gracious host who believes that no party is successful without it. I was once at a party in California where everyone was smoking grass but me. People looked askance in my direction. Although I was definitely odd man out, I would not be pushed into doing something I really didn't want to do because of peer pressure.

De gustibus perhaps, but I do want to say that no host should be pressured either into feeling it necessary to be "with it" and pass around marijuana or other drugs or to tolerate its use by guests. If someone lit a joint in my house, I'd ask him to please put it out; it is inappropriate for a guest to take the lead. The choice of offering drugs is the host's to make, but for the protection of her guests she should be aware of the laws pertaining to drug use in her community.

3 TABLE MANNERS

THE ELEMENTS OF GOOD TABLE MANNERS

Good table manners derive essentially from common sense, from what is most logical. The main thing to remember is to eat naturally and unself-consciously (self-consciousness will spoil your dinner) and unobtrusively (obtrusive eating habits may well spoil the meal for others). Natural, unaffected table manners are an acquired art, however, and take practice. The best place to practice is at home. If manners at the table are insisted upon at home they will become second nature. Even a formal dinner won't put you off course, because you'll have the fundamental rules which are basically all anybody needs; your table manners will be automatic, and you can therefore spend an enjoyable meal savoring the food and the conversation instead of worrying about the mechanics of eating.

Sitting at the Table

Aristotle in his *Ethics* quotes an ancient proverb which states that you cannot know a man until you and he have eaten a peck of salt together. Dining, no matter how elegant the surroundings, is a social occasion. Even gourmets who savor each mouthful do so in groups so that they may discuss the merits of the food before them. Though I was always told as a child to "sit straight" at the table, one needn't sit stiffly. Hands may be in your lap when you're not eating, or, if it makes you more comfortable, rest your forearms on the edge of the table. Don't rest your upper arms on the table or you'll tend to sprawl. You may rest your elbows on the edge of the table in between courses. Resist the temptation to play with the silverware or rearrange the place setting, and don't straighten your hair at the table, as a stray hair may land in your food or in somebody else's.

When you eat, bring the food to your mouth, don't bend to meet it halfway between your plate and your chair. Don't eat with your elbows bent out, as if you're about to take flight, but rather keep your elbows close so that you don't interfere with those sitting beside you. A hand that isn't in use may rest in your lap or on the table. The elbow of an idle arm is kept off the table while you're eating, as it not only will contribute to sloppy posture but may also set up a conversation barrier, if all that your dinner partner can see of you is your arm. While everyone is eating, the form, though not exacting, is similar. Elbows on the table or other sloppy eating habits during the meal tend to make you out of sync with the precision of a tightly knit group. In this respect, dining may be viewed as a team effort.

Don't call attention to your eating by making noise either with your mouth or by scraping silverware against your plate. I think the worst of bad table manners is talking with your mouth full. Not only is it disgusting for the rest of the company, but your words will be lost amid the contents of your mouth. Of course, everyone talks at the table while eating, but only when little or no food is left in the mouth and one is mindful of the situation.

You may reach for the salt and pepper or the butter if it is close enough so that you can grasp it in a simple motion. If you must reach across your dinner partner or so far across the table that you have to dodge the centerpiece, ask instead, "Please pass the salt."

Which Fork to Use

Though the main criteria for good table manners are how you sit, talk and eat at the table, knowing which fork to use does tend to make one less self-conscious, more relaxed. The simple rule to follow is to begin with the silverware on the outside of the place setting and work your way in with each course. If you end up with a large meat fork for the salad course, such a small error on the part of your host or yourself is no cause for dismay, no one is watching. Even if you detect eyes glancing your way, no one is making a judgment about something so trivial. When in doubt about the silverware, watch your host or someone else at the table who is eating with an air of authority and follow that example.

American and European Styles of Eating

To eat using the European style, one holds the fork in the left hand, tines down. Cut the meat with the knife in your right hand. Then bring the fork, tines down, in your left hand to your mouth. To use the American style, cut a bite of meat, place the knife on the side of the plate, resting the blade and the handle across the top rim of the plate (the knife handle should not rest on the table, as it looks messy when a knife isn't clean), then switch the fork to your right hand and bring the food to your mouth. Use either style, whichever is more comfortable for you. Both are equally correct. When eating small bits of food such as peas or cut-up vegetables, hold the fork with tines up and push the food onto the side of the fork with a knife.

Left-handed people who must live in a right-handed world may adapt the use of knife and fork so that it is most comfortable and easiest for them.

PREPARING THE TABLE

Table Settings

A formal table set with a white damask cloth, exquisitely polished silverware, china and crystal is certainly a beautiful sight. Nevertheless, table settings using a bit more imagination and unorthodox flair can be equally beautiful and festive. If you don't have silver or good china and crystal, brightly colored place mats and napkins and an inventive centerpiece can give your table a festive and formal touch. Printed bedsheets can take the place of white tablecloths, centerpieces might be made up of fruit or vegetables instead of flowers. One memorable centerpiece at a dinner for six was a flowering cauliflower (and the napkins were hand-woven lace towels from Czechoslovakia). Bud vases with a single flower set at each place setting are perfect for crowded tables. One thing to keep in mind: do make sure your centerpiece is not so high that it obstructs the guests' view of one another.

Buffet tables, rarely elegant in the fine-silver-and-glassware category (few people have enough matching pieces to accommodate more than twelve guests), can be made to look gay and inviting. Don't worry about mixing and matching plates, silverware and glasses. Brightly patterned tablecloths or sheets substituted for tablecloths will do wonders to blend together your buffet table.

The Buffet

A buffet is a good way to give guests the opportunity to circulate: a guest can wander from one group to another as he serves himself different courses. When serving a group of more than eight, set out two sets of dishes, napkins and silver and two serving platters so that guests can serve themselves two at a time from the buffet table.

If you are serving salad as part of your buffet, you may wish to offer salad plates, though the guests will almost always serve themselves their salad on their dinner plates at buffets unless you offer a separate salad and cheese course.

With a free-standing table you can use each end for serving platters. A table against the wall can also be used in this way by putting two stacks of plates next to each other in the center and the serving dishes one at each end. Glasses and bottles of wine should also be on the serving table, and guests can help themselves. The host can refill glasses during the meal or she can put open bottles of wine in strategic places about the room so that guests will be able to refill glasses on their own.

Make sure you have enough room for everyone to find a comfortable place to sit. To avoid the plate-on-lap dinner, provide small trays and end tables in areas where no tables exist. After most of the guests have served themselves, the buffet table will be fairly uncluttered and remaining guests can be encouraged to sit down with their plates at the table. If guests are reluctant to do so, the host may have to sit down and ask guests to join him.

If you have leftovers, don't think it's because guests weren't happy with your cooking. I've found that people eat more at a seated dinner than they ever do at a buffet, possibly because a buffet gives people the chance to circulate and therefore they concentrate more on the conversation than on the food. Also, at a buffet, guests have to work to get their dinner, whereas at the table all is presented to them. When it comes to a choice between, on the one hand, getting up to refill your plate and, on the other, continuing a conversation, many guests opt for the conversation.

If your party is large and you have no help, plan on serving dessert and coffee from another area so that you won't have to worry about the table being spick-and-span immediately. A host at a buffet meal does best by serving each guest dessert and coffee, as guests are usually too comfortable and content by this time to rally round once more to serve themselves.

The Formal Dinner

Traditionally, a formal dinner included a waiter to serve every six guests a five-course meal. At a formal dinner a plate remains at every setting throughout the meal.

Plates for the first course and for dessert are the only plates which can be carried two at a time. Plates for every other course must be exchanged; therefore each service requires two hands. So you see the amount of help it takes to present such a dinner.

Today, a seated dinner at an elegantly set table where guests are served is considered a formal dinner. Place plates are at each setting as guests arrive at the table. The plate containing the first course, soup or fish, for instance, is set down directly on the place plate. Place plates are removed along with the plate from the first course.

The formal table is never set with more than three knives and three forks. Additional silver, a fork for the salad, for instance, is placed beside the plate when the course is served. The spoons for an appetizer such as fruit or soup are placed to the right of the knives. The dessert spoon and fork are placed above the plate. No serving dishes are ever put on the table except dishes of fruit or candy. Condiments are served and returned to the kitchen.

DURING THE MEAL

When sitting down at the table each man holds the chair for the woman sitting at his right, pulling the chair back from the table and pushing it foward carefully as she sits down. Although such ritual formality isn't always observed today, as women rarely wait for the courtesy, men do wait until the women have begun to sit down before they themselves take their seats. Generally at today's informal gatherings the men sit down after they have seen to it that the women are just about seated—men's chairs are the last to scrape in.

Saying Grace

Though some families say grace at each family meal, many more families today say grace only on special days: Jews on Friday nights and on religious holidays, Christians at Sunday dinner and on holidays. If you aren't familiar with the customs in the household, take your cue from your host. Don't unfold your napkin until your host does, as grace is said directly after everyone comes to the table, before napkins are touched or a sip of water has been taken. If all the people at the table say grace together and you don't know the words, remain silent with your head slightly bowed. When one person says grace, generally everyone at the table joins in the amen.

Napkins

Wait until the host begins to unfold his napkin before you do, as this is the signal that the meal is to begin. If the napkin is a very large one you may leave it folded in half on your lap. A smaller napkin is unfolded completely. Always use your napkin before drinking so that you won't leave food on the rim of the glass. When eating with your hands, don't lick your fingers, use your napkin.

Though ideally after eating with our fingers we would be offered finger bowls, in our modern world the extra time and trouble of introducing finger bowls need not be taken—except when serving lobster or corn on the cob, after which a finger bowl is a necessity. Otherwise, after eating a pickle or a sandwich or picking up a chicken leg, use your napkin.

Generally only children use napkins as bibs, though a napkin may be tucked under your chin in specific circumstances: when you're eating lobster, or when you're eating with chopsticks in a Chinese restaurant. When you're a guest in a private house, it's best to wait and see if your host converts the napkin into a bib before you do.

To hosts: if you serve a dish with a great deal of sauce it's perfectly all right to tuck your napkin under your chin or in your shirt. The host sets the tone at the dinner table, and it is courteous to let your guests know that they are welcome to take such an inelegant though often necessary precaution.

Your napkin remains in your lap until after the meal. When your host puts his napkin on the table, that is the signal the meal is over and it's time to leave the table. Don't refold your napkin, whether it's cloth or paper, but rather place it loosely gathered next to your plate. A napkin is folded after a meal only if you are replacing it in a napkin ring. If you have to get up during the meal, leave your napkin on your chair, not on the table, where it may get in the way of your dinner partner. Also, a napkin that isn't spotlessly clean lying on the table is not a pleasant sight during a meal.

Napkin Rings

Members of the family each fold up their napkins and replace them in their napkin rings. House guests are generally given a clean napkin for each meal. When a guest's stay will be a fairly long one, she is also given a napkin ring. During the meal, the ring is placed above your plate to the left.

Serving

At an informal meal when the host serves, she or he passes each dish to the right. The woman closest to the halfway mark keeps the first dish, then others on the right keep each successive dish. The host then serves to the left, serving him- or herself last. Vegetables, gravy, salad and so forth may be passed separately among the guests. In fact, decorative serving dishes, such as a casserole or a bowl filled with a colorful salad, can take the place of a more traditional centerpiece. When serving dishes are passed by the guests, each guest holds the dish for the person next to him if the platter is too heavy or cumbersome to hold in one hand and serve oneself with the other.

When you've finished eating or you pass your plate to your host for a second helping, knife and fork (tines up) are placed together on the plate. Be sure silverware is placed securely on the plate and the handles aren't extending precariously.

When a household worker is serving, she presents each platter to the guest's left, because for the right-handed it is easier to serve yourself from the left. The guest seated to the right of the male host will be served first. At a family meal with only one or two guests present, look to see if those already served have taken one chop or two, as the platter may not be coming back again. At a larger party the platter is brought in again and second helpings are offered.

To help yourself from a serving dish, use the spoon to cut and lift the portion, placing the fork on top of your portion to insure a safe and secure transfer to your plate. When small bits of food, such as mushrooms, are served on toast, take up the toast with the spoon as well. Don't scrape off the food and leave a soggy piece of toast on the serving platter. (You don't have to eat the toast.)

It's wasteful to take more than what you intend to eat. If you don't like a particular dish or you're allergic to the food, don't take any. Leave such food on your plate if it's been served to you by your host. You needn't give an explanation, as it will only call undue attention to a minor problem. Don't take food only to be polite and then leave it on your plate. That is more conspicuous than refusing the dish in the first place, and it might lead your host to believe there is something wrong with his or her cooking. However, if what you can't or don't like to eat is served as the main course, make an exception and take just a small portion. You can fill your plate with larger portions of the other dishes served, and thus put your host at ease.

When a household helper is serving, as much of the entire course of the meal as possible should be on the serving platter. Ideally, meat, vegetable and potato or rice would be offered from one platter. Otherwise, by the time a guest has waited for the separate platter of vegetables or potatoes, his meat is already cold before he can begin eating. Of course, if dinner is for more than four or six at most, one serving platter is not possible. A host may decide instead to have the meat and vegetable served from a platter. Guests then pass the potatoes and gravy around the table themselves.

For a dinner of more than twelve, two serving dishes must be presented to guests simultaneously so that serving will take a minimal amount of time.

Service begins with the woman seated at the right of the male host. When two serving platters are passed, the other begins to the left of the male host.

When to Begin Eating

When you're seated at a table of about six people it's courteous to wait until everyone has been served before you begin eating. At a larger table, you may begin to eat after three or four people have been served. The host generally gives the go-ahead by saying, "Please don't wait, the food will get cold." Take your host at his word and do begin eating. If you're one of the first few to be served, eat slowly to let others catch up. If cold food is being served I think it's polite to wait until everyone at your table has been served.

Soup

Soup may be served in a cup or in a wide soup plate. Soup in a cup may be sipped with a spoon until the soup is cool enough, then drunk from the cup if you'd like. Use your spoon to eat any vegetable or meat at the bottom of the cup. When nearing the bottom of a cup or a soup plate, tip the dish away from you (the spoon may be tipped either toward you or away from you, it makes no difference) to eat the last few spoonfuls. After you've finished, rest the spoon on the saucer or plate under the bowl. If the soup plate is a large one and the plate beneath it isn't much larger, rest the spoon in the empty soup plate.

Oyster crackers or croutons, when served with soup, are put into the soup whole. Drop oyster crackers in with your fingers, since they're dry. Use a spoon to drop croutons into your bowl, as they might be buttery. When large crackers are served with soup, eat them separately. Don't break them up and sprinkle them into your soup unless you're eating alone at home. It certainly tastes good but it is too messy a practice when others are dining with you.

Bread and Butter

The butter plate is on the left of the place setting. To butter your bread, break off a bite-sized piece of bread, and butter it holding the bread against the side of the butter plate. (In medieval times bread was broken at the table and each piece was eaten separately, because it was the custom to give the leavings at the table to the poor.) Hot rolls, muffins or toast are buttered all at once while the bread is still hot—taste isn't sacrificed for daintiness. To serve yourself from a butter dish, use the butter knife, not your own, unless your knife is clean and there is no butter knife, in which case ask your host for one—it may possibly have to be retrieved from the butter plate of an absent-minded guest. Butter plates are not mandatory. In fact, at formal dinners traditionally butter was never served. Sets of European china include no butter plates for this reason.

In order to simplify certain aspects of my dinner, I don't use butter plates. They take up a lot of room, and in our weight-conscious society people don't eat as much bread as they used to. I do sometimes serve bread that has already been lightly buttered and heated—fast food is becoming a way of life—and guests put the bread on the side of their dinner plates.

Gravy

Though gravy is made essentially from and for the meat, gravy lovers may pour or spoon gravy on potatoes or vegetables as well, as it's a compliment to the host to show your enthusiasm regarding the food.

Bread and Gravy

To dip bread into gravy on your plate, break off a small piece of bread, put it into the gravy with your fingers, then eat it with your fork, tines down.

Salad

When salad is served with unmanageably large pieces of lettuce, use a knife to cut the leaves. (Traditionally, lettuce was never cut with a knife because before knife blades were made of stainless steel the vinegar in the salad discolored the blades.) You'll be living dangerously if you try to fold the lettuce with your fork. When cutting lettuce, cut each bit separately. You're bound to scatter the salad from the plate if you attempt to slice up all the lettuce at once, and your chopping will imitate a chef's behavior more than a guest's.

Salt Cellars

Generally there is a tiny spoon resting in each salt cellar. If not, use the tip of a clean knife to take your pinch of salt, or use your fingers, since you must taste the food (and dirty your knife) before you salt it. If there is an individual salt cellar at each place setting, it is expected that the guests will take salt with their fingers.

Condiments

When helping yourself to condiments on the table, put each condiment on your plate beside the food, not directly on the food itself; cranberry sauce or horseradish is placed on the dinner plate, not on the meat; butter, jam or honey is put on the butter plate and not directly on the bread.

Dessert Served with Spoon and Fork

The dessert fork and spoon may be placed on the plate with the dessert when the plate is served or they may be placed above the plate in the table setting, spoon handle facing right and fork handle left, fork below the spoon. When your dessert is served in a bowl with a plate underneath, let the silverware rest together on the plate after you've finished eating, unless the plate is small in relation to the bowl and the silverware would make a tight fit. In that case, place the silver in the bowl.

When eating a dessert with spoon and fork, use the fork to hold the food in place and to push the food onto the spoon if necessary. The spoon is used to cut the dessert and to bring each bite to your mouth. It's perfectly all right to use just the spoon or the fork (spoons for fruit desserts, forks for pies) if you're not accustomed to manipulating both and attempting to do so will make you self-conscious about eating "correctly." Ice cream and cake may be eaten with only a spoon or spoon and fork.

Drinking at the Table

Drink when your mouth is empty and after you have wiped it with your napkin, so as not to leave food on the glass. When drinking from a water goblet, hold it at the base of the bowl.

Today, with simplified service for do-it-yourself parties, you need include water glasses at place settings only if you're serving a salty dish such as ham.

Hold a red wineglass similarly at the bowl's base. A glass of chilled white wine is held by the stem so that your hand won't warm the wine. Brandy snifters are first held with the bowl in both hands in order to warm the brandy. Sip holding the snifter cupped in one hand.

Coffee and Tea

When serving coffee, the host pours and adds cream and sugar, asking each guest, "How do you like your coffee?" At a large party, cream and sugar may be passed. If coffee has been served in the living room, leave the empty cups where guests have laid them down. A meticulous host who likes everything in its proper place will have to bear the clutter. If you begin cleaning up at such a late hour in the evening, it will seem to guests as though you're telling them the party is over. (Help hired for a party may certainly remove cups while guests are present.)

As often happens, if liquid has jiggled into the saucer, ask for a clean one. If for some reason a clean saucer isn't easily obtainable, pour the liquid back into the cup, then place a (paper!) napkin in the saucer and put the cup on top to dry both the saucer and the bottom of the cup. Remove the napkin. This rather unseemly device is better than dripping tea or coffee each time you take a sip.

Iced Tea or Iced Coffee

Place the long-handled spoon in the saucer before drinking. If there is no saucer, hold the spoon handle against the side of the glass while you drink.

Mugs

When you're served coffee or tea in a mug, remember that your host wouldn't choose this manner of service if slightly sticky spoons lying on the table were anathema. After you've served yourself cream and sugar, sip the excess liquid off the spoon so that the spoon won't leave a puddle when you put it down next to the mug. If the table is covered with delicate place mats or a tablecloth and you can't bring yourself to set down your not-too-clean spoon on the finery, or if you're served a tea bag in a mug, ask your host for a small plate. Don't drink from a mug with a spoon in it, as you'll find there is not enough room for both your mouth and the spoon. Such an attempt might prove to be dangerous to your eyes as well.

Clearing the Table

Dishes are removed from the guest's right. Carry only two dishes at a time, one plate in each hand, no matter what you remember from your waitressing days in college. Don't stack dishes at the table and then carry off the entire pile. Though it may be the easiest way to get a dirty job done, it is not a pleasant sight for your guests to watch you treat your table as though it were the kitchen sink. Dishes may be stacked on a rolling cart which goes directly into the kitchen.

In old English houses kitchens are often in the basement just below the dining room. I once dined in a house which was equipped with the most magical device for disposing of dirty dishes. After the meal the dishes were placed on the serving table that stood adjacent to the dining-room table. Then this *deus ex machina* (the entire serving table) descended through a trapdoor into the kitchen, leaving not even a suspicion of our feasting.

SITUATIONS AT TABLE WHICH NEED EXTRA THOUGHT

When to Pick Up Food with Your Fingers

Foods such as corn on the cob and spareribs are of course eaten with the fingers. Some shellfish, such as shrimp and lobster, depending on how prepared, are also eaten this way. If you're not sure that it would be acceptable to pick up food with your fingers, wait and follow your host's example. One way to decide for yourself is to rely on your own pragmatic instincts: ask yourself which would be the neater and easier way to eat the food.

A thoughtful and alert host of an informal gathering where guests seem hesitant to pick up food that is most easily eaten with the fingers should set an example and be the first to offer a hand-held demonstration. For instance, when crisp duck is served it's a shame not to be able to pick up the bones in order to eat the parts of the bird which to some are the most delectable.

When cookies, fruit or other finger foods are served, take the food from the serving dish and place it on your plate before eating it. Don't take food from a serving dish and put it directly into your mouth.

Finger Bowls

Finger bowls are sometimes served after shellfish or corn on the cob. To clean your fingers, first dip in the fingers of one hand and then the fingers of the other. Then wipe your fingers with your napkin. Don't clean your mouth with the water from a finger bowl. In some houses finger bowls will be served directly after the main course, whether or not you touched food with your fingers. I often serve finger bowls in my house, a holdover, I suppose, from the routine in the house in which I grew up. Finger bowls are served on the dessert plate, with the dessert spoon and fork placed on the plate on either side of the bowl. A doily, either paper or cloth, lies under the bowl. After you've used the bowl (there's no reason to use it at all if your fingers are clean), pick up your dessert spoon and fork and place them on the table on either side of the plate. Then simultaneously lift the finger bowl and the doily and place them to your left above your plate. This maneuver takes two hands and ten fingers. If finger bowls arrive at the table and you're not sure what to do next, watch your host or another guest who seems to project some authority on the subject. If you've forgotten to watch, just ask your host or another guest what you should do next.

Taking Food Out of Your Mouth

When removing a bit of food or a small bone from your mouth, try to take it out the same way it went in. For instance, a pit in a dessert fruit is removed with your spoon and placed on the service plate. A bit of gristle in the meat is taken out with your fork and put on the side of your plate. Small bones from fish or meat are most easily located and removed with your thumb and forefinger. The important thing to remember when removing food from your mouth is to do so unobtrusively. Therefore, if you can accomplish the task with your fingers much more circumspectly than with silverware, remove unwanted bits that way—the point being to make as little show about it as possible.

If you take a bite of food which is too hot, take a sip of water or whatever is being served with the meal, to put the fire out, then swallow. When you eat something which you unhappily discover you don't like at all, swallow as quickly as possible, don't spit it out. If you do happen to take a bit of food which is spoiled, you certainly may spit it out as inconspicuously as possible.

Food Caught Between the Teeth

Never use a toothpick at the table. You may ask your host for a toothpick after the meal, but use it in privacy.

Smoking at Table

There is generally a pause for relaxed discussion after the entrée has been completed and before the dessert is served. If cigarettes and ashtrays are provided at the table, you may smoke before dessert. Don't, however, smoke between courses. It has been proven that cigarettes dull the awareness of the palate; however, scientific proof should not be needed as a deterrent. Smoking is simply not a good accompaniment to food. Therefore, smokers should always be conscious of others around them. When you're in the company of those who aren't smoking at table, let others enjoy their meal before you enjoy your cigarette. Refrain from smoking until the meal is finished. (For more on smoking at table, see Chapter 1, "Everyday Manners in Public Places." For smoking abroad, see Chapter 18, "Travel.")

Silver That Isn't Quite Clean

When dining at a restaurant, if you're served silver that is a bit dirty ask for a new piece. In a private home you'll have to use the silverware the way it is. Never wipe silverware on your napkin. That your napkin may be clean at the time makes no difference.

Dropping Silverware

Retrieve fallen silverware directly if possible or wait until after the meal. In a restaurant, ask for a replacement. If you can't conveniently pick up the piece you've dropped and the waiter isn't terribly rushed, you may tell him you've dropped it and he will pick up the piece after everyone has left the table.

Accidents at Table

A bit of spilled food on the table may be scraped up with the edge of a clean knife or spoon. A really bad spill on a really pretty tablecloth should be called to the host's attention. Not that there is too much that can be done at the moment. However, some hosts have ingenious remedies for spills of all sorts, and they should be warned so that they can work their magic. For that most popular mishap, spilled red wine, one antidote is to pour soda water on the spill; another is to sprinkle salt on the stain and then pour on water. A wine connoisseur once assured me that the only way to clean up a red-wine spill is to pour white wine on the stain.

Sneezing and Blowing Your Nose at Table

Being set at meal scratch not neither
spit cough or blow your nose except
there's a necessity for it.

—GEORGE WASHINGTON,
"Rules of Civility and Decent Behavior"

Try not to blow your nose at table. If you must, make it a quick and quiet blow, turning your head to the side. When you sneeze, hold your handkerchief or at least your hand in front of your nose and mouth, as germs travel in the droplets of moisture from a sneeze. Napkins are not used as handkerchiefs at the table.

FAST FOOD

There's nothing like it—a purely American invention facilitating speed and economy, it serves our needs when we're traveling or when we want a quick, inexpensive bite to eat, though most children and teenagers would be happy to fit fast food into their daily routines. Such food is certainly fast and informal; however, buying a Big Mac is not license to become a boor. The abundance of paper and plastic used to package the food is certainly not helping the country's conservation efforts, nor the fast-food customer's cleanup efforts. Don't treat the restaurant or its parking lot as a litter basket. Throw all nonedibles into the trash baskets. In fact, I've noticed them to be the largest and most evident feature of the décor in all fast-foot restaurants. They are designed so as not to be missed.

HOW TO EAT CERTAIN FOODS

Artichokes are always eaten with your fingers, one leaf at a time. Dip the pulpy base of each leaf into sauce (generally melted butter is served with hot artichokes, and a mayonnaise dip or vinaigrette is served with cold artichokes), and scrape the pulpy part off the leaf with your teeth. Place the leaf on the side of your plate or in a dish put on the table for the purpose of holding discarded leaves. When you reach the prickly part (the choke) under the leaves that surround the heart, scrape it away with a knife. Then eat the heart with knife and fork.

Asparagus

Small, slender asparagus may be picked up and eaten with the fingers. Eating the longer, thicker asparagus with your fingers is generally a messy job, as excess liquid from the vegetable will tend to run over your hands. It's easier, therefore, to eat the large asparagus with knife and fork. Do not take a knife to a dish of asparagus and immediately cut off all the tips at once. Cut and eat each asparagus a bit at a time, leaving the tough, inedible stalk on your plate.

Avocado

Sliced avocado is eaten with a fork. Use a spoon to eat a halved avocado that is still in the shell.

Bacon

Crisp bacon is always eaten with your fingers, as its very crispness defies any attempt made with knife and fork. Bacon served with meat loaf, for instance, which is less well cooked and rather limp, may be eaten with knife and fork.

Bird's and Frog's Legs

Use your knife and fork to cut off as much meat as you can from pieces of duck, quail, squab and Cornish hens. Disjoint the leg and wing pieces, using your knife and fork, then pick up the pieces to eat with your fingers, holding the small bones in one hand. At a formal dinner you must do the best you can with knife and fork only. Whole pieces of chicken are picked up only at picnics or other very informal meals. Disjoint large frog's legs with knife and fork before picking them up.

Cheese

Cheese served as hors d'oeuvres are spread on crackers with a knife. When cheese and fresh fruits are served for dessert, the cheese is cut and eaten with a fork. Runny cheeses such as Camembert or Brie are always spread on crackers with a knife.

Corn on the Cob

The only way to eat corn on the cob is with both hands. First butter the corn with a knife, spreading a pat of butter over the corn until the whole ear is buttered while it is still hot. A large ear may be broken in half to make eating it a bit simpler. Though meals at which corn on the cob are served are by their nature informal, take care not to eat with so much abandon that bits of buttery kernels stick to the side of your mouth. If you'd like you may cut the kernels off the cob with a knife by holding the knife in one hand and the cob in the other at an angle with one end against the plate. But this is generally a hazardous business for the inexperienced.

Filleting a Fish

When a small fish is served to you whole, first cut off the head and the tail, then slit the fish from one end to the other lengthwise and lift the meat (fillet) away and up from the backbone. Put the tip of your knife under one end of the bone and with the knife and fork gently lift out the entire skeleton. Place the bones on the side of your plate or on your butter plate. Eat the fish with knife and fork or only with a fork. Be careful to take small bites and to chew carefully; even the most expertly filleted fish will have tiny bones still remaining in it. If you do find a bone in your mouth take it out with your thumb and forefinger.

Fruits and Vegetables

Apples and pears, when eaten at the table, are quartered and cored with a knife. Remove the peel if you prefer to do so. You may then eat them with your hands or cut them into even smaller pieces to be eaten with a fork.

Grapes. Break or cut a section from a large bunch of grapes; never pick off single grapes from the bunch that is being served. When eating a grape with seeds, put the whole grape into your mouth, drop the seeds into your fist and then put them on the plate.

Concord grapes. If you don't like the skin press the grape with your thumb and forefinger, stem side against your mouth. The pulp and the juice will pop into your mouth. Leave the skins on your plate.

Bananas. When at the table, peel the banana, break off each bite and eat it with your fingers.

Grapefruit. When grapefruit halves are served, no matter how tempting, don't pick up the fruit to squeeze the last bit of juice onto your spoon. If a whole grapefruit is served in a fruit bowl you may peel it and eat it in sections just as you would an orange.

Mangoes are deliciously juicy and worth the trouble they are to eat. Cut them into quarters and pull the skin from each quarter, holding each slippery section down with a fork. Then cut the mango into bite-sized pieces and eat with spoon or fork.

Melons served in balls are eaten with a spoon. When a quartered melon is cut in sections from the rind, eat it with a fork. When it is not, cut away from the rind and eat it with a spoon.

Oranges. Maître d's and gourmets are able to peel the skin from an orange in one continuous spiral. The rest of us can section the skin with a knife and pull it off with our fingers. Break the orange apart and eat it a section at a time. When eating a large orange you may cut each section in half rather than biting it and taking the chance of having juice dribble down your chin. Oranges are sometimes served halved in the skin like grapefruits and are eaten with a spoon just as you would eat a grapefruit. If there are seeds in each orange section, drop them into your fist and then put them on the side of your plate.

Watermelon is generally served on the rind and is usually eaten held firmly in both hands. Or you can lay the slice on its side, remove the pits with the fork tines and cut each bite, cutting it with the side of your fork.

Stewed fruit. Drop pits of plums, cherries, prunes, etc., onto the spoon and put them on the side of your service plate under the bowl.

Celery, Pickles, Olives

Take them from the dish with your fingers when they are served as a garnish. Take small bites around the pit of a large olive. Put small olives into your mouth and drop the pit into your partially closed fist. Celery, olives and pickles in salads are eaten with a fork.

Potatoes

French fries are eaten with a fork if you're at the table. Cut the french fries with the side of your fork into manageable pieces; don't nibble at them from the end of your fork. When eating them with other finger food, such as hamburgers, eat French fries with your fingers. Eat potato chips with your fingers.

Shellfish

To eat raw oysters and clams served on the half shell, hold the shell steady in one hand and lift the oyster or clam with the fork held in the other. Dip it into sauce and pop it whole into your mouth. You may pick up the empty shell and tip the remaining juice into your mouth. Oyster crackers are dropped whole into sauce and also eaten with the fork. When eating steamed clams, remove the clam by the neck with your fingers. Holding it by the neck, dip it into the clam broth and then into melted butter. Eat the whole clam in one bite. On the neck of the clam is a sheath which slips off easily and is discarded on your plate, or you may want to eat the clam, neck sheath and all. Put the empty clamshells on your butter plate, or in the bowl on the table which is meant for empty shells. If broth for dipping clams is served in a bowl, you may drink the broth directly from the bowl after you've eaten the clams.

Fried clams are eaten with the fingers or with a fork. Fried clams and forks, however, don't always get on too well together, as clams tend to be a bit rubbery and difficult to cut.

A shrimp cocktail is eaten with an oyster fork. Large shrimps are speared with the fork and a mouthful at a time is bitten off. Redip the shrimp in the sauce before each bite.

To eat fried shrimp, hold the shrimp by the tail and bite off a mouthful at a time. Then place the tail on the side of your plate.

Mussels: When they are served in a sauce, take out the mussel from the shell with a fork. You may pick up the shell and quietly sip the remaining juice from it. The broth remaining in the plate is eaten with a spoon, or you may dunk bite-sized pieces of bread into the dish, one at a time, and lift them out with a fork just as you would eat bread and gravy. Discard empty shells on your butter plate or on a plate provided for such a purpose.

Hard-shelled crabs: Take off the legs with your fingers and quietly suck out the meat. Then turn the body on its back on the plate and pick out the meat with an oyster fork or a nut pick. Crack the claws with a nutcracker.

Lobster: It's easiest to first tackle a lobster by twisting off the front claws. Crack the claws with a nutcracker and remove the meat with an oyster fork or a nut pick. Next, break the tail off the body. The meat in the tail can generally be lifted out with a fork fairly easily (compared with the meat of the rest of the lobster). You can then cut up the tail with a knife and fork or, more informally, since by this time you're probably up to your elbows in butter and lobster, pick up the tail and bite off a mouthful at a time. Then break off each leg and quietly suck out the meat. The parts of the lobster body that are edible are the green tamale and the red roe.

Snails: Grasp each snail in the special tongs that are always served with the dish and pull out the snail from its shell with a snail fork. The delicious garlicky butter left in the dish may be eaten by dropping in bite-sized pieces of bread, one at a time, and lifting them out with a fork.

Spaghetti

Twirl the spaghetti around the fork and then lift the forkful (carefully) to your mouth. If spaghetti is also served with a spoon, hold the spoon in your left hand and twirl the spaghetti into a nest in the spoon. A spoon makes spaghetti eating easier, because it helps the spaghetti to hold its twirled shape. Leave the spoon resting on the plate and bring the spaghetti to your mouth with the fork.

4 OVERNIGHT GUESTS

HOW TO BE A POPULAR GUEST

What Clothes to Bring

If you're a confirmed city slicker who's been invited to the country, or a nonskier who's due to spend a weekend at a ski house, ask your host when you're invited what clothes you'll need. Your host may need prompting, because he probably knows the lay of the land so well it doesn't occur to him that you don't. The answer will serve a double purpose. First, you'll learn the weekend dress code, and, second, it will give you some insight into the activities planned.

Breakfast

Some people feel strongly that breakfast is the most important meal of the day. If you subscribe to this belief, make your needs known. Find out the night before what your host's morning routine is. Ask to see the kitchen layout if you're staying in a house where breakfast means fend for yourself. If you and your host are breakfasting together, let your host organize the meal.

On the other hand, maybe you enjoy sleeping late or are a morning misanthrope and don't want to join your host and family for an early breakfast. Just tell your host you had planned on treating yourself to a late morning and you'll get your own toast and coffee. Don't count on the late morning, however, if there are young children in the house. A host cannot be expected to keep children quiet until that unknown hour when his guests wake up. Paula has a beach house, and all summer friends come and go. After a few weekends of being shushed all morning, Paula's three children rebelled. They complained that it was their house, too. Paula saw their point and warned guests that unless they were heavy sleepers they'd probably hear the children in the morning.

Role reversals have been known to occur in which the host becomes the guest's problem at breakfast time. In Bob's large summer house where the hospitality is gracious and relaxed, there is but one unbreakable rule: Don't wake up Bob. One sunny Saturday, Bob's four house guests were breakfasting none too quietly. Bob burst upon the scene, clad only in his Japanese housecoat and raving like a samurai warrior. His guests slunk sheepishly out of the house and to the beach. Sunday's breakfast was conducted in whispers. That Bob overreacted need not be overstated. When four or five people are sharing a house, there is no room for short tempers or fits of pique. Had it been my house, I'd have been delighted that my guests were enjoying themselves so thoroughly and without any help. But then, I'm an early riser.

Staying Out of the Way

Naturalist Jane Goodall spent years living among the chimpanzees in the wild in Africa. Months of observation made it possible for her to enter into a few of the chimpanzees' daily activities. An overnight guest, not unlike Ms. Goodall, must devote considerable energies to adapt successfully to unfamiliar surroundings. Members of a household participate in a choreography that originates from family routines. Each family member has his or her own activity and territory. For instance, whoever is making dinner would naturally claim the kitchen. In some households, the cook may chat with other members of the family; in others, the cook may prefer to spend the time making dinner alone. In the morning, all family members know who takes a shower at exactly what time and who makes the toast. Even in a small household, patterns are fairly rigidly set, though they are not usually too intricate and are therefore easier for a guest to work around.

Be aware that these patterns exist and you'll be less likely to stumble into the middle of one of them. Pay particular attention during customary heavy traffic hours, such as mornings and before meals. Try to stay out of the mainstream of activity. Just because your host is busy doesn't mean you have to disappear, however. If everyone is in the kitchen, you can certainly go in to chat. But don't infringe on the domain of the cook and lift lids or taste the food.

Using the Telephone

When making a long-distance call, bill the call to your home number or use your credit card. Don't have your call billed to your host's phone and then casually say, "Please let me know what I owe you." A host will have great difficulty in asking for the dollar thirty-five when the bill arrives three weeks later—and will be rightly put out, though his asking will be made easier, if you called Guadalajara instead of Main Street. A host shouldn't be put into the position of seeming to be a Scrooge, and you shouldn't expect long-distance hospitality from your host.

What You Can Do to Help

Making your bed and straightening up the bathroom after you've used it are part of an overnight guest's unspoken duties. Putting books you've read back into the bookcase and records back into their jackets are secondary duties not to be overlooked. Make yourself useful around the house when the time is right; watch carefully and you'll pick up the signal. For instance, wait for your host to initiate the washing up after dinner. Jane's mother-in-law, under the guise of helpfulness, is always the first one to clear the table. In doing so, she has made the decision for Jane, the host, that dinner is over. So that you won't be accused of acts of aggression, simply ask what you can do to help instead of taking it upon yourself to decide what needs doing.

Don't volunteer for things you can't do. If you're accident prone, it's safer to peel potatoes or help with the shopping than to clear the table or dice the vegetables. Explain your problem; your hosts will be sympathetic—nobody wants his dishes or his guests broken.

Some hosts are annoyed if they've been made to feel they've become the guests' servants for the weekend. Others enjoy doing everything for their guests. Therefore, if your hosts respond to your offer to help by suggesting you sit down and relax instead, take them at their word.

Visiting Friends Without Your Host

Sometimes my guests have friends living close by. As long as I'm told far enough in advance so that plans I've already made aren't disrupted, I'm perfectly happy to see guests go off visiting on their own, and I provide them with transportation if I can. If I'm invited to join them, I feel free to say yes or no. If my guests have given their friends a rave review, I will generally go with them. On the other hand, I might decline the invitation and use the time to be by myself on an especially hectic weekend. Sometimes, in an expansive mood, I'll ask my guests' friends to join us for lunch or a swim.

If guests cheerfully spring the news that they are going visiting alone, the host may interpret this to mean his guests expect to have a better time with other friends. Tell your host of your plans when he first extends the invitation—just say you'd like to keep an hour or two free to visit other friends in the area—and your host won't feel used or jealous.

A Guest in a House with Full-Time Help or Live-in Help

When you are an overnight guest in a house with live-in help, tip about three to five dollars a day. At the end of your stay the amount depends on how much the household worker has done for you. If you've been home for every meal during the weekend and your host has entertained, you would give more than if you'd been out most of the time and the help had only made your bed and straightened your room. I tip the household help even when I stay with my mother, just as she tips my help when she stays with me.

Leave the tip in an envelope with a note, "Thank you for all you've done for me (us) this weekend," and sign your name or write "Mr. and Mrs. Ferguson." You may leave the envelope in your room, deliver it personally or leave it with your host to pass along. A guest staying in a house with help should always say "Please" and "Thank you" when someone in the house does anything to help him.

If you're weekending in a house with a fairly large staff it's best to tip everyone two or three dollars at the end of your stay: for instance, two dollars to the cook, two dollars to the person who took care of your room, and two dollars to the person who brought you your breakfast and who sees to the comfort of the house. You may put each separate amount in an envelope with each person's name on it and leave them with your host, or, if you know them well, give the envelope directly to each person.

The host will tip the household help after a busy guest-filled weekend if guests themselves have not done so.

Overnight guests in the house with full-time help are responsible for keeping the guest room neat. A household worker should not have to literally pick up after guests. Guests are, of course, expected to hang up clothes and put away cosmetics.

Guests in a house with one household helper should also make their beds and tidy up their room. In a house with anything less than a household staff it is only considerate to look after yourself as much as you can.

(For more on household help, see Chapter 13.)

Visiting with Children

Martha and Doug were hesitant about spending the weekend with friends who had no children of their own but insisted their guests bring along their eighteen-month-old son. Martha ended up spending most of the time protecting the baby from her hosts—removing filled glasses and lit pipes from the coffee table just before the baby did. Her male host was clearly irritated and sang a constant litany of "When I have a child he's going to learn not to touch glass," "My kid is going to learn not to touch cigarettes," and on and on.

Visiting with small or even medium-sized children can be more trouble than it's worth, unless, of course, there are children where you're going. People, young or old, who aren't used to children might savor the concept of a Weekend with the Children; but their fantasy is easily shattered when the children shriek with delight one minute and with murderous intent the next, and when they bolt from the table, trailing grape jelly on their heels. Your children's everyday mishaps may be viewed as calamitous in an adults-only household. If you're thinking of taking your child along on a weekend you're planning to spend with friends who don't have children, arrange a test run before the major event. Ask your friends for a family lunch or brunch. Watch their reactions carefully. Are they cheerful, if a bit haggard, when it's time for them to leave? Do they leave early? Consider the good signs as well as the bad (do the bad signs outweigh the good after only a few hours?), and you'll have a fair indication of how your weekend will go.

Thank-You's

You as an overnight guest should contribute to the household in some way. If you like, you may bring something to your host when you arrive. I've found that safest and the most pleasing to your host is something that, though pretty, has a utilitarian purpose. Bring something delicious to eat. Even if your host doesn't like marzipan, he won't have to take it out of the closet and put it on the mantel every time you come to visit—someone will be happy to eat it. Note pads with your hosts' name printed on them or pretty pencils or felt pens are also good choices. You can't go wrong with a present that is usable. When you're visiting a family with children, bring the children something, in which case it's not necessary to also bring a gift for their parents.

You may wait until after your visit and send a house plant or cut flowers again—safe presents that everyone is pleased to receive. You can reverse the order and arrive with the plant or send the food after you stay. Keep in mind, however, that flora doesn't travel well. To give a thank-you gift is a generous gesture. It is not a necessity. A thank-you note shows your appreciation just as well, if less extravagantly.

There are many ways to say thank you during your visit. John, an excellent cook, is in demand as a house guest because he always volunteers to prepare one of his perfect dinners. If your cooking is less perfect than John's, you can offer to make the lunch sandwiches or the pancakes for breakfast.

A movie buff, addicted to the silver screen, travels with his projector and his favorite old classics. Bill's visits include such highlights as *The Thief of Bagdad* with Douglas Fairbanks, Sr., and *Ozzie and Harriet* reruns.

If you'd like to say thank you by inviting your hosts out to dinner during your stay, give them enough advance warning so they won't have already begun plans for dinner at home.

HOW TO BE A POPULAR HOST

Invitations

When you issue an overnight invitation, let your guests know what time you expect them to arrive and, just as important, when you expect them to leave. Janet thought her weekend invitation to her in-laws was clear when she suggested only that they arrive on Friday evening. By Monday morning, Janet was a little put out that her guests were making no motions to leave; by Tuesday, she was desperate. Janet's mother-in-law picked up her vibrations, and that evening she and her husband made their overdue and by now somewhat brusque goodbyes. Confusion, resentment and crossed signals could have been avoided on both sides if Janet had been definite about the length of time her invitation covered. Include in your invitation a mention of any activities that call for special clothes. Tell your guests if they'll be playing tennis or swimming or if you have a party planned so that they'll plan their weekend wardrobe accordingly.

At the time you invite your guests, be sure to discuss with them any specifics your invitation may hold. Paula works in the city but spends every weekend during the summer at her beach house. When Paula asked two friends to come for the weekend, she was hesitant to mention that she expected them to share the food costs. Paula got around to explaining the situation only after the weekend had begun. Her guests were understandably resentful; they felt they'd been conned into signing a seemingly standard contract only to discover they had not been advised of the loophole. Now they had no choice but to agree to an additional expense they had assumed their host would shoulder. Explain simply to your guests what your situation is *when you invite them:* "Mary, I'd love to have you up to the ski house this weekend. The Burkes are coming, too, and we're all splitting the food and liquor costs." Mary now has the chance to decline the invitation if she can't afford to or doesn't want to spend the extra money.

Also let your guest know if he or she is going to be sleeping on the living-room couch or sharing a room with one of the kids. People aren't usually fussy about accommodations, but your guest, unbeknownst to you, might suffer from a bad back or perhaps insomnia and may be petulant—at best—in forced to lie wide-eyed in the dark for fear of waking a roommate, instead of spending the hour reading as he or she is used to.

When Guests First Arrive

When a guest first arrives, you as host must demonstrate that your guest is very welcome in order that he immediately begin to feel comfortable in your house. If guests arrive at mealtime your problem is solved; if they come at other times, be sure to ask if they would like a drink or a snack, thus exhibiting your concern for their well-being. Jerusha, who tends toward intermittent but extravagant moods, greeted a blizzard-weary traveler to her ski house with a bubble bath and heated towels (heating towels in the dryer takes only a minute). Though most hosts don't extend their hospitality to the far reaches Jerusha does, all hosts must pay special attention to making guests feel at home.

Who Sleeps Where: Unmarried Couples

Sleeping arrangements for unmarried couples are clearly up to you, the host. Friends have voiced the problem of what to tell their children if an unmarried couple shares a room. Small children generally aren't interested in who is sleeping where and why. Teenagers know what's going on anyway. But if you think certain arrangements would make you uncomfortable and would not be easy to explain to your twelve-year-old child, put the couple into separate rooms. It's best to clarify the arrangements with your guests before they arrive. Call the half of the couple you're most comfortable with and explain how you feel. If your friend seems offended, postpone your weekend entertaining with the hope that eventually they'll marry or go their separate ways.

When you're entertaining an older married couple, ask the half you know best what arrangements he or she would prefer. When I asked engaged friends who were coming for the weekend, the woman wanted a room of her own. (If lack of space makes such a request sometimes difficult to fulfill, possibly you could free a child's room and have one half of the couple sleep on the couch.)

A couple who are living together would unquestionably share a room when they visit you. If you can't condone their behavior, you probably aren't very good friends to begin with, and it may be more comfortable for everybody if your time together did not include an overnight stay.

If you're entertaining two people you don't know well and you have no knowledge as to the extent of their relationship, don't assign rooms according to your assumptions. It's better to make available to them two separate rooms (even if one is bunking in with your eight-year-old twins) and let the couple (if indeed that is what the two people constitute) make their own choices.

House Rules

Alice was startled when her good friend and host for the weekend informed her that she didn't like guests going into the refrigerator. Alice had played host to her friend more than once and had always given her free run of the kitchen. Alice considered her host's policy inconsistent and said so. It was her friend's turn to be surprised. "But those are your rules," her friend reasoned. "When you're at my house, I expect you to follow my rules."

If certain things guests might do would cause you mental discomfort, define your rules at the beginning of their stay. Be straightforward and announce, "I have a thing about anyone doing the dishes, going into the fridge, messing up the morning paper." You, as host, are entitled to your idiosyncrasies as long as you don't put your guests in a straitjacket. So are your guests. When guests have habits which are not your own but which aren't disruptive to the organization or the peace of mind of your household, it's rude and dictatorial to try to curtail them. Also, the more strictures you put on your guests' freedom, the more you'll be reduced to waiting hand and foot on thankless souls with penetrating, glowering stares. A guest is a captive, more or less at your mercy. If you can't abide the slightest change in your routine, don't invite guests to spend an extended period of time with you.

Maxine spent a long weekend in the guest house of well-to-do friends. Everything was beautifully arranged: there was coffee and breakfast food in the guest house so that Maxine could have breakfast at her convenience. In return for such grand hospitality, Maxine had brought a very lavish present: a case of wine. As she was helping to prepare an informal lunch on the first day of her visit,

Maxine began to open a bottle of the wine. Before she could offer a glass to her hosts, they announced they did not have wine before lunch or even with lunch. They had wine only with dinner. In this case, the enforcement of house rules crossed the border into hostility. Maxine, after all, had brought the wine her hosts were forbidding her to drink. That they made a further issue about when they considered it fitting to drink the wine told Maxine they did not appreciate her extravagant present or her extravagant presence. The other side of this story is that the wine, after all, was a gift and Maxine had no claim on the gift after it was given. Though weekend hosts must learn to be flexible about their "rules," self-assertive guests must, in return, learn to hold back.

Does a Host Have to Double as a Maid?

When I have guests, their suitcases are unpacked, wrinkled clothes are pressed, beds are turned down in the evening. I do it because I have the help. I don't think most people expect such treatment. It isn't necessary to provide these kinds of services for your guests if you manage your household by yourself.

Guests cannot expect a host to iron for them, to pick up after them or to turn down their beds. Guests take care of their own belongings and tidy up their own rooms. (If a guest does need ironing done, he may certainly ask his host if he can borrow the iron and do it himself.)

Suggesting That Guests Lend a Hand

Ideally, your guests will help you out as much as possible. But this is not always the case, especially with male guests. One friend, whose husband always pitches in, has taken to making disparaging but amusing comments to men who sit on the sidelines. When their indolence is thus pointed out to them, the properly abashed guests ask what they can do. If you're not the type to cajole gently or you don't have a husband you can hold up as a model in this regard, just ask your guest, "Would you set the table?" as you hand over the silver, in a natural, straightforward manner. I don't consider it rude to ask guests for help if a guest doesn't volunteer. Begin delegating small chores soon after your guests arrive so that they'll learn you run your household through joint effort. Don't spend your weekend inwardly fuming and doing everything yourself. People are usually glad to help. It's difficult to know what to do in a house that is not your own, so you, as host, may have to take matters in hand.

Do You Have to Plan Every Minute?

Some hosts are comfortable when entertaining a house guest only if the day is filled with planned activities. Keep in mind that your needs do not necessarily duplicate the needs of your guests. Don't become a cruise director and organize every minute of your guests' visit. Let visitors structure some of their own time; let them swim or play tennis or loaf when they'd like to. Time spent away from home is often looked upon as a leisurely mini-vacation. Guests are happy to spend some of that time fending for themselves.

Alice's most memorable overly structured weekend was spent at the mercy of friends at their beach house. The morning sun was glorious. Alice had made herself comfortable on the patio with a book and a cup of coffee when her hosts cast their long shadows over her plans. The time was right, they insisted, to stroll along some distant dunes to see the terns nesting. After a lengthy car ride and a grueling walk through driftwood and marsh—Alice's clothes for a relaxed weekend included nothing sturdier than a pair of backless sandals—the party was suddenly surrounded by low-flying, hissing terns and sea gulls, protecting their nests against the intruders. By this time Alice was doing some hissing of her own, but it went unnoticed. Once back at the house, it was low tide and time to slide down the clifflike dunes of yet another beach to gather mussels for dinner. The pounds and pounds of shellfish were carted in pails up the cliff, and Alice spent the afternoon with her host in the kitchen cleaning mussels. She concedes that dinner was delicious, but *moules marinière* did not compensate for a day spent under the lash of her well-meaning but Legree-like hosts.

When a Guest Gets Sick

As *The Man Who Came to Dinner* illustrates only too well, if a guest gets sick in your house, you become the nurse and caretaker until the sickness or the guest departs. A guest who has taken sick cannot be left languishing in the guest room. The host summons forth the appropriate remedy, be it chicken soup or an ambulance. A host does not abandon a guest in distress.

Making the Kitchen Available to the Guest

Though you may be perfectly content with three meals a day eaten at regular mealtime hours, your guest may be in the habit of eating a late-night sandwich or of drinking a glass of milk before bedtime. Ask your guest before bedtime if he is hungry or thirsty. If the answer is yes, make the kitchen available to him so that he can prepare the food himself. As a courtesy, I always leave a bowl of fresh fruit and some cookies in the guest room.

When Inviting a Gay Guest

When you invite a gay friend for the weekend and the friend has a lover, invite the couple. In other words, apply the same rules to a gay family as you would to any family. If your personal moral code is against their rules, don't consider them your friends. You can't acknowledge the characteristics you admire in someone—wit, charm, intelligence or whatever those qualities may be—and leave others unacknowledged.

The Single Host

A single person carries out all the duties of a host. Julius, one benighted single host, was in the habit of expecting his women guests to do the cooking. The guests, if they wanted a meal, could hardly fail to oblige. Julius, however, was rude indeed and, it turned out, presumptuous as well. One hungry weekend he discovered that all women were not born knowing how to cook, after twenty-four hours of bologna and cheese sandwiches which Alice prepared for every meal. Julius' criticism unleashed in turn some harsh criticism from Alice, who didn't much care for bologna, either. She suggested that if he, as host, did not or would not cook he must provide enough cold food or dine out. Alice's advice was perfectly correct. Single men cannot expect a woman guest to fill the traditional female roles, nor can single women hosts expect male guest to make drinks or to barbecue steaks. Though it's wonderful if a guest does volunteer to do a few hostly chores, it's the host's job to provide the hospitality.

OVERNIGHT GUESTS IN THE CITY

City dwellers may find they are hosts more frequently than they'd like. Friends living out of town may ask to stay with them when in town for business or pleasure. You are expected to be a gracious but not a full-time host when your friends' primary reason for staying with you is not for the pleasure of your company. For guests who are unfamiliar with the city, it is thoughtful to put a map and a city guide in the guest room. If your guest is sleeping on the couch, clean out a drawer and make hanging space in a closet. This makes things easier for both of you; otherwise you'll find yourself tripping over shoes which have been poorly concealed under the sofa.

You aren't responsible for planning your guest's entertainment unless you'd like to do so. If you've already made plans that don't include your guest, there's no need to cancel them. Just let him know well enough in advance for him to make plans of his own. City guests often go off on their own. Give your guest a set of house keys so that no one will be inconvenienced. (Just make sure you introduce him to your doorman first.)

A guest who stays for more than a couple of days may want to add a few of her usual food staples to your kitchen. Don't feel you've neglected your duties when you see a box of crunchy Granola in the cabinet. Your guest is right to make herself comfortable by supplying her own breakfast; you couldn't possibly have guessed that she wasn't satisfied with toast and coffee.

When you invite yourself to stay with friends, you must take the initiative and make your own plans. Assuring friends that you can take care of yourself and then locking yourself in the guest room for hours at a time will make your hosts feel responsible for you and, at the same time, angry at having been duped. If you're single, don't expect your host to provide escorts or dinner invitees of the opposite sex or even that they will have masses of friends over to meet you. Your social expectations may not fit in with their life style or their pocketbook. Taking you out to dinner or having people over for dinner more than once or twice may be inconvenient or too expensive.

A guest takes a chance of alienating his host if without giving previous warning he entertains friends in the apartment where he's staying. A guest alone can be an imposition—though a pleasant one—in a crowded apartment. A living room filled with friends of friends can strain a relationship permanently.

5 THE BUSINESS WORLD

It might be helpful to understand a strange dichotomy present in the business world: though the profit motive insists on the innovative, social situations in the office are usually governed by the dead hand of tradition. Old equipment, whether last year's or last century's, is discarded in a moment in the wake of the magic words "new and improved." Yet when it comes to questions of dress, speech and manners in the office, the business world is a most conservative one. The factory floor points toward the year 2000, but the social customs in the executive suite seem anachronistic by comparison.

Nevertheless, offices do run smoothly on the well-greased, old-fashioned machinery of custom. And this conservative attitude about social situations does have value—as long as gradual change is permitted. The machinery that no longer runs so smoothly is being discarded, but much of the manners taken for granted in the office, such as the importance of correct speech and deference to superiors, prevail because they help to soften the bumps brought about by day-to-day personal contact and the anxieties of the business world.

OFFICE INTRODUCTIONS

Whether or not your office is run on a first- or last-name basis depends on the customs in your field. Wall Street still relies on the comforting traditions of formality, whereas newer businesses such as data systems and television tend toward a more relaxed, shirt-sleeve style. Whatever the surface style, the business hierarchy underneath is definite and pronounced, and those within the hierarchy know or try to know where they stand. When one is being introduced, however, the hierarchy, though certainly not forgotten, need not be alluded to. If an executive is introducing his secretary to the company's most important client or to a new member of the firm, the executive uses both first and last names of both people she is introducing: "Richard, I'd like you to meet Jane Wyler. Jane, this is Richard Parrish." (It is courteous to defer to the client or the other executive and introduce your secretary or assistant to him first.) It is then up to the two people who have been introduced to decide whether to use first names or not.

(For more on Introductions, see Chapter 1, "Everyday Manners in Public Places.")

Shaking Hands

Traditionally, a man waited until a woman offered her hand in greeting. Today, when a guest comes to your office for an appointment, you stand and offer your hand whether you are a man or a woman. After the meeting, you rise and again offer your hand. It is courteous to escort a guest out of your office and to the elevator if the office is labyrinthine.

THE WOMAN IN THE OFFICE

Despite the drive for equality of the sexes, in the modern office women are often still expected to be the motivators and arbiters for the touches of sensible politeness we call etiquette. Actually, this expectation is often a fine opportunity for a woman to show both manners and good business sense. For example, one woman executive, the only woman present in a meeting, was also the only one to get up and get a chair for the president of the company, who had arrived late to a crowded board room where the only remaining place to sit was a radiator. The woman secured a chair for the president out of graciousness and a sense of good manners. The men, she reasoned, did not get up because to do so might be interpreted as a slip in status. Because of her combination of good sense and good manners the room took on a more relaxed air as soon as the president was comfortably seated.

Small Courtesies in the Office

In the office men will treat women associates with a backstage familiarity which does not include the small courtesies the same men may accord the same women outside the office. A woman can no longer assume that what she may view as proper manners will be carried out during the working day. Assuming that because you are walking with a man you'll be the first one out the door might well cause a collision. The men you work with may see you solely as a business associate, and they may not extend a courtesy which was not so long ago taken for granted. Whether or not a male business associate does remember or elect to exercise the small social courtesies during business hours is now an individual decision. Young men, especially, are not brought up to believe that women need doors opened and cigarettes lit for them. Although they are thoughtful gestures, those and other small deferences are no longer mandatory in male–female relations— especially during business hours. A group of men, for instance, need not stand when a woman enters a room for a meeting. Again, when she takes a seat, the men on either side of her are not expected to rise, though it certainly is nice and, I'm sure, appreciated.

On the other side of the spectrum is the man who clings to his chivalry and may be offended if he is lunching with a woman and she slips out of her coat unaided or if she opens the door before he has a chance to reach for the knob. There is a happy medium reached easily enough through mutual respect. Neither a man nor a woman should barge through a door without taking others into consideration. One friend or business associate might naturally help another with a coat. However, women who are very used to making their own way and are proud of their independence cannot be expected to change gears in order to please a man who enjoys being overly solicitous to the opposite sex.

When a Woman Is Asked to Do "Woman's Work"

Just as men aren't standing back to let women pass through the door first, they should no longer presume that a woman in business will naturally take on jobs which were once traditional in both the home and the office. It is poor manners indeed to take for granted that a woman who attends a meeting will get the coffee or take the minutes. One of the best ways for a woman to deal with such anachronistic thinking when she's asked to get coffee (or, more likely, if someone mentions coffee and all eyes turn to her) is to respond, "Could you see if someone else could get the coffee?" and turn to the man sitting next to her. Or try "Why don't you ask your secretary?" if secretaries in that office routinely serve coffee or take the minutes at meetings.

Getting the Coffee

Because this chore has been held up as the symbol of the female secretary as servant to the male boss, in most offices it has demeaning connotations which Xeroxing or ordering office supplies does not. Better for a boss to ask a secretary if she minds getting the coffee and for a secretary to answer honestly. If she does mind, perhaps another system could be worked out and hidden resentment could be avoided. The staff could take turns getting the coffee or everyone may get coffee for himself.

A Woman Traveling on Business

When a woman travels with a male business associate, the expense each incurs, such as meals and taxis, are split, as each person will record expenses and be reimbursed by the company separately. A woman is expected to arrange for the handling of her luggage and do her own tipping.

It is common today for women to travel alone. Although a woman traveling alone on business can excuse herself from unwanted company easily by saying, "I have work to do," the rules for a woman traveling alone whether for business or pleasure are similar.

(For more on women traveling alone, see Chapter 18, "Travel.")

SEX AND THE OFFICE

Entwining romance with business has long been thought of as at best scandalous. Even in these days of more relaxed attitudes about sex, the guideline to still keep in mind is that sex and business mix about as well as oil and water. Of course, your personal life is your own; if you form a romantic attachment with someone who happens to work in your office, let common sense as well as discretion be your guide.

Confusing romance with moving up the corporate ladder can only be to your detriment. You should realize that in using sex for your advancement you are breaking all the rules of good business practice and therefore you can't expect others to play by the rules in their dealings with you. When you break a taboo you're not protected by the traditions of the tribe.

How a Woman Can Handle a Pass Made by a Male Superior

If a male superior or a client in the office makes a sexual pass at a woman co-worker, her response should be diplomatic. Though she may be surprised or annoyed, the office hierarchy cannot be forgotten. Women should not ignore sexual advances; they should acknowledge a man's behavior and at the same time make their feelings clear, but in a nice way. A woman may tell the man that his behavior is not what she expected and that it also makes her uncomfortable, but she may add, "Are we still friends?," which implies that they have a good business relationship and that she would like it to continue.

To Male Executives Who Make Passes in the Office

If you are attracted to a woman who has a lesser rank, there is no harm in inviting her out. If she rebuffs you, it is unconscionable for you to use your position in the company to make her business life unpleasant, or to force the issue. And it is also illegal: sexual harassment is a form of sexual descrimination.

OFFICE TELEPHONE COURTESY

A secretary or an assistant answers the office telephone saying, "Steve White's office." Steve White answers his own phone with "Steve White" or with the less brusque "Hello, this is Steve White." (In England, the common version is "White here.")

Though it is most polite for a caller to identify herself immediately with "Hello, this is Mildred Pearlman. Is Mr. White in?," if the caller fails to give that information the person answering the phone says, "May I ask who is calling?" Because it is often possible for a secretary or an assistant to help the caller, he is responsible for finding out what the call is specifically about. "May I ask what this call is in reference to?" asks the question if a bit bluntly. I think a smoother way to ask would be: "Would Mr. White know what this call is about?"

When you call and an assistant asks you what the call is about, don't be disgruntled and evasive. The person answering your call is only trying to save the boss time, and possibly he or she will be able to help you directly. Offer the information if it's a business call; otherwise state that you're calling on a personal matter.

Although it is proper business procedure to place calls for the boss, executives today often make many of their own calls. Robert Townsend, the former board chairman of Avis Rent-A-Car, advises in his book *Up the Organization* that an executive makes all his own calls; the most important thing in an office is to make the best use of time. A call coming directly from or answered directly by a business associate not only is accepted and convenient but is sometimes a clever strategy known to disconcert the person at the other end.

If you as an executive, however, prefer to have your secretary or assistant make calls for you on certain occasions, be sure to take the call immediately once your party has been reached. It is very discourteous to keep him waiting on the line.

SMOKING

In the office, nonsmokers, unless they cannot physically tolerate others' smoking, should have an ashtray on their desks for guests who do smoke. For smokers confronted with the ashtray as objet d'art it's a good idea to ask if what you are about to put your ashes into is designed for that purpose. Smokers should also make a point of locating an ashtray before striking the match. Matches, ashes and cigarette butts belong only in an ashtray.

(For more on smoking, see Chapter 1, "Everyday Manners in Public Places.")

CHRISTMAS PRESENTS

Giving something personal but fairly inexpensive to those one or two people with whom you work closely is a thoughtful gesture as well as a much practiced custom. Perfume, a pretty ashtray, a paperweight or any other small but obviously thoughtful gift are all suitable. You may prefer to give something for the home, especially if you know the spouse of your business associate. Pretty candles or a gourmet treat are safe selections if you don't know their taste.

An executive who has had the same secretary or assistant for many years may want to give her a more expensive gift, though an expensive present from a boss puts a secretary in an awkward position. It's obvious that a secretary can't equal the dollar value of the boss's gift, but a little present at Christmas time will be appreciated.

In some instances an executive giving gifts without having the giving reciprocated can be charming and most appropriate. The late Bennett Cerf, co-founder and president of Random House, played Santa Claus every Christmas and gave each one of his (female) editors a long string of pearls, a chain necklace or a bottle of perfume. The presents weren't expensive, and his joy in giving was so contagious that everyone loved it and no one was made to feel uncomfortable by the gesture, though today it might be considered by some to be chauvinistic.

When You Receive an Unexpected Gift

It may happen that you receive an unexpected present from someone in the office. Quash the temptation to run out during your lunch hour to buy a present to reciprocate. Instead, thank the giver and tell him how much you like your gift. Reciprocating with a late present can only make the person who gave you the gift feel uncomfortable about giving you something in the first place. One of the lost arts is being able to say a simple, sincere and unself-conscious "Thank you."

LETTERS OF REFERENCE

An example of a traditional enthusiastic letter of reference:

> To Whom It May Concern:
> I'm very happy to have this opportunity to give George Pappas a reference.
> He was an efficient and conscientious assistant and was always pleasant and tactful as well. Mr. Pappas is unquestionably a talented and intelligent young man whom I can recommend without reservation.
> Sincerely,

Following is an example of a radically different sort of recommendation. This letter was written specifically with those in the motion picture business in mind, as the young lady referred to in the latter wanted a career in film production. Such a letter is not recommended for conservative professions.

> To Whom It May Concern:
> Melanie Weinberger's many fine points as a student and a person tend to give me pause. Her work is superior, conscientious, and very often inspired. She is honest, pleasant, and quite thoroughly sweet, attributes which at times render her an old-time serial heroine, in the clutches or under the heels of the ruthless, the weak, and the unscrupulous persons in this vale of wrath and tears. She is becoming a shrewder judge of character, more inclined to Pickford's goal of revenge through mischief than the fixed amazement of the Griffith ingenue. I applaud her courage. You are advised to change your plans, swing from trees, and derail trains in order to be useful to her. She is worth it, and much more.

A less than enthusiastic letter of reference:

> To Whom It May Concern:
>
> Martin Martinson was a salesman for one year with Dalton and Company. He was enthusiastic and outgoing and his work was always satisfactory.

If your former employee was an unsatisfactory worker, instead of writing a damning letter of reference, refuse to write one at all. Instead ask that a prospective employer telephone you. If you do receive any inquiries by phone, tell of your reservations about your former employee, but do so calmly and include only the facts.

(For greetings and signatures on letters, forms of address and written business invitations, see Chapter 6, "Correspondence.")

A THANK-YOU NOTE AFTER A JOB INTERVIEW

After a job interview it is a good idea to write a thank-you note to your interviewer. This way, you will stand out if there are several applicants for the same job, and, morever, your interviewer will know that you are interested. Try to mention specifics of the conversation, to fix the interview permanently in the interviewer's mind, and be sure to mail the letter the same day, before the hiring decision is made. Use a standard business format. A letter might read:

> Dear Mr. Anderson,
>
> I very much appreciated your taking the time to meet with me today to explain the opening in Anderson & Coyle as a copywriter.
>
> I felt confident after our meeting that my experience suits the position you have available, particularly since I have been writing frozen-foods copy for the past two years at Smith & Belding. I do hope that you will have a chance to look over the sample ads I left with you, especially the newer ones, which reflect the innovative packaging we discussed.
>
> I thank you for your consideration, and look forward to hearing from you.
>
> Sincerely,

And, should you not get the job, feel free to write another letter, expressing interest in the company. You never know when another position might open!

BUSINESS ENTERTAINING

When an "Extra" Is Invited

Once when Barbara Walters and I planned a lunch I brought along at the last minute an aunt of mine who is a big fan of Barbara's—unannounced. Barbara was most gracious during the meal, and my aunt was most impressed with her and had a wonderful time, but afterward Barbara did call me to say, "Please, don't do that to me again." Barbara taught me a valuable lesson. All too often, when we plan a casual lunch with a friend or a business associate, we invite a third party to join us. Unless you've checked the addition with your original lunch date, this is not good business practice. Your lunch date was planning on spending time with you alone, and an "extra" could be an imposition. When someone does call you just before your appointment to ask, "Is if all right if Shirley joins us?" and you really don't think it is all right, just say, "I'd love to have lunch with Shirley some other time, but today I'd rather it be just the two of us."

When a Woman Picks up the Check

When a woman invites a man to lunch, even though the reason is strictly business a man may still feel uncomfortable in his new role. To end embarrassment and uneasiness, a woman should stand firm in her role by establishing herself as the host. She should start by issuing a straightforward, unambiguous invitation: "Could you have lunch next Wednesday, the twelfth?" She should choose the restaurant and make the reservation herself, and call her guest on the morning of her lunch date to let him know what time to meet her and where. With the reservation in her name and the arrangements in her hands, there can be no doubt as to who is the host and who is the guest.

When sharing a taxi to the restaurant, the lunch host pays the fare. In order to do this smoothly she must be prepared to pay;

don't begin digging in your purse for change when you're already at your destination. If her guest attempts to pay, she may simply say, "I'm paying for this," in a light but firm manner. If she waivers she'll lose command of the situation.

If you're meeting your guest at the restaurant and the two of you have never met, come to the restaurant a few minutes early. Give your guest's name to the maître d' so that the maître d' can escort him to your table when he arrives. Both of you will be spared the embarrassment of trying to recognize each other. When meeting in a fairly large bar or hotel lobby, give the maître d' your name and ask him to page your guest.

Ordering the Meal

As the host, a woman may ask the waiter for the menus. She gives the waiter her order and may then say to her guest, "What would you like?" He then gives his order directly to the waiter.

Ordering the Wine

The host asks the waiter for the wine list and orders the wine herself. When the wine is brought, the host quietly points to her glass—waiters need help, too, in these situations—so that she can also be the one to taste the wine. Of course, a guest may be asked to order the wine and to taste it.

Paying the Check

For a small business lunch, the host signals for the check and pays it at the table. Having an account at the restaurant or a credit card makes it easier to pay, since the process then involves merely signing the bill. There is no reason not to pay in cash, however. If your guest reaches for the check, be firm and say, "No, you are my guest today. I invited you." If the waiter mistakenly presents the check to your guest, say directly to the waiter, "The check is for me." A man who is the invited guest of a woman should not make a grab for the check. He must learn to play by the new rules—women have egos, too.

A woman who is host to a group of men may prefer to dine at a restaurant where she is well known. When making the reservation she may add that she would prefer that the bill be sent to her instead of it being brought to the table. She must remember to specify the amount of the tip (fifteen percent is usual, twenty percent in a more expensive restaurant), which is added to the bill. Or she may excuse herself after the meal to pay the check away from the table. These minor subterfuges are generally used only in certain social gatherings. For instance, if I'm taking a group of men or an older man to lunch and I foresee a slight uneasiness regarding the check, I will make sure beforehand that the check doesn't come to the table. Although it's simpler to settle the bill at the table, as host I'm most concerned about making my guests feel comfortable. Older men who have lived so long with certain customs are easily embarrassed if those customs are ignored, just as a group of men can become self-conscious when their traditional roles are reversed by the mere presence of a woman.

A Woman Hosting in the Evening

The business lunch is by now an established procedure, and a woman paying the check is no longer seen as an anomaly. Yet, dining out in the evening is still considered by many to be worthy of traditional formal courtesy. For instance, a woman host may find a male guest attempting to give her order to the waiter, even though the same man would not do so at lunch. This is one of the amenities which are still more often than not reactivated only in the evening. Though a man may give the woman host's order to the waiter and may order the wine or taste the wine, if she prefers, a woman may perform these courtesies in the evening as well, since they are the responsibilities of the host.

If guests arrive at the restaurant before the host, they may wait at the bar if there is one or ask to be seated at the table. When the party is to be seated all together the maître d' escorts the guests to the table and the host seats the guests.

If a woman is hosting a business evening and her husband is also present, he would of course act as co-host. The check would not be brought to a co-hosting husband, though he may order and taste the wine. Many women who pay the check directly to the waiter when they entertain at lunch prefer to have the bill sent or to excuse themselves from the table to pay it in the evening.

(For more on entertaining in a restaurant, see Chapter 1, "Everyday Manners in Public Places.")

Social Obligations of a Spouse

Not long ago, the wife of a man in a career which demanded he attend frequent social functions was often expected to accompany her husband. Conversely, a husband with an executive wife in a business with similar demands was not necessarily expected to accompany her; it has long been assumed that a man has a busy life and will not always be free. Today, busy wives who can't find the time to attend their husbands' business evenings may bow out with the valid excuse of having work or engagements of their own. If the husband has been issued the invitation he is responsible for answering it. He may say, "I'm very sorry my wife won't be able to come. She has to go to a conference in Chicago." Or, "Jane would love to come, but she simply can't. She has a commitment for next Thursday."

Of course, if the wife is issued the invitation (for instance, if the wife of the president of her husband's company calls and asks them both to have dinner), the busy wife may say, "Let me check with Bobby. I'm sure he would love to be there, but I have a meeting that night, so I won't be able to come." To remain unassailable, remain firm. People will hear the ring of confidence very clearly in your voice, and they'll respect it.

When husband and wife whose last names are not the same attend each other's business entertainment, the wife would introduce her husband this way: "I'd like you to meet my husband, John Fredericks." Similarly, the husband would introduce his wife, "I'd like you to meet my wife, Jane Barnes."

(For at-home business dinners, see Chapter 2, "Entertaining.")

6 CORRESPONDENCE

Since your correspondence reveals more about you than merely the words on the paper, it might be helpful to know something about the papers and the printing processes that determine your "unseen message."

The first paper we know about was produced by the Egyptians about 2,500 years ago from the split and pounded stalks of the papyrus plant (thus the word "paper"). Basically, despite technological advances, this is still the way paper is made. The quality—or "feel"—of the paper depends on its weight and the materials used in making it. The best papers for stationery are made from new, unlaundered and undyed cotton rags that produce a strong, sparkling white or richly dyed paper. Less expensive papers are made from vegetable fibers or various types of wood pulp alone or in combinations. However, the higher the rag content, the better the paper.

You can often tell the quality of stationery by looking for a watermark and occasionally an imprint about the paper's composition. A true watermark is the manufacturer's symbol or trademark and is applied by a wire-mesh screen to the top of the paper as it is being made. Not apparent when the paper is being used, the watermark can be seen if the paper is held to the light. Since a watermark is usually a sign of a quality paper (along with a paper's weight and snap, or "rattle," when shaken briskly) some manufacturers put an artificial watermark on less expensive papers. These are characterized by a sharper, more artificial appearance than the slightly blurred natural watermark of a fine bond paper.

Another characteristic of stationery that reveals quality (or, at least, expense) is the nature of the printing. The most expensive and durable form of printing is metal engraving. The image—words, crest, etc.—is cut onto a metal plate and then transferred to the paper in a process that resembles illustrative etching. True engraving—which has always marked the highest-quality printing —has an embossed, or slightly raised, image on the paper. Another way of identifying true engraving is to look for the indentation (debossing) of the image on the other side of the paper. This indentation is caused by the pressure of the engraving plate on the paper when the engraving is made.

Naturally, because the individual metal plate is made by hand, the process is costly and time-consuming—adding additional expense for the consumer. However, once the plate is engraved, it is yours to own and can be used over and over again without additional plate-making expense.

Because the distinctive raised-letter look and feel of engraving have become associated with fine-quality work, a less expensive, imitative process known as thermography has been developed. Using a dense ink and a special resin which is dusted on, the thermographic process produces raised letters which look much like real engraving. However, the stickler-for-the-best who runs safe-cracking-sensitive fingers over the lettering can detect thermography. It is shinier and less delicate than genuine engraving, the image is easily scraped off with a fingernail, and there is no indentation on the other side of the paper.

By far the most unusual and least expensive method for putting an image on paper is the widely used printing process called offset lithography. Almost all magazines, advertising flyers and business stationery and most books are printed this way. Though standard offset printing does not have the feel or cachet of engraving or thermography, it offers conveniences of both economy and ease in use. Offset-printed stationery can produce any one- or two-color design you might desire both quickly and cheaply. Though offset printing is used more often for business stationery than for personal stationery, its convenience and ability to reproduce complicated designs certainly makes it as acceptable as the other, more expensive methods.

WHEN TO TYPE AND WHEN TO WRITE BY HAND

Although the typewriter can be used for almost any correspondence, there are three kinds of notes which must be handwritten:

thank-you notes, formal invitations and replies, and letters of condolence. However, you should write rather than type other notes or letters when you want to convey an air of informality and personal feeling. For example, a letter of congratulations or a note accompanying a gift or any correspondence which is specific and personal is handwritten. Letters to friends can, of course, be typed, but writing a letter by hand today gives it a specialness in our age of increasing impersonality.

THANK-YOU NOTES

Traditionally thank-you's for entertaining and for wedding presents were always written by the woman of the house and were addressed to the woman of the house, as social correspondence was a woman's domain. The men were mentioned in the body of the letter. Today, however, the man and the woman are often equal co-hosts in their homes—men and women divide the household chores, social correspondence included. It has become an accepted practice to address a note to both the man and the woman of the house, and the man of the house may just as well write the note as the woman. Whoever does write the note may include in the signature the name of his or her spouse or the person he or she is living with.

The sooner you write a thank-you note, the more lively and spontaneous your note will be. If you put off writing, your appreciation may sound false, as you'll have had to try to conjure up your initial delight after it has begun to fade. A thank-you note should be sent within a week. You may write on informal paper, with the exception of thank-you's for wedding presents, which are generally written on formal (plain or engraved) stationery. (See Chapter 7, "Weddings," for more on thank-you's for wedding presents.)

When a Thank-You Is Obligatory

Although you're never out of place sending a thank-you note, there are certain instances when a thank-you note is obligatory, when you must reciprocate thoughtfulness and acknowledge another's consideration on paper:

When receiving by mail a present (birthday, Christmas or any gift for a special occasion such as a congratulations gift for a graduation or an anniversary).

After a weekend visit.

After being given a gift when you're sick (see the section on hospital visits or in Chapter 1, "Everyday Manners in Public Places").

For wedding presents (see Chapter 7, "Weddings").

For letters of condolence (see Chapter 14, "Funerals").

When you're the guest of honor at a party.

After dinner at your boss's. Send a note to the house address, and address it to both hosts if your boss is married.

When a Thank-You Is Up to You

When in doubt, it's always better to write and say thank you than not. The telephone is not a substitute for a note, except when you're thanking a friend whom you see often. Here are some situations when a thank-you note may not be expected but will come as a welcome surprise:

After a dinner party.

After a business entertainment. Though a written thank-you isn't usual, it may cement the business relationship. A note is sent even if the tab was paid by your host's company. The person who entertained you did make the time and take the trouble to do so. Similarly, a thank-you note sent to a stranger or an acquaintance who has entertained you for lunch or dinner may help to lay the foundation for a new friendship.

After receiving a note of congratulations for a birthday, an anniversary or some other special occasion. (When you receive a printed card with no personal message you needn't write a note.)

After a job interview. You'll leave a more lasting impression if you write a note. (See Chapter 5, "The Business World.")

When as a host you receive a gift after your party, you might phone your thank-you. No need to thank elaborately someone who has thanked you elaborately, or the thank-you's may never end.

Printed Thank-You Notes

Printed cards are often funny or sweet to send, but they don't take the place of a personal message. So if you choose to send a card, be sure to include a line or two of your own.

Thank-You's for Presents

Though you are under no obligation to send a thank-you note for a present if the giver has already been thanked in person, a note would be a most welcome surprise, especially if the present was given at a party. A thank-you at a party is fairly quick and is mixed in with the general oohing and aahing about all the presents received. A note shows your specific and lasting appreciation for each gift. If a gift has been sent to you, your thank-you note should be sent as soon as possible. Your note is an acknowledgment that the package has been received, so don't delay or you're likely to be asked that embarrassing question "Did you ever get those mittens I sent you?," after which no thank-you, no matter how superlative and sincere, can ever be enough. When you write, be sure to mention the present specifically and just how and why you like it —that it looks so pretty in your living room or it's just what you've been needing. For instance:

> Dear Augusta,
>
> Your lovely fruit bowl has become the centerpiece on our dining-room table. The blue-and-white pattern goes beautifully with our china, and now there is fruit always within easy reach. I've found that the children naturally help themselves from such an enticing dish, and my nagging about an apple a day has stopped completely. We all

thank you for your perfect present, which is also keeping
the family in fine health.

Love,
Alicia and Albert

When you're given something which you don't love nearly as
much as Alicia and Albert love their fruit bowl, try to be as generous in your acknowledgment as the giver was in the attempt to
please you with the perfect gift. Let your note reflect your generosity. Phrases such as "unique," "interesting" and "quite out of the
ordinary" should do the gift justice and make the sender quite
happy with your appreciation.

When You Receive Money

Money is generally a most welcome gift, and it's not at all unseemly to mention the amount received in your thank-you note.
Along with the amount, always be specific about what you'll do
with the money—how you'll convert the cash into goods. If you
really aren't sure, you may be so general as to mention that you're
planning on including the gift in your furniture fund or your
spring-holiday money.

Weekend Guests

A weekend guest, even if he brings a present to the host, writes
the obligatory bread-and-butter letter after his stay—thanking the
host for "bread or butter," essentially the hospitality afforded him.
The note need not be a long one but should stress the highlights of
the weekend:

Dear Ursula and Roberto,
I want to thank you for the absolutely perfect weekend.
The brunch was such fun, and I especially enjoyed meet-
ing the Riveras. Fishing Saturday was a special treat for

me, something I haven't done since I was a child. Thanks
for offering me part of the catch; we've just finished a
delicious bluefish dinner.

Jackie and I hope you'll come for dinner as soon as you
get back in the fall—don't be surprised if it's a bluefish
special.

Love,
Annabel

Thank-You's After a Party

Guests rarely call to say thank you after a party these days—
unless it's to hear what happened after they left. Getting no rever-
berations from guests after the work and exhilaration of a party is
disappointing for the host. A short note, just two or three lines, is
most welcome. One friend of mine keeps a box of plain white cards
for just this purpose. A card received a week or even ten days after
the party shows the host that the party was enough of a success to
linger on in the mind of the guest. If you think that the party was
less than a success you may prefer to put your thanks over the
phone. A guest's thank-you, however, is optional, unless you were
the guest of honor, in which case you're obliged to write; it is also
a good idea to give the host a present if the party is in your honor.

Children's Thank-You's

One friend says she feels the same way about thank-you letters
as she does about playing the piano—she wishes she'd been forced
to do both as a child. She regrets all those letters she didn't write
to those who were especially kind to her as a child almost as much
as she regrets not having practiced the piano. I think a child must
be taught the importance of writing thank-you notes for each present he receives. To encourage your child, don't give him a set form
to follow, just suggest that he tell Cousin Antonia how he feels
about the model kit she sent him—why it makes him happy. In
this way your child will learn to write spontaneously and sincerely
and he won't be plodding along in order to simply fulfill a set of

rules you've prescribed for him. Do, however, insist that your child write the thank-you's within a couple of days after receiving the gift, so that the delight is still fresh enough to put down on paper easily and artfully.

STATIONERY

Your writing paper, like any accessory you choose, reflects your style and taste. You may prefer variously sized and colored note papers and cards or simple, unadorned white paper. Unless you entertain both frequently and formally, you needn't keep a supply of all the papers mentioned here. You can manage nicely with personal business paper or household stationery, personal note paper, visiting cards, and formal writing paper. (See the "Invitations and Replies" section in this chapter for examples of visiting cards, informals, and formal writing paper.)

Women's Personal Writing Paper

Personal writing paper is used for writing informal invitations and replies, thank-you letters, and letters to friends; it is the paper to use for all informal social correspondence. This kind of stationery is generally folded note paper about five by seven inches, in white, off white, gray or a pale pastel with a contrasting border. You may use any combination of colored stock and ink, though it might be wise to save "decorator" combinations (mint green and navy blue, for instance) for the more informal, casual type of personal paper—single sheets instead of folded paper. Single sheets are about five by seven inches, with or without a border. They are considered a more casual kind of paper because, until fairly recently, Great Aunt Hattie would have raised an eyebrow upon opening a letter from a "lady" written on anything other than folded note paper.

Note paper (folded or single sheets) may be printed or engraved with your name and, if you wish, your social title; if you're a married woman, this could be either the traditional "Mrs. Charles William Quales" or the contemporary "Mrs. (or Ms.) Vivian Fein Quales." (See "Issuing an Invitation" in this chapter for a list of traditional titles and contemporary titles.) Or note paper may be

Mrs. Charles William Quales

Folded note paper with formal engraving

VIVIAN FEIN QUALES

Single-sheet note paper with contemporary engraving

VFQ

Small seminote paper—monogrammed

marked with your address only, or with your monogram in the center or the upper left-hand corner. (Although the combined initials of husband and wife are often marked today on all household items which are engraved, on writing paper the initials of the woman only appear, presumably because a man would not correspond on such delicate stationery and because historically women attend to all social duties.)

The name of your city and state are always printed or engraved in full without any abbreviations. If your street number is twenty or under, you may have it written out, though numerals may always be used. Always include your zip code.

Matching envelopes are lined or unlined. The back flap is marked with your address. If your paper is engraved, it is acceptable to include your name as well as the address in order to save an additional engraved plate.

Another popular paper is the seminote, a folded paper about five by three and a half inches. Don't order note paper any smaller. The smallest envelope the Post Office will accept is three and a half by five inches. The seminote is usually marked with either your monogram in the center, your monogram at the top left and your address at the right, or just your address in the center. On the seminote, use the inside and the back for the message (unless only the address is on the front, in which case you'll have room enough to begin the message on the front).

Men's Personal Writing Paper

The traditional personal writing paper for a man is white, tan or gray. His name is engraved at the top in a gray, navy or brown shade to complement the color of the paper. A home address or business address may be included under the name, though a company name is never used. The paper is of the size that when folded once across the center will fit into an almost square envelope.

As business stationery has become more innovative and informal, the change has been reflected in men's personal stationery. The size of the paper and the colors, type styles, special designs or logos printed or engraved on the paper are now a matter of individual choice. Today a man's writing paper may include a fine border in a corresponding color to the color used in the engraving or printing, or the paper may be decorated with a specially designed

Charles William Quales
102 East 75th Street
New York, New York 10021

Personal writing paper with full address

C.W.Q.

Personal writing paper—monogrammed

monogram in place of the name. The paper is usually a single sheet about seven by ten inches which is folded twice before fitting into an oblong envelope. In addition to personal stationery, some men use correspondence cards with matching envelopes for short notes.

A Coat of Arms

During the Middle Ages, knights wore their colors and insignias into battle and in tournaments so that they could be recognized individually as more than just iron men. Their devices were called coats of arms because they wore them embroidered on sleeveless jackets which were worn over their armor. Heralds organized the tournaments and kept records of the various colors and insignias of the participants—hence the term "heraldry."

The coat of arms is inherited by every direct male descendant. When there are no sons, daughters inherit (they become heiresses or co-heiresses with sisters) and pass their inheritance to their sons. Even by the fifteenth century so many social climbers had assumed a coat of arms for their families, though they were not entitled to, that the College of Arms was legally chartered in 1484 to regulate heraldry in England, which it still does today. In America the New England Historic Genealogical Society in Boston will rule on a family's claim to "bear arms"; however, the Society does not grant coats of arms, since in America we have no history of aristocracy. The right to "bear arms" is inherited individually; don't be fooled into buying a coat of arms based simply on your family name. The design might be pretty, even majestic, but its meaning is based on wishful thinking—on somebody else's idea of what will play on one's vanity and presumption.

When a coat of arms or a part of a coat of arms can be used:

The crest can be engraved or embossed on wedding invitations and announcements if the father's family has the coat of arms and if his name appears on the invitation.

The crest can be embossed or engraved on place cards and on menu cards at a formal dinner.

The full coat of arms, or just the crest and motto, may be engraved on large pieces of silver and embossed or engraved on stationery.

The coat of arms can be painted (blazoned) and framed and hung on your wall as a decoration.

A woman can use her father's or her husband's coat of arms in a diamond-shaped lozenge, the feminine version of the shield. She may use a crest on personal possessions, such as writing paper, linens and accessories on her dressing table.

If a woman whose family has inherited a coat of arms marries a man who has not, she does not use her coat of arms after her marriage. Her husband and her children are not entitled to use the device. They have not been entitled in the past, anyway. Today with women becoming equal in marriage it's possible that they will be given the right to "bear arms." (Possible, but not probable, as the College of Arms, which is still involved solely with what is essentially a medieval practice, is not very likely to burst forth into twentieth-century progressive thinking.)

Ted Morgan, *né* Sanche de Gramont, wrote in his autobiography *On Becoming American:* "It seems to me every American's secret wish is to trace his origins back to a Saxon cave . . . But to me, being American means starting my own family tree . . ." Ted Morgan can speak with such offhandedness about his roots because his speech resonates with the echo of that very cave. But I think Ted Morgan is right, most Americans are held in thrall by royalty and the outside chance that they may be descended from such grandness. This is a claim very few can make. This country was founded on very solid stock indeed, but, I'm afraid, not on royal stock, as most of those with even a trickle of royal blood were comfortable enough in Europe not to have to uproot themselves in search of a better life. I think the fashion of looking for our past as a key to our present in this unstable and fast-forward-moving world is valid. Our name needn't, however, come with a logo attached. The past is important for its own sake; it matters not how important each person in our historical past was in his or her society. Every person becomes important when analyzed individually.

Personal Business Paper

Paper used for business correspondence would, of course, be larger than the note paper and would be marked at the top with name and address. A woman may use her professional name without a title if she wishes: Vivian Fein Quales.

VIVIAN FEIN QUALES
102 EAST 75TH STREET
NEW YORK, NEW YORK 10021

AREA CODE
TELEPHONE NO.

Personal business paper

```
102 EAST 75th STREET                    AREA CODE
NEW YORK, NEW YORK 10021               TELEPHONE NO.
```

Household stationery

Household Stationery

This stationery is for the entire household to use. It is marked with the address and, if you wish, your telephone number. The envelopes have the address on the flap or they are left unmarked and the return address is handwritten on the front left corner of the envelope.

Conserving Out-of-date Stationery

Because printed stationery is generally ordered in large amounts, most of us at one time or another have been left with a drawer filled with writing paper which is no longer accurate. Unless you've moved and the only thing correct about your paper is your name, try to bend toward conservation instead of insisting on one hundred percent accuracy. Using what you have is a better solution than throwing out dozens and dozens of sheets of paper, which, unless absolutely necessary, is plain wasteful. A business letter I received announcing an associate's promotion included an explanation that the new vice-president of the sales department would continue to use the stationery which was printed with the former vice-president's name, because she couldn't bring herself to throw out hundreds of sheets of perfectly good paper. I've even received a party invitation, the engraved fill-in kind, from a friend just separated from her husband with the "Mr. and" in "Mr. and Mrs. Peter A. Campbell" simply crossed out, in order, I presume, to inform her guests of her new social standing and to forestall rumors of reconciliation.

SIGNATURES ON YOUR LETTERS

One always signs correspondence with one's full name, "Vivian Fein Quales," not "Mrs. C. William Quales." Titles are never included in the signature. If a woman prefers to be addressed by her husband's name, she may write underneath her signature in parentheses:

> Signature
> (Mrs. C. William Quales)

If the letter is typed, "Mrs. C. William Quales" is typed beneath the signature, and the parentheses are omitted:

> Signature
> Mrs. C. William Quales

When writing on stationery marked "C. William Quales," the signature stands alone. A woman may also include her title Mrs., Ms., Miss, in parentheses before her signature to indicate how she is addressed.

Sign your formal and social correspondence with your full name, or the name by which you prefer to be addressed. Your name is your own and you may sign any way you like. President Carter fought for the use of his nickname—as Governor of Georgia he received a ruling from the Georgia Secretary of State that he could legally use his nickname, and he went on to become the first President in history to use his nickname officially. Though Washington fought against the use of "Jimmy" Carter, the White House insisted on it again and again, until "Jimmy" was accepted.

FORMS OF ADDRESS

Ms., Mrs. or Miss

Because "Ms." is a relatively revolutionary change in address and its use has not yet been formalized by textbook rules, decisions as to when and where to use it are left up to the individual. Marina, a business associate of mine, has staunchly refused to adopt the title at all—for herself or for anyone else. She's sure "Ms." is a passing fad which will fade out before it ever becomes entrenched in the language. Marina insists on being addressed only by her married name, Mrs. David J. Brockner. She signs her name "Marina Katherine Richards Brockner." Only her checks are printed with her full name, preceded by "Mrs." It took the bank's computer to push her from what she considers a very important social pedestal by insisting on *her* name and not her husband's name. But another friend of mine insists on addressing all women as "Ms." Finally, she says, she can address a woman in her own right!

When it comes to using "Ms." most women fall somewhere in between always and never, with a large number leaning toward almost never, possibly because many of us are hesitant to try something new. In certain instances "Ms." is most appropriate. My business name is Charlotte Ford and my mail is too often addressed to "Miss Charlotte Ford" or "Mrs. Charlotte Ford," when in this case "Ms." would be the most appropriate title.

A woman who writes under her signature "Mrs. C. William Quales" should be addressed in that way out of simple courtesy, since that is what she would obviously prefer. A woman who uses her full name, "Vivian Fein Quales" or "Vivian Fein" should be titled "Ms." Whether or not she is married is beside the point. "Ms." should be used when you're in doubt as to how a woman prefers to be addressed. When you're not sure whether a woman is married, single or divorced, again, use "Ms."

Addressing a Woman in Business

Many married women use their maiden names as well as their married names professionally. A woman who makes her professional reputation using one name will not usually change it because her personal life has changed. Women in business who marry or remarry do sometimes add on to their name their new married name. This is a fine idea as long as the name doesn't become too unwieldy.

Until recently, a married woman always had more than one identity. Mrs. Vivian Fein Quales at the office was Mrs. C. William Quales at home. Some women, however, don't want to relinquish their own identities—their professional name—especially in their own homes. A woman today might prefer to be addressed by her own name socially as well as professionally, whether or not her last name is the same as her husband's and whether or not she and her husband are being addressed simultaneously in a letter of invitation. Since different people follow different rules for different occasions, you may wish to refer to the list of traditional and contemporary titles in the "Invitations and Replies" section of this chapter.

Addressing People by Their Full Names

Sometimes letters in business are addressed to "Dear Deborah Dowling" or "Dear Paul Young." This seems to me a bit indecisive. I think it's better to err on the side of formality and address the person by title and last name if you don't think your relationship is ready for first names.

Addressing a Widow

A widow keeps her late husband's name and is addressed traditionally as "Mrs. Jasper Murray" or, if she prefers, "Mrs. [or Ms.] Joline Murray."

Addressing a Divorced Woman

A divorced woman does not, of course, continue to use her former husband's full name. Traditionally she puts her maiden name before her married name and becomes Mrs. Furgeson Jaeger, an impersonal form of address which is fast disappearing. Today it is usual for a divorced woman to address herself as Mrs.

or Ms. Hazel Furgeson Jaeger, Hazel F. Jaeger or simply Hazel Jaeger. Some divorced women may prefer to return to their maiden names.

Addressing Envelopes

Traditionally addresses on all social formal envelopes were properly written out in full with no abbreviations, "Cornelius Paul Snape" or "Cornelius Snape," not "Cornelius P. Snape." The state was also written out: "Connecticut," not "CT." or "Conn." These days, I think it is perfectly acceptable to use abbreviations if you wish, since most people today act as their own social secretaries.

Type or write the address on the envelope depending on whether the letter itself is typed or handwritten: the address is written in a block, with each line beginning directly below the next, or each line may be slightly indented.

> Ms. Angela Lowry Snape
> 375 Drew St.
> Hinsdale, Ill. [zip code]

> Mrs. Cornelius Piper Snape
> 375 Drew Street
> Hinsdale
> Illinois [zip code]

Addressing Envelopes to Couples Who Use Two Different Names

When addressing an envelope to an unmarried couple, write their full names on separate lines or, if they have reasonably short names, write them on the same line, separating the names with a comma or an "and."

> Ms. Sandra McGougal
> Mr. Jonathan Segal
> 428 Rover Place
> Dover, DE [zip code]

FORMS OF ADDRESS

PERSON	CORRESPONDENCE (Business or Social)	LETTER OPENING (BUSINESS)*	LETTER CLOSING (BUSINESS)†	IN CONVERSATION	INTRODUCTIONS
The President of the United States	The President The White House Washington, D.C. 20500	Dear Mr. President:	Most Respectfully,	Mr. President or Sir	The President
The Vice President of the United States	The Vice President Old Executive Office Building Washington, D.C. 20501	Dear Mr. Vice President:	Very truly yours, or Sincerely yours,‡	Mr. Vice President or Sir	The Vice President
Member of the Cabinet	The Honorable Jack Quinn Secretary of Commerce Washington, D.C. 20230	Dear Sir:	Very truly yours, or Sincerely yours,	Mr. Secretary or Mr. Quinn or Sir	The Secretary of Commerce, Mr. Quinn; or the Secretary; or Mr. Quinn
The Attorney General	The Honorable Mary Smith Attorney General Washington, D.C. 20530	Dear Madame:	Very truly yours, or Sincerely yours,	Miss/Mrs. Attorney General or Miss/Mrs./Ms. Smith	The Attorney General, Miss/Mrs. Smith; or the Attorney General; or Miss/Mrs./Ms. Smith
Assistant Secretaries	The Honorable Vernon Zimmerman Assistant Secretary of Defense The Pentagon Washington, D.C. 20301	Dear Sir:	Very truly yours, or Sincerely yours,	Mr. Zimmerman	Mr. Zimmerman

Position	Address	Salutation	Complimentary close	Informal address	Introduction / Conversation
Head of a bureau or division	Mr. Richard Zeff [Business Address] Washington, D.C. [zip code]	Dear Sir:	Very truly yours, or Sincerely yours,	Mr. Zeff or Sir	Mr. Zimmerman
Chief Justice of the United States	The Chief Justice The Supreme Court Washington, D.C. 20543	Dear Mr. Chief Justice:	Very truly yours, or Sincerely yours,	Mr. Chief Justice or Sir	The Chief Justice
Associate Justice of the Supreme Court	Mr. Justice Priber The Supreme Court Washington, D.C. 20543	Dear Mr. Justice:	Very truly yours, or Sincerely yours,	Mr. Justice or Mr. Justice Priber or Sir	Mr. Justice Priber
Speaker of the House of Representatives	The Honorable Emily Levine Speaker of the House of Representatives H-204, The Capitol Washington, D.C. 20515	Dear Madame Speaker:	Very truly yours, or Sincerely yours,	Madame Speaker or Miss/Mrs./Ms. Levine or Madame	The Speaker, Miss/Mrs./Ms. Levine; or the Speaker
United States Ambassador	The Honorable David Balin Ambassador of the United States [Address] Paris, France	Dear Sir:	Respectfully yours, or Sincerely yours,	Mr. Ambassador or Mr. Balin or Sir	Ambassador or Mr. Balin
United States Minister	The Honorable Ryan Amburn United States Minister to China [Address] Peking, China	Dear Sir:	Very truly yours, or Sincerely yours,	Mr. Minister or Mr. Amburn or Sir	The Minister of the United States or Mr. Amburn

PERSON	CORRESPONDENCE (Business or Social)	LETTER OPENING (BUSINESS)*	LETTER CLOSING (BUSINESS)+	IN CONVERSATION	INTRODUCTIONS
Lesser American diplomatic officials	David Adnopoz, Esq. United States [Title] [Address]	Dear Sir:	Very truly yours, or Sincerely yours,	Mr. Adnopoz or Sir	Mr. Adnopoz
Judges	The Honorable Carol Baum Recorder's Court [Office Address]	Dear Judge Baum:	Very truly yours, or Sincerely yours,	Madame Justice or Madame	Judge Baum
Lawyers	Anthony Burton, Esq. [Office Address]	Dear Mr. Burton:	Very truly yours, or Sincerely yours,	Mr. Burton or Sir	Mr. Burton
University professor	Professor [or Mr., or Dr. if he holds the degree] Barry Bernstein [Office Address]	Dear Sir:	Very truly yours, or Sincerely yours,	Professor [or Dr.] Bernstein [in the university]; Mr. [or Dr.] Bernstein [elsewhere] or Sir	Professor [or Dr.] Bernstein
Physician	Edward Bleier, M.D. [Office Address]	Dear Sir:	Sincerely yours,	Dr. Bleier or Sir	Dr. Bleier
Dentist	David Brown, D.D.S. [Office Address]	Dear Sir:	Sincerely yours,	Dr. Brown or Sir	Dr. Brown
Foreign ambassadors	His Excellency The Ambassador of France [Address] Washington, D.C. [zip code]	Excellency:	Sincerely yours,	Mr. Ambassador or Sir	The Ambassador of Brazil, Mr. Felix Milan; or the Ambassador of Brazil; or Mr. Felix Milan
Foreign ministers and envoys	The Honorable Gustl Breuer Minister of Switzerland [Business Address]	Sir:	Very truly yours, or Sincerely yours,	Mr. Minister or Mr. Breuer or Sir	The Minister of Switzerland, Mr. Breuer; or the Minister; or Mr. Breuer

	Address	Salutation	Complimentary Close	Informal Address	Reference/Introduction
United States and State Senators	The Honorable Julie Tanner United States Senate [or other] [Office Address]	Dear Senator Tanner:	Very truly yours, or Sincerely yours,	Miss/Mrs./Ms. Tanner or Madame	Miss/Mrs./Ms. Tanner
Representatives and Assemblymen	The Honorable Knox Burger House of Representatives [or other] [Office Address]	Mr. Burger:	Sincerely yours,	Mr. Burger or Sir	Representative Burger
Governors	Honorable Gloria Safier Governor of New York The Executive Chamber, Capitol Albany, N.Y.	Dear Governor:	Sincerely yours,	Governor Safier or Madame	Governor Safier or the Governor
Mayors	12224 Honorable Leonard Sims Mayor of Detroit [Office Address]	Dear Mayor Sims or Dear Mr. Mayor	Sincerely yours,	Mayor Sims or Mr. Mayor or Your Honor	Mayor Sims or the Mayor
Protestant Clergy: Bishops of Episcopal Church	The Right Reverend George Snowden Bishop of New York [Office Address]	Right Reverend Sir	Respectfully yours,	Bishop Snowden	Bishop Snowden or Dr. Snowden, the Bishop of New York
Clergymen with Doctor of Divinity degree	The Reverend Roderick Thorp, D.D. [Office Address]	Reverend Sir:	Respectfully yours,	Dr. Thorp	The Reverend Doctor Thorp

PERSON	CORRESPONDENCE (Business or Social)	LETTER OPENING (BUSINESS)*	LETTER CLOSING (BUSINESS)†	IN CONVERSATION	INTRODUCTIONS
Clergymen without doctor's degrees	The Reverend Calvin Ramsey [Office Address]	Reverend Sir:	Respectfully yours,	Sir	The Reverend Calvin Ramsey
Methodist bishop	Bishop Will Clark of the Los Angeles Area [Office Address]	Reverend Sir:	Respectfully yours,	Sir or Bishop Clark	Bishop Clark
Mormon bishop	Bishop Frank Comaford Church of Latter Day Saints [Office Address] or Mr. Frank Comaford [Home Address]	Sir:	Very truly yours,	Sir or Bishop Comaford	Bishop Comaford
Jewish rabbi	Rabbi Howard Kaminsky Temple Beth-El [Address] Brooklyn, N.Y. [zip code]	Sir:	Very truly yours,	Rabbi Kaminsky or Rabbi	Rabbi Kaminsky or Rabbi
Jewish cantor	Cantor Albert Goldman Temple Israel [Address] Detroit, Michigan [zip code]	Sir:	Very truly yours,	Cantor Goldman	Cantor Goldman
Roman Catholic forms: The Pope	His Holiness, the Pope John X Vatican City Rome, Italy	Your Holiness or Most Holy Father	Your Holiness' Most Humble Servant,	Your Holiness or Most Holy Father	His Holiness, The Holy Father, The Pope, The Pontiff

	Envelope	Salutation	Complimentary close	Speaking to	Introduction
Cardinals	William Cardinal Ryan Archbishop of New York [optional] [Office Address]	Dear Cardinal Ryan	I have the honor to be,	Cardinal Ryan	Cardinal Ryan
Bishops and archbishops	The Most Reverend Robert Cifu [title optional] [Office Address]	Dear Bishop [Archbishop] Cifu	I have the honor to be,	Bishop [Archbishop] Cifu	Bishop or Archbishop Cifu
Priests	The Reverend Father Douglas Graham [Address]	Reverend Father or Dear Father Graham	I am, Reverend Father,	Father Graham	Father Graham
Catholic brothers	Brother Thomas Harmon [Address]	Dear Brother Thomas or Dear Brother	I am, respectfully yours,	Brother Thomas or Brother	Brother Thomas
Catholic sisters	Sister Maryanne Holston [Address]	Dear Sister	I am, respectfully yours,	Sister Holston or Sister	Sister Holston or Sister
Eastern Orthodox priests	The Very Reverend George Harpootlian [Address]	My dear Father Harpootlian	Yours respectfully,	Father	Father Harpootlian
Secretary General of the United Nations	His Excellency Paul Huang Secretary General of the United Nations United Nations Plaza New York, N.Y. 10017	Dear Mr. Ambassador or Dear Mr. Secretary General	Very truly yours, or Sincerely yours,	Mr. Secretary General	His Excellency the Secretary General of the United Nations

* For social correspondence, "Dear [Title]" or "Dear [Name]" is correct.
† For social correspondence, "Sincerely yours" is always correct.
‡ More informal.

Ms. Ann Fatt and Mr. Jack Spratt
4 Rush Terrace
Manhattan Beach, CA [zip code]

When sending formal announcements or invitations you may send one to an unmarried couple, addressing it with both their names.

When addressing an envelope to a married couple with different names, follow the same formula. Which name comes first is a matter of personal preference.

Addressing Envelopes to Children

A little girl or a pre-teenager is addressed solely by her name. A title, "Miss" or "Ms.," is added when she is thirteen. When a boy is thirteen he begins to be addressed with "Mr." Until then, he is simply "Benjamin Bliss." A little boy or a pre-teenager may also be addressed as "Master Benjamin Bliss."

The Return Address on Envelopes

The Post Office prefers that the return address be on the face of the envelope at the upper left. It may be handwritten, or one may use a printed sticker. On personal or business stationery the return address (with or without name) is generally printed or engraved on the back flap of the envelope. In this case tradition is stronger than the desire to facilitate automation.

When the name is included with the address, a woman's title (Mrs., Miss, Ms.) is generally included in the return address. However, "Miss" is rarely used on engraved envelopes, because it is expensive to have another die cut solely for the envelope, as would be necessary since "Miss" is omitted from the name engraved on the stationery itself. A man uses a title only if it is a professional one. "Mr." is not used on the envelope.

LETTERS OF INTRODUCTION

In the days of leisurely travel, neither rain, sleet, hail nor dark of night kept the mailman from his appointed rounds, though they certainly delayed him—sometimes for months. Consequently, in order to introduce a friend who was traveling from New York to Philadelphia, one would write a letter of introduction—in effect, a voucher of the person's good character and worthiness. The letter was important in a society much more concerned with social standing. Today, a quick phone call usually takes the place of the letter of introduction. The old-fashioned letter was given to the person being introduced. He or she would then, upon arrival, either send a messenger with the letter or call in person to deliver it. The recipient of such a letter was bound to make some gesture to share hospitality with a stranger, albeit a stranger with references. Now if a letter of introduction is written at all it is generally sent directly. The traveler, the person whom the letter is concerned with, is not entrusted with it. This is done for the sensible reason that if the person to whom you're writing cannot or simply will not comply, the person you're introducing will be none the wiser—and you won't be embarrassing anyone into doing what he may not want to do.

If a friend of a friend who is visiting your city has been given your number and you're taken by surprise, you can simply excuse yourself from any obligation by saying you're busy. If you're curious but hesitant, extend an invitation for a contained period of time: for a drink or for coffee. If the person turns out to be not quite your cup of tea, hopefully she'll leave after a cup of her own.

For the visitor: when you do arrive at your destination and call the friend of your friend, why not invite him to have a drink or a meal with you? If you're prepared to extend your hospitality instead of waiting to receive the hospitality of a stranger, you'll possibly feel less shy about making the call in the first place.

LETTERS OF COMPLAINT

The successful letter of complaint is the one that gets results. To write a letter of consequence, to get your way at least, you have to be straightforward. Stick to your story. Keep to the facts; they are on your side. Don't wander from the point or give extraneous information. Most of all, be polite. No matter how indignant you are, try to keep your venom out of your letter—it would only antagonize the very person who is in a position to help you.

Here is an example of a straightforward letter showing disapproval with the poor service of an airline:

April 18, 1980

Mr. Jason Seldom,
Chairman,
Trans American Airways
671 Park Avenue
New York, N.Y. [zip code]

Dear Mr. Seldom:

It is not my practice to complain, but it seems that I had more than my share of disappointments with your airline last month, and I feel you should know about it.

In planning my return to New York from Hong Kong, I personally went to the Trans American office in the Peninsula Hotel to discuss flight arrangements with your representatives. It was confirmed that I would fly on Flight 800 to Tokyo, and that I would occupy seats 1-A-B. Further, that on the stretch from Tokyo to New York I would occupy seats 7-A-B on your Flight 747SP. These arrangements were specifically confirmed by the young lady with whom I spoke.

However, the confirmations appear to have been good only when face to face. Five telephone calls later I learned that my reservations were only for any available space rather than for the specific seats I had chosen.

I feel that the success of a business depends, to a large extent, on how well it keeps its commitments. Although the commitments made to me by your representative in Hong Kong may not be considered major, nevertheless the plans I had worked out with your representative were of some major importance to me, and I would far rather have been told early on that I could not have the seats than go through the aggravation and frustration to which I was subjected.

I would like to believe that Trans American is more competent and more concerned with the comfort of its passengers than my recent experience would indicate.

Sincerely,

Large companies may not respond to a straightforward letter such as the one above, especially if your complaint isn't a major one. For a minor complaint you might want to embellish the facts with a story line or an interesting or unusual style, something that will make your letter stand out. Here is a letter concerning the kind of small complaint which often receives only cursory attention, but which in this case was satisfactorily settled—possibly because of the unusual letter.

September 19, 1977

Mr. Eli Simmons
Simmons Ford
919 Grand Avenue
St. Paul, Minn. [zip code]

Dear Mr. Simmons:
   Whatever you are doing at this moment, please stop. Sit down, relax, because the story I am about to tell you is a sad one. It will no doubt bring tears to your eyes.
   I thought the Pinto was a cute little car, so I talked my husband into test-driving the little charmer. It was love at first sight. We said goodbye to our faithful station wagon, got into our "brown beauty" and brought it home to live with us. I can safely say our entire family loves our Pinto, even our dog, Pebbles.
   Now brace yourself, here comes the sad part of this story. At midnight we were roused from sleep by a loud blasting. It was our "brown beauty" blasting away with her horn. The next night brought about an instant re-play. Tonight we will definitely disconnect the horn before retiring, but this doesn't solve our problem.
   Can you give us an explanation as to why our horn starts blasting in the middle of the night and never in the daylight hours? Can you offer a solution?
                                                    Respectfully,

Hints for effective complaints:

   In the library you may find the names and addresses of appropriate corporate officials.
   The library (or your stockbroker) will have a copy of the company's annual report. If your letter shows knowl-edge about the company in regard to your complaint,

your complaint will be taken more seriously. Also, the more you know about the company, the more ways you'll have to approach your own particular problem.

Type your letter or write it carefully by hand, to make it easy to understand and answer.

CHRISTMAS AND NEW YEAR'S CARDS

Some people like to spread their good cheer during the holidays by sending cards to everyone from Great Aunt Hattie to nice Mr. Cornwall at the hardware store; others send cards only to their closest friends and family who live far away, because the cost of postage has become prohibitive; still others send none at all. If you send a sufficient number of cards to have them printed, they should be printed with the most informal form of address: "Elsie and Bob Cratchit" (or "Bob and Elsie," which follows the time-honored "Mr. and Mrs." form of address; the choice is yours), not "Mr. and Mrs. Robert Cratchit."

When the whole family sends a card and children's names are included, the father's name has traditionally come first. Today, however, since the father *and* the mother are being recognized as joint heads of household, this rule has been relaxed; put first the name you would prefer: "Bob, Elsie [or Elsie, Bob], Matthew and Timmy Cratchit." If children in the family come from a previous marriage, list only first names. One type of card may be sent to everyone on your list. Printed cards sent to close friends should include a handwritten message, which may be as brief as "Have a Happy Christmas." If you know only the husband or the wife of a couple, address the card to both; Christmas is a family time.

As a sender whose list includes both close friends and mere acquaintances, you'll be aware by now that you won't receive a corresponding card for everyone you send. A nonsender need not, at the last minute, send a card to the woman down the block who waves every autumn when she's raking her leaves. If you don't send Christmas cards, there's no reason to dash one off to the leaf-raker just because you're included on her list, but be sure to acknowledge her thoughtfulness the next time you see her.

Your business-related Christmas-card list may be enormous, but is it essential? A word of warning: It's easy to add a name to your list, but once you have someone on your list it's risky removing that person, who may take your change of heart as a slight even though you haven't done business in years.

PERSONAL LETTERS

Etiquette (and a certain amount of paranoia and mistrust of our own feelings) has admonished us from time to time to refrain from writing anything in a letter that we wouldn't want read in court or printed in the newspaper. Just think if Abelard and Heloise or Ellen Terry and George Bernard Shaw had adhered to such constricting advice! As long as what you put down isn't dishonest, I think you may say whatever you'd like. If you are apprehensive about being read aloud in court, either a U.S. court or a kangaroo court of friends' devising, if you're afraid a letter of yours or the emotions and sentiments expressed therein may get to the wrong person, one safeguard is to date your letters, since letters themselves often outlast our own convictions. Your best precaution is to write what you truly believe and, just as you wouldn't whisper over the back fence retelling tales retold to you, don't gossip in a letter. Only *your* secrets are yours to confide.

The tone of a love letter and the feelings expressed cannot be governed by a set of rules. The only criticism that one must follow when writing a love letter is to speak sincerely from the heart. All or any feelings may be expressed as long as they are genuine.

INVITATIONS AND REPLIES

Issuing an Invitation

The wife issues and replies for almost every kind of party for herself and her husband. The only exceptions are invitations for formal dinners, dances, debuts and weddings when invitations are issued from "Mr. and Mrs.," or when an invitation is sent on an informal which is marked with "Mr. and Mrs."

Not so long ago a married woman issued her invitations using only her married title, but it was understood that her husband would be there. Today women, married or single, have the choice of using their own names socially. Following is a list of traditional titles and contemporary titles to be marked on note paper, informals and visiting cards.

TRADITIONAL AND CONTEMPORARY TITLES TO USE

	TRADITIONAL	CONTEMPORARY
Girl under 13	Vivian Fein	
Girl over 13	Miss Vivian Fein	Ms. Vivian Fein
Married woman	Mrs. Charles William Quales	Ms. Vivian Fein Quales
Husband and wife	Mr. and Mrs. Charles William Quales	Ms. Vivian Fein Quales and Mr. Charles William Quales
Couple living together or married couple when wife has retained her maiden name		Ms. Vivian Fein Mr. Charles William Quales
Widow	Mrs. Charles William Quales	Ms. Vivian Fein Quales
Divorced woman	Mrs. Fein Quales	Ms. Vivian Fein Quales

FORMAL INVITATIONS

On formal invitations (on the invitations themselves as well as the envelopes) abbreviations are never used when there is room to write out the complete word. Initials in names are omitted: "Mrs. Michael Sargeant Peters" or "Mrs. Michael Peters," or "Ms. Jeannette Holly Peters issues an invitation," not "Mrs. Michael S. Peters" or "Ms. Jeannette H. Peters," unless, as in Harry S. Truman, the initial is part of the full name. This is generally the case when the first name is the one given the initial: "R. Phillip Wagner." "Junior" may be abbreviated "Jr." Roman numerals (II, III, etc.) are written as such after the name. However, you may prefer to write out "Second," "Third," etc. A comma is placed after the name and before the "Jr.," "Second" or "Third." No comma is used before Roman numerals.

In street addresses, the number may be written out if it is twenty or under. Names of cities and states are also written out in full. However, if you do abbreviate state names, use the official abbreviations the Post Office has established.

"R.S.V.P."

In order that your guests will know to answer your invitations, write in the lower left-hand corner "R.S.V.P.," which stands for the phrase *Répondez s'il vous plaît* ("Please answer"). "R.S.V.P." or "R.s.v.p." are both correct. You may translate the phrase and write instead, "Please reply," though "R.s.v.p." is most often used.

If your party is to be held in a club or a hotel and replies are to be sent to your home, write your home address under the R.S.V.P.

> R.s.v.p.
> 12 Oakdale Ave.
> Wooster, Ohio [zip code]l

For an invitation to a large cocktail party or an open house to which guests aren't expected to reply, omit the R.S.V.P. To elicit replies from those who cannot come, write "Regrets only" under the R.S.V.P.

Response Cards

A response card is enclosed with a stamped, self-addressed envelope in invitations to very large parties or to business functions, to encourage prompt replies. Response cards are printed. Example:

> M [fill in your name]
> _____accepts
> _____regrets
> for Saturday, December eleventh

Or:

> M [fill in your name]
> accepts   regrets
> [cross out word which does not apply]
> for Saturday, December eleventh

Cancellations

When it is unavoidable and you have to cancel an invitation you've already accepted, phone your regrets as soon as possible. Stress how disappointed you are to miss the event. Don't apologize too strongly for your absence. I've heard an annoyed host complain that a canceling guest sounded as though her failure to appear would be the most important event of the party. Your host deserves nothing less than an iron-clad, plausible excuse; that you are sorry is taken for granted by a host who was nice enough to ask you in the first place and has been counting on you.

When canceling a more than casual invitation where your host has gone to some trouble, a note must follow your phone call.

> *Dear Kitty:*
> *We were so sorry to miss a much-looked-forward-to evening with you and Doug. As I told you on the phone, Jim had to fly to Chicago unexpectedly and I had to drive him to the airport. When he gets back, I hope the two of you and the children can come for a cookout now that the weather is warm at last.*
>
> *Love,*
> *Leslie*

If you have to cancel on the day of the party, you might add something extra to your apology. I've found that a nice touch is to send flowers (which the host can add to his party decorations) with a note saying, "Please forgive me." Although the flowers are an extra and are up to you, a note is mandatory.

Business Invitations

Formal business invitations follow the general rules for social invitations, with some slight additions and adjustments. It may be necessary to give a title and a company name after the host's name so that it is clear to all those invited who the host is.

> Ms. Geraldine Palmer Borrell
> President of Tin Roof Productions
> requests the pleasure of your company . . .

Invitations are addressed to guests as they are known profession-ally. A married woman in business would be addressed by her professional name and not her married name, if the two are different.

Although one replies to formal invitations with a formal written reply, such an invitation sent by a company will usually include a response card, or a phone number will be printed under the R.S.V.P. for simpler and easier replies. In fact, in these more informal times many invitations that traditionally were written are delivered by telephone. I can recall my initial surprise when I received a dinner invitation from a foreign embassy by phone. Now, this kind of practical informality is becoming increasingly frequent.

Informal business invitations may be sent in a letter, by mail-gram or night letter, or by telephone.

Visiting Cards and Their Uses

Mrs. Charles William Quales

Ms. Vivian Fein Quales

102 East 75th Street
New York, New York 10021

Visiting cards, which once were left by afternoon callers on the butler's silver salver in Grandmother's parlor, are a tradition that became a convenience and are still used today for invitations and replies. They are also enclosed with flowers or any small gift.

The visiting card is about two inches by three inches—there is no exact size it should be. Your name is engraved in black on white or off-white paper. Your address may be engraved in smaller letters in the lower right-hand corner, or you can be Continental and have your name in the upper right-hand corner. Because the Post Office will accept no envelope smaller than three and a half by five inches, the envelopes will be larger than the cards if you're going to use your cards for invitations. You can order larger cards to fit the envelope. These larger cards are easier to use for invitations, though a large card would not be left when paying a call.

The address is not marked on the envelopes of visiting cards, informals, or formal invitations, though it may be written on the back flap or the upper left-hand corner of the envelope.

When you send the card with a gift, a few personal words are written on the card and a line is drawn through the engraved name. To use this card for sending invitations, write the pertinent information at the lower left.

```
┌─────────────────────────────────────────┐
│                                          │
│     Mrs. Charles William Quales          │
│                                          │
│                                          │
│   Dinner Sat., the 23rd, at 8            │
│   R.S.V.P.                               │
│                                          │
└─────────────────────────────────────────┘
```

If your address isn't marked on the card, write it in the lower left.

A reply can also be sent on a visiting card:

```
┌─────────────────────────────────────────┐
│                                          │
│     Mrs. Charles William Quales          │
│                                          │
│                                          │
│   Sorry, we can't make it                │
│   on the 23rd                            │
│                                          │
└─────────────────────────────────────────┘
```

Visiting cards can be used as "To Remind" cards if invitations have been phoned.

The Uses of an Informal*

An informal is just right for thank-you's. Begin writing on the inside sheet. If the note is to be rather a long one, start at the top

* For more about informal writing paper, see page 177 in this chapter.

of the paper inside. For a shorter note, begin inside under the fold. Your message can extend onto the back page.

An invitation written on an informal may be written on the outside or the inside.

Mrs. Charles William Quales

Dinner
Saturday, Sept. 24th, at 8

Mr. and Mrs. Cornelius Piper Snape
R.S.V.P.   135 Drew Street
           Hinsdale, Illinois [zip code]

Or send your reply:

Mrs. Charles William Quales

We accept with pleasure
Sat., Sept. 24th, at 8

Or:

> *Mrs. Charles William Quales*
>
>
> *Sorry we can't make it*
> *Sat., Sept. 24.*
> *We'll be away.*

When inviting or replying on the inside of an informal, there is no reason to restrict your note to the shorthand needed when using the limited space on the front. You might say:

> *Dear Evelyn,*
>   *We're hoping you and Jared can come*
> *to dinner on Saturday, Sept. 24th,*
> *at 8 o'clock.*
>   *Love,*
>   *Sarah*

A reply might read:

> *Dear Sarah,*
>   *We're looking forward to dinner*
> *on the twenty-fourth at eight.*
>   *Love,*
>   *Evelyn*

The Card Informal and Its Uses

The card informal, an all-purpose informal note card, is just like an informal except that it is a single card made of heavier paper. It is handy for quick notes and thank-you's. Use the card for invitations and replies just as you would a visiting card.

"To Remind" Cards

Follow up telephoned invitations with "To Remind" cards. Those who entertain very frequently may have on hand a supply of printed cards. You may also use note paper or informals for reminders. Write on the card or paper all the information about the party. Then write "To Remind" or "A Reminder" at the top of the paper.

A Reminder

Dinner, Thursday, September 24, at 8 o'clock
Mrs. Vivian Fein Quales

Formal Invitations and Replies on Note Paper

To answer formal invitations, use seminotes or the larger note-paper size with matching envelopes. Conservative formal writing paper is perfectly plain white or cream with no artwork or borders; it may be engraved, however. Matching envelopes are also unmarked. The paper may have a monogram at the top center or the top left if you prefer your papers personalized.

Note paper which is monogrammed or marked with name and/or address in a traditional script may be used for formal invitations and replies. If your note paper is printed in big block letters or sans-serif type and is obviously on the casual side, I wouldn't use it for formal correspondence. When your full name is marked in the center on your note paper, begin your reply on the inside below the fold with "accepts [regrets] the kind invitation of . . . ," since the first line of the formal reply, your name, already appears on the face of the note paper. When only your monogram or address is on the front, or only your name appears and you're replying for both yourself and your husband, reply in full inside.

An Engraved or Handwritten Invitation

Mr. and Mrs. Cornelius Piper Snape
request the pleasure of your company
at dinner
on Saturday, the twenty-first of September
at eight o'clock
375 Drew Street
Hinsdale, Illinois [zip code]

R.S.V.P.

An Engraved Fill-in Invitation

Those who entertain regularly have a supply of fill-in invitation cards:

Mr. and Mrs. Cornelius Piper Snape
request the pleasure of your company
at [dinner]
on [Saturday, the twenty-first of September]
at [eight o'clock]
375 Drew Street
Hinsdale, Illinois [zip code]

R.S.V.P.

Or:

Mr. and Mrs. Cornelius Piper Snape
request the pleasure of
[Ms. Otis']
company at [dinner]
on [Saturday, the twenty-first of September]
[and so forth]

In all succeeding examples of invitations the impersonal form, "request the pleasure of your company," is given. You may use that form or the more personalized form which is given directly above in which you write in each guest's name on the invitation.

Handwrite in the lower right-hand corner "Formal," "Black tie" or "Informal."

(For an extra touch you may have your monogram or family crest embossed in the top center of engraved or fill-in invitations.)

When the Party Is for a Special Guest

Mr. and Mrs. Cornelius Piper Snape
request the pleasure of your company
at a dinner
on Saturday, the twenty-first of September
at eight o'clock to meet
Mr. Julien Sorel

R.S.V.P.
375 Drew Street
Hinsdale, Illinois [zip code]

Or:

Mr. and Mrs. Cornelius Piper Snape
request the pleasure of your company
at a dinner
in honor of Mr. Julien Sorel
on Saturday, the twenty-first of September
at eight o'clock

R.S.V.P.
375 Drew Street
Hinsdale, Illinois [zip code]

If you're using fill-in invitations, write at the top of the invitation "For Julien Sorel" or "To meet Julien Sorel."

An Engraved or Handwritten Invitation to a Formal Dance

Mr. and Mrs. Cornelius Piper Snape
request the pleasure of your company
at a small dance
on Saturday, the twenty-first of December
at half after nine o'clock
Hinsdale Country Club
R.S.V.P.
375 Drew Street

The word "small" modifying the dance is generally included whether the dance is enormous or is in fact a small dance; however, it is not mandatory.

Friends Issuing an Invitation Together

Ms. Adela McPhee and Mr. Jonathan Langsam
request the pleasure of your company
at a small dance
on Saturday, the twenty-first of December
at half past nine o'clock
[or: half after nine]
486 West 83rd Street
R.S.V.P.

When a Guest May Bring Along a Guest

Ms. Adela McPhee
and
Mr. Jonathan Langsam
request the company of
Denise Knobey and guest
[or: Dennis Knobley and guest]
at a dance . . .

An Invitation to a Debut Ball or Dance

Mr. and Mrs. Cornelius Piper Snape
Miss Cornelia Snape
request the pleasure of your company
on Saturday, the sixteenth of June
at ten o'clock
Hinsdale Country Club
R.S.V.P.   Dancing
375 Drew Street

Or:

Mr. and Mrs. Cornelius Piper Snape
request the pleasure of your company
at a dance
in honor of their daughter
Miss Cornelia Snape
on Saturday, the sixteenth of June
at ten o'clock
Hinsdale Country Club
R.S.V.P.
375 Drew Street

Invitation to a Debut Afternoon Tea

Mrs. Cornelius Piper Snape
Miss Cornelia Snape
will be at home
Saturday, the sixteenth of June
from five until seven o'clock
375 Drew Street

(No response required, therefore no R.S.V.P.)

FORMAL CANCELLATION

Mr. and Mrs. Cornelius Piper Snape
regret that it is necessary to
recall their invitation for dinner
on Saturday, the twenty-first of September
because of the illness of Mrs. Snape

FORMAL POSTPONEMENT

Mr. and Mrs. Cornelius Piper Snape
regret that it is necessary to
postpone their invitation to dinner
on Saturday, the twenty-first of September
to Saturday, the twenty-fourth of November
at eight o'clock
375 Drew Street
R.S.V.P.

FORMAL ACCEPTANCE

Mr. and Mrs. Michael Piccoli
accept with pleasure
the kind invitation of
Mr. and Mrs. Cornelius Piper Snape
for dinner
[or: for a dance]
on Saturday, the twenty-first of September
at eight o'clock

Or:

Mr. and Mrs. Michael Piccoli
accept with pleasure
the kind invitation of
Mr. and Mrs. Cornelius Piper Snape
for Saturday, the twenty-first of September
at eight o'clock

FORMAL REGRETS

Miss Ida Otis
regrets that she will be unable to accept
the kind invitation of
Mr. and Mrs. Cornelius Piper Snape
for Saturday, the twenty-first of September

Or:

Miss Ida Otis
regrets
that because of a previous engagement
she will be unable to accept
Mr. and Mrs. Snape's
kind invitation
for Saturday, the twenty-first of September

Or:

Miss Ida Otis
regrets
she cannot accept
Mr. and Mrs. Snape's
kind invitation for
Saturday, the twenty-first of September

7 WEDDINGS

Marriage today has become a matter of individual choice, not an inevitable fact of life. No one has to get married because it's "the thing to do." People nowadays are thinking more seriously not only about whether or not they want to marry, but about what kind of marriage they want—and what kind of wedding they want to celebrate the event. You might get married in a church, on the beach, in a ball park or at the home of the justice of the peace. Still, there are some basic guidelines which make life easier for everyone.

GETTING ENGAGED

Telling Parents

The first people to tell when you become engaged are your parents. Tell both sets of parents your plans without delay. If you won't be seeing them immediately, it's better that *you* phone them with the news rather than your Aunt Helen who has already been congratulated by the pharmacist. The paths along which gossip gallops are intricate and diffuse. Avoid hurt feelings by taking the direct route yourself. Similarly, if your parents are divorced—no matter how well your mother and father communicate when it comes to your needs—tell each of them yourself. One parent should not have to hear your good news from the other parent, which might be the case if you neglect to notify them both.

When You're Afraid They'll Be Less Than Delighted

This is a time of congratulations and delight—if your parents know and like your fiancé and have been eagerly awaiting the news. If you can't predict your parents' reaction accurately, or if you know that their reaction will be stony, you may wonder how you can best approach the lion's den. One couple took the parents of the bride-to-be by surprise. Nancy's fiancé believed in old-fashioned diplomacy and, with Nancy present, asked her parents for their blessing. The nicest thing Nancy's mother found to say—lips trembling and voice quavering—was that she was bitterly disappointed. Nancy's father chimed in with similar congratulations of ill will. The engaged couple countered with speeches concerning their love and respect for each other, making it clear *they* knew what was best. Their serious, nondefensive tone indicated they were not to be dissuaded. Nancy's parents began to accept the marriage as inevitable and were forced to look at the forthcoming event with something less than their original consternation.

A united front can work the miracle you can't manage on your own. Your parents, like Nancy's, will probably be impressed that your future spouse has enough love for you and enough courage to stand up to them. A couple's forthright declaration of their love and concern for each other's happiness under such adversary conditions will at least demonstrate to willful parents that you mean business and will not be thwarted easily. They may not be pleased with your choice at the outset, but console yourself with the knowledge that you have managed to convince them you are an adult, free to make your own decisions.

It's true that the adult posture needed to persuade your parents is sometimes easier said than done. Most of us, in the face of a forbidding parent, react unconsciously in childish ways. Your voice gets stuck somewhere in your throat and comes out three octaves higher than it should, shrill and whiny—the voice of the child you are busy telling your parents you are not. Try taking deep breaths before you present your arguments. Just follow your natural breathing and keep your attention on it. One friend who has been through natural childbirth finds those breathing exercises extremely helpful in stress situations. Since you undoubtedly have not yet had this training, a simple yoga exercise will suffice.

Discussing Your Finances with Parents

Some fathers and mothers expect their daughter's intended to explain roughly how he plans to make a living and support a wife. Because most marriages today begin with both partners working and therefore sharing financial responsibility, the chat in the study will often include the concerned parents' daughter as well as the future son-in-law. One father, confused by the new marriage roles, asked the young man, who was still in graduate school, if he planned on ever working or if his wife was always to be the sole support of the family. To put jittery parents at ease, outline your short-term financial prospects. Parents with a son-in-law still in school may foresee a dark future in which they will be asked for money they cannot afford to give.

If you do plan on beginning your marriage with parents' help, don't take that help for granted. Both of you should speak with your would-be benefactors to get your finances in order and out into the open. Parents can then tell you how much help to expect or that you have been living in a fantasy world. Both of you should be in on the discussion. Work out your financial problems as a couple from the start.

How Much to Tell Your Parents About Your Relationship

Now that you're engaged, your parents may be happy for you with no strings attached. They may be relieved that you're finally getting married to the man they think, or are afraid to think, you've been spending weekends with for the past six months. Some parents would rather be kept in the dark when it comes to particulars about your personal life. If you have such parents, be sensitive to their needs.

On the other hand, your parents may not want to know but can't stop themselves from trying to find out—hoping all the while that there's nothing to find out. Brenda, newly engaged, lived with a roommate in the city. She spent a few nights each week at her fiancé's apartment. Brenda's mother took to calling Brenda's apartment early in the morning. On those mornings when Brenda wasn't there, her roommate would say that Brenda had already left for work. Brenda's roommate didn't like lying and, to cover up her nervousness, would launch into complicated embroideries about early meetings and the pressures of Brenda's job. To ease her mother anxiety's and to quiet her own conscience, Brenda began calling her mother before she left for work. She thus avoided a confrontation she knew would result in her mother's unhappiness. Brenda could have staged a showdown, but she realized that the truth was a weapon not recognized by her mother's own Geneva Convention.

If you have never been able to keep a secret, tell your parents privately about your relationship with your fiancé. Don't wait until the middle of an argument to declare your independence; your revelation should not be an act of defiance but rather an assertion that you are now grown up enough to take Jiminy Cricket's advice and let your conscience be your guide. Once you've told them, there's no need to refer constantly to your confession. They'll remember. Don't expect them to start seeing things your way. True, you have cleared the air by getting things out in the open; but that doesn't mean they will restructure their standards to conform to your own.

(For more on unmarried couples spending the weekend with parents, see Chapter 10, "Children.")

Introducing Your Fiancé to Your Friends

By the time you become engaged, you and your fiancé will probably have come to know most of each other's friends. It's possible, however, that you haven't had the opportunity to introduce old friends who live far from you. Old friends should find it easy to adjust to your news, at least from your point of view; but this is not always the case. While your friends will want to like the person who has made you happy, people's instincts aren't always as pure as they would like them to be. It can happen that your oldest friend, whose allegiance you've always counted on, seems to take an instant dislike to the one person you want so much for her to get along with. Your friend may be direct and tell you how she feels. Though you may be hurt, try not to be defensive. Some of the time and attention you now give to your fiancé was once reserved for her. She may be jealous. She is no longer a part of the in-jokes which you now share solely with your fiancé. Tell your friend you hoped she and your fiancé would get along and you still hope she'll come to see in him all those qualities you love. Spend time alone with her. Don't try to push their friendship. Let the two of them work it out for themselves. On the other hand, you may be unable to understand why a man as interesting as your fiancé has a best friend with every bad quality your fiancé lacks. Your fiancé's friend may be less than courteous to you, the person his buddy is now spending his poker evening with. Don't set up a him-or-me situation. If you don't like him, don't spend time with him. Your fiancé can see his friend without you. Don't try to change or end a friendship you are not a part of.

A somewhat sticky situation may result when an old friend of yours, in an attempt to win your fiancé's friendship, takes on the role of his confidante. She may tell him all about you, much more than you wanted him to know—from her anyway. Your fiancé may be upset after hearing bits and pieces from your past life. His fantasy may fit those pieces together innaccurately. And the information need not concern past romances to be upsetting and/or misleading. When Leslie threw a small party to introduce her old friend, flamboyant Gina, to her fiancé, fastidious Mark, she was relieved to see these two disparate types talking the night away. Several days later, while shopping with Mark, Leslie noticed that he was watching her oddly. When she teased him about it, Mark admitted to being concerned about her shoplifting. Nonplussed— to say the least—Leslie asked him what he was talking about. It turned out that Gina, in her rambling, stream-of-consciousness narrative about Leslie—Leslie as a little girl, Leslie now, Leslie as a teenager, etc.—had recounted a "hilarious" episode concerning a shoplifting attempt. She had neglected to mention that it was an isolated incident and had occurred when the two women were fifteen. Gina had assumed that Mark, like her own friends, had acted out in this way as a teenager and would place the story in its proper perspective. She was wrong.

Luckily, Leslie found out what was bothering Mark and was able to reassure him. The opportunity may not arise for your fiancé to repeat to you stories confided in him that he found disturbing. The easiest thing to do if you are concerned that an old friend might have overplayed her hand as confidante is to ask your fiancé straight out if he heard anything he would like you to explain. And don't hold anything she may have said against your friend; remember, she was only trying to share her love for you with your fiancé.

Meeting Your Fiancé's Family

If an engaged son or daughter lives far from home, parents may wish to phone their prospective daughter- or son-in-law to introduce themselves and say how pleased they are at the prospect of a new member joining the family. You may prefer to write a note, as that leaves no room for awkward silences and is a more official form of welcome.

> *Dear Louise:*
> *We're so delighted with Sebastian's good news! He has told us so much about you I feel as though you're part of the family already. Uncle Robert says how kind you were to show him Chicago when he was there last spring, and I confess he did say after his trip that he hoped you and Sebastian would proceed to a more permanent relationship. We do so look forward to meeting you in June and hope that you'll have time to spend at least a week here so we'll have a chance to get to know one another.*
> *Love,*
> *Clarisse and Alfred Freeman*

Introducing Parents to Parents

Traditionally, the groom's mother wrote to the mother of the bride to say how happy she was about the engagement and to ask when it would be convenient to visit. The groom's family may not be aware that such a tradition exists. Today either family phones or writes to break the ice. (I think it's easier to write if you don't plan on extending an invitation.) Either family may have a small lunch or dinner so that both sets of parents can become better acquainted. An engaged couple often visits each family separately. If parents would have to travel a great distance to meet one another, it may not be possible to introduce them until the wedding.

It is fairly common today for an engaged couple to come from opposite ends of the country or opposite ends of the social scale. When Sandra and Jim got engaged, they looked forward to their parents' eventual meeting with some apprehension. Jim's parents live in the Midwest. His father is quiet, diffident, subdued. His

mother is an avid clubwoman, highly respected for her organiza-
tional skills and her precise efficiency. She projects an air of such
authority that Sandra was thunderstruck when she discovered, on
her third or fourth visit, that her future mother-in-law, who she'd
always thought was about her own height, five feet nine, was actually an unimpressive five two. Sandra's own mother lives in New
York. She is a well-traveled, sophisticated, always fashionably
dressed career woman. She has an Auntie Mame expansiveness
and a love of slightly off-color gossip which would not amuse Jim's
hard-working, no-nonsense family.

Jim and Sandra feared that even a short meeting would be tense
and silent. Sandra's mother said, "Nonsense." The next time Jim's
parents were in town, she asked them, along with Jim and Sandra,
of course, for cocktails. Jim's teetotaling parents politely swirled
the ice in their sherry while Jim and Sandra worked hard to start
the conversation off on some middle ground. The ensuing hour or
so of polite discussion, while a bit awkward for everyone, served its
purpose: the parents had a chance to learn a little about the family
into which their child was marrying. It was obvious from the start
that a friendship would not develop between the in-laws; however,
their sense of propriety (and, I'm sure, their curiosity) was satisfied.

If you find yourself with a similar in-law conundrum, you might
forgo the one-on-one introduction. In its place, a cocktail/dinner
party to introduce your friends to your parents as well as your
parents to one another will be much less work psychologically. It
will take the pressure off you and your fiancé, and the in-laws can
meet in a less charged atmosphere.

Cementing Your Engagement: Engagement Presents

Many couples seal their engagement with something tangible.
The most popular manifestation of an engagement is, of course, a
ring. If your fiancé plans on giving you an engagement ring, you
may want to go together to pick it out or discuss it with him beforehand. Since you'll be the one wearing it, you should love it from
the beginning. There are many varieties of engagement rings.
Your budget or your taste may rule out diamonds as a possibility.
Semiprecious stones make beautiful engagement rings. If you're
not sure what you want, ask a jeweler to show you a number of

different stones and settings. It's possible that your family or your fiancé's family may have a stone which you can have reset. Again, ask the jeweler to show you a number of settings. If you fall in love with a setting that won't accommodate your wedding ring, or if the wedding band you'll be wearing is a very wide one, you can wear your engagement ring on your right hand after you are married.

One woman whose fiancé surprised her with a ring insisted on having the setting changed. Her attitude didn't sit at all well with her future mother-in-law, who had picked the setting, or with her fiancé, who felt she should have left well enough alone and not embarrassed his family. If your ring is a surprise you are not wild about, you might wait to change the setting until after the wedding or even after an anniversary or two. Console yourself with the knowledge that you'll have the ring forever. Waiting a bit to get just what you want is certainly much kinder than sacrificing the feelings of those close to you.

Although a ring is the traditional engagement present, you may prefer a pair of engagement earrings or some other piece of jewelry. You may not want jewelry at all; you may prefer a more functional gift. One man whose fiancé loves to sew gave her a super sewing machine she'd wanted for ages.

If your fiancé gave you a present, you may want to give him something in return. Why not an engagement ring? If his eyes pop out at your suggestion (you might leave out the word "engagement"), give him a different type of jewelry or a different kind of present entirely. The two of you might want to pool your resources and buy something jointly. One couple decided on engagement presents they could both use in their new household; they gave each other a stereo speaker each.

Engagement Parties

The bride's family or the groom's may want to honor the couple with an engagement party. Invitations can be printed, handwritten or telephoned, depending on the size of the party. Although the guests may know the reason for the party, it is not specifically stated on the invitations; therefore, no gifts are expected. The host usually announces the engagement at the party with a toast. The form of the party can be anything from a formal sit-down dinner to a barbecue or a cocktail party. Sometimes, a lunch or a tea for the bride takes the place of an engagement party. The mothers of the bride and the groom, the bridal attendants and close female relatives are invited.

If you're concerned about the nature of the invitations, the people you should be sending them to and the kind of party to which you are inviting them, remember that an engagement party is a celebration, not a duty. Share your planning with the engaged couple so that you'll agree on the guest list and the atmosphere you wish to create.

A note to those who are organizing pre-wedding parties: it is up to those who are giving the parties to decide upon the style and tone. Friends may want to give a casual after-office-hours cocktail-party shower, whereas the groom's parents may have their hearts set on a formal, seated rehearsal dinner. The success of any party depends largely on how comfortable the host feels with the surroundings; if the host feels comfortable it's fairly certain guests will, too.

Announcements

To announce your engagement in the paper, call and ask what information they would like you to include. If you and your fiancé are from different towns, send the announcement to both papers. Divorced parents who would both like to announce the engagement can include their names separately. Such an announcement would read: "Mr. George Smith and Mrs. or Ms. Martha Smith (or Mrs. Robert Jones, or Mrs. or Ms. Martha Jones, if she has remarried) announce the engagement of their daughter, Sarah, to John Quinn, son of Mr. and Ms. Paul Quinn of San Jose, California."

In a second paragraph you may mention where the bride and groom went to school, any honors they received there, and the positions they now hold. If you've already set a date for the wedding, you can add the time and place at the end of your announcement. You may want to include your picture or a picture of both yourself and your fiancé. Be sure to attach a caption to the picture (don't write on the back) with pertinent information.

Although engagements are generally announced by the bride's parents, the parents of the groom, especially if they are participating in the wedding plans, may want to co-announce the event. If you and your fiancé are planning your own wedding, you may announce your engagement jointly. (See "Wedding Announcements" in this chapter for wording suggestions.)

Some newspapers, mainly those in the larger cities, will print your engagement announcement or your wedding announcement, but not both.

Broken Engagements

When an engagement is broken, call friends and, with as much grace and dignity as you can muster, given the situation, tell them, "We've broken our engagement." There's no need for long explanations, and, to discourage others' open curiosity, say no more about the situation. Return wedding presents already received. It's preferable to send presents back to avoid face-to-face confrontation in which the giver can really only say, "Please keep this, it was for you." What to do with unreturnable gifts? Hang the monogrammed towels on your towel rack, thank the giver and don't expect anything very lavish from him or her if you attempt marriage again.

If formal wedding invitations have already been sent, you'll send a formal cancellation.

Mr. and Mrs. Geoffrey Salinas
announce that the marriage of their daughter
Regina
to
Reginald Kirkpatrick
will not take place

When informal wedding invitations have been sent, write a note regarding the cancellation.

WEDDING PLANS

Wedding Announcements *sent after a small wedding.*

Announcements are sent just after a small wedding to friends and acquaintances. After a large wedding which could even have been larger, announcements are sent to distant social and business acquaintances who were not invited.

A formal announcement is engraved or printed and reads:

Mrs. Frederick H. Meyers
has the honour of announcing
the marriage of her daughter
Sharon Leigh
to
Mr. Michael Goldstein
on Sunday, the twenty-seventh of July
Nineteen hundred and eighty
Pumpkin Blossom Farm
Warner, New Hampshire

A couple who planned their own wedding send their own announcement. It may be written informally in the first person. This announcement is also engraved or printed:

Catherine Kelly
and
Peter McShane
with pleasure announce
our marriage
Friday, the twenty-third of May
Nineteen hundred and eighty
New York

Announcement of the Wedding in the Newspaper

To send information to the society page of your local newspaper send a release about three weeks in advance. The release begins with the bride's maiden name and the name of the groom; then the hour, date and place of the ceremony; the name or names of the officiates; names of those in the wedding party and their relationship, if any, to the bride and groom; a description of the bride's dress and flowers and the bridesmaids' dresses, and where the reception will be held; the names of the parents of the bride and their occupations and the grandparents of the bride; where the bride went to school and to college and where she is employed; and the essential facts about the groom and his family. Finally, mention where the couple will live after the marriage.

You may send a portrait of the bride or, more in keeping with the times, a photo of the bride *and* the groom; attach a caption to the photograph, with specific information—don't write on the back of the photo. If the bride will be keeping her maiden name after the marriage, mention this fact in the announcement: "After her marriage, Ms. Krensky will retain the use of her maiden name." If the bride and groom will be sharing a hyphenated name: "After their marriage, Mr. Moore and Ms. Krensky will be sharing the surname Krensky-Moore."

In larger cities, newspapers publish a wedding announcement only if it is of some news value. If you live in a large city, you need only send the society page a note to advise them of your marriage and the date of the wedding. Include the names of the bride and the groom and the date and location of the ceremony. Should they want more information, they will contact you before the wedding.

Wedding Arrangements

If your parents are sponsoring your wedding, don't make the mistake of handing over all the responsibilities to them. Become involved as much as possible. Wedding plans can turn into a baroque disaster if you abdicate your responsibilities and at the last minute decide you'd like different arrangements from those which have already been made. One friend, whose parents planned her entire wedding in Cleveland while she was working in the East, ran up enormous phone bills trying to convince her family to give her the kind of wedding she wanted. At the point where her father shouted, "This is *my* wedding and I'll do it *my* way!" my friend gave up in despair. If you don't participate in the preparations, you and your fiancé might well end up like the bride and groom on the wedding cake, present but uninvolved. In order to fully enjoy your wedding, you must make it yours.

If you are living far from your parents and can't be in on the day-to-day plans, you and your fiancé should sit down with them in the beginning to discuss exactly the kind of wedding the two of you have in mind. No matter who is paying for the wedding or arranging most of the details, this is your day—my friend's father had it wrong—so be sure you're all in agreement with the type of wedding you've leaving them to plan. It might be helpful to choose as an attendant a friend who still lives in the vicinity of your parents. Making her an attendant gives your friend entrée to act as your representative in the wedding plans.

Wedding Expenses

Weddings are expensive today, and therefore wedding costs are often being shared more equally between the families of the bride and the groom. Traditionally the bride's family paid for the wedding invitations and announcements, the photographs at the wedding and the reception, flowers for the wedding party, the expense entailed by the ceremony itself (flowers, canopy, music, cars and so forth) and all reception expenses.

The groom was responsible for the marriage license, the bride's ring and any gift to the bride, the officiate's fee, gifts for his attendants, and the honeymoon. The groom sometimes paid for the bride's bouquet and going-away corsage, the corsages for the mothers and grandmothers, and the boutonnieres for his attendants and the fathers, but today brides often pay for all flowers. The groom's family paid for their own hotel accommodations, the rehearsal dinner and the hotel accommodations for the groom's attendants.

To split the costs a bit more evenly, a working bride and groom may pay some of the wedding costs. The groom's family may offer to pay for the liquor at the reception (or for the entire reception if they are in a better position to do so).

The easiest and most workable way to divide up wedding costs is for the bride, the groom and their families to sit down together and discuss the costs openly, so that everyone has the same wedding in mind.

It's a good idea to split the responsibilities from the beginning. If it is decided, for example, that the groom's parents will pay for the flowers and the liquor, those bills should be sent directly to them. Otherwise, conflicts may arise when the bride's family must later "bill" the groom's family for their share. Plan a wedding and a reception at which all hosts are comfortable, and the guests are bound to be comfortable too.

The Guest List

Your guest list is the deciding factor for the type of wedding you will have; it determines the site of the wedding and the cost of the reception. The list is usually divided equally between the two families. It's difficult, in the early stages of planning, to predict the exact number of guests before the bride's family and the groom's family both have made up their lists.

Kathleen and John had originally planned a wedding with just the immediate family. It soon grew to include the relatives to whose weddings they had been invited. Then the couple decided it would be silly to invite relatives just for the relatives' sake and exclude those they were close to. Inviting friends posed another problem: if they invited Tanya, whom they liked, she would be telling Michelle, whom they didn't. So they asked their Michelles as well. By now, the guest list was snowballing sufficiently for John to use the occasion to entertain business acquaintances. What began as a tiny wedding ended up with a guest list of over one hundred.

Although your guest list may not jump quite so erratically, it's best to estimate the outside limit. When the lists are in, they can be combined, duplicates can be eliminated, and then the list can be shortened. Keep in mind that for a large wedding you'll be asking people from out of town who won't be able to accept.

Invitations

The formal wedding invitation conforms to a specific standard. It is engraved on the top half of a piece of white or ivory paper which has been folded in half. The engraving is protected by a loose piece of tissue paper, and the invitation is inserted into an inner envelope on which is handwritten, in black ink, the full name of the recipient. This envelope is then inserted into another envelope which is addressed by hand and stamped.

A formal invitation reads as follows:

Mr. and Mrs. Robert Fine
request the honour of your presence
at the marriage of their daughter
Sara
to
Mr. George Francis White
on Sunday, the seventh of September
one thousand nine hundred and eighty
at four o'clock
Temple Emmanuel
Chicago

(For an invitation to a military wedding, see the "Military Weddings" section in this chapter.)

How to Invite a Guest to Bring a Guest

If you word an invitation to read ". . . and guest" you'll have no idea how many guests of guests will be expected. Instead, ask your friend whom he or she would like to invite and send an invitation to that person. Properly, each invited guest receives a personal invitation to a formal wedding.

Variations Almost Within the Limits of Tradition

At traditional weddings, the invitations are engraved and worded in a formal traditional style. If you're having a more informal, personalized wedding, your invitations will most probably indicate that to the guests.

You may want to have your invitations printed rather than engraved; printing is less expensive. One kind of printing process, called thermography, looks very much like engraving. Your great-aunt can run her hand over the print and still not be able to tell the difference. (Only if she turns the paper over and looks at the back will she notice that the paper is smooth and not indented as it is when engraved.)

If you decide on printing, you may want your invitations printed on colored stock. Your printer can show you a variety of colors to choose from.

If you're conservation-minded, you can eliminate the extra envelope. When that tradition began, no one knew that paper would one day be an endangered commodity.

You can also change the traditional wording of the invitation. When I got married, both my parents, who are divorced, were included on the invitation. (In the past, only the mother's name appeared.) My conservative printer tried to dissuade me, but I held my ground. Don't be inhibited by your printer. If he's Victorian, it's up to you to advise him of your preferences.

An invitation issued by divorced parents reads as follows:

Ms. [*Mrs.*] *Jane Thor*
[*or Ms. Jane Wiggins or Mrs. Christopher Wiggins if remarried*]
and
Mr. Peter Thor . . .

Divorced women, if they kept their married name, have in the past been formally addressed by their maiden name plus their married name: Mrs. Hickey Thor. This seems a bit unmanageable, even for such a formality as a wedding invitation. It's perfectly acceptable to use your first name in place of your maiden name, as in the above example. A woman may also use her first name if she is remarried.

If you and your fiancé are sponsoring your own wedding you may want to send the invitations in your own names. They can read:

[*Ms. or Miss*] *Martha Graves*
and
[*Mr.*] *Jonathan Wagner*
request the pleasure of your company
at their marriage . . .

or, more informally, " . . . invite you to their wedding . . . "

Today, with the high cost of weddings, more and more grooms' families are splitting the costs with the brides' families, in which case invitations are sent in the name of the groom's parents as well as in the name of the bride's. Such an invitation might read:

> *Mr. and Mrs. Walter Balin*
> *request the honour of your presence*
> *at the marriage of their daughter*
> *Judith*
> *to*
> *George Tanner*
> *the son of*
> *Mr. and Mrs. Robert Tanner . . .*

Or:

> *Mr. and Mrs. Walter Balin*
> *and*
> *Mr. and Mrs. Robert Tanner*
> *request the honour of your presence*
> *at the marriage of their children*
> *Judith and George . . .*

When the children help with the financial plans of the wedding, the invitation might read:

> *We join our parents*
> *Jean and Frederick Josephs*
> *and*
> *Shirley and Herbert Mayhew*
> *in inviting you*
> *to share our happiness*
> *as we exchange marriage vows*
> *Sunday, December twenty-eighth*
> *nineteen hundred and eighty*
> *at two o'clock in the afternoon*
> *Huntington Town House*
> *341 East Jericho Turnpike*
> *Huntington, New York*
>
> *Paula and Errol*

These latter two examples can be confusing to acquaintances who don't know the families well. Close friends and relatives will be able to sort out kinship ties.

If all guests are invited to both the wedding and the reception, you add, after the place of the wedding on your invitation:

and afterward at
The Inn of the Clock

Or you can enclose a printed or engraved reception card with the invitation. The card reads:

Reception
immediately following the ceremony
The Inn of the Clock

It's helpful to send Xeroxed hand-drawn maps with the locations of both the ceremony and the reception to out-of-towners who accept your invitation.

For small weddings of fewer than fifty guests, you'll have the time to write each invitation. Handwritten invitations are sent in the form of a short personal note.

Writing Your Own Invitations

Many couples feel that traditional invitations are not an appropriate representation of their informal life style. In order to share their happiness and feelings of celebration, they write their own invitations. What you say in your individualized invitations is up to you. Meredith and Ted's invitations began:

Meredith Sanford and Theodore Stein
would like you to share in the celebration
of their wedding . . .

If your parents are sponsoring you, their personal invitations might begin:

George and Ann Sanford
would like you to come and share
in the wedding celebration
of their daughter
Meredith
to
Theodore Stein . . .

The invitations may be written or printed on any size or color paper you wish. If there's an artist in the family, the invitations *can* be hand-lettered and -decorated.

Invitations to a small wedding may be handwritten or even phoned or telegrammed.

A note might read:

Dear Jack,
Judy and I will be married at two o'clock on Saturday, the
seventeenth of November. The wedding will be at Judy's
mother's and we do hope you can come.
Please do let us know if you can be there.
                    Yours,
                    David

Answering Invitations

Few people know the correct form of a formal reply. It is perfectly acceptable to send a short note to either accept or regret, even if the invitation you receive is a formal one. If you'd like to reply in kind to a formal invitation, you write:

Mr. and Mrs. Paul French
accept with pleasure
Mr. and Mrs. George Sanford's
kind invitation for
Sunday, the twelfth of September
at four o'clock

Or:

> *Mr. and Mrs. Paul French regret they are unable to accept*
> *Mr. and Mrs. George Sanford's kind invitation for . . .*

Invitations to large weddings often include response cards. These printed cards do hasten replies and simplify your filing system, although some consider them just another reminder of an increasingly impersonal world where so much of our mail is a computer-printed form addressed to "Occupant."

If you are one of those people who learned the alphabet without the letters R.S.V.P. and don't respond, keep in mind that responding to a wedding invitation is not just a formality. Without your response, the wedding party cannot make their plans. The only time a reply is not necessary is when you're invited only to the wedding ceremony and not to the reception.

Addressing Invitations

Printed or engraved invitations should be ordered about three months before the wedding so that they will be ready in plenty of time for you to address them. You may want to pick up the envelopes early from the printer to get a head start.

In the past, no abbreviations except "Mr." and "Mrs." and army rank were used on wedding invitations. Names of cities and states were written out in full. If your wedding is to be large and you don't have the patience to follow such rules, abbreviate. The mailman will deliver the letters just the same.

When you're sending a formal invitation to a family with young children, address the outer envelope with only the parents' names. On the inside envelope, under "Mr. and Ms. Jones," write the first names of the children. Children of thirteen and older should receive their own invitations.

A couple living together may be sent a single invitation. Both names should be included: "[Mr.] Charles Bennett and [Ms.] Lydia Fine." Use the same form when inviting a married couple if the wife has kept her maiden name.

Clothes for the Wedding Party

DRESS FOR THE BRIDE

If you plan to wear a traditional wedding dress, begin shopping about four months in advance. Most wedding dresses are made to order. It can happen that shipment of material is delayed or that complicated alterations are needed. The bridal shop will need plenty of time if last-minute panic is to be avoided.

Choosing a wedding dress is something that the prospective bride has had no practice in. A woman might shop for a formal dress or even a fur coat with no intention of actually buying, but what woman has taken a practice run at buying a wedding dress? Practice isn't needed, as it turns out, yet the "never before" aspect is an added anxiety, so a bride-to-be should take her time when shopping.

More and more grooms-to-be are coming along on shopping trips and are more than just a little surprised when their future brides step out of the fitting room, since most of the grooms-to-be have never seen their future brides so dressed up before. I think it's a good idea to take the groom along so that he'll catch a little of the excitement of the pomp and circumstance of the occasion.

Wedding dresses are expensive, considering they are worn only once. If you can't find one you like in your price range, it might be less expensive to have yours made. Ann, who was married in December, chose a dress of heavy satin, so she almost didn't miss her coat when she traveled by car to the church and then to her reception. She wore no gloves with her long-sleeved dress. Even if your dress is short-sleeved, gloves are not necessary; they obstruct the basic part of every ceremony: the exchange of wedding rings. Ann wore a long veil, which lent an extra air of formality to her wedding. Some women, instead of a veil, wear flowers in their hair.

If you want to look like a traditional bride but your groom can't be talked into anything more formal than a navy-blue suit (for an informal church wedding), you may wear a long white dress but without the train.

You may be more comfortable in a dress which feels less like a costume than the traditional wedding gown. Kathleen wore a long print chiffon dress in a modified peasant style with sandals. Meredith wore an antique white lace dress she'd been saving for her wedding since she was twelve. Any pretty, festive dress is a good choice. It's important that you feel at ease as the star attraction.

DRESSES FOR BRIDAL ATTENDANTS

The dresses of the bridal attendants are usually identical, although the maid or matron of honor sometimes wears a dress in a different color and style than the bridesmaids. Bridal attendants pay for their dresses and shoes. I've always heard that money spent on a bridesmaid's dress isn't lost because you'll wear the dress again. I've never seen it happen. The trouble with traditional bridesmaids' dresses is that they make you feel like a bridesmaid.

If attendants are dressing alike and live out of town, call them a couple of weeks before the wedding to make sure they have their clothes in order. Don't rely on them to follow through without a little prodding on your part. Also, out-of-town attendants should be safely in town the night before the wedding so that you won't have to confront the transportation delays, snowstorms, floods or locusts on that most important day.

Contemporary weddings are usually smaller than traditional ones. The bride may have only a maid or a matron of honor to attend her. If the bride and her honor attendant can't shop together for their dresses, they should look at their dresses side by side long enough before the wedding to make changes. Even the most down-to-earth blues can clash. Or the dress the attendant thought was so simple may turn out to be more formal or more of an eye-catcher than the bride's dress.

CLOTHES FOR THE GROOM AND GROOMSMEN

For traditional weddings held during the day, the men in the wedding party generally wear cutaway jackets, gray waistcoats and dark striped trousers for a formal wedding or, more informally, gray sack coats, gray waistcoats and dark striped trousers. Evening weddings (after six o'clock) are the most formal of all. The men may wear white tie and tails in true Fred Astaire tradition. Men's wedding fashions have changed considerably. Cutaway coats and tails are being replaced by ruffled colored shirts and variously styled Edwardian jackets or tailcoats, also in a wide variety of colors. Just as the bride always stands out from her attendants, the groom of today has begun dressing a bit differently from his ushers and best man. For a formal wedding, he might wear a tailcoat while his groomsmen will be in tuxedos of the same color and similarly styled.

Colors present the traditional problem of having to coordinate the dress of the groomsmen with that of the bridesmaids. The men in Kathleen's contemporary wedding party had all agreed to wear dark suits, but had not consulted one another beforehand. As a result, there was an assortment of brown, blue and gray. This is one more detail which shouldn't be left to chance. If the men can't color-coordinate their suits, possibly they'll all have blazers and dark slacks to work with.

The groom may want to dress more flamboyantly. John complemented his bride, Kathleen, by wearing a peasant shirt with full sleeves and a colorful vest instead of a jacket. The trend, even in men's formal wedding clothes, shows a tendency for the groom to want to look as festive and dazzling as the bride.

DRESS FOR THE MOTHERS

Each mother should dress in a style which is most natural and comfortable for her. One may be comfortable in a cocktail dress with a hat and gloves. The other may prefer a long dress, especially if the wedding is outdoors or at home. Such diversification is perfectly acceptable. There is no need for both mothers to dress in a similar fashion, unless they have similar tastes. At Meredith and Ted's wedding, Meredith's mother wore a beige pants suit and Ted's mother had on a long Indian silk dress. Garlands of daisies in their hair identified them as the mothers.

WHAT THE GUESTS WEAR

For a formal wedding held during the day, women guests may wear a cocktail dress or a long skirt and a pretty blouse or sweater. The men generally wear suits, as they do for evening weddings. If an after-six wedding is very formal, the men don dinner jackets and the women wear long dresses.

There has long been a make-believe restriction on women wearing black to a wedding. One friend was appalled when a guest informed her she was wearing a black dress to the formal wedding. Of course women can wear black to weddings; a black dress is certainly not suggestive of anything less than celebration. (Of course, if all guests wore black, they would tell another story, but the odds are against this.) A guest may also wear a white dress—as long as it's not *her* old wedding gown. Even though she may be endowed with a cheery disposition and a perfect complexion, it's doubtful that she'll outdazzle the bride's radiance or that the groom will mistakenly sweep her off to the altar.

JEWISH WEDDINGS

Jewish wedding ceremonies range from the Orthodox to the Reformed and vary accordingly. There are, however, parts of the ritual which are common to all Jewish weddings. A wedding canopy (*huppah*) covers the bride, the groom and the rabbi. Originally *huppah* was the word for the bridal chamber itself, and the modern *huppah* symbolizes the entering of the couple into the chamber. The wedding ring must be plain gold, with no stone, and is placed on the bride's finger by the groom as he says, "You are sanctified to me with this ring according to the religion of Moses and Israel." Both the bride and the groom sip from a wineglass after appropriate blessings have been said over the wine. A final note: the Jewish ceremony includes the groom stepping on a wineglass (the glass is usually wrapped in a cloth napkin) to symbolize Jewish mourning for the destruction of the Temple.

MILITARY WEDDINGS

A groom who is a member of the armed forces may choose to be married in uniform. Full-dress military uniforms make the wedding a formal one in which the bride wears a long dress. Though several of the groom's attendants may be in uniform, the wedding party may also be mixed, with some civilian ushers. Those ushers who aren't in uniform wear whatever is appropriate to the formality of the wedding. Men in uniform wear military decorations but never boutonnieres.

Only commissioned officers on active duty can wear the saber, or sword as it's called in the Navy, with which the ushers form the traditional arch of steel for the bride and groom to walk under at the end of the ceremony, and with which the couple later cuts the cake. The arch is formed inside the church (some churches will not allow this) as soon as the bride and groom turn to face the congregation just after the ceremony. The head usher commands,

"Center face!" and the ushers form two facing lines on either side of the chancel steps. On the command "Arch sabers" (or "Draw swords") each usher raises his sword, the cutting edge on top. After the bride and groom pass under the arch, the ushers walk with the bridesmaids in the recessional or they leave by the side door and reform the arch on the church steps. When the arch is formed outside, the bride and groom, followed by the bride's attendants, walk to the vestibule, where they wait until the ushers take their places. To form the arch, at least four military ushers are needed. Civilian ushers may line up in formation with the military ushers or they may stand on one side with the bridesmaids.

Invitations to Military Weddings

The rank of the groom is printed in the invitations and announcements. The title is used before his name if his rank is equivalent or higher than captain in the Army or the Air Force or commander in the Navy. If his rank is lower, it is listed with his branch of service:

John Paul Butler
Lieutenant, United States Army

If the bride is an officer in the armed forces the invitations would read:

. . . at the marriage of their daughter
Carmen
Captain, Women's Army Corps . . .

A WEDDING IN TIME OF MOURNING

When a death occurs in the family of the bride- or the groom-to-be, the wedding may be postponed. Or if the wedding is already some time off it may take place as scheduled, but the reception would not be extremely large. Since a marriage is a time of great joy and offers the promise of a new beginning, the wedding should reflect these sentiments. There is no need to curb the gaiety; you certainly may have dancing. The bride and groom should scale the wedding according to their own needs and feelings.

A WEDDING POSTPONEMENT

Mr. and Mrs. Elliot Mauser
announce that the marriage of their daughter
Elaine
to
Mr. Robert Greenlief
has been postponed from
Sunday, the twentieth of May
until
Sunday, the twenty-second of August
at twelve noon
Randall Hall
1230 Peachtree Street S.E.
Atlanta

A CIVIL CEREMONY

A civil ceremony follows the procedures for an informal wedding. It generally takes place in a private home, in a judge's chambers or, if performed by a justice of the peace, in a registry or at the justice's house. A civil ceremony is generally a small one, though the reception following may be quite large. Sometimes a civil authority officiates at a large wedding in a club or a hall. Rows of chairs are set up on each side of the aisle, and the formal wedding procedures are followed.

A ceremony by a justice of the peace takes just a few minutes and is informal and efficient. The bride and groom have to bring their own sense of romance with them, as the justice and the registry provide only the legalities. Dress should be appropriate to the dignity of the occasion.

FLOWERS

Traditional flowers for the bride to carry include white roses, gardenias, carnations, stephanotis, and orchids. The bride may wish to carry an all-white nosegay (roses and baby's breath, perhaps) and have each of her attendants carry a single white rose. The men in the bridal party wear white boutonnieres.

A bride may also wish to carry flowers in season freshly picked from her own garden or the garden of a friend. Flowers often are carried loosely tied and are placed in vases after the ceremony. Many brides today wear garlands of flowers attached to their veils or in their hair. The bride and her attendants may carry or wear the kinds of flowers and arrangements which suit them best. A bride who has no definite idea regarding her flowers should describe her dress and the dresses of her attendants to a florist, who will surely help to solve the problem.

PHOTOGRAPHS

The formal photographs of bride and groom, attendants and parents are taken after the receiving line at the reception or may be taken several hours before the ceremony. Candid photos are taken throughout the reception and during the processional and the recessional of the ceremony as well. You might decide on a professional photographer. Another fine alternative is to hire a photo-reportage photographer from your local paper.

Asking a dear friend who is also an amateur photographer may well save money, but there is no guarantee that even one photograph of this, "one of the most important days in your life," will be realized. One couple thought their photographic problems were solved because half a dozen guests all volunteered to take photographs. Most of the photographs were charming, but the guests with the cameras didn't know who was who in the cast. Therefore most of the photos were of guests who were essentially the extras and not the supporting cast. It's best therefore to hire a professional who will ask first who's who and has developed an eye for what is important at such an event.

WEDDING PRESENTS

The bride and groom receive presents from everyone who has accepted their wedding invitation. Those who come to the wedding, eat the cake and toast the bride and groom are obliged to reciprocate the kindness of the invitation and to contribute to the couple's new life together.

I don't think it's necessary for invited guests who do not share in the wedding celebration to send something, though they certainly may do so. Presents may be sent before the wedding or up to a year afterward. You may want to wait until after the couple are settled before you choose a gift for them. Weddings conjure up pictures of silver, crystal and fine china—hardly the necessities of life, which may be just what the couple have overlooked. One newly wed couple, when asked, requested an iron and an ironing board after the honeymoon was over.

The Bridal Registry

Many couples register their preferences at certain stores. A bride and groom make an appointment with the bridal consultant at the store when they are ready to register their choices for presents. Bridal registry is a free service provided by most department stores and small stores, such as those specializing in kitchen wares and housewares. Guests invited to the wedding may call the store or go there personally to choose a wedding present. The store keeps a careful record of what has been bought so that duplications won't occur.

If the bride is registered, friends will have no trouble selecting something the couple will like. If not, ask the bride, the groom or one of their mothers for suggestions. When buying a present for someone you know only slightly, it's safest to stick to categories such as kitchen equipment—a salad bowl or a casserole—which have a function as well as being pretty. Don't buy something which is solely decorative. Your taste may not be theirs.

Possibly the bride and groom will be living in a small apartment, are still in school, plan to travel after the wedding or are otherwise not yet ready or willing to settle down with silver, china and matching monogrammed bath towels. They may be happier receiving money in place of wedding presents. Any amount you wish to give is fine. There's no need to feel embarrassed if you can afford only a small sum. If you're dead set against giving money, for whatever reason, send a present which you think would be appropriate to the couple's life style. One group of friends chipped in and bought a delighted student couple an army-surplus inflatable pontoon. The couple use it every summer when they vacation at the bride's family's summer house. Another couple, who had been living together before their marriage and therefore already had most of what is usually given as wedding presents, organized a color-television fund. Close friends and family felt their cash gifts to be less impersonal when they knew that their money was going toward something specific.

Recently, an acquaintance of mine was confounded by a gift problem none of us had previously encountered. She has a favorite niece to whom she had promised, as a wedding present, a prized piece of Dresden china that had been in the family for years. She regretted the promise, made years ago when the niece was a child, when she heard that the prospective bride and groom were moving into a commune in which all personal possessions became community property. I could sympathize with her dilemma; I shared her concern for the safety of this heirloom and also felt that in choosing a life style which disapproved of personal property the niece had relinquished her right to the china.

Nowadays, some young people do choose communal life styles, some cooperative, some fostered by a parent organization which claims title to all personal property. Friends and relatives may want to make gifts to the bridal couple but not to an organization to which they have no relationship and, in certain instances, no sympathy. One solution might be to make your gift a bond that is due to mature in five to ten years.

Exchanging Presents

As a bride-to-be, in all likelihood you'll receive some presents you'll want to exchange. If you don't tell people what you want, you'll have more exchanging to do than if you make specific requests. Kathleen made what, in retrospect, she considers a silly mistake by not registering and also by telling friends and family that any present they wanted to give would be fine. She ended up with a lot of white elephants, many of which she was unable to exchange. The ones sent from out of town she and her husband have learned to live with or they take up needed storage space in their small apartment.

Kathleen solved the additional problem of what to do when friends surreptitiously cast their eyes about her apartment trying to locate their present—which she has long since exchanged—among her belongings. Every time she invites the couple who gave her the crystal water glasses, she makes a point of using her Swedish-design plastic to dress down the dinner table so that her friends will be led to understand that this is not a formal, crystal evening. Before her aunt who gave her the decanter arrives, Kathleen takes down all her decanters from their place on an open shelf so that her aunt won't notice that her decanter is not among them. There's no need to offend someone who cares enough about you to send a gift, whether or not you're as pleased with the gift as with the thought behind it.

Monograms

A bride used to come to her marriage with her trousseau. Because the trousseau belonged to the bride before her marriage, items were monogrammed with her initials. Today parents may furnish a bride with a part of her trousseau, and wedding presents may make up the remainder. The beautiful designs on sheets, towels and tablecloths often take the place of monograms. If you would like to have monograms on your silver and some of your linens, you can use your maiden initials, your married initials or a combination consisting of your first initial, your husband's first initial and the initial of your married name. It is not necessary, however, to hold to a uniform monogram. For instance, your silver might be comprised in part of family heirlooms, some marked with your great-aunt's initials and some with the initials of the groom's family. Parents of one bride gave her a set of flatware, including only dinner knives and forks, monogrammed with her family initials. The set was completed with unmonogrammed pieces in a similar design found in a secondhand-silver shop. (If you want silver but you find the prices prohibitive, try looking in shops which sell old silver. Don't be put off by what seems to be old and dirty castoffs. Ask for a piece or two to be polished, and you'll discover under the tarnish beautiful silver which looks like new.)

Acknowledgment Cards

If you're planning a very large wedding and therefore receive so many presents that you won't possibly be able to thank everyone shortly after the wedding, you may send a formal acknowledgment card, engraved or printed, after you receive each gift. Though in the past these cards were always sent by the bride, as she was ostensibly the one to receive the presents, I think that today both the bride and the groom should send the cards together. They can be mailed just after the wedding.

> *Mr. and Mrs. Harry Groner gratefully acknowledge the receipt of your lovely wedding present and will write you a personal note at the earliest possible date.*

Send such cards only if you absolutely must, since they are a very impersonal means of acknowledging a personal consideration. So unless you're planning a cruise around the world or a six-month back pack through South America, I think a three- or four-month delay in thank-you notes is preferable to acknowledgment cards.

Please note that acknowledgment cards in no way replace your personal thank-you notes; they serve only as a confirmation that the gift has been received.

Thank-You Notes

It's important to set up a file to keep track of each gift you receive and who sent it. This way, you can mention the present specifically in your thank-you note. A thank-you note should be sent to everyone who gave you a gift. Even close friends you see often and have probably thanked in person deserve a written note. Your notes should be addressed to whoever gave you the gift. If it is a couple, don't write only to the woman, which has often been done in the past. The signature should only be that of the person who wrote the note. Your spouse may be included in the body of your letter; for instance, ". . . Johann and I both love the brandy snifters." When you are thanking someone for a check, make the note personal by mentioning what you plan to spend the money for.

Thank-you notes may be written before the wedding, if you have the time and the presence of mind, or up to three or four months after, if your wedding was very large. Otherwise two or three months are all the time you have to complete the task.

Your note need only be a few sentences. Mention how much you liked the gift, that it adds a bright touch to your new house. Include one or two additional sentences unrelated to the gift—a thought about the wedding or how much you're looking forward to having your friend visit.

Don't take advantage of what you hope will be your friends' understanding of thank-you-note blues. They'll all realize you have many notes to write; but no one, after taking the time and the trouble to pick out something for you, will understand if you short-change them with a one-sentence note or a note that reads like mimeographed copy.

Thank-you notes can be written on paper designed for brief messages; but don't try to save time by sending notes on paper small enough to double as a place card. One offended friend received a note written on such a miniscule card that there was room for only a thank-you-very-much and a signature. While you can buy thank-you notes already printed—all you have to do is fill in the blank with the specific gift and sign your name—I don't suggest you take this decidedly easier way out. Again, friends and family can only be offended by such an impersonal reply.

Thank-you notes have previously been considered the woman's work. I see no reason why you and your husband can't share the responsibility, especially if you're both working and are similarly pressed for spare time.

If you don't have the time to begin your notes before the wedding, you should start on them immediately afterward. Put aside a certain amount of time each day so that you will get them all out before your mother-in-law begins receiving phone calls inquiring whether or not you received certain gifts. Delayed thank-you notes have often been the first bone of contention between a defensive bride and a mother-in-law made equally defensive by having to explain away her new daughter-in-law's rudeness to her friends.

Displaying Wedding Presents

If you have the space, you may want to display your presents at home for a few weeks before your wedding. You can set up tables covered with white tablecloths or white sheets in the basement, the family room or the dining room. The gifts are separated into categories: silver, glass, kitchen equipment, etc. The half-dozen butter dishes and salt and pepper shakers you receive should be scattered about diplomatically.

In front of each present you may want to put a card with the name of the giver. This is up to you; if you think that bad feelings and subtle competition may arise when all can see that your Aunt Rose gave a more expensive present than his Aunt Ruth, then omit the cards.

Checks are placed one on top of the other in such a way that the signatures are visible but the amounts are hidden. On the top check, you will place a piece of paper over the amount.

If your reception won't be at home, you may want to give a lunch or a tea to display your wedding gifts.

SHOWERS

Showers are generally given by a bridesmaid or a close friend of the bride. The bride is consulted ahead of time so that she can specify the type of shower she wants. It's important for her to remember that shower gifts are given in addition to wedding presents. She must take into account the limits of her friends' budgets. A tactful way to set a price range is to suggest some of the things she would like to receive.

The shower for today's bride can be anything from an afternoon tea for a linen shower to a garden party for a gardening shower, with bags of fertilizer and perennial bulbs among the most valued gifts.

Showers are no longer given only for the bride. Joint showers for the couple, either for cocktails, for dinner or for a weekend brunch, are making pre-wedding parties less separatist occasions. It's old-fashioned to assume that only women are interested in decorating and equipping the household. Today, men are taking a similar interest in these activities, possibly out of necessity if both partners are working. The groom will probably be changing the new sheets and cooking in the Chinese wok. Since "his and her" chores around the house are fast becoming "theirs," joint showers give the wedding couple a chance to share equally in the fun of setting up the new home they will both be managing.

Showers are fairly small, so you will have a chance to thank everyone at the party. Nevertheless, short thank-you notes should also be sent soon after the shower to all who attended and especially to the host or hosts who gave you the shower.

THE APPOINTMENT WITH THE OFFICIATE

You should set your meeting with your officiate well in advance of the wedding to explain the kind of ceremony you have in mind and, possibly, to avail yourself of the advice of an expert. Kathleen and John, who were to be married by a priest in a nondenominational chapel, originally thought they'd have a simple service with only the traditional vows. After they discussed their plans with the priest, their ceremony came to include elements of the new wedding: friends were asked to speak, and John and Kathleen wrote their own marriage vows, all of which lent an air of community and informality to their wedding, something which both of them had wanted but were hard put to achieve without suggestions from their officiate.

A clergyman may also want to discuss marriage with you. Many believe that brief counseling before marriage saves many couples from counseling later on. The clergyman will also want to discuss any religious problems peculiar to your marriage, For instance, Ann, who is Jewish, and David, who is Catholic, were to be married in a Unitarian church which Ann had attended on a few occasions as a child. Neither Ann nor David had strong religious convictions, but they wanted a church wedding. They felt that a nonsectarian service would be meaningful to them and would also reflect their personal religious views, which were not bound by specific doctrine. When the couple spoke with the clergyman before their marriage, he initiated a discussion of the kinds of problems involved in a mixed marriage. He was informative and supportive. When the time came to discuss the ceremony, he told them what he had planned, a simple ceremony including quotations from Shakespeare and a discussion of the family of man, and asked them to feel free to comment or to request changes. Ann and David thought the service quite personal and responsive to their views.

If you do not speak with the officiate beforehand, you'll be leaving the wedding ceremony to chance. One couple did not speak with the rabbi who was to officiate at their wedding, because the bride had known him since childhood and therefore assumed he would have something meaningful to say at her wedding. Instead of talking about the bride when she was ten, saying a few personal words appropriate to the couple, the rabbi gave a sermon on truth and righteousness which seemed clearly to be his standard marriage sermon. It had nothing to do with the spirit of this wedding or the two people getting married. The service was impersonal and formal, not at all the tone the couple were trying to set for their wedding.

In another instance, the couple met the officiate only minutes before the ceremony was to begin. During the service, he spoke of the Spanish groom as coming from Argentina. In the hurry and confusion, the officiate had mixed his information, and he embarrassed the bride and groom as well as the congregation.

THE REHEARSAL

If your wedding is to be anything more complicated than two witnesses, you'll probably have a rehearsal. The service isn't read at the rehearsal, but the officiate puts all the participants through their paces to learn their parts. The rehearsal is a good time for the officiate to become acquainted with members of the wedding party and to iron out any last-minute questions or problems. (When Ann was over an hour late for her rehearsal, leaving her groom to wait and worry, the minister, fearing habitual lateness on Ann's part, nipped a potential problem in the bud and instructed her to arrive a half hour early for the ceremony.)

THE REHEARSAL DINNER

Many weddings include a dinner immediately following the rehearsal. Invitations are mailed or phoned. The rehearsal dinner is usually given by the parents of the groom. It can be a buffet or a more elaborate sit-down affair. The dinner can be fairly small and include the families of the bride and groom and the members of the wedding party; or, if many of the guests are coming from out of town, it can include those who have arrived early for the wedding. At the rehearsal dinner, the bride and groom give their attendants small presents as mementos of the wedding. Gifts are simple: bracelets or charms, possibly engraved with the wedding date, for the bridesmaids, cufflinks, a desk set or the traditional silver shot glass for the groomsmen. One groom gave each of his ushers and his best man a glass-bottomed beer mug.

If you're living away from home and have planned your own wedding, you may want to use the tradition of the rehearsal dinner as an opportunity to introduce out-of-town relatives to your friends. Because Kathleen didn't want her parents, who live in another city, to be strangers at her wedding, she gave a night-before cocktail-dinner party. She cooked a ham and a turkey, and friends brought the side dishes and dessert. It turned out to be a successful evening, but for Kathleen it was the last gasp before exhaustion in a long line of wedding plans and parties—it was two o'clock before the last guests left and she could begin loading the dishwasher. If you are thinking of giving your own party just before your wedding, think again. The night before is not the time to entertain on a large scale. If your situation is similar to Kathleen's, your friends might give the party as a wedding gift to you and your groom.

THE WEDDING TAKES PLACE

Seating

At traditional church weddings, ushers escort all guests to their seats. Friends and relatives of the bride sit on the left of the aisle, the groom's guests sit on the right. The mother of the bride, the last to be seated, is escorted to the first pew—the signal that the ceremony is about to begin. If the wedding is small and there are no ushers, guests seat themselves. They need not divide their ranks but may sit where they like, leaving the first few pews for immediate family.

At less formal weddings taking place out of doors or at home, guests stand in a semicircle, leaving space for an aisle if one is not marked by boxed flowers or ribbons. Ted and Meredith, who were married at home, stood on an Oriental carpet surrounded by garlands of daisies which served to further define the space. Guests stood in a semicircle around the rug.

The Processional

In a formal wedding, the bride walks down the aisle on the arm of her father (if the bride's father is dead, she may choose her brother, a favorite uncle or a close family friend to walk with her down the aisle), preceded directly by her flower girl or ring bearer, then by her maid or matron of honor and finally by the bridesmaids and the ushers. The bride meets the groom, the best man and the clergyman, who have appeared as if by magic at the front of the church. When the clergyman asks who is giving the bride in marriage, her father answers: "Her mother and I."

Some brides no longer want to recreate the symbolism of being owned by the father who is now giving her to her husband. Kathleen, who had been living on her own, felt this tradition inappropriate as well as demeaning. Her father, on the other hand, was counting on it. They worked out a compromise popular today. Kathleen's father walked her down the aisle and stepped into his seat in the first pew, leaving Kathleen to take the last few steps alone to the altar.

Some brides prefer to walk with both their parents, one on either side, down the aisle. Sometimes, the groom as well as the bride participates in the processional. Those who include their parents in the processional are borrowing a tradition from the Orthodox Jewish ceremony, where both bride and groom are flanked on either side by their parents.

Sometimes, especially if the bride and groom have been living together before their marriage, the couple may want their ceremony to indicate that they come to their marriage as a unit. In such a case, the bride and groom may wish to walk down the aisle hand in hand.

The Ceremony (The New Wedding)

No matter how contemporary you make it, no matter how many old traditions you cast aside, your wedding still contains certain basic elements, otherwise it wouldn't be a wedding. The face of the wedding ceremony has undergone plastic surgery, but the bone structure hasn't been touched. You may not want to wear a long white gown or say, "I will," or swear to obey. Many couples, in view of the increasing number of divorces and remarriages, have done away with "till death us do part" or "as long as we both shall live." Couples are getting married on beaches, in meadows, at sunset and, woe to the guests, at dawn. But they're still exchanging vows. Public affirmation of love and commitment hasn't changed.

Meredith and Ted's wedding is a fine example of the free-flowing, personal expression many weddings have today. In order to stress that they were marrying each other and were not "being married," they wrote their entire ceremony and officiated with the help of both sets of parents.

Meredith and Ted walked down the aisle together and stood facing each other before their parents. (Although Meredith's parents were divorced, neither felt it necessary to make an acknowledgment of this fact. They were standing up as Meredith's parents, not as husband and wife.) Each father made a welcoming speech and gave a short explanation of the ceremony. Meredith's mother then asked Ted to voice his commitments, and Ted's mother asked Meredith for her vows. The couple exchanged rings carried on pillows by Meredith's young nephews. Although wedding rings have taken the place of crowns (still used in Eastern Orthodox and Polish weddings), which symbolize the eternal circle, Meredith and Ted crowned each other with simple crowns of silver wire, again carried on a pillow, this time by Meredith's niece. The crowns had been made for them by a friend who is a sculptor. The couple then declared themselves to be husband and wife, and the guests tossed daisies which they had been given at the door.

To legalize their marriage, a rabbi conducted another ceremony toward the end of Ted and Meredith's reception, which was held at the same place as their do-it-yourself ceremony—at home. Meredith spoke her vows in English, and Ted spoke his in Hebrew. The rabbi called it a Universalist service.

Kathleen and John, while not altering their ceremony quite as drastically as Meredith and Ted, also took pains to see that their wedding service reflected their personal values. Because they felt that the way they related to those close to them was connected, in part, to the way they related to each other, they wanted all those present to participate as a community, not as an audience. At the altar, the bride, the groom, the maid of honor and the best man turned to face the congregation in a semicircle, with the priest standing off to one side. All the members of the bridal party were to speak at some length, and they felt that the traditional stance of the bride and groom with their backs to the congregation would be inappropriate as well as downright unfriendly.

Because Kathleen and John saw their wedding as a union between the old and the new—a melding of old friends and family with their new life together—they had asked both an old family friend and a young friend of their own generation to stand and speak from the congregation about what marriage meant to them. The speeches had not been monitored beforehand, and Kathleen, who has an active career and does not live in accordance with ancient Biblical commands, was indeed surprised when the older man read a dark passage from the Old Testament in which the woman's place is described as being to spin and to toil. The young man then spoke extemporaneously about the couple, adding a few words about John's previous marriage, saying that he hoped this one would endure. Although some guests were offended by such bluntness, Kathleen and John felt the speech appropriate—they were standing before their friends and family as people, not just as bride and groom.

This kind of spontaneity makes a wedding informal but also may make the guests and perhaps even the bride and groom a bit nervous. To eliminate chancy free-form style, pre-select prose speeches and poems or have your rehearsal at least two or three days before the wedding and ask all those who will speak to attend. If their speeches are not in accordance with your views, they'll have time, with your help, to modify them.

I'm giving an example here of a much simpler ceremony than either Meredith and Ted's or John and Kathleen's. This ceremony is, I think, to the point and charming. It was written by a bride and groom who felt that the "standard" ceremonies were excessively long and formal and contained phrases they described as "too sanctimonious."

REVEREND: We are gathered here to celebrate the marriage of Catheryn
Cheal and William Clark. Cathy has suggested that the ceremony be dignified, simple, and traditional in form. Bill has
recommended brevity balanced by whimsy, to which she
agrees, asking only that his wit not undermine their purpose.
Let us proceed.

    Bill, do you take Cathy as your beloved wife, to share your
life with her? Do you pledge that you will love her, honor her,
and tenderly care for her, in sickness and in health, in sorrow
and in joy, in prosperity and in adversity, living together in
this way to provide the firmest foundation for married love?

BILL: I do.

REVEREND: Cathy, do you take Bill as your beloved husband, to share
your life with him? Do you pledge that you will love him,
honor him, and tenderly care for him, in sickness and in
health, in sorrow and in joy, in prosperity and in adversity,
living together in this way to provide the firmest foundation
for married love?

CATHY: I do.

[*The couple join right hands.*]

BILL: I take you, Cathy, to be the wife of my days,
    The mother of my children,
    Together with me always.

CATHY: I take you, Bill, to be the husband of my days,
    The father of my children,
    Together with me always.

REVEREND: What pledge do you offer that you will fulfill these vows?

B. AND C.: These rings.

REVEREND: These rings are symbols of truth and are offered as a pledge
that the love here declared shall be like them, pure and en-
during.

    Do you, Cathy, accept this ring?

CATHY: I do.

BILL: (*placing ring on her finger*): This ring is a symbol of our union,
a token of my faith and love. With this ring, I do thee wed.

REVEREND: Do you, Bill, accept this ring?

BILL: I do.

CATHY   (*placing ring on his finger*): This ring is a symbol of our union,
a token of my faith and love. With this ring, I do thee wed.

REVEREND: Here we may borrow from a ceremony written by Jonathan
Swift:

> Within this chapel in bonny [stormy] weather
> I marry this man and woman together;
> Let none but Him who rules the thunder
> Put this man and woman asunder.

[*Pause.*]

> I do now pronounce you husband and wife.
> May peace dwell in your hearts and wisdom in your minds.
> May your days be good and long upon this earth. Amen.

[*Cathy and Bill kiss.*]

Old Problems at New Weddings

As long as you're improvising your wedding, you may have to improvise answers to questions which used to be taken care of by formal rules. Older people often can't understand why anyone would want anything other than an established ceremony. Some are embarrassed to witness public declarations of love. For them, the wedding itself is enough of a declaration; no elucidation is needed. "If the couple don't have those feelings for each other, they shouldn't be getting married in the first place," I overheard at a new wedding reception. For those guests who are squeamish about what they possibly consider a public display of affection in the new wedding, it may help to discuss your plans with them beforehand. Explain why you want your wedding your way; explain how you feel about the person you're about to marry. In other words, tell your guest essentially what you'll be telling the congregation at the wedding. Your speech, given from the heart, should turn on the emotions of the most avid anti-new-wedding-ite.

Sometimes you must direct your attention to the most basic question of all, "Is this really a wedding?" Kathleen and John planned a Catholic wedding mainly for the sake of their families. However, they altered so much of the identifiable rituals that their families weren't at all convinced they had witnessed a wedding. After the service, Kathleen's father, needing reassurance, asked a priest cousin, "Well, are they or aren't they?" John's father, a Latin American, asked the priest who had officiated what Protestant denomination he was. The families might have been put at their ease if the officiate had explained to the congregation the basic elements of the new ceremony or if each of the guests had been given a program so that they could acquaint themselves with the unfamiliar parts of the service.

Religious differences have always created question marks for guests, especially now, in the new wedding, when specific rituals have been reinterpreted by the bridal couple to reflect their personal convictions. If you're a guest at a wedding of a different religion from yours, ask ahead of time if there are any codes of dress you should follow—whether or not you should wear a hat or long sleeves, for instance. During the ceremony, remain silent and seated if your religion—or lack of it—forbids you to kneel at certain times or to recite specific liturgies.

Because most religions are becoming more liberal, it is sometimes acceptable to take part in a religious rite which is not your own. For instance, after the vows at Kathleen and John's wedding, the priest poured wine into a chalice and began breaking French bread. He suggested that anyone who wanted to celebrate could take Communion. The Communion could be viewed either as a sacrament or simply as a part of the wedding celebration. The parents of the bride and the groom came up to the altar first, and then the entire congregation followed their lead. The Communion became an impromptu receiving line. Some of the guests drank the wine and ate the bread in celebration of the bride and groom, while others, even with the priest's urging that the wine and the bread in this case need not be considered Communion, only congratulated the couple. It's interesting to know how deeply religious sanctions are ingrained in all of us.

Kathleen and John had emphasized the concept of community throughout their wedding. Their guest list was necessarily diversified; John works for a multinational company, and among his colleagues invited to the wedding were Moslems and Buddhists. So that the improvised ceremony, which had few of the traditional landmarks, should not be confusing, John began by speaking of the various groups present: the two families, the friends, and his international business associates. By introducing each group to the others, John brought the separate elements of the congregation together. However, the priest had not been told of the varied makeup of the congregation. During the ceremony, he made a short speech to the interdenominational gathering about his views of the wedding ceremony as a sacrament to be shared by the community. He included in his statement, "All of us, Christians and Jews, make up this community." Moslems and Buddhists were not mentioned. Had the priest discussed the wedding in more detail with the bride and groom, he would have known to include everyone.

The Recessional

In the recessional of a traditional wedding, the bride takes the groom's right arm and is followed by her flower girl, then the maid or matron of honor, on the right arm of the best man, and, finally, the ushers and the bridesmaids, who are also paired. Pairing is usual in the recessional, as it symbolizes the union of the marriage. If the women and the men in the bridal party are not paired, the bridesmaids and then the ushers follow after the bride and groom.

If your wedding is a small one and is held at the same place as the reception, there is no recessional, for the simple reason that there is nowhere to recede to. After the groom kisses the bride, the couple are congratulated by the officiate and then by the immediate family. This is usually the signal for the other guests to say a few words to the couple, and, instead of a recessional, an impromptu receiving line may form.

THE RECEPTION

Generally, a formal wedding is followed by a formal reception with hors d'oeuvres, a sit-down meal or buffet, a wedding cake and champagne. An informal wedding reception ranges from champagne or wine and wedding cake to a complete meal.

Your reception may be a picnic in the park or a hotel extravaganza. If you decide on a hotel, you'll be supplied with plenty of help and advice. So much so that a little advice on the advice you'll be getting is in order. Banquet managers and wedding consultants tend to come up with a steadfast rule for every detail you are not in agreement with. Don't be cowed by the experts. If you don't want doves flying out of your wedding cake, or a twenty piece orchestra, or food served which you can't pronounce, be resolute. This is your wedding; you're the expert.

If your reception is to be at a hotel or catered, ask to be served the meal you are planning on serving at the reception. Some hotels and caterers may not *offer* sample meals, but all will accommodate such a request at no charge. After all, you're willing to spend a great deal of money, so be willing to make sure you'll be getting what you want. Also, ask to see the caterer's equipment to make sure the chairs, china, etc., are all in good condition.

The Responsibilities of Bride and Groom at the Reception

The purpose of the wedding reception is for the bride and groom to share their happiness and celebrate with those close to them. The bride and groom must be more than just objects to be admired and clucked over. Even if parents are actually hosting the event, it is also the responsibility of the bride and groom to make sure that all those gathered in their honor are enjoying themselves. This is a doubly difficult task: first, because the married couple must fulfill their roles as stars of the show; and, second, because guests are generally comprised of diverse groups. Wedding receptions always include a few odds and ends you're afraid won't fit in at all. How do you see to it that those who know only one or two others present will have a good time?

One mother of the bride, to make sure that everyone would celebrate and not sit alone in the corner, decided on seating plans only at the parents' table, at which she sat all those guests who knew only one or two others present. This thoughtful woman called each of these guests a few days before the wedding to let them know they would have a place card at her table. She knew that family members and friends of the bride and groom knew enough people present to take care of themselves.

Kathleen and John were worried about how Kathleen's suburban, comparatively unworldly family would get along with John's South American diplomatic family and his Middle Eastern and Far Eastern business associates. As it turned out, the striking diversity in the guest list proved to be more of a help than a hindrance. The usual self-consciousness which tends to inhibit guests who are strangers to one another was lessened because the various groups of guests were culturally so diverse that curiosity outweighed formality. Social barriers were down because nobody knew anybody else's rules of behavior. Kathleen introduced her Aunt Ruth to an Arab sheik hesitantly and was amazed to see the two still engrossed in conversation fifteen minutes later. Kathleen had assumed her aunt would regard the sheik as a Martian and would therefore be reluctant to converse with him. What she hadn't taken into account was that there was a "Martian" to every group, but a friendly Martian. The sheik was just as curious about Kathleen's Aunt Ruth as she was about him.

I'm not suggesting that you import extras to your reception to stimulate conversation. This story does illustrate, however, that the most unlikely mix of people will get along. Don't look for similarities between two people when making your seating charts or to ease an introduction. You might be more successful putting together a dissimilar pair. If your reception is too large for you to make sure everyone is being looked after, ask bridesmaids and ushers to make a special point of mingling.

Guests at a reception are expected to take matters into their own hands and introduce themselves. The shared joy and celebration makes it easier for people to open up to new faces and gives them a common ground on which to start a conversation.

The Receiving Line

The receiving line starts off the reception. The bridal party arrives at the reception site first (since they are the first to leave the ceremony) and is, therefore, ready to greet the guests as they arrive. The receiving line always includes the bride and groom, the two mothers and the maid or matron of honor. Whether or not the fathers and the bridesmaids are in the line is optional. If yours is a large reception, you may prefer to keep the line as short as possible. The line forms near the entrance in this order: first, the mother of the bride; next, the mother of the groom; then the bride and groom; and, last, the honor attendant. Bridesmaids are the last in line, and fathers stand on either side of the mothers. If fathers aren't in the line, they may station themselves in proximity to it and greet the guests.

As a guest going through the receiving line, introduce yourself to the mother of the bride, the first in line, adding your relationship to the bride or groom if she doesn't know you. You're expected only to say a few words to the mothers about how nice or how touching the wedding was, and to congratulate the bride and groom. (In the past, the congratulatory remarks were reserved for the groom. It was rude to congratulate the bride, because it implied she had caught her man. Congratulations to the groom were in order because he, the pursuer, was expected to do the catching. I think we can dispense with such distinctions and congratulate both husband and wife.) Usually, the people on the receiving line will take responsibility for introducing you to the next person on line. If they are too busy or have forgotten your introduction, reintroduce yourself.

At small receptions—about fifty people—guests will have the opportunity to greet the bride and groom and the parents individually at the party, so a receiving line is not necessary.

Special Problems

Ann and David's wedding reception presented some special problems. Ann's parents had been recently divorced, recently enough for Ann to feel that certain reception traditions might become awkward situations. For instance, to seat her mother and father at the same table she thought would be ridiculous, and to put them at separate tables would make them conspicuous. So Ann didn't have place cards at any table except the bridal table at her reception lunch, and her parents were therefore able to sit where they chose to, among their respective friends and relatives. There was also no dancing at the reception, because Ann did not want to put her parents through the traditional dance they would be expected to have together.

I think Ann's consideration for her parents is an extreme case. A bride and groom are not expected to modify their wedding for the sake of their parents. If anything, parents should bend over backward for their children's needs. If you find yourself in a predicament similar to Ann's but you want your wedding to include those traditions your parents might find uncomfortable, discuss it with them and let them come up with alternatives which would be acceptable to all of you.

Janet had an additional problem with her divorced parents. Her father had recently begun living with a woman whom he had not yet introduced to the family. Janet's semi-stepmother eased any question which might have arisen by not attending the wedding. She felt it would be an inappropriate time to meet grandmothers and aunts as well as the bride's mother. She also realized that the wedding was a special time for the mother of the bride and that there would be other family gatherings she could attend in the future.

Conversely, one groom's stepmother, who had arranged the wedding and the reception, seated herself next to the groom's real mother at the small reception dinner. Did she feel that seating the groom's mother at the opposite end of the room would seem antagonistic? Even though the two women certainly had enough in common to make conversation, I think side by side is a bit drastic. Possibly the groom's mother, even though she may be on very good terms with his stepmother, may feel ill at ease finding herself with such a dinner partner. Her feelings, as a guest, must be considered. I think a separation of mother and stepmother by three or four guests may be more diplomatic—if the two women are to be seated at the same table. Another reason to split up mother and stepmother: these two women sitting side by side may upstage the bride and groom.

Throwing the Bouquet

The tradition of tossing the bridal bouquet to the unmarried women at the wedding need not be upheld. At my wedding, there were few guests in their late teens and early twenties—the bouquet-catching age—so I threw mine to the children. Some brides may want to keep their bouquet as a memento of their wedding or may want to give it to someone special. In one instance, the bouquet was not thrown, because one member of the bridal party had recently canceled her wedding. The bride felt it would be tactless to put her friend in the position of possibly catching what, in this case, would be an unlucky symbolic offering.

A Do-It-Yourself At-Home Reception

If you have your heart set on celebrating your wedding with friends and family but don't see how your budget can stretch to accommodate so large a guest list, there are many ways to cut the costs instead of the people. When friends ask what you'd like for a wedding present, suggest that the perfect gift would be their help at your reception. Enough willing and able volunteers can see you through your entire reception, from making the wedding cake to lending a hand on the cleanup crew. Or your friends can assist around the wedding cake and the caterers. They can arrange flowers (loose flowers are less expensive than arrangements), tend bar, make music if you're lucky enough to know a guitarist or a pianist. For a wedding present, one friend supplied a do-it-yourself reception with hired help for the day.

The food you serve doesn't have to be the equivalent of a Roman feast. Simple hors d'oeuvres or tea sandwiches served on paper plates with plastic utensils are fine. If you plan on having a caterer or live in a metropolitan area, you might follow Kathleen and John's example: for a light buffet lunch, they hired a Japanese caterer. The food was superb and could be eaten easily while the guests were standing. There were a few raised eyebrows when guests discovered that the delicious tidbits were raw fish, and a few more guests were astonished to see Japanese women in kimonos pouring the champagne.

Liquor can be one of your highest expenses. Because Kathleen and John wanted to keep costs down they served only domestic champagne. Meredith and Ted served a wine punch for the same two reasons. This solution is much friendlier than limiting guests to a certain number of drinks apiece. Your guests should be able to have their fill of whatever you're serving.

A Reception at a Friend's House

Kathleen and John's reception took place at the penthouse apartment of friends. The lady of the house, after inquiring whether Kathleen had enough champagne glasses, silver and china, swallowed hard as Kathleen explained that the champagne was to be served in plastic glasses and the food on paper plates. If friends are kind enough to loan you their house for your reception, explain beforehand just what kind of reception you have in mind. Everyone has ideas about the way things should be done. There's no reason to assume that your silent host would have the same kind of reception you want. And though it is your reception, your host can't help feeling that the reception reflects on his taste. Iron out all differences of opinion beforehand.

It's also important to make clear just who is doing what. Don't assume your friend will provide any of the services you need, unless she has specifically volunteered for a job or two. Make sure, for instance, that your plans include an adequate number of people to help clean up. Even if you're using paper and plastic, you'd be surprised at the amount of work needed to put the house back into the condition in which you found it. In fact, don't expect to find the house in perfect order. It's unfair—and unsafe—to rely on your friend's generosity and presume she will spend the time or the money to put her house in immaculate condition. This is also your responsibility.

MARRYING AGAIN

Second weddings are designated thus only if the *woman* is marrying for the second time. A groom can participate in a big, lavish wedding as many times as circumstances demand. A woman who has been married before was supposed to be circumspect her second time around. I hope this part of the double standard is coming to an end. Every bride should be able to have the kind of wedding she wants, though it's doubtful that she'll want six attendants and four hundred guests more than once. If she hasn't had an extravagant wedding, it's unlikely she'll be able to afford such a bash, now that she's on her own. However, the decision is hers and her groom's.

Generally, second weddings include an informal ceremony, a guest list of no more than fifty or sixty, and informal, handwritten invitations. The reception following can be as large as the couple would like. If the couple want a large wedding (and the officiate agrees), they may plan such a wedding complete with long white dress, bridal attendants, processional and all the traditional trimmings. A bride who chooses a simple wedding and a large reception might wear a short and simple dress for the ceremony and a long dress to the reception.

Telling the Children

When you tell your children the news of your impending marriage, it's best to tell them by yourself. Even though they may get along well with your future spouse, he or she is not yet part of the family. No child will disclose uncomfortable feelings with an outsider present, especially if that outsider is the person about whom the child has uncomfortable feelings to begin with. If your children don't live with you, it's worth making an extra trip to see them or to have them spend extra time with you in order to tell them your plans. A phone call might be easier—the children won't have a chance to ask questions or to state opinions you'd rather not discuss—but it's not as honest. You may find it more difficult to tell your children in person, but it will give them a chance to react openly and to talk things over with you.

Getting to Know Future Stepchildren

Even though you aren't the wicked stepmother (or stepfather) of fairy-tale lore, your future spouse's children, because of their ambivalence about the marriage, are apt at first to cast you as such. The hostility they exhibit toward you is most probably misdirected. Children often feel hostile toward their parent for marrying again and will take it out on the person they see as the cause of the problem—you. Given a little time and a little encouragement, the children will come to terms with the new situation. Be warm and loving, but not overwhelming. They will need space to find their new ground with you and to learn to like you in your new role. They also need reassurance. Children, like the rest of us, are creatures of habit; they must be reassured that you'll bring about as few drastic changes in their lives as possible and that the ones that do occur will be for the better.

Whether you're marrying someone who has been widowed or someone who is divorced, don't enter into competition with the absent parent. Trying to take that parent's place can only be regarded as a usurping of power. Instead of immediately becoming a new Mother or Father, begin by being a comradely adult, interested and supportive but not overly demanding.

Just because your future spouse's children are grown and on their own, don't take it for granted that they will welcome you into the family wholeheartedly. A friend of mine surprised herself with all sorts of "baby feelings" when she found out that her father was remarrying. For the six years her father had been widowed, she had expressed her hopes that he would find someone else. When he finally did find a woman who was, my friend admitted, "irresistible," my friend did her best to resist her and grumbled a bit about "the disposition of goods." Normally a sympathetic person, my friend was embarrassed by her own lack of grace and appalled that, at thirty-one, she could be so childish. But the truth is that as far as our parents are concerned we will always be children to some extent. Fortunately, in this instance, my friend's stepmother-to-be understood this and with patience and good humor helped her to adjust to the new situation.

Telling Your Ex

Someone on good terms with his or her ex-spouse will have no trouble telling him or her of current wedding plans. If, on the other hand, your divorce decree was a declaration of war, it's still important to get the news through the front lines and into enemy territory. If you've been receiving alimony and your husband reads the good news of your remarriage in the paper or is told by a friend, he may have good cause to be angry—he may already have sent your next month's check (which, of course, you'd return). Why put him through even a short-lived paroxysm? Write him a letter, if speaking to him directly will be upsetting; or, in irreconcilable cases, have your lawyer notify his lawyer.

If you're the one sending the alimony, it's just as important to tell your ex-wife of your plans to remarry. If she hears the news elsewhere, she may assume you failed to tell her because your new wife will be the one spending the money meant for alimony payments.

If you have no children or financial ties to your ex-spouse, whether or not you tell him or her of your remarriage is up to you.

Invitations

For a small wedding of fifty or so, your invitations may be handwritten in the form of a short note. If your wedding is to be larger, you may send personalized invitations or traditional printed or engraved invitations. (See the "Invitations" section earlier in this chapter.) A woman marrying for the second time may wish to issue her own invitations jointly with the groom.

I think it's more relaxed for the bride to use her first name together with her married name or her maiden name, whichever she has been using. The stiffness of the traditional use of maiden

name plus married name—Mrs. Samuels Sherman, for instance
—I think is out of date and can be confusing. Presumably the bride
is not addressed in such a formal and distant manner by close
friends and family, those whom she will be inviting to her wedding.
After your first marriage, you probably use the combined form,
Mrs. Gail Sherman, and you may use this address on your invitations.

Often second weddings including only immediate family are followed by larger receptions. If you'd like to send traditional formal
reception invitations, they may be issued by your family or jointly
by you and your groom. An invitation sent by the bride and groom
would read:

> *Ms. [Mrs.] Gail Sherman*
> *and*
> *Mr. John Meyer*
> *request the pleasure of your company*
> *at their wedding reception*
> *on June twenty-first at four o'clock*
> *The Old Coach House*
> *Cincinnati*

If parents are giving the wedding, they may issue the invitation:

> *Dr. and Mrs. Robert Ash*
> *request the pleasure of your company*
> *at the wedding of their daughter*
> *Jane Ann Ash Yankowsky*
> *to*
> *Dr. Frederick Simpson, Jr. . . .*

An invitation to just the reception would read:

> *Dr. and Mrs. Robert Ash*
> *request the pleasure of your company*
> *at the wedding reception of their daughter*
> *Jane Ann Ash Yankowsky*
> *and*
> *Dr. Frederick Simpson, Jr. . . .*

Wedding announcements may also be issued by the bride's parents or by the couple themselves. (See the "Wedding Announcements" section earlier in this chapter.)

What to Wear

What a woman chooses to wear for her first or her third wedding depends solely on her taste and the kind of wedding she's planning. A white dress, once symbolic of the bride's purity, has now come to symbolize the wedding itself; therefore many second-time brides wear white. For a fairly large and formal second wedding, it is not unusual for the bride to wear a traditional wedding gown, albeit without the veil. Because the traditional wedding dress does require an equally ornate and formal setting, which second weddings rarely have, the bride generally wears a simple white dress or a dress of a light color. For my own, a small at-home wedding, I wore an off-white long chiffon dress. A friend, who is an expert seamstress, made a long cotton print dress for her wedding, which took place outdoors on the lawn. She carried a bouquet of fresh flowers from her garden. Many brides who have previously been married forgo carrying a bouquet or wearing flowers of any kind. This decision is, again, a personal one, as it affects only you.

The dress of the groom depends on the formality and style of the bride's dress. (See the section headed "Clothes for the Groom and Groomsmen" earlier in this chapter.)

The Ceremony

Religious distinctions between first and subsequent marriages, while less stringent than in the past, are still very much in evidence. Your clergyman will instruct you as to what, if any, particulars your second ceremony may involve.

If you're planning a small and simple wedding, you may choose not to include some of the rituals of a first wedding. If, however, you don't want a simple wedding, you may include any or all of the rituals that go hand in hand with a traditional wedding, providing you have the approval of your clergyman. That this is your second marriage is not reason enough to dispense with what are the distinguishing features of a wedding. Abbreviations or adaptations of nonreligious elements such as the processional, giving away the bride, and the recessional are a matter of personal choice.

Second-wedding services, though generally brief, tend to be among the most personal. Many divorced people who go into marriage for the second time, try to ward off repeating past mistakes in their personally written vows. If, for instance, empathy had been lacking in a previous marriage, the vows might stress its importance. A second marriage of someone who has been widowed is also often intensely personal, for that person is so much more aware of just what a marriage entails than those going about it for the first time.

Your Children and Your Wedding

The distinguishing characteristic of today's second wedding is the participation of the children of the bride and/or the groom. Small children can be flower girls or ring bearers. At one second wedding, the groom's two little girls acted as ring bearers and brought the rings to the parents of the bride and groom. The parents, saying a silent prayer, placed their hands over the rings. In this way, the parents became actively involved in the ceremony and symbolically gave their blessing to the marriage. At one charming wedding, the bride's daughter and the groom's two little girls were the flower girls. Because their marriage certainly included the children, they thought it important that the children be included in the wedding. Older children may also be included in the wedding as the maid of honor or the best man.

Another way to let your children share in your wedding is to give them special mementos of the day. A small silver cup for odds and ends, engraved with the date of the wedding, a silver ashtray, or, for small children, charms for the girls and cufflinks for the boys, also engraved, are a tangible way to show them you want the day remembered together.

Sometimes, the way to show your children that you care is less tangible but even more important: special consideration for their feelings. Everyone knows that words can be devastating weapons. What appears innocent in one context can cut to the heart in another. Amanda, attending her widowed father's wedding, was witness, along with her three siblings (two of whom were still adolescent), to her father's repeated rejoicing, "This is the happiest day of my life." Sentiments expressed in such circumstances must be weighed beforehand—be sure your joy doesn't translate as the poison on the tip of the arrow. There are many ways to express your happiness; pick a neutral one.

Thank-You Notes

With second marriages, in some instances, it is an added courtesy for both the bride and the groom to send separate notes for the same gift. A friend felt most put out when her father's new wife, whom she knew only slightly, sent a note to thank her for her wedding present though she heard not a word about the gift from her father. This is a case where one thank-you note was not enough. Separate notes from you and your spouse to your children or to close relatives of a previous spouse, show your appreciation in a most thoughtful and personal manner.

8 MARRIAGE

BEGINNINGS

Changing Your Name—Or Not

Traditionally, the change of status from single person to married person was most dramatic for the woman, who took her husband's name and became Mrs. Marc Eigen instead of Miss Sarah Cotsworth. Now not only is "Ms." supplanting "Miss" and "Mrs.," but it is no longer taken for granted that the husband's last name will be the family name after marriage. Not infrequently, married women are retaining their surnames. And some couples are joining their last names together with a hyphen, the most popular order being the wife's surname followed by her husband's—Sarah Cotsworth-Eigen—proof that the patrilineal line is still the most important; most husbands will not lose their names to a prefix.

There are exceptions. The Queen of England, though she herself has no surname, must have given the issue some thought, as she has changed the family name from Windsor to Mountbatten-Windsor. In complicated instances, the wife's last name will be comprised of her husband's followed by her own—Sarah Eigen-Cotsworth—while her husband will prefix his own surname with that of his wife—Marc Cotsworth-Eigen.

If you'll be using a nontraditional surname, it's a good idea to enclose a separate card in your wedding invitations or your announcements. For women who wish to keep their names, the card may read:

After marriage,
Sarah will retain
her surname Cotsworth.

A more persuasive announcement might read:

Sarah Cotsworth
wishes to announce that she
will retain her surname
for all legal and social purposes
after her marriage to
Marc Eigen.
The co-operation and understanding
of friends and family would
be appreciated.

For couples who are combining names, the card may read:

After marriage,
Sarah and Marc
will share the surname Cotsworth-Eigen.

Or a fuller explanation may be given by adapting Sarah Cotsworth's persuasive announcement above.

You'll still probably receive wedding presents addressed to Mr. and Mrs. Eigen from people who refuse to accept your decision. To meet their resistance, refer to yourself exclusively by your preferred name, correcting those who refer to you by any other. Remind the people with whom you deal on a regular basis what you'd prefer to be—insist on being—called. There will, of course, be some instances where you'll have to accept established tradition— a great-aunt need not be expected to bow to your progressive ways.

If you are afraid your decision is not going to sit well with your parents, take the time to discuss your reasons with them and ask for their support with other relatives. One woman I know who was so uncomfortable with her in-laws she didn't even know what to call them solved both problems in one fell swoop by blurting out, "We're going to call ourselves Harold and Diane Brooks-Kroger, and, by the way, what would you like me to call you?" Her in-laws were so relieved that the subject of their names had come up they accepted Diane's choice of last name without a second thought.

What to Call Your In-Laws

If your in-laws fail to speak up in the beginning and tell you what they'd like to be called, you must take the initiative. Don't let shyness force you into silence. If you wait too long, it will be inappropriate to bring up the subject (unless you use Diane's somewhat awkward gambit), and you'll end up having to tap them on the shoulder to get their attention and consistently referring to them as "you." Either refer to them as "Mr." and "Mrs."—they may feel this is too formal, in which case they'll tell you what they would prefer—or simply ask what they'd like to be called. If your mother-in-law says she wants to be called "Mother," and you think one mother for you is enough, it is not good form to refuse to comply after you're the one who asked. To be on the safe side, ask, "May I call you Anna?" She'll either say yes or steer you toward a more formal address or, possibly, a nickname.

Sharing Bed and Board

It's best to start a marriage with a special sensitivity—not something you can look up in a book for handling special occasions but something that starts at home, and with your day-to-day living.

Do you absent-mindedly drop your shoes in your closet each night, letting them fall where they may, perfectly content in the knowledge that tomorrow morning you'll have to weed out a matching pair? Such casualness could bring out the worst in your new spouse who grew up in a house where, as one friend has put it, "godliness was child's play compared with cleanliness." Your spouse may assume that all's right with the world only when shoe trees are snapped snugly in place. In a new marriage, all of us must wrestle with this kind of surprise. Sharing your decorating ideas or a closet or the same bed may not turn out to be the idyl you've imagined. There are ways to make it easier.

Decorating: Starting from Scratch

If you're newly married and both of you have previously been living at home or with roommates, you'll probably start fresh in an apartment or a house you've picked out together. With hope, joint perusal of wedding presents will have shed some light on differences of taste, so the shock won't be so great if one of you has dreamed of a living room to rival Liberace's and the other leans toward the architectural philosophy "Less is more." Decorating from the carpet up is expensive enough to make it a slow process —it takes months and sometimes years to finish the job—so you have time to decide on what you really like and needn't make snap decisions you may later regret. Since you'll be living with that sofa for years and years, it won't hurt to sit on folding chairs for a while instead of rushing to buy what you only halfheartedly like.

What's Mine Is Yours

For those who bring their furniture to their marriage, each of you will already be familiar enough with the other's belongings either to have grown accustomed to certain items you initially disliked—or at least didn't love—or to suggest that certain pieces be stored or sold or put out on the stoop.

When two people combine their furniture, there is no guarantee that the checks on his favorite armchair will get along with the print on her sofa. Again, it's more important that the two of you get along. The couch or chair can be reupholstered or moved to another room in the years to come.

The Second Time Around: Redecorating

If you've been married before, your new spouse may be moving into the house you shared with your former spouse. In order for your new spouse to feel at home, redecorating to some extent is a must. Otherwise, you will not be sharing a household so much as entertaining a permanent guest.

In redecorating to accommodate a new partnership, you must also consider the feelings of children and stepchildren. I know of one instance where the new husband of a widow with teenaged children moved in all his furniture and moved out all the old familiar furniture. The children were attached to some of that furniture and to the family portraits now relegated to the attic.

When embarking on a major redecorating job, involve the children. Generate their excitement and interest by including them in your plans. Show the children the fabrics you have chosen; ask them what they think of your overall color scheme for the living room. It's a good idea to let them make a few changes in their rooms so that they won't feel they've been shunted aside. They can pick out a new bedspread or curtains, paint their dresser or worktable or rearrange their furniture.

If the children don't live with you full time, let them know you're making changes, so that they won't walk into a house they've felt comfortable in and been a part of to find it has all been changed now that "he" or "she" has moved in. If the room the children use when they come to stay doubles as a guest room or a workroom when they aren't with you, let them put up posters or pictures of their choosing. The anonymity of a guest room can make a child feel more like a guest than like a member of the family. Confer with grown children on any furniture you want to store or otherwise discard. They may want it.

If you are the new member in the household, don't try to make the house solely your turf. Bend a little; it's the children's house, too. Don't enforce your rules when existing family traditions will do as well. If the Christmas tree has always been in the living room, don't insist on putting it in the front hall. In the same spirit, it won't do to shift dinner into the dining room in a family which is used to eating informally at the big kitchen table. If you'd be happier with a little more formality, ask your family to indulge your whim and eat in the dining room at least occasionally.

Sharing Closets

Unless you and your new spouse countenance the same degree of neatness (or sloppiness), sharing a closet is not a good idea. If there's only one closet in your bedroom, one of you can use another closet, even if it's at the other end of the house. The next question, of course, is who gets the bedroom closet. The closet outside the bedroom might best be used by the one who gets up earlier, so that the one still sleeping will not be disturbed.

Sharing a Bathroom

All of us have shared bathrooms with parents, siblings, roommates, so we're all familiar with the hiss or bellow (depending on individual style) emitted through a locked bathroom door at 7:25 A.M. Some men seem to be more relaxed about bathroom privileges than women (a lot of those relaxed men have been in the Army, so they know that things can be worse). Men also seem to spend much more time in the bathroom with their hot combs and hot-lather shaves than is generally supposed. Since there is rarely a bathroom down the hall to which one of you can escape, some pounding on the door is inevitable. Here are a few suggestions which will help to ease recurring tensions:

Agree on division of shelf space in the medicine cabinet, or put up additional shelves. You might put up a second medicine cabinet when one isn't enough or when further demarcation of properties is necessary: when your tweezers didn't survive the last time they were substituted for pliers, or when you look like a German dueling champion after your razor has been used without your knowing.

Sharing a Bed

Does sharing your life with the person you love include sharing your bed? It seems so. One bed, no matter how large, shared by two people, no matter how large, has come to symbolize successful marriage. Bed-sharing has come all the way from the bundling board to the king-sized bed. Although *Playboy* afficionados would hint that king-sized beds inspire king-sized sexual exploits, I think larger beds were inspired by disgruntled couples worn out by continual struggles over sleeping territory—the larger the bed, the better chance two people have of attaining a good night's sleep.

One couple intent on sharing one bed has solved their seemingly never-ending war of the blankets by simply equipping the bed with two of everything: two top sheets, two sets of blankets. The one drawback: there is simply no way to make the bed. The couple in question feel that an unmade bed is a small price to pay for a good night's sleep. For those of us who could tolerate a night's lost sleep more easily than an unmade bed, this is obviously not a solution.

For those who have tried to but can't sleep together in one bed, twin beds will not prophesy the end of your marriage. (Friends and neighbors are more apt to discuss your chronically unmade bed than they are your twin beds, if gossip worries you.) For those who can't sleep together in the same bed, twin beds are a satisfactory answer.

If your spouse is perfectly happy in one bed and you are the one who wants the twin beds, present your argument tactfully. Don't blame his snoring, take it on yourself: "I love the idea of our sharing a bed, but I can't seem to sleep." Once you have made the switch, work to make the togetherness of twin beds as alluring as your togetherness in one.

I have one final comment on beds for those who are beginning their marriages with two sets of furniture. While the overflow—two sofas, two dining tables—can be a blessing in terms of extra chairs and enough drawer space, the question of whose bed will be *the* bed has been known to initiate more than one dialogue. Though most newly married couples have made no secret of their pasts, many are reluctant to carry the past into the future: they insist that the bed they will share must be new. Beds are expensive, however. If you don't have the extra money or think it foolish to spend extra money duplicating what you already have, agree on the most comfortable bed, buy a new bedspread and let the bed's former life be damned.

Redecorating the bedroom is a must if you're beginning a marriage with one or two sets of children. The future life of your bed can be cursed by children who remember its rightful past. Again, if you can't afford a new bed, make the smaller purchase which in this case would ease the minds of your children: a new quilt and bedspread will issue in a new beginning.

FINANCES

All couples fight about money. Intangible problems in a marriage often take hold in the very real problem of money—who makes it, who spends it and how. Now that sex is out on the line with the wash and Masters and Johnson, money is the dirty secret left in marriage. Though you'll overhear discussions of sex at every cocktail party and movie line, talk of hard cash is considered unseemly and is seldom heard outside the family. Money problems are openly discussed by the unmarried. I know of one woman who asked the advice of friends regarding financial disagreements she had with the man whom she was seeing. Once married, she stopped talking about her financial complaints entirely. That the marriage corrected the disagreements is doubtful. Marriage seems to force financial disagreements underground; it doesn't help them to disappear.

Traditionally, the husband has been the one to manage the money and to make decisions regarding large sums. With the new women's consciousness has come the beginning of the end of the belief that the housewife is performing a volunteer service and not a very important service at that. It is now generally accepted that a woman's work in the home entitles her to a larger portion of the family money than that which she can scrape together for the cookie jar. Some women's groups are advocating wages for their housework. They define the role of caring for a husband and children as an important contribution to the labor force, and they want the government and business, in turn, to provide the housewife with a wage for her work. Although the government and the business community do not recognize such a right, independent studies have evaluated a housewife's labor to be worth about $250 a week. While few housewives would insist on being paid such a high salary, they can take heart from these studies which recognize them as being equal partners in the marriage.

That men are taking on some of the household chores is an important step toward equality in marriage. As important, though less visible, is who has control of the money—not who actually makes it, but rather who decides how it will be spent or saved. If one partner must be accountable to the other for every penny spent, then arguments over who takes out the garbage or who oversees the laundry are merely straw men in the fight for equality in marriage.

Managing Money Jointly

One of the first things an engaged couple does is open a joint bank account. Sharing a bank account can be likened to sharing a bed: whether it works or not, we are loath to abolish such outward manifestations of togetherness. Unless you both have the financial management skills of a J. Pierpont Morgan, results may be more satisfactory if you each are responsible for a share of the family finances. To simplify matters, decide first who is going to take care of what bills and purchases, and open your accounts accordingly. You may wish to maintain separate accounts, joint or personal, depending on who pays what bills, and each have a personal account in addition.

I think it's important that one spouse not be at the mercy of the other for every personal expenditure, no matter who is making most of the money. If one of you is managing the household full time or going to school, you should not be penalized and the threat or punishment of withholding money from you should never even come up. Your work, though unpaid, is a valuable contribution. (Education can be looked upon as an investment. Theoretically, your earning power will increase once you're back on the job market. The mother of one friend maintains that college students should be paid for their studies, thereby recognizing the investment for what it is.)

I'm not suggesting that if one of you likes to spend the day at the race track the other must sit back quietly while the grocery money is put on the wrong horse. Within reason, however (and "reason" is a loaded word here—you'll both have to sit down with pencil and paper and decide what, after all the bills are paid, is reasonable on your budget), each of you should be able to spend some money each month the way you'd be happy spending it—on yourself, on your house or on a luxury for the two of you—even if the other doesn't fully agree. Each should allow the other his or her own small extravagances, whether it's an abundance of parking tickets or an extraordinary bottle of wine.

Investments and Savings

Ignorance as to how much money there actually is and where it goes causes dependency. Both of you should be fully aware of your financial holdings. If only one of you manages savings and investments, the other will realize severe problems in case of divorce, bankruptcy or the death of the spouse who did the managing. One stockbroker suggests that, though traditionally the man in the family handles investments, the woman, generally the primary consumer of smaller items, is often the one in a position to most correctly determine just what company to invest in. The stockbroker pays particularly close attention when his wife extolls a new product. That the public—i.e., his wife—likes the product is a sign that the company is moving forward, that its sales will increase and its stock will soon go up.

Two-Career Families: Keeping Your Money Separately

When both husband and wife have careers, it is not unusual for each to keep his or her money separately. Financial autonomy does not preclude the possibility of sharing. Frank and Janet, who lived together before their marriage, had always shared every expense equally. Their system worked so well—it successfully short-circuited almost all arguments about money—that they saw no reason to adopt a new one after they were married. They each pay half the rent and split even the weekly cost of the household helper. Frank pays the liquor bills and the other items he shops for. Janet pays for groceries, the cleaners and the necessities for which she is responsible. At the end of the month, both add up what they've spent. Whoever comes out ahead is reimbursed by the other. When they needed a car and Janet had the ready cash, Frank paid her a certain amount each month until the car was half his.

More and more women working outside the household realize the distinction between "our money" and "my money." Many women who insist on keeping their money separately from their husbands or the men they live with have come to their hard line the hard way. Janet's first husband emptied out their joint savings account; Kathleen, in a previous relationship, found herself left with thousands of dollars in debts run up by both Kathleen and the man with whom she had been living—but on her credit cards.

When a Woman Supports a Man

Men have been taught that to support a wife and family is a further indication of virility: the more money their wives can spend, the taller they feel. Don't let this be confused with innate generosity. An expensively dressed wife can be but a symbol of a husband's worth. Women, on the other hand, feel no pride in supporting a man, but just the reverse. Even the most unconventional women balk when they are called upon to support their men. They become resentful even if the measure is necessary and/ or temporary—if, for instance, the husband has lost his job. One woman explained to me that she severed a long-term relationship because the man had become a luxury she could no longer afford.

A fairly successful actor, he had fallen on hard times, and the psychological strain of supporting him had been too much for the relationship.

That men as well as women resent being supported sometimes can't be helped. Women have been indoctrinated from early childhood with the idea that any man worth loving will make a decent living and support them. In cases where the situation has been reversed, women may dole out allowances grudgingly, with none of the characteristic expansiveness of a man.

A woman who is making the most sizable contribution to the household may do so with grace and a budget based on a realistic appraisal of the needs of both husband and wife. Again, the one making most of the money should not parcel it out in bits and pieces. When the person on the receiving end doesn't have to ask for money, the breadwinning role is seen as less of a manipulative power source.

If you do have resentments about supporting or being supported, try to contain them. A woman who refers to her supporting role or a man who makes bitter jokes in public about being supported embarrasses not only the other but the company as well. While it is no longer *de rigueur* for the man to carry the checkbook at all times, a woman who makes it known in public that she is the one buying his shirts and his evenings out by paying for everything is misusing her money at his expense. In times past, a supporting woman would have made sure before leaving the house that she had given the man money enough to pay both their ways. I don't think women have to be quite so conscious of outward appearances —no one is surprised when a woman pays for a meal or for movie tickets; however, the budget should take entertainment into account so that he will have money on hand for such occasions as often as she.

Men who are being supported need not stop being generous. Scrimp a little on your expenses one week and buy her a present with your savings. You may both feel better for it.

MARRIAGE CONTRACTS

Many couples who don't think of marriage in terms of "contracts" actually have nonverbal contracts they have built over the years and can skip the following section. But for many newlyweds marrying in the midst of changing attitudes and ethics, a written contract at the outset may pave the way for those good years ahead. The traditional contract, based on the husband as bread-winner and fix-it man around the house and the wife as home-maker and child raiser, does not necessarily apply today, though many of us still take these roles for granted. For instance, Linda, who had lived with her husband for some time before their mar-riage, once married, felt she had to be a proper wife, which to Linda meant the same sort of wife her mother had been—devoting all her time to her home and family. That she had a career of her own and that she and her new husband had established equal responsibilities in the household (before their marriage) were real-ities of lesser importance than her new role as "wife." Luckily, Linda's husband, who wanted Linda more than he wanted a "per-fect wife," insisted that they reevaluate their marriage with a mar-riage contract. Their respective responsibilities, when put in writing, assured Linda that her role in their marriage was a valid one, even though it did not follow the same pattern as the marriage of her parents.

If your marriage is not structured along traditional lines or if you wish to amend certain obligations customarily taken for granted, drafting a marriage contract may help you to define your specific marriage relationship.

Most engaged couples don't discuss their expectations and roles before marriage. How money will be managed or who will do the marketing does throw a pall over romance. But after the wedding a couple may find that romance has a better chance to flourish if grievances and disagreements are aired. Joanna and Peter were married just out of college. Although both were working full time, Joanna took on all household responsibilities. It was months before she questioned her great expectations of marriage—that they might not rise or fall on an overflowing hamper. Peter didn't real-ize there was a problem, since the problem clearly wasn't his. Joanna finally threw down her pot holders and guiltily admitted that she couldn't handle the responsibilities of being a wife. They both came to the realization that the old-fashioned roles in mar-riage were not going to work for them. In essence, they began to redefine their marriage contract. This time, they put the terms of their contract in writing, which helped them to be specific about revisions.

There are many women who don't work outside the house and

whose husbands can't understand what "housewife" means. I overheard one husband compare his wife to a French poodle, remarking that only housewives and poodles lead such pampered and splendid lives. Another husband said belligerently that he didn't see any reason to lift a finger around the house. After all, he had to work all day, and his wife just stayed home; no matter that she was caring for the house and two preschool children. For these women, sitting down and reciting a list of chores in an attempt to enlighten the husband will not be enough. Your contract could consist of a complete list of chores and household maintenance. Possibly a timetable could be included so that when your husband sees you sorting the laundry at ten at night, he'll realize it's a continuation of your work and not a kooky impulse.

Whatever your reasons for deciding on a written contract—I hope they won't be as chilling as upgrading your status from that of a poodle—the contract helps bring to the surface unspoken resentments and desires. Once these have been acknowledged and validated, many couples, when adding to or changing parts of the contract, find that a verbal agreement is sufficient. Many written contracts become ongoing verbal dialogues.

What Does a Marriage Contract Contain?

A marriage contract might define the rights and obligations of the marriage partners in ways which will differ from customary rights and obligations. Marriage contracts might reject, by common agreement, certain rights held both legally and socially by the community.

Names

The contract might specify that the wife will retain her own surname or that husband and wife combine their last names with a hyphen, as described earlier in this chapter.

Careers

A section of the contract might outline the demands that careers place on a marriage. A frequent consideration is the possibility of

a job opportunity for either husband or wife which would necessi-
tate a move. The "whither thou goest" clause—the husband, in
most states, has the legal right to decide where his family will live
—can be amended. The contract could specify what would make
such an opportunity desirable; possibly, a higher salary would not
be the deciding factor. The overall advantage to be gained by one
of the parties in pursuing a new career opportunity might be
weighed against the disadvantages, economic and otherwise, in-
curred by the other.

Finances

A couple's financial agreement may be as simple as specifying
that all income will be held in common, or as complicated as a
corporate merger, depending on how much money is involved.
One couple, at their lawyers' insistence, had a complicated contract drawn up which dealt solely with their quite large financial
holdings. The lawyers convinced the couple to put romance aside
for the moment in order to avoid problems later on. The couple in
fact were so impressed with the good sense of their financial agreement that they went ahead on their own and developed a marriage
contract regarding their personal expectations in their marriage,
addressing themselves to questions concerning decision-making
and their mutual responsibilities in the household.

Most couples don't need lawyers to clarify their financial decisions. Here are a few points to cover if you're working it out on
your own:

Both parties may state that they have made a complete financial
disclosure to each other concerning all assets and liabilities. The
parties may refute the customary role of husband as sole provider
and agree instead to be both responsible for each other's debts and
for the support of the household. In one case, where both parties
are making a fairly equal contribution, the contract might stipulate
that each party will maintain separate savings and checking accounts; a joint account will be established to save money for joint
projects. One may not tell the other how to spend his or her money
unless the money is to be placed in a mutually agreed-upon fund.
If one or the other is unemployed, the other will share his or her
earnings.

Children

This section of a marriage contract might include agreements on whether or not to have children or adopt them, whether the wife will continue to work after a child is born and decisions in the event of an unwanted pregnancy. If there are stepchildren included in the marriage, visitation rights and child support might be discussed, as well as other rights and obligations involving the children.

The contract may reject the concept that the primary responsibility for raising children rests with the woman and may, instead, agree that child raising will be a mutual responsibility. In allocating time and duties, the parties might take into account the demands of their respective careers.

In the case of one couple I know, the husband didn't want to have children for a while because of the time and energy he felt he must invest in his new and blossoming career. His wife, who very much wanted a child, made an agreement with him that she would be solely responsible for the child's care. They wrote out an agreement complete with the reasons for the decision. After the baby was born, the wife, Ellen, realized that a baby was a lot more work than she had initially bargained for. She began feeling resentful until she read over their agreement—in the hope of finding a loophole—and saw that the conditions motivating her husband's decision remained the same; his career didn't let him take time to help with the baby, something he realized fully from the beginning, so she had to live up to her part of the bargain. After a couple of years and before another baby, the demands on her husband's career leveled off and the contract was renegotiated.

Divorce

Marriage contracts usually include a section on divorce which states generally whether one party is to be financially responsible to the other, how common property will be divided, whether one party can contest a divorce, and provisions for children. I know of at least one couple, Pam and John, who initially rebelled against a clause on divorce in their marriage contract, decrying it as "self-fulfilling prophecy." Having finally included it, however, Pam is glad. She claims that now, when she has a fight with John, she doesn't worry for days about what the prospect of divorce would mean for her. She already knows what it would mean and gets over the fantasy in ten minutes.

Care of the Household

Newly married couples may wish to add to their already existing contract or draw up a contract to alleviate areas of stress in their relationship which were not previously considered. A contract drawn up after the first year of marriage can clarify expectations which have turned into unsatisfactory compromises. Problems which seem insoluble may be set right when negotiated in concrete terms. Couples who find that their house and their lives are not in perfect order can specify household responsibilities from who takes out the garbage and when to an agreement that one party will stop nagging the other to throw out old magazines or walk the dog. Responsibilities can be divided to some degree on the basis of who does what best. Joanne thinks nothing of fixing clocks, stopped-up sinks and vacuum cleaners, of building bookshelves or kitchen tables. George enjoys marketing on Saturday mornings and prefers to go without Joanne, whose impatience gets in the way of his careful, if time-consuming, formula for comparison shopping. Their contract reflects this natural division of labor.

Other Items to Include in a Marriage Contract

If you have come to resent your in-laws dropping over on a whim or the unspoken but mandatory rule of dinner with them every Thursday, you and your spouse might work out an agreement as to how much of a role parents will play in your marriage. Other bones of contention—where you'll go on vacations, time spent with friends, whatever your problems are—might be solved by drawing up a contract. Though some parts of your contract address themselves to legal questions, such as a wife's choice to keep her surname, or joint decision-making as to where the family will live as well as how divorce settlements and/or child support might be worked out (you should know that the marriage laws in most states may override personal marriage contracts, just as the states' divorce laws may override the best intentions in such a contract), most contracts deal with the daily workings of a marriage. Drawing up a marriage contract, whether or not it is legally binding, will help to clarify and define your problems. As you discuss certain issues, specifics you may not have considered previously will come to light and you'll then be able to resolve them.

CHILDLESS OR CHILD-FREE

Many couples nowadays are deciding to remain "child-free"; the term indicates that their decision is based on positive choices rather than negative conditions (e.g., they can't afford it, they're waiting until they can move to the country, etc.). It can be difficult, however, to remain positive about your choice in the face of the flak you may get. One couple who had lived together for years told me that questions from contentious family and friends regarding their unmarried status paled beside remarks which arose later as to why the couple didn't have children. Not being married turned out to be a small sin compared to not having a child.

Deciding not to have children is classified as aberrant behavior which requires constant explanation. If you don't want children, friends and family will begin, sooner rather than later, to ask why. It is a rare mother, mother-in-law or even friend who has enough courtesy and enough of a sense of privacy to let you live your own life with no questions asked. The questions will be asked and you will have to fend them off. That you're firmly committed to zero population growth or that you don't want to bring children into an already overcrowded world with a soon-to-be-nonexistent ozone layer are realistic enough answers for acquaintances but not personal enough for those close to you to accept quietly.

For those who do have personal reasons for not wanting to have children, include those reasons when answering inquiries from friends and family. If you feel you aren't capable or aren't willing to assume the demanding responsibility of children, say so. If you simply don't like children, say so. The more well-disposed to answer questions you are, the fewer "buts" and "ifs" you'll hear and the sooner your conversation will end.

You may add a line to your explanation to the effect that you think it's inappropriate to inquire into the private lives of others, even if they're family. I must admit, I'm curious as to why friends of mine don't have children; but I'm patient enough to wait for them to bring up the subject—eventually, I've found, they all do.

9 LIVING TOGETHER

     In the next few pages I will discuss the social problems of couples who have chosen to live together without the sanction of marriage. Used here, the term "living together" does not include couples who spend long weekends together or who keep toothbrushes in more than one residence. We must assume that a couple who live together have made some commitment toward the future, whether it be for the run of the lease or for a lifetime.

     Couples who live together have tacitly agreed to a kind of trial marriage, although the agreement is rarely verbalized as such. With divorce so prevalent, couples may want to work out their relationship—questions of money management, in-laws, children and stepchildren, small likes and dislikes—without the pressures of "forever." Many couples live together with a contract similar to the marriage contract,* but with an additional clause stipulating that after a certain period of time the contract can be renewed, renegotiated or terminated. Some couples think that marriage is no longer relevant in today's society, but most couples who live together for a prolonged period of time do eventually marry when they begin making long-range plans to buy a house or to have a baby.

     Living together, then, is representative of commitment, whether it's made publicly in a wedding or privately between the two people involved.

     In fact, an unmarried couple is today recognized by the courts. Since the Marvin decision in California, an unmarried cohabiting

---

* For those couples living together who wish to draw up an agreement similar to a marriage contract, see Chapter 8, "Marriage."

couple has the legal right to a trial to determine property rights based on an oral or implied contract.

The United States Bureau of the Census figures show that the number of people living together without benefit of marriage has increased more than seven hundred percent in ten years, compared with only a ten percent increase in legal marriages. The Bureau's statistics do not only include young people. A large group of people in their forties and fifties have also chosen to live together. (Some of these people were outraged ten years ago when their children came home from college wanting to share a room with a friend of the opposite sex.) Older people are deciding on living together because society is no longer so conventional and suburban and rural communities are now accepting couples who live together, and the couple's own children are grown and approve of their parents' decision.

Before 1979, other citizens—senior citizens—were also living together, because to marry would mean a loss in Social Security. Older people living on fixed incomes literally couldn't afford to get married, though they might have wanted to. I will discuss the problems of younger people living together, though similar problems exist for unmarried couples regardless of age.

MOVING IN TOGETHER

My Place or Yours

Because living together often begins as an experiment, the experimenters are apt to be cautious. When Kathy and Peter decided to live together, Peter was the one who did the moving. Kathy wanted her apartment to be their apartment in case the union was dissolved. She had been the one to move out in a previous relationship, and she did not want to be inconvenienced again. A friend of Kathy's, on the other hand, moved into her partner's apartment for the opposite reason. If the relationship was to break up, she didn't want to be the one left alone in an apartment with belongings and memories he'd surely leave behind.

A Living-Together Announcement and Change-of-Address Card

The two of you, when moving into a new house or apartment, may want to send printed address cards which will dispatch two messages at once: the obvious information of your address changes and the announcement that the two of you are living together. The card might read:

> Louise Meyer and Ted Lewis
> have moved to
> 1185 Harbor Drive
> San Diego, California [zip code]
> [Phone number]

When one of you has moved in with the other, you may also like to send cards. These might read:

> Louise Meyer and Ted Lewis
> are living at . . .

Telephone and Mailbox Listings

I believe you must list both your names in the phone book and post both names on the mailbox* and on your bell, whether you have moved into your partner's apartment or vice versa—unless one of you wants to be silent partner in this new merger. Some people do opt for anonymity to hide their living arrangements from neighbors, family et al. I advise against it. If you don't want to be obvious about your living arrangement, use your last names and first initials.

Outside of a large city, anonymity is not even a realistic option. Whether or not both your names are on the mailbox, you can't camouflage your living arrangement in a small town, and, very possibly, it's unnecessary to even try. While your neighbors may find your style a bit unorthodox, there's no reason to expect overt

---

* For more on addressing mail to an unmarried couple, see Chapter 6, "Correspondence."

hostility, especially if both of you are members of the community in good standing. One friend, a New Yorker, summering in Vermont, asked a neighbor where she got her delicious homemade preserves and was surprised to hear that they were made by "the companion" of a local farmer. My friend had previously believed that only city people, cloaked in anonymity, indulged in such living arrangements.

Moving into a New Apartment Together

Janet and Frank thought that the added commitment of an apartment which was "theirs" from the outset was symbolic of a more permanent relationship.

Janet and Frank had been warned by another tenant in the building that the landlord did not smile on liaisons such as theirs. Therefore, they never said they weren't married and they never said they were. There's no reason to mention that you aren't married, especially if the truth will lead to discrimination. This won't work if you feel uncomfortable without both your names on the lease. And if you feel your unmarriage is a political statement, you'll be fighting the battle for all of us by making it public knowledge and insisting on your rights. In a case such as Frank and Janet's, however, you'll probably end up going to court with the landlord. The Constitution is on your side, but existing prejudices are not. I see no reason to announce your personal convictions in such cases if they will result in additional problems for you.

Do tell building officials your surname to avoid confusion. Janet was known as "Mrs." in the building by the doorman and the maintenance people. Her own surname was on the mailbox and on her front door. The people in the building either assumed that she received mail and visitors who knew her by her professional name, which, in fact, was the case, or overlooked the idiosyncrasies. (Janet also didn't wear a wedding ring, a fact which, again, could be considered part of a modern marriage.) However, women shouldn't let themselves be fooled into thinking they've done the fooling just because people in the building refer to them as "Mrs." Other people can easily read the signs and interpret their real meaning, but it's doubtful that they care, and, in any case, it's easier psychologically to address a woman as "Mrs." when she is known to be living with a man. Calling you "Mrs." is probably saving *them* from embarrassment. Allowing them to do so is, therefore, common courtesy.

There are times when it is necessary to make sure that people's assumptions about you conform to your needs. Gerry Steele lived with Hal Moffet and was known as "Mrs. Moffet" in their apartment building. After Gerry registered to vote, a policeman routinely came to the building to inquire if Ms. Gerry Steele did indeed live there. The doorman, fearful that all was not well if the law was calling, stated that she did not live there. After Gerry's trip to the precinct to resolve her fugitive status, she assured the doorman that it would be all right in the future to admit to her whereabouts. The doorman apologized for causing her trouble, something he was trying to keep her out of in the first place. He said he had assumed she wasn't married but thought she wanted people to think she was.

The assumption that marriage is better and anything else may be illegal is as close as your own front door. The incident above never would have occurred if Gerry had told her doorman who she was. You don't have to divulge your secret life to your doorman; he probably knows too much about it anyway. You can simply tell him you use your surname professionally. He'll thus be advised if visitors give him that name or if parcels come in that name.

Establishing Yourself in the Community

Corinne, known as "Mrs." in the supermarket (she writes Alan's name on the delivery slip) is greeted with a profeminist speech whenever she pays for the groceries by check. The checker is delighted with the evidence of Corinne's feminist orientation as manifested by her "maiden" name on the check. Although the climate seems right for Corinne to divulge her true identity, she sees no reason to alert the market that she is unmarried.

Since Peter moved in with Kathy Evans, he is known in the neighborhood as Mr. Evans. To keep matters simple, he goes along with it. In order to set the record straight, he'd have to discuss his personal life—a step he thinks would cross the existing boundaries between buyer and seller. To avoid any misrepresentation which may lead to problems involving lengthy explanations, it's best to use your full names from the beginning in all situations. Correct anyone who uses another name the first time he or she uses it.

A Housewarming

Those who aren't willing to play by the rules of the game may still reap some of its rewards. If two people get married, they are congratulated with presents and, generally from close family, with cash as well. The same two people if they choose to live together without marriage have to struggle along with their Melmac. For an unmarried couple firmly committed to each other, there is a way of "going public," however: they may give a housewarming. Of course, this can't be done unless the two of you move into a new house or apartment or finish refashioning the one in which you already live. And don't expect to be given champagne glasses or expensive enameled casseroles—housewarming gifts are traditionally much less extravagant than wedding gifts. A housewarming will net you small but useful items, plus it will announce your living situation to close friends in a manner which is not brash and with just enough fanfare to make it "official."

DEALING WITH FAMILY

Telling Them the News

Though some parents may be against the idea of their son or daughter living with someone without being married, for moral or religious reasons, others may be disturbed with the news because parents often tend to see marriage for a son or daughter as a sign that he or she is settling down—in other words, that the emotional and financial responsibility for that child has now been lifted from the parents. When there is no actual marriage, parents may be confused as to their responsibility to their child.

If you live far from your family you can possibly live with someone discreetly. However, if you don't want your family to be unaware of such a major part of your life but you think they might be upset with the news, there are ways and means of telling them which make it easier for everybody.

Eileen didn't want her living situation to be a secret from her parents, but she also didn't want them to think, as she put it, that "it was a youthful act of arrogance." She confided in them that she was planning to move in with Paul, whom they knew and liked. To allow them to get used to the idea gradually, she involved them in her search for an apartment, asking for their suggestions on the merits of specific locations and buildings.

Paul, expecting more difficulty from his more conservative parents, visited them by himself—they had never met Eileen—and approached the situation from a purely practical point of view. He told them that he didn't think he was ready for the full commitment of marriage, that he was afraid of making another mistake (Paul was divorced). Paul's mother interrupted him by saying, "Why don't you think about living together? I hear that a lot of people are doing it these days." To date, neither set of parents has said, even once, "Why don't you get married?" Paul and Eileen think this has to do with the way they handled the situation rather than with who their parents are. Because they both discussed their plans with their parents at some length, the parents were able to feel that their children were acting in an adult and responsible manner.

Family Telling Others in the Family

Although Eileen's mother was sympathetic to her daughter's new living arrangement, she didn't think the rest of the family would be. Therefore Eileen's mother didn't tell the family (they all lived in another state), and, since her mother would be the one most affected by the family's response, Eileen honored her mother's preference.

One set of parents living in a city distant from their son, Sam, asked if they might tell friends and family that Sam and Flora were married. Sam foresaw the possibility of receiving wedding presents from relatives and friends, and he and Flora realized that if they ever did decide to get married the ceremony would have to take place without the circle of friends and family so important to a wedding. Therefore he and Flora asked that Sam's parents accept their choice. They suggested that Sam's parents needn't tell those who might be upset with Sam's living arrangements, but that lying about such an important event would only cause problems for all. Sam told his parents he respected their values, but asked them in turn to respect his.

Winning Over Unaccepting Parents

When Amy and Chris moved in together, Amy's parents, who were divorced, were very supportive of Amy, whose caution they thought might save her from difficulties with which they were only too familiar. Chris's parents, however, were shaken with the news. They told Chris they hoped he'd reconsider his improvident act and come back to God. They also refused to acknowledge Amy, and they never mentioned her in their correspondence or phone conversations with Chris. In turn, Chris diplomatically never mentioned to them his life with Amy. Amy began to feel she'd become an issue instead of a person.

Though Chris's two sisters, with whom she'd become friendly, assured her, along with Chris, that their parents would never accept her without marriage, Amy decided to act on her own to change her nonperson status. She wrote a letter to Chris's parents. She began by introducing herself, explaining that in spite of the way she knew they felt about her living with their son she felt they couldn't make a fair judgment until they knew something about her. Providing a brief summary of her background, Amy told them where she grew up and went to school, that her parents were divorced, and something about her work. She went on to say how much she cared about Chris, that the two of them had a firm and loving relationship which was growing on a daily basis and on a long-term basis. She also mentioned how much she liked Chris's sisters and that now that she knew part of the family she looked forward to meeting the rest.

Chris's mother, in her prompt reply, thanked Amy for having taken the time to write to tell them about herself. She said she'd heard wonderful things about Amy from all her children. She explained that she and Chris's father had grown up in a certain way and held certain beliefs about marriage and family. Chris's mother did not compromise her position, but her letter was warm and loving and established a sound basis for further communication.

Amy could have remained invisible or she could have given an ultimatum to Chris to choose between her and his parents. But because she knew how close he was to his family she didn't want to create a rift in his relationship with them, or in his relationship with her. Instead, she forced his parents, in the nicest and most thoughtful way, to acknowledge her. They were flattered and impressed that she had done so. Amy had a good grasp of the situation and was sure enough of herself to discern that it was not she they disliked—they knew nothing about her—but, rather, her circumstances. Once they got to know Amy, their disapproval of the situation became secondary.

That Amy was friendly with Chris's sisters helped a great deal. In an analogous instance, parents finally welcomed the woman with whom their son was living after they received a glowing report from a nephew who had met her and liked her. Again, once the person against whom the parents' opposition has been directed is separated from the circumstances, he or she becomes an individual in their eyes.

You can ease relationships with parents by being sensitive to the possibility that they are uncomfortable, not antagonistic. Parents who used to phone you freely or routinely every Sunday at the dot of six may stop calling you entirely once they are told you are living with someone. It may be that they don't want to interfere in your new life or they are afraid that "he" or "she" will answer and they won't know what to say. Suddenly, parents don't quite know how they fit in. You will have to be the one to put them at ease. Why not mention that you miss their calls?

If his or her parents live far away and haven't yet met you, they may be shy when confronted with their child's new situation via your unknown voice at the other end of a telephone line. In this case, to put them at their ease, introduce yourself: "Hello, this is Karen. No, Roger isn't home from work yet, would you like him to call you?" If you make yourself accessible to parents, they'll begin to form a picture of you as an agreeable person instead of that standoffish someone who may be a threat to their relationship with their son or daughter.

WHEN TO BE SPECIFIC ABOUT YOUR RELATIONSHIP

Though most people to whom you have been introduced on a first-and-last-name basis will figure out your relationship sooner or later without your telling them in awkward phrases, there are instances where you must find a way of getting the information across—most notably when you are talking about the person you live with, if he or she is not there to be introduced.

Failing to be specific about your relationship when conversing with social acquaintances and business associates may cause confusion. Discussing particulars about the person you live with—his or her taste in clothes, taste in foods, friends from out of town—may be perplexing to those who don't know who he or she is. But not being specific about your relationship invites confusion through misinterpretation. Cat lovers may assume you are speaking about an adored pet. Or take the case of one woman I know who, failing to come up with anything more appropriate, always used the term "roommate" to define her relationship to the man with whom she lived. "Roommate," she said, always got a laugh at least and was often a catalyst for further conversation.

(For more on introducing unmarried couples, see Chapter 1, "Everyday Manners in Public Places.")

LIVING TOGETHER AND YOUR PROFESSIONAL LIFE

Your professional face certainly differs from your private one; to what degree it differs depends upon your personal style and on the style set in the place where you work. Large companies tend toward the formality engendered by a complex, hierarchical structure. Your friends at your job will no doubt know at least a bit about your personal life; whether your boss and the boss's boss know depends on the climate in the office. One boss in a multinational company invited his subordinate to bring the woman he lived with to a company conference in London. This is unusual. In most companies, those on the periphery, unless they are husband or wife, remain unacknowledged. Often a man or woman who lives with someone is still considered single in the office. Most employees of large companies tend to be less cavalier and more concerned with maintaining a veil of formal propriety in the office.

Many companies count an employee as single unless he or she is actually married. Frank's work demands that he attend a considerable number of social/business functions. The social evenings hosted by Frank's contemporaries always included a specific invitation for Janet, with whom he was living. Janet was rarely invited to functions planned by senior members of the firm, although they had met her on a good many occasions and certainly knew her relationship to Frank. To older business associates, only wives were invited. Both Frank and Janet were aware that Janet was not being personally slighted but merely overlooked in a world where only wives counted, so Frank would, every so often, ask if Janet might accompany him. After Frank and Janet were married she was, of course, invited to every social function.

WHEN ONE OF YOU IS A PARENT

"Stepchildren"

Living with someone when you have children has, obviously, its own set of problems. The "stranger" occupies an ambiguous place in the lives of the children. These relationships are difficult for all concerned, particularly without the authorization of the person you're living with being a true stepparent, in itself a vague and ill-defined role. It is up to you and the person you are living with to give as much definition to the circumstances as you can.

If the children live with the other parent but visit you for occasional weekends and some vacations, the first thing to make clear is that you are living with someone—and to explain this before their arrival. I've heard more than one story in which children are not told the truth from the outset and are therefore invited to form their own conclusions. They are bound to sense the secret and to snoop into closets and drawers for easy confirmation. If the children visit you infrequently, you may think it best to hide the fact that you are living together until they have gotten to know the "stepparent." Children are smart. It's almost impossible to keep such pertinent information from them. Don't make children live with your deceptions. A large part of the resentment a child can build up against a "stepparent" can result from feelings that something is being kept from them. Children will take longer to like your friend if they sense an undercurrent of deception during the initial period of acquaintance. It won't help your relationship with the children—or with the person you're living with—to lie.

For the parent who interprets the children's behavior to mean they don't really want to hear the truth—and many children won't —better take the chance that they'll be angry with you when you tell them than the chance that they'll feel betrayed by you when they find out later.

If you let the children discover the truth for themselves, your talk with them may also take on overtones of a confession rather than a discussion. This in turn may imply you are doing something you may not be altogether happy about. In a talk of this kind, the parent must explain that the two of you are living together because you care about each other. You must reassure the children that you both care about them: you want the children to be part of your relationship; the relationship between the two of you isn't competitive with your relationship with them; the children aren't left out, they are included.

There's no need to bring up marriage unless the children do. In that case, again, tell them the truth: either that you will probably be getting married or that you don't want to get married again, at least not now.

Lies, which end up hurting the children most, occur most frequently when parents don't want the children carrying back the news to their other parent. Whether he or she feels that the ex-spouse would be morally outraged (that the children's values were being sullied) or will just use the information as another weapon in an ongoing battle is a moot point. The children are the ones who will suffer. Under no circumstances should you let your children do your lying for you. Your ex-spouse should be told of your new arrangement in person, by phone or by letter, whichever is easiest for you, whether you think he or she will approve or not.

If you are the ex-spouse who has just been told (preferably by *your* ex-spouse and not by your children or by a neighbor), put your own feelings aside if you have to in order to help the children accept the new situation. You won't ease them over their hostilities and ambivalence if you join them in their disapproval. This doesn't mean you must wax ecstatic; simply keep your negative feelings to yourself while you reassure the children that their other parent's love for them will not be lessened because he or she loves another person. Wait until your children have been told by your ex before you discuss the situation with them.

One very real fear you may have is that the "stepparent" whom your children may grow to love will not be a permanent fixture in their lives. No one wants children to grow up assuming that marriages split up and that relationships split up even more easily. But unless your ex has had a number of such relationships, there's no point in predicting disaster. If you're worried that the relationship lacks commitment and is unstable, discuss your fears with your ex.

"Stepparent"

Most children accept new living arrangements, provided you compensate for your part as the interloper and take care to make them feel a part of the new household. When one woman began living with a divorced man whose children spent weekends with him, the children made it apparent by their frequent temper tantrums and rudeness that they were not completely happy with their new "stepparent." In a successful attempt to overcome their resistance, she sent the children a package of books and included a letter saying that she wanted very much to be friends with them, that relationships such as theirs didn't just happen but had to be nurtured. She hoped that they would feel as she did and would give it a try. After the letter, the tantrums ended magically and the children were more amenable toward their "stepmother."

When you become a part-time member of a ready-made family, you and the children's parent must decide at the outset how large your part will be. You may not look upon this as a voluntary decision—I agree you must do all you can to give the children a good time when they are visiting—but you are the one responsible for defining the structure in which you'll be working, from occasional dinners and afternoons together to entire weekends and vacations spent together. If you don't like children, or you don't like these particular children, and you feel burdened spending any more than a minimal amount of time with them, you needn't accompany them on every afternoon excursion. Make your own plans to shop, have lunch with friends or catch up on your work. To come right out and tell the person you live with that you want to be only a limited part of the weekend can pose problems in your relationship —if the children live close by and you see them often, this, obviously, means that their parent wants them to be a very central part of his or her life—but the relationship can become more problematical if you spread your hostility over the children as well as their parent. You must consider your own feelings as well, and if you prefer limiting the amount of time you spend with the children, the time you are with them can be spent more graciously.

I think it's best, no matter how good your relationship with the children is, no matter if you live with them part time or full time, to let them spend time alone with their parent, as they have in the past. On the other hand, if there is tension in your relationship with the children, one way to ease it is for you to spend time alone with them. Going with them to the movies or taking them to lunch or shopping will help you to begin an independent dialogue with them. As you and the children's parent develop a deeper relationship which includes routines and needs in common, the children will become used to your presence, while you and the children will become more compatible.

Introductions

Children introducing you to their friends or parents of friends need to say only, "This is Karen." A fuller explanation offered by a child would be awkward for all concerned. If the child is prodded for more information, as will most likely be the case after you leave, the child can say, "Karen lives with us." If the two of you do marry, you'll be surprised how pleased—and relieved—the children will be that you have an official title. One woman couldn't help but notice that her new husband's delighted children referred to her as their stepmother as often as they could possibly use the word.

LIVING TOGETHER AND HAVING A CHILD

Your decision to have a child without getting married cannot be made independently of the foreseeable reaction in your community. If business opportunities will suffer or your social circle can't tolerate the circumstances, you'll probably get married before the ninth month. Even if you live in a laissez-faire community, you'll find yourself hurdling obstacles in areas you were sure would be hurdle-free.

Friends who were one hundred percent accepting of your living arrangements will begin to question them once a baby is expected: "Why don't you get married?" or, from the more optimistic, "When are you getting married?" Friends emerging from divorce traumas will most likely be the only ones who don't ask such questions.

Telling Your Family

Either your mother will reach for the smelling salts and your father for the shotgun or, if you and your partner have been living together for a few years already, they'll most likely put on a brave face in front of you and console each other after you've gone. Because parents who have been counting on your marriage must now accept that their wish may never be granted, they may give you things they've been saving for your wedding. One couple were surprised to receive a set of the family silver. Another couple took a more active role with grandparents who had hinted for years that a check would be forthcoming only in the event of a wedding. They simply asked for their long-promised gift by stating the obvious: the decision to have a baby is just as much as if not more so than marriage the tie that binds.

Now is the time parents may ask if they can tell friends and family you are married. If this is not acceptable to you, they'll have a lot of explaining to do to keep you, and therefore themselves, respectable. Your parents will be coming up against the same kind of critical response you are encountering. An incipient grandparent spreading the good news will not have it mirrored with "That's wonderful!" but more likely with "That's wonderful?" To all parents and grandparents faced with this predicament, I suggest you begin your good news with a brief explanation of the circumstances, even if they are well known, so that you can build to the punch line rather than have it completely deflated by quizzical looks or pitying shakes of the head. Just say, "I've told you about Jennifer's wonderful young man, Robert. The two of them are so modern, such a free and independent couple. I don't think they'll ever get married. But they've decided to have a baby. Jennifer is pregnant." This kind of positive declaration wil stop condolence calls before they start.

Fortunately for parents who never pictured themselves winning an Oscar Award for best acting, the need to explain may not arise. If you don't volunteer information about Jennifer's marital status, others may well assume she and Robert did get married somewhere along the line.

How to Head Off Criticism

What you'll hear more than anything else is, "What about the baby?" Although we all know that expectant parents aren't having the baby for the baby's sake, this doesn't mean that parents don't want to give their children every advantage. Annette, when asked, tended to let her ambivalent feelings about marriage show. She explained and overexplained just why she didn't want to get married. Some friends responded with shrugged shoulders and raised eyebrows. They were suspicious. Suspicious about Annette and Tom's relationship, suspicious about their motives for having a child, suspicious about Annette's mental state or lack of it. Other friends weren't suspicious at all: they did little to conceal their annoyance. After all, everyone gets married first. They got married first. What made Annette and Tom so special? What were they trying to prove, for Heaven's sake?

Annette and Tom worked out a public statement which did away with silent accusations and suspicions. When either was asked "What about the baby?" they explained that they had thought out their somewhat idiosyncratic situation and had, after much discussion, come to the realization that the circumstances would not bring about undue suffering to the child. To give weight to their argument they briefly outlined the current divorce rates, the remarriage statistics, the growing propensity of mothers to retain their maiden names. They said they had considered the possibility of their child being ostracized and had realized that such a backward conscience was old-fashioned. That the child would have a hyphenated name made up of both parents' last names or the last name of only one parent shouldn't surprise other children or the teachers. People were much more accepting of others' differences these days, especially in their community, New York City, and what problems they did foresee were minor ones. The lack of defensiveness in their explanation, offered to friends taking an adversary position, melted friends' criticism and left the couple secure in the knowledge that, although the situation was unconventional, it was not careless or destructive.

(For birth announcements and ceremonies for the newborn, see Chapter 10, "Children.")

Your Doctor

Annette's obstetrician knew she wasn't married—she'd been a patient of his for years—so she was concerned about how he'd take the news of his positive diagnosis. As it turned out, he was interested in the baby's progress and in Annette's truly remarkable consumption of doughnuts and spaghetti and lectured her about the fallacy of eating for two. He wasn't at all interested in her matrimonial status.

When she first thought she was pregnant, Annette could have chosen to tell her doctor that she had gotten married. Annette and Tom knew that their disregard for convention might bring some rough weather and were, in fact, rather surprised by how little the outside world cared about their personal lives. Most of the opposition they'd gotten had come from family and friends.

If your obstetrician is less of a free-thinking spirit than Annette's, find another doctor who will be more sympathetic to or less interested in your personal life.

Children's Last Names

You have a variety of last names to choose from for your child. Most popular is the father's last name, which, of course, will demand the least amount of explanation. Some alternatives are becoming common. Your child can carry a hyphenated last name made up of both your last names. In a complicated variation of this, the daughter's hyphenated name will be comprised of her father's last name followed by her mother's, to carry on the matrilineal line; the son will have his mother's name followed by his father's. The mother's surname alone is rarely used if the parents are living together, most probably because Father is feeling left out enough in the birth process and is obliged to be given some credit —and because paternity is such an important part of our male-dominated culture.

Unmarried Parents Fitting In

One unmarried couple with a young child spent a summer vacation in a beach house. They were clearly Mommy and Daddy on the beach; but they introduced themselves to the clique of other mommies and daddies using their respective last names. If people thought it peculiar, they kept it to themselves. You may often find yourselves in a similar situation. I think being straightforward is the best approach. If you are confident and comfortable in your situation, others will not presume to question it.

Overhelpful Friends

Friends may try to compensate for what they consider your unconventional life style. When the social occasion is their responsibility, as an evening at their home, don't be surprised if someone whom you have just met opens a friendly conversation about marriage and its alternatives. Obviously, this person is working from a scenario supplied by an overly anxious host, a scenario designed to circumvent any faux pas which might have come your way had other guests not been previously briefed about your situation. Too much knowledge in the hands of a guest can inspire tactlessness, though the intent is to put you at ease. As a host to an unmarried couple with a child, there is no need to alert your guests to the intimate details of your other guests' lives. They can't be pleased at being catered to and treated as one might treat an aberration.

10 CHILDREN

BABY SHOWERS

A baby shower is generally given by a friend or relative of the new mother. The shower may be any kind of a party, a small lunch at a restaurant for a handful of close friends and family or a simple at-home afternoon with coffee and snacks. Others are more elaborate, with thematic decorations: miniature bassinets or cradles which hold flowers, place cards decorated with baby carriages on an elaborately decorated luncheon table—at an all-out bash. Invitations are handwritten notes or stationer's cards made specifically for the occasion, or they are issued by phone.

No matter how fancy the shower is or how many guests are invited, presents for the new baby should be inexpensive. An appropriate present for a baby shower is something for the baby to wear or a small, cuddly toy. Babies grow so very quickly that clothes may be for the baby's first or second year. One friend of an expectant mother had a shower to which guests were asked to bring something their children or a friend's child had outgrown or no longer used. The guest of honor went away with a newly painted bassinet, a crib and even a small indoor swing which a veteran mother promised would keep a six-month-old contented long enough for a mother to spend a good five uninterrupted minutes on the telephone or in the tub.

Showers need not be for women only. One shower was a large buffet dinner given for the expectant parents of twins. Guests were asked to bring a part of the buffet dinner, and their present to the parents was a joint gift of a washing machine.

Although each guest is thanked at the shower as gifts are opened, thank-you notes written afterward are a must. The host of the shower should definitely receive a thank-you note and possibly a small gift, a plant for instance, or the guest of honor may say thank you by entertaining the host for a meal at home or in a restaurant.

A host may want to give a shower after the baby is born. It gives the new mother the opportunity to show off her new baby, and it also gives her a chance to socialize, something a new mother often misses. (Feminists are staying away from pink and blue as the only choice in baby clothes and are leaning toward yellow, pale green or other non-sex-specific colors. Admittedly, this isn't an easy plan to follow, since the color choice offered in ready-to-wear, easily washable clothes for small babies is minimal.)

It's also thoughtful to give a shower for the single mother. Independent and new-thinking as she may be, she may value the shared support and the small things for the baby that the shower will bring.

BIRTH ANNOUNCEMENTS

New parents may send birth announcements to friends, relatives and business acquaintances. The announcements don't have to be sent directly after the baby's birth. At least a few days are needed for a stationer to print up the announcements if they are to be the traditional kind, or until parents have the opportunity to create a contemporary announcement—indeed, a newborn baby does have world enough and time. A traditional announcement is made up of a very small card printed or engraved with the baby's full name and birth date. The card is tied with a ribbon to a larger informal card printed or engraved with the parents' names. I'm seeing more white and yellow ribbons these days than the traditional pink or blue.

The Traditional Birth Announcement

Neil Armstrong Marino
July twentieth

Mr. and Mrs. Paul Marino
187 Cross Highway

You may take pleasure in designing your own personal announcement. One such announcement sent by parents who gave their newborn daughter their combined surnames read:

Michael Surrey and Pamela Graham
joyfully announce the birth of
Anna Graham-Surrey
April 23, 1979
78 Radcliffe Avenue
Oak Park, Michigan [Zip Code]

I received one from a journalist friend which was composed on various kinds of newspaper type. One couple sent a photo copy of the baby's birth certificate. You may also send a fill-in card to convey the good news; there are many varieties available in a stationery store, from sentimental to cute to just plain cheerful.

If your baby is born in the fall or early winter, a few handwritten lines added to your Christmas card serve as a birth announcement.

Receiving a birth announcement does not oblige one to send a gift to the baby; it is thoughtful to reply with a note of congratulations or a telephone call.

Birth Announcements for Unmarried Parents

Birth announcements from unmarried parents are especially thoughtful because they let friends know what the baby's last name is. You may like to send an announcement in which both your full names, and the baby's full name, appear. (Similar cards may be sent by a married couple when the wife has retained her surname.) A middle ground would be a card which did not include your last names—the card will be sent to friends and relatives who know perfectly well who you are. A charming and simple birth announcement sent me by married friends is readily adaptable for unmarried parents. It reads:

Lenor and Stephen
are happy to announce the birth of
Alissa Beth Eigen
September 5, 1980

Birth Announcements for the Single Mother

Birth announcements sent by a single mother would include her name and the name of her baby. They could read:

Susan Miller
happily announces the birth of
Jessica Ann Miller
March 21, 1980

If you're feeling vulnerable and unsure of your new circumstances, you may think it preposterous to send announcements in reply to which some may feel inclined to send a reproach instead of congratulations. A public announcement indicates your confidence and will, therefore, help to eliminate ambiguous, embarrassed responses to your situation.

Announcing a Baby's Birth in the Newspaper

You may telephone or send an announcement to your local newspaper: "A daughter, Deirdre Yvonne Francis, was born to Mr.

and Mrs. Sidney Francis (or Mr. Sidney Francis and Ms. Carol Graham) of Cambria Heights, New York, on April 8 at Montefiore Hospital. They have one son, Brett, aged two. (If the mother uses her married name, she may wish to add her maiden name.) Mrs. Francis is the former Ms. (or Miss) Carol Graham."

Give the paper your name, address and telephone number in case they should want further details. The paper will take the trouble to contact you to inquire about the names of the baby's grandparents and possibly the occupations of the baby's parents if they'd like to include them in the announcement.

ANNOUNCEMENTS OF ADOPTION

If you adopt a child, a traditional announcement might read:

Hampton and Adele Hunt
are happy to announce
the adoption of [or: the arrival of]
Sara Jane
born November 23, 1980

When Adopting a Child from Another Country

Friends who adopted a one-year-old Korean child sent this announcement:

We joyfully announce the adoption [arrival]
of Kara Custin
Born Sept. 23, 1977, in Seoul
Arrived in New York City on December 19, 1978
Samuel and Veronica Custin

I prefer the use of the word "adoption" instead of "arrival," which is euphemistic and better used on train schedules.

Adoptive parents have reported to me that friends and strangers alike view the reasons for adoption as a public matter. Friends, no matter how close, should not be moved to inquire, "I assume you couldn't have children?" If you have to assume, do it silently. Reasons for adoption concern only the parents and the agency with which they are working. Friends also need not remind the adoptive parents of their wonderful deed of adopting across racial lines. Approval expressed with fanfare becomes patronizing.

Adoptive parents of children of a different race than their own have told me the frequent tactless remark addressed to them by strangers: "Is she yours?" And their succinct answer: "Yes, she is." Newly adoptive parents may lack the self-confidence wrought from experience and may feel they must explain the adoption. There's no need to.

To friends, acquaintances and strangers alike: congratulate the new parents and fuss over the baby.

CHRISTIAN RELIGIOUS CEREMONIES FOR THE NEWBORN: CHRISTENINGS

Most babies are christened in infancy. In the Catholic Church early baptism originated because many children died in the first few months, so baptism took place as soon as possible after the baby's birth. If one wasn't baptized in infancy, however, one may be baptized at any age.

The Christening Ceremony

A Protestant christening takes place during the regular church service or just after the service. If the christening is to be a large gathering, schedule it on a weekday when the church is not being used. Catholic baptisms are generally scheduled for a certain time on Sunday in the afternoon, and parents make an appointment for that time in advance.

The godmother holds the baby and stands before the priest or minister. Other godparents stand next to her. The clergyman asks questions, and the godparents answer in the child's behalf. The questions and answers are printed in the prayer book, so they need not be memorized before the service. When the godmother is asked the child's name, she answers with only the given names and does not include the surname. If the name is unusual or very long, it should be written out before the service and given to the officiate to insure that the baby will be baptized with the name the parents intended. The clergyman then takes the child from the godmother, dips his fingers in the baptismal water and makes the sign of the cross in a Catholic ceremony, or touches the baby's forehead while naming the baby.

Baptism is a sacrament of the church, and there is never a fee. However, one of the parents may give the clergyman a donation just before or after the ceremony. The size of the donation depends on the size and style of the christening. If you're not sure how much to give, ask a friend who is active in the church or one whose baby has been christened there.

Invitations to a Christening

Invitations are given over the telephone or in a short note:

> Dear Jeanette,
>
> We are having Belinda christened next Sunday, the 12th, at 2 P.M. in St. Luke's. We would be very pleased if you and Pierre could come to the ceremony and then to our house for a small celebration.
>
> Love,
> Gerry

Godparents

Godparents are chosen from among one's closest friends or favorite relatives. Some faiths require that a child have a godmother and a godfather; others require three godparents—two godmothers and one godfather for a girl, and two godfathers and a godmother for a boy. A godparent should be of the same faith as the child. Catholics are not allowed to be godparents for a child of another faith. A friend is usually asked to serve as godparent just after the baby is born, or even before. If a godparent cannot be present for the christening, he or she may be represented by a proxy.

A Godparent's Responsibility

Traditionally, a godparent is responsible for a godchild's religious instruction. The term "godparent" has a special significance today. Even those who do not have their baby baptized may ask a friend to be a "godparent" to their child. A godparent's obligation is mainly a social one: a godparent becomes an additional relative and remembers to send a godchild a present at Christmas and on the child's birthday, and takes a special interest in the child as the child grows up.

Clothes for a Christening

Those who attend a christening wear what they would wear to church. The baby is generally dressed in white (this is a social custom and not a rule of the church). The dress may be long or short; it may have been worn by the baby's great-grandmother or it may be brand-new.

Christening Presents

Only the godparents are expected to give the baby a christening present. The present is generally one of a lasting nature: a silver spoon and fork, a silver mug engraved with the child's name or initials and possibly the date of the christening, or a savings bond. Those invited to a christening are close friends and family who will probably give a baby a present in any case. A guest at a christening who has not yet given the baby a present may give it at that time.

A Christening at Home

A christening ceremony at home would take place in the living room in front of a table covered with a cloth or left bare. A bowl, either silver, china or glass, is used as the font. It may be surrounded with white flowers which are laid stems toward the bowl and blossoms facing outward in a circle. The clergyman and the godparents wait until the guests have arrived before they come into the room. The clergyman enters first, the godmother holding the baby comes in next, and she is followed by other godparents. After the ceremony, the clergyman, if he is wearing vestments, changes into his street clothes in a room provided for him and then joins the christening party.

The Christening Party

A party is generally held just after a christening. A buffet lunch if the baby is christened in the morning or, more usually, an informal reception in the afternoon with tea sandwiches and sweets is appropriate if the ceremony is in the afternoon. The style and type of party may be whatever the baby's parents prefer. Every ethnic group has its own traditions. The food once served at an English christening party was the caudle, a hot eggnog punch, and a christening cake, a white cake delicately and elaborately iced. Today a champagne or wine punch takes the place of the caudle, while a christening cake is a rarity. The baby may join the party for a bit if she isn't too tired or cranky.

Contemporary Christenings

Just as with other traditional ceremonies, some parents are altering the christening ceremony to fit their own individuality and way of life. I've heard of a christening which took place in a spring meadow. The baby was baptized with water from a stream, held in a small silver pitcher. The surroundings and in fact the informal and charming novelty of this baptism took nothing away from the dignity of the sacrament.

JEWISH CEREMONIES FOR THE NEWBORN

Brith Milah (Bris)

Baby boys on the eighth day after birth are named during the circumcision ceremony called the Brith Milah or, less formally, bris. The ceremony usually takes place at home, but it may take place in the hospital. The circumcision is done by a mohel, though Reform Jews may have a doctor perform the circumcision with a rabbi present. The bris initiates the boy into the Biblical covenant between God and Abraham that is one of the foundations of Judaism. After the ceremony, there is a celebration with wine and cake. Guests are generally invited by note or by phone.

Baby girls are named in the synagogue on the Sabbath after they are born. The father is called up during the reading of the Torah, and the rabbi says a prayer for the baby and her mother and then announces the baby's name. In some Reform congregations boys are also named this way in the synagogue in addition to being named at the bris.

Pidyon Haben

According to Biblical injunctions in the Old Testament, the first-born, if a boy, was dedicated to serve God in the Temple. He could be redeemed by his parents if they paid a fee to a *cohen* (a man of priestly lineage—usually someone with a family name of Cohen or a close equivalent. *Cohen* is the Hebrew word for "priest"). Today, thirty days after the baby's birth, a *cohen* conducts a small cere-mony at home in which a symbolic payment is given to the cohen (five shekels in Biblical times—today, often five silver dollars), which he usually donates to charity or gives back to the child as a present.

RELIGIOUS CEREMONIES FOR BABIES OF UNMARRIED COUPLES OR SINGLE MOTHERS

Logically, we might assume that all those who aren't married, as well as those who were married in a civil ceremony, wouldn't be interested in a religious ceremony for their new baby. However, attitudes toward religion or toward babies aren't directed by logic, necessarily; you might still want a christening or a brith for your baby.

When you meet with the clergyman, you may introduce your-selves, each using your own name. Explain your family situation to the clergyman. The ceremony is being performed for your child; your morality is not in question here. I assume that the godparents responsible for your child's moral and religious upbringing will also know you are not married. People who disapprove of you would hardly make satisfactory mentors for your child.

The celebration after the christening may be of any type you'd like. The joy a newborn child brings cannot be dampened by soci-ety's outdated rules.

CHRISTIAN CEREMONIES FOR THE OLDER CHILD

First Communion

A Catholic child receives First Communion, a sacrament of the church, when he is about seven years old, the age at which the church considers that the child is able to know right from wrong. Children are given instruction in the Roman Catholic doctrine and make their first confession, also a sacrament, before First Communion. The children in the class of instruction take their First Communion together at a Mass. The girls generally wear white dresses and veils, the boys dark suits and white shirts and ties. Parents invite close friends and relatives to their home for a small party after the First Communion Mass, or the family might go out to a restaurant to celebrate. Guests give the child presents of significance, such as a cross on a chain, a religious medal or a small Bible.

Confirmation

To Catholics and some Protestants, Confirmation is a sacrament; to other Protestants, though it is not a sacrament, it is still an important occasion. Most children are confirmed at eleven or twelve, but actually, if one was not confirmed as a child, it can be done whenever an adult enters into full membership of the church. Before Confirmation, the candidate is instructed in the tenets of the faith, and, if Catholic, and in many Protestant sects as well, it is customary to have received Holy Communion. Confirmation is administered by a bishop or a priest, and normally it takes place in the spring and is akin to a school graduation. Though Catholic Confirmation is not part of the Mass, it is often performed in conjunction with the Mass. To most Protestant denominations, it is made part of a regular Sunday service. Girls usually wear white dresses and veils, though some Protestant ministers allow dresses in quiet colors. Boys wear dark suits with white shirts and ties. Sometimes the Confirmation is marked by a celebration immediately following the service at the church if there are facilities. Or the celebration may be held at home. Gifts are given by parents and guests. Though this rededication to faith should certainly be treated as an occasion for rejoicing, its religious rather than social aspects are emphasized.

JEWISH CEREMONIES FOR THE OLDER CHILD

Bar Mitzvah and Bat Mitzvah

According to Hebrew law, a boy reaches his religious adulthood on his thirteenth birthday and a girl on her twelfth birthday. On that day a child becomes "subject to the Commandments of God" (in Hebrew, Bar Mitzvah for a boy and Bat Mitzvah for a girl). It has become customary to mark the day with a special ceremony. Traditionally, a boy plays a part in the Sabbath service, reads a section of the Torah aloud to the congregation and in some cases actually conducts a part of the religious service. Since women do not participate in synagogue service, no formal ceremony has developed for girls. However, in these days of growing feminist awareness, individuals and religious groups have developed a ceremony to allow young women to have a significant equivalent to the traditional male Bar Mitzvah. Though the nature of the ceremonies of the Bat Mitzvah differs, they are all valid as long as they do not violate any religious laws.

Today a festive celebration almost always accompanies a Bar or Bat Mitzvah. The extent of the celebration varies widely according to the taste and desire of the parents of the child and the traditions of the community. Sometimes the celebration is a simple one with light refreshments served directly after the synagogue service; sometimes there is an elaborate and expensive sit-down dinner the day of or after the ceremony. However, most celebrations strike a moderate course reflecting a combination of parental pride and family joy in the child's "coming of age." Many people feel that the Bar/Bat Mitzvah is the Jewish equivalent of the Christian Confirmation. However, the Bar/Bat Mitzvah differs in that it is almost always a social occasion in addition to being a religious one.

Invitations to a Bar or Bat Mitzvah are usually sent well in advance of the occasion. Only those who attend the celebration are expected to send or bring a gift.

DISCIPLINE

A contemporary of mine confided to me that she grew up in a household with no discipline and naturally equated her parents' nonchalance with noncaring. Consequently she is a fairly strong disciplinarian with her children; she is trying to show them she is involved in their lives and is a concerned and caring mother. I too believe in disciplining children, paradoxically because my parents believed in strong discipline for their children and I think their methods were successful in instilling in us their values and manners. I'm bringing up my daughter according to the blueprint I received at home. I don't use the words "discipline" and "strictness" interchangeably. "Strict" to me means severe, whereas discipline is a system that includes consistency, firmness and a refusal to turn away from or ignore a problem which involves you and your child.

The most important parts of the manners and standards imparted by disciplining your children are those of consideration and respect toward others. Given these tools as a child, a young adult will have the awareness when developing his or her own value system to adopt those precepts to his or her way of life. Parents shouldn't make rules arbitrarily. A rule should have a reason, though that reason may be as dogmatic as "Because I want you to" or "Stop, because what you are doing is annoying me." Nor should children be able to rely on "But everyone else does." That everyone else stays up late or goes out on school nights isn't reason enough for parents to capitulate to their children's demands. But in some cases "everyone else" is a valid argument; if "everyone else" wears blue jeans, or wears their hair in a certain style, it is a matter of contemporary taste, not standards. Parents should be able to make the distinction.

Children, especially teenagers, may not always look the way you'd like them to. Remember that they are in the process of developing their own style, a process which takes some experimentation. Criticism won't help their self-esteem, nor will it help to encourage self-discovery. And a parent's constant prodding has never been known to force a child to conform to the parent's wishes.

Teaching manners to a child is a vital parental duty. Children who are taught specific rules to meet varying situations will find an easier path into the society of their peers and later on into the society of adults.

Teenagers especially need explanations of the rules you're trying to enforce. A teenager finds himself expected to behave in ways he was never expected to before. To help him make the transition from child to adult, give him reasons as to why his consideration is so important. A teenager should be told that this is his house, too, his car, too, and he must help maintain the things he shares with his family. When he borrows the family car he should not return it with an empty gas tank; borrowed clothes should be returned promptly and should be in the same condition as they were when borrowed. Records should be put back in jackets, books returned to the shelf, and so forth.

While discussing the fundamentals of parent–child relationships a mother of four children said of the generation gap, "I think there is a gap and I'm glad of it. Children and parents aren't friends. I don't consider my children my friends, I'm their mother." An overly permissive parent does not give a child direction or boundaries, which all children need and want. A child must have the freedom to try out her own independence, but at the same time that child must be aware of how she is affecting others. Making some of the rules for children means they don't have to take on responsibilities they may not be ready for and may, in fact, be happy you've shouldered. "There are things about my life that my children are just too young to know, and there are things about their lives that I'm too old to know," my friend concluded. The generation gap need not create misunderstanding or a lack of acceptance. To acknowledge such a separation is to allow both parents and children to properly respect one another's ideals and privacy.

Parents attempt to pass on their own standards and values intact to their children. Although children may alter those standards to fit their own needs, by and large they conform to the customs of their community—the customs of their parents. Since American communities differ considerably in their customs and values, American standards are relative rather than absolute. I've spoken with parents who thought it premature for their fifteen-year-old daughter to date and with other parents who were at ease with the boy friend of their sixteen-year-old daughter living with their daughter in their home. I will not attempt here to legislate morality

—morals are always a personal choice. However, I will discuss what is considered polite behavior for children, whether they are at home with their family, with friends or among adults. A well-mannered, considerate child will find cheerfulness and cooperation among peers and adults alike.

Saving Children from Embarrassment

Parents certainly may correct their children's manners in front of others. How can a child learn without guidance? Though corrections may be made in public, punishments should be meted out in private. Spanking especially is too humiliating for a child to be done publicly.

When a young child is to be confronted with a special situation, tell the child beforehand what will be expected. A quick run-through of saying hello and shaking hands is good practice before setting off for a visit with Great-Aunt Marianne who was famous in her day for having the cleanest and quietest children in town. Just before setting out for a birthday party a reminder that the present is for Annie because it's her birthday is a good idea.

Though very young children may not be able to articulate all they know, they understand more than many adults realize. Think of this if you're inclined to tell stories about a young child in front of her. You may regard the child's behavior as funny or cute, but the child may interpret your words as ridicule or embarrassment.

CHILDREN CALLING PARENTS BY THEIR FIRST NAMES

Some children call their parents by their first names. One young child I know calls her mother Marianne. Mother and daughter do at times hear from their public. "That's your mommy," a shopper might say to Darlene in the supermarket, "so call her Mommy." To which Marianne wisely replies, "It's fine with me if she calls me by my first name. She knows I'm her mother." If someone suggests that Darlene is being disrespectful, Marianne addresses the stranger and states that she doesn't think Darlene is being disrespectful in the least. To someone even more insistent Marianne says, "Please do not interfere in the relationship between me and my child." I agree with Marianne that the names by which children address their parents are a matter to be decided by the family and not to be questioned by outsiders.

CHILDREN AND INTRODUCTIONS

A small child of about four is expected to say hello when she meets someone new, unless the child has an attack of momentary shyness, very common among the young, in which case there is no point in trying to persuade the child to let go of your leg or peek around from behind you to greet a newcomer. Save the lesson for next time. Most little children only have to be reminded occasionally to say hello, since they enjoy acting grown up. When a child is a bit older he may begin to personalize a greeting with "Hello, Nancy," or "Hello, Mrs. Lazaar."

Introducing Your Friends to Children

When introducing a child to an adult, begin by presenting the child to the grownup: "Elizabeth, I'd like you to meet my son John. John, this is Mrs. Cummins." The traditional courtesy children extended to adults by addressing them by their title, Mr. or Mrs. or Miss or Ms., is no longer being used exclusively, though it is not yet in any danger of becoming extinct. If the adult you are introducing prefers being addressed on an informal basis, she may say to the child, "Please call me Elizabeth." Whether or not the child actually does call Mrs. Cummins Elizabeth is dependent upon the formality of the child's household. Children who are brought up in traditional houses, when presented with an unprecedented "Please call me Elizabeth," may not feel comfortable in doing so, in which case the child will skirt the issue of address and not call Elizabeth anything at all or will backslide to "Mrs. Cummins." When given the option of a first name, I think a child may address an adult in whatever manner is most comfortable for the child.

As children grow up they often remain in contact with or reestablish contact with friends of their parents. It's up to the older generation to suggest that the young adults now address them by their first names. However, addressing someone by title may be more personal and familiar than to change the long-held custom.

"Aunt" or "Uncle"

A special friend of the family may be called Aunt Maria or Uncle Jasper by the children. "Aunt" and "Uncle" are titles reserved for special adults in the child's life, and some children may balk at using this term, which implies a certain amount of intimacy, for many friends of their parents. Also, some children, and I was one of them, have so many relatives that they have no room in the family for an honorary aunt or uncle. Unless an adult is almost a member of the family it is best for the adult to ask the child to address him or her in the same manner he or she would prefer to be addressed by other children, either Mrs. Oliver or Midge, whichever is preferred.

Children Introducing Their Friends to Their Parents

Children introducing a friend to a parent may, by way of introduction, alert the friend to the manner in which the parent prefers to be addressed, especially important if the parent's last name is different from the child's. The child making the introduction may say, "Mom, this is Julian Bradbury. Julian, this is my mother, Mrs. Medina." A correct introduction once meant that the child be presented to the adults first. This may still be carried out, but I think the order of introduction is secondary in importance to teaching the child to make a proper introduction.

If your child has forgotten to introduce a new friend, you may help by saying, "George, is this Julian? Julian, I'm Mrs. Medina, George's mother. It's nice to meet you."

Children should stand when an adult enters a room, just as younger adults stand when an older person enters. Offer your hand to a child when you are being introduced or when you introduce yourself. This is a good habit to start with young children. The seated child will quite naturally have to rise and walk over to you to shake hands.

Children of parents who prefer to be addressed by their professional title should be taught to make a complete introduction, "This is my mother, Dr. Glass," otherwise the parent has to correct the person acknowledging the introduction with "Hello, Mrs.

Glass," and either sounds pompous or makes the other person look foolish.

(For children introducing an adult who lives in the household but isn't married to their parent, see Chapter 9, "Living Together.")

Children and the Telephone

It is frustrating to make a call which is answered by a child too young to adequately communicate on the telephone. Therefore, a young child should be discouraged from answering the telephone. When the child is a bit older, he should be taught to be polite when calling a friend and when answering the phone at home. (See also "Telephone Manners" in Chapter 1.)

BABIES AND YOUNG CHILDREN

Table Manners

It's best to err on the side of leniency regarding the very young baby. A baby may begin to learn the basic rules at about ten months or when she begins to feed herself. A baby still in a high chair who mushes food and seems interested in the consistency of the food and its properties is learning about tactile sensations, a more valuable lesson at this age than a lesson in anything but the most rudimentary table manners. It is necessary for the baby's development that she have the freedom to experiment with the food on the plate.

A toddler will drop the spoon or fork as soon as your back is turned and use fingers instead, which gets the job done in half the time. Encourage the child to use fork and spoon even though utensils aren't used exclusively. Don't be too strict. Rigid adherence to grown-up rules can make meals a tense and anxious time, for both your child and you. This atmosphere may create picky eaters. Leniency at first on the part of parents is necessary in order to keep mealtime a pleasant time.

A three- or four-year-old may also be told, with some success, to chew with his or her mouth closed. Quite frankly, chewing with a closed mouth is what I consider one of the basics of successful table manners. Success may be achieved through fairly constant repetition—but not harassment. "Please chew with your mouth closed" may be said in a neutral voice, even if it's the sixth time you've said it in the last three mouthfuls.

A parent can also express his or her own feeling: "I don't like to see the food in your mouth." Expressing a feeling is honest, and it also lets the child know that part of living in the world is respecting other people's feelings. However, for some children, telling them what you don't want will only provoke the undesirable response. In that case, revert back to the simple polite command.

I think parents should insist that children come to the table wearing clean clothes and that their hair be combed and face and hands washed.

The extent of how perfect a child's table manners should be is determined by each family. I was brought up with strong discipline and, in turn, tend to be the same way with my daughter, Elena, especially when it comes to her manners at the table. I've spent endless meals, when she was smaller, sitting at the table insisting on elbows off the table, knife and fork used properly, no slouching and so on. I know people who won't eat with their children just because they aren't willing to spend the time getting indigestion playing drill sergeant at the table. They can't remain silent when they do see the way their children eat and yet they don't want to take the time and trouble to correct them. Who, then, will teach the children their table manners? I think if you insist on correct manners at the table from your children it's up to you to teach them.

Be discreet when you correct a child's manners in front of others. Children should learn their table manners privately with the family. Guests shouldn't be put through the annoyance of sharing a meal with a child in training. Say what you have to say quietly and in a neutral tone. "Elbows," or "Please put your knife and fork together," is enough to make your point. There is no need to embarrass the child, or anyone else at the table for that matter. After the child has finished his meal, if he is eager to leave the table, he asks, "May I please be excused?"

There are some parents who take an extremely lenient attitude toward their children's table manners. In one laissez-faire household, dinners with the children generally mean spreading a tablecloth on the living-room carpet and picnicking on pizza or hamburgers. The family enjoys these picnics, everyone is relaxed. Paper plates preclude the necessity of washing up. On the children's many nonpicnicking nights they eat without their parents and with a mother's helper.

When the mother of this household took her children with her on a business trip over the summer holidays, she was most surprised when her ten-year-old asked to have the steak she'd ordered in a restaurant cut for her. "Robin," her mother inquired, "now that you're ten isn't it strange that you don't know how to cut your meat with a knife?" Robin sensibly answered that it wasn't strange at all, since nobody had ever taught her. Robin and her two brothers are warm and outgoing and very polite, and somehow they've been eating all these years. When I asked the children how they learned the proper table manners they said that, although they'd never been specifically taught at home, they observed at an early age that it was permissible to eat a certain way at home, and that when they are in company or in a restaurant they eat in a more conservative way. Robin's skill with a knife was mastered, she said, when she began eating foods other than hamburgers, French fries and other assorted finger foods, and fork foods, tastes she admittedly acquired somewhat late in her young life. I think a balance must be struck between a no-knife policy and rigid protocol; if the steak had been ordered in the company of non–family members, the child might have been acutely embarrassed.

When Eating in a Restaurant with Children

When eating in a restaurant with young children, parents will do well to abandon some of the rules which are a matter of course at home. Children will inevitably fill up on rolls and bread and order dinners which they cannot possibly finish. If rolls are forbidden, the children are apt to become boisterous and bored while waiting for their dinner. For the parents' sake and the sake of others in the restaurant, rolls are the better alternative. As for trying to explain that a selection from the children's menu is a more realistic choice than a large steak, I'm afraid the argument falls on stubbornly uncomprehending ears. The simplest solution is to ask that the uneaten portion be packed to take home. Parents' insistence will only lead to arguments, pouting and bad feelings all around.

"Please" and "Thank You"

"Please" and "thank you" are a vital part of everybody's vocabulary, children—even small children—and adults alike. Children are too often taken for granted. In an instance where an adult would automatically say "please" or "thank you" to another adult for a small favor or courtesy, an adult often delivers a command to a child without a "please" and accepts the courtesy of a child without a "thank you." Some adults reserve "please" and "thank you" for those outside the family. If the words aren't part of your child's vocabulary, it's possible it is because they are not part of your own at home. Family members should make a special point of being polite to one another. Such small courtesies help children to remember that everybody, especially other members of the family, should be treated with respect and consideration. "Please" and "thank you" help children and their parents as well to remember not to take those closest to them for granted.

Swearing

Small children are delighted when in the course of their discourse they repeat a four-letter word and receive a stunned silence or a gasp from their audience. Adults may encourage swearing by stating absolutely that the child may not ever say such a word; repetition, no matter how frequent, becomes a show stopper. An arbitrary rule which makes as much sense to the child as the four-letter word does won't stop him or her from using it. I don't think it's necessary for adults to change their speech habits because a child is present. If the child doesn't hear the word used by another member of the family, be sure she will hear it elsewhere. One friend got her three-year-old to delete expletives from her conversation by simply telling the child that grownups use these words but that children may not. Just as grownups stay up late at night and children may not, she explained, there are lots of things grownups may do that children may not do, and swearing is one of those things.

Older children use four-letter words among themselves and learn very quickly to clean up their language when they visit Aunt Mim. If you're in doubt that your children are capable of making the distinction between Aunt Mim and recess, make it for them and remind them that at certain times and places their manners are different from those at other times and places.

Should Children Be Seen and Not Heard at Grownups' Parties?

That children should be seen and not heard is an outmoded concept now that the full-time nurse or nanny has dwindled down to a part-time mother's helper or baby-sitter. Children are no longer presented clean and shining from the nursery for ten minutes before their bedtime. The nursery, complete with nanny, is a thing of the past. Today children are a part of our everyday lives, and the family room, if not the living room, has become a part-time nursery.

It is expected that children of the host, unless they are babies, will come in to say hello to the guests. Young children may come in clean and scrubbed and ready for bed to say good night and may give a special kiss to those guests they know well. It's not necessary that a child say hello and shake hands with each guest individually. It may be embarrassing for the child to greet each guest, and it is out of place at a party to make the child the center of attention. It's best for the child to slip away to bed from a party that is in full swing.

A small child may be told before company comes that he will join the grownups for a few minutes before bedtime, but that this is the parents' time to talk with their friends and the children's time to listen. (Parents who have no help for their small children schedule dinner parties for a later hour than they ordinarily might, to coincide approximately with the children's bedtime.) A well-behaved child visiting the party for fifteen minutes or so may relax the company and give people who have just met a mutual topic of conversation—the problems and delights of their own children, nephews and nieces or grandchildren. Do talk about the evening beforehand with your small child so that he will not expect to be the center of attention. Otherwise your guests and your lack of patience with the child's interrupting and scene-stealing ploys which work so well when the family is alone might precipitate a tantrum or at best a confused and unhappy child, which will make for unhappy company. I don't mean to suggest here that I expect children to remain mute in the presence of adults. I just don't think children should dominate adult conversation, and discussion should not center around them. But children may be introduced to company; it will help them to gain self-confidence and ease when saying hello to and conversing with adults.

If they join the adults at the table, they should abide by the old rule, "Speak when you are spoken to." Children sometimes help their parents by passing hors d'oeuvres or cleaning the table at dinner. (For more on children helping at grownups' parties, see Chapter 2, "Entertaining.")

How to Treat a Small Child When You're Not Used to Children

Children, even very small ones, have distinct personalities, likes and dislikes. They react to new people in much the same way as an adult would. Therefore, those who aren't used to being around children will get along very well with a small child if they act as though they are meeting an adult. Don't condescend to a small child. Don't talk baby talk or attempt to ingratiate yourself. Be direct when saying hello. Then it's best to wait for a sign from the child that she is ready for an exchange. Children are naturally curious and will most likely give you an opportunity to engage them in some form of conversation. If you're uneasy around small children, it's best to smile and say hello and leave it at that. There is an old saying that horses can smell the fear of a human. I think little children have the same ability. An intense overture from someone who isn't fond of children can make for an unhappy, even tearful child and an embarrassed parent. If you feel cool toward children, don't overcompensate to camouflage the feeling; it won't work.

If you'd like to make contact with a toddler, he will be an instant friend if you let him or her look in a mirror you may be carrying, play with your keys, try on your gloves or, if you're carrying a handbag and don't object to the potential hazards of disorganization, snoop around inside it. A good conversation start which will bring a glint to the eye of a three- or four-year-old is to point to his or her blue sweater and say, "What a pretty red sweater." The child will be flattered if a new grownup takes the time and trouble to begin a friendly, teasing conversation. And don't forget, small children, just like anyone else, love compliments. I once complimented a mother of a two-year-old on her little girl's pretty shoes. The little girl gave me a happy, proud grin, and I realized I should have directed my compliment to her. Children, even tiny ones, must be treated politely and be given respect. Take their feelings into account. Once, while I was visiting friends, their two-and-a-half-year-old ran across the lawn crying, into his mother's arms. In between sobs he told her that the mother of the neighbor's slightly older children had dinner ready and had told this little boy in a perfunctory manner to simply "go home now." He felt the unexplained rejection acutely. You can explain to children more than you think you can. They understand more than their articulation would lead you to believe. It's better to overexplain to a child than to leave the child without an explanation.

Traveling with Children

A friend who has traveled the world with her two small children tells me that people expect children and babies to misbehave on planes and trains, and therefore when children do behave themselves fellow travelers are delighted, and when they don't others are generally resigned to the trouble. My friend has kept her children, and consequently other passengers, happy by traveling with lots of food. If a child acts up, she gives in to demands with lollipops and other surprises she has on hand.

When traveling with a baby, always keep diapers within easy reach. Dirty diapers must be changed promptly as a courtesy to other passengers. During takeoff or landing or a bumpy flight, diapers can be changed at your seat. Dirty diapers may be temporarily stored in bags provided by the airlines. (For more on traveling with children, see Chapter 18, "Travel.")

Breast-Feeding in Public

A mother would probably feel more comfortable nursing her baby in private without suffering the withering glares or the averted eyes of embarrassed strangers; women today, however, are out in the world, and their needs and the needs of their babies should be respected.

Nursing mothers do try to plan their activities around the baby's feeding schedule. Babies, however, aren't predictable. A nursing mother whose baby becomes hungry while in a public place such as a restaurant, while traveling or in a waiting room, may breast-feed her baby there. A mother need not banish herself and her baby to a public restroom to nurse—unless the restroom is clean and has a separate lounge area. No one should have to eat in a bathroom. A mother soon becomes so adept at nursing that she breast-feeds her baby with a minimum of fuss and exposure. The curious will watch, and women who have breast-fed their own children will look on smiling and remembering the joys of the experience. Those who disapprove should do so silently.

Children and Public Restrooms

A father, grandfather, uncle or male friend who takes a little girl on an outing should take her into the men's room when she has to use the bathroom. It's unlikely that she'll be distressed by anything she sees there, but a man might distress a woman and be embarrassed himself if he attempts to take the little girl into the women's room. Women have been taking little boys into the women's room for generations now. Men's rooms aren't designed with modesty in mind, but a small child is naturally curious and will not be easily alarmed there—especially if she has a brother at home. Most families live in fairly close quarters which preclude complete privacy, so the little girl will take her trip to the men's room in her stride. If she does ask questions, answers should be straightforward.

Playground Problems and Resolutions

The protocol of the playground—the rules the children adhere to—may not seem to invoke the best of all possible worlds. They are more like the proverbial rules of the jungle, the main difference being that even the most violent encounter lasts possibly a few minutes. Crying, fighting children will more than likely be fast friends tomorrow or even later today. Children don't hold grudges (as their parents might), and doing battle is all part of an afternoon's play.

When a parent sees two children in the midst of battle, the first instinct is to scream at the one that is yours. Unless blood is being shed or the fight is getting particularly nasty or one of the children is older and is obviously winning hands down, let the children solve their own problems. Toddlers aren't necessarily polite to one another. They don't get insulted (not for very long, anyway), and they can settle their differences within a matter of minutes and sometimes seconds. Children's disagreements may be more disagreeable to their parents than to the children themselves, but try to suffer in silence before interfering. A parent is not impartial and therefore cannot be an effective referee; children may fight even harder if parents are involved, to save face in front of adults. When toddlers fight, their parents, in essence, should make a treaty. If they discuss their feelings they will come to a decision about how to act when their children act up. Take heart from the words of a friend of mine who travels a great deal with her two small children and reports that playground problems and resolutions are the same whether in a park in Israel, France or Texas.

Tantrums in Public Places

I do know one mother who, when her child's screeching filled the snowsuit department of a large department store, looked up at the circle of disapproving salespeople and customers and then retorted to the child, "Wait until we get home and I tell your mother." But in most instances you should not worry about saving face. Your responsibility is to your child, not to your public. An out-of-control child is frightened and is counting on a relatively calm adult to help him or her regain control. An out-of-control parent screaming at the child will only fan the flames of a tantrum. If you feel yourself going over the edge, take a deep breath and let the child scream, until you have regained what will pass for composure. Then step in with a steady and compelling manner and insist that the child accompany you out of the store, away from the swings, or away from wherever the tantrum is occurring. If necessary, pick up the child and transport him or her to new environs. In a different location, with a precise and steady parent at the helm, the child will feel safe enough to begin to calm down. This means that a parent needs a will of iron and tunnel vision to block out a disapproving public. This is not the time to depend on the kindness of strangers. Most of those people staring rudely have been in the same situation themselves and are curious to see how you'll handle it. Ignore your audience and concentrate on what is happening on your stage.

Interfering in Public Battles Between Parent and Child

In a public place, passersby sometimes have the bad luck and disturbing displeasure of seeing a parent lose control and berate a child. The parent has obviously overreacted to the child's naughtiness and is having a tantrum of his or her own. Don't interfere by criticizing and reprimanding the parent. Righteous indignation has no place here. A stranger may interfere only in order to help the child—and the parent. Carla, a warm and loving woman, when witnessing such extreme behavior on the part of an adult, feared for the child and still felt compassion for the parent. Carla walked over to the mother, put her hand on the mother's arm in order to make her presence concretely felt and said to her, "Oh God, I know how you feel." In this way Carla diffused the mother's rage and deflected it from the child. At the same time she had validated the legitimacy of the mother's anger. The mother turned to Carla and confessed, "You don't know what my morning was like." Carla told her she was the mother of two and had had fifteen years of those mornings. Carla's honest concern was a source of comfort to the mother, and her rage subsided.

Birthday Parties for Young Children

It's best that parties for small children not be too elaborate. Too many bunnies popping out of hats or the opening of too many presents from too many guests may be so confusing that the birthday child ends up in bewildered tears.

Parties should be about two hours long, plenty of time to open presents and for the children to play a bit and have their fill of ice cream and cake.

If the children are so young that an adult has to accompany each guest, guests shouldn't number more than four or five. At one such party celebrating a second birthday an observant parent noted that there was an adult standing behind each child's chair as they ate cake and ice cream. The parent remarked that there hadn't been so many in attendance for so few since the court of

Czar Nicholas II. This astute observation should make parents think twice before planning too much of an extravagance for toddlers who are still too young to appreciate fully and enjoy the celebration.

Children of any age don't need an extravagant party. Hired magicians and clowns are festive; they are also expensive. Just as festive is a room decorated for a birthday with balloons and crepe paper and a smiling, enthusiastic adult or two to get things rolling. If your children have their birthdays in outdoor weather, they (and you too) are very lucky. Parties outside offer more possibilities than indoor parties for the children and are more easily managed for the adults. My daughter, Elena, has her birthday in May, and she always has a large outdoor party.

I have one friend, Ruth Anne, whose four children were all born during warm-weather months. Ruth Anne and her family live in New York City. On the birthday of each of her children when they were pre-teens, she carried balloons, lollipops and other small favors to a little tree in Central Park which became known after a few successful birthdays as "Our Tree." Ruth Anne spent the morning decorating "Our Tree," and in the afternoon the birthday child had a party in the park. The children always preferred to organize their own games—tag or baseball and other games. They ate pizza which the pizza shop delivered to the tree, or hot dogs the year Ruth Anne made arrangements with a hot-dog vendor to pass by "Our Tree"; the Good Humor man passed by, too, so the children had ice cream with the cake Ruth Anne had brought. The party always had an alternative date in case of rain.

There are a variety of successful birthday parties which may take place outside the house: an evening of dinner in a restaurant and the theater, or a special movie with one or two friends and the family, or a bowling party, or a skating party followed by sundaes at an ice-cream parlor. These kinds of parties with packaged entertainment are easier for some parents than parties at home, and they are a special treat for the children.

INVITATIONS

Parents may write or phone party invitations for their young children. Older birthday children may like to pick out the invitation and fill it out by themselves. A phone invitation needs a parent to remember all the details and to give the invitation credibility. One ten-year-old insisted that she phone her own invitations, and only three guests out of a possible seven actually arrived for the event.

PRESENTS

Parents sometimes complain that their children's social lives are more complicated than their own—and almost as expensive. I think that if it's customary in the community for each child to have a birthday party, parents might add on the invitation that presents shouldn't exceed more than two dollars or so. If an invitation includes such a preference, the idea may fast become a neighborhood tradition. There is quite a selection of toys for the price: paperback books, puzzles, a flashlight, crayons, watercolors, magic markers, a kite or a Frisbee, hobby books for the child with a special interest. If a child or a parent is handy, a T-shirt or mittens can be embroidered with the birthday child's name or initials.

THANK-YOU'S

Though thank-you's have never been an acknowledged custom for birthday parties, I thought it charming when my six-year-old daughter received a special note from the host after she had been a guest at a birthday.

The card was printed with a message of special thanks, and the birthday child had signed her name. Although this isn't mandatory, a note of thanks from the small host or from the guest thanking for the party is a delightful extra, especially among young children who love to send and receive mail. It also teaches young children the importance of thank-you's.

Young Children Visiting One Another

When a young child has been invited to spend the afternoon at your child's house, it's best for you as the host parent to mention to the guest's parent what the children have planned. I remember one particular instance when the parents of a nine-year-old guest did not approve of their child going to the park alone, whereas the mother of the host did allow her child to do so. The children spent their afternoon together playing Ping-Pong instead of playing in the park. It's important that parents be advised beforehand of what their children will be doing when they visit their friends, in order that they can refuse the invitation if they'd prefer, or come to a compromise with the parent of the young host. If a parent is not told of the plans and finds out from her child after the event has taken place, unnecessary bad feelings may develop between the parents, which could have been circumvented if plans had been discussed in advance.

TEENAGERS

Parties for Pre-Teens and Early Teens

INVITATIONS

Invitations are the responsibility of the host. They are mailed and include the time the party ends as well as the time it begins. Some young hosts may wish to make the party a "grown-up" celebration. In that case the type of dress should be included on the invitation. Invitations also must specify whether or not the guest is to bring a date. It may be considered only proper in some young teenage circles to bring a date. However, finding a date may be a problem for some, enough of a problem to stop them from accepting the invitation. An early-teen party is much more relaxed and less exclusive if both boys and girls are invited by the host.

Even if the party is for eleven- or twelve-year-olds, a parent must be present. Don't leave the record changing in the hands of a baby-sitter. When my daughter was eleven she planned her first big boy-girl party, at a time when I was to be traveling. One of the invited guest's parents said their child could not go if I was not going to be there, even though the party would have been properly chaperoned. I changed my travel plans and learned how important and necessary the voice of a parent is when ten or fifteen pre-teens have become rambunctious.

HOW TO BEGIN THE PARTY

Younger teenagers and pre-teens tend to be ill at ease in these early social experiences. How does one pull together the girls standing and whispering on one side of the room and the boys shuffling and pushing on the other side of the room? You need an extroverted adult who likes and understands children. For my daughter's party of eleven-year-olds I arranged with a family friend to drop in, in order to get the party off to a good start. He put himself right in the middle of the empty floor, clapped his hands and announced above the roar of the music that there would now be a dance contest. The children couldn't have been happier for the excuse to get together and dance. The winning couples, and there were plenty of those—the best fast dancers, the best slow dancers, the most energetic dancers, etc—were all given gift coupons from an ice-cream parlor. Once the dancing and the fun started it didn't stop again until it was time for guests to go home.

WHEN GUESTS ARRIVE

Parents are present to greet guests when they arrive and to make their presence known. Parents need not linger on the outskirts of the party once guests have arrived. Unless the adults are contributing to the fun they will make the guests self-conscious.

WHAT TO SERVE

A fruit punch or lots of soft drinks and snacks such as pretzels and potato chips should be placed on a table which is easily accessible. The supply should be replenished as it depletes. Sandwiches or a cold-cut platter and cookies or some sort of sweet may be offered at about the halfway mark. Just as Ozzie and Harriet always served refreshments to David and Ricky's friends, it's a good excuse for you too to see how the party is progressing.

The daughter of a friend was mortified at her twelfth-birthday party because her parents planned to serve the hot dogs. This brought the parents into the party, which, God knows, was not "done." The parents insisted and inadvertently made a success of the party. The group of twelve-year-olds had separated according to sex, unsure of how to act. The sudden presence of adults and food, which everyone had to gather around, broke the ice.

If the party is for dinner, guests most likely will be eating from trays or eating while sitting on the floor, so be sure the menu you serve is easy to eat; hamburgers or hot dogs or things which can be managed with only a fork are always popular. The daughter of a friend of mine who had been to her first "dinner party" was excited to tell me that guests—there were a dozen twelve-year-olds—sat at card tables set with checkered tablecloths and marked with place cards. Because of the grown-up seating plan, this was voted the party of the year by the guests.

Teenagers and the Telephone

When children become teenagers they seem to spend more time on the phone than do most gossip columnists. Parents may tell their children that telephones are not for visiting, that their purpose is to transmit information. In households with teenagers, family telephone regulations may include no receiving or making calls after a certain hour in the evening, no answering phone calls during dinner, and limiting phone calls to ten minutes. Parents who can afford it sometimes have a separate phone installed in the teenager's room. While this may seem a luxury for a teenager, parents find that they are the ones who luxuriate in the quiet and relative peace a private line brings to the house.

Though teenagers are the ones charged with telephone abuse, I also must include a list of telephone rules for parents:

1. Parents should take the time to write down and remember to give phone messages that children receive.

2. A parent should not pick up an extension and reprimand a child while the child is in the midst of a conversation. If parents have complaints about their children's telephone behavior, they should air the complaints when the child is not on the phone.

3. Parents should respect their children's right to privacy. If the telephone is located in a public area of the house—the front hall or the kitchen, for instance—a sensitive parent, aware that a child is trying to conduct a private conversation, will, if possible, discreetly move away from direct listening proximity.

(For more on the telephone, see Chapter 1, "Everyday Manners in Public Places.")

Allowances

A child's allowance increases with his or her age and responsibilities. The amount is generally prescribed by the allowance received by his or her peers. It covers the small extras in a child's entertainment such as candy or comic books and saving for Christmas presents for parents and the rest of the family. Essentially, such an allowance is mad money. Today, even "extras" such as movies are so expensive that some parents dispense with a formal allowance and give their children money as they see fit. Teenagers who may in the past have been given a clothes allowance are given a modified clothes allowance to be spent on specific items of clothing, since a full clothes allowance would by necessity have to be enormous. Today, many children of high-school age work part time in order to have extra money.

An allowance has been used as a way to teach a child the value of money and the necessity for thrift and saving; it teaches a child basic economics. The patterns by which adults spend or save is begun in childhood. However, I don't think that it is money itself which will teach a child good money habits, nor do children learn to save or spend by the example set by their parents.

Some children drop every penny of their pocket money in their piggy bank. Others spend their entire allowance in a few extravagant moments, and when they need a bit extra they borrow from siblings or parents. Saving carefully or spending recklessly seems to be formed as a part of one's character and cannot be taught simply by reading wise, but poor *Poor Richard's Almanack*.

An allowance is necessary because it gives a child a sense of independence and privacy. Some parents don't believe in giving their children an allowance at all. One set of parents I know reasons that the children are part of the family and that therefore when a child needs money for something special the child may ask for it; whether the children are allowed to do that something special—going to the movies, eating out after school—is not decided according to the money involved, but rather it is a question of discipline and privilege: Have they done their homework? Are they eating out too much after school? Have they just seen a double feature? For smaller items of necessity and entertainment, the parents keep a container filled with change in a kitchen drawer. This, they feel, gives the children the responsibility and freedom of making their own decisions about how they will spend their money. These parents have reported that the children are quite careful to take only as much as they need.

Friends or Relatives Giving Money to Children

Children are thrilled when they receive a bit of extra money. It's perfectly suitable to give a child a present of money for a holiday or a birthday. Parents need not be consulted in advance as to what type of present someone outside the immediate family may give to a child.

Family Dinner Conversation

I once spoke with a man who was a volunteer in the teenage crisis center in his suburban town. He said the center was busiest during dinnertime; that is when the family gets together, and unfortunately when the family gets together they take the time to air their grievances. Dinnertime in many households, he reported, became the catalyst for family arguments. I believe that mealtime should be a time of pleasant conversation. If a parent looks across the table only to be confronted with a sullen teenager, possibly the teenager is sullen because she has come to expect parental complaints during meals. Keeping personal interfamily disputes out of family situations may help in maintaining dinnertime tranquility. Have your discussions privately with the family member in question at another time. Family digestion will most likely improve if civility is restored during mealtime. Children should learn that mealtime is a social time, and parents are responsible for keeping the tone, an impossible lesson for children to learn if they sit down at the table of parents who assume the gathering to be a call to arms.

Dating

WHEN TO BEGIN DATING

Children in their early teens begin to go out together in groups. When "real" dating should begin is a bone of contention in some families. While some parents may forbid their child to begin dating until she is a certain age, other parents may try to pressure their child to date before the child is emotionally or psychologically ready to do so. I don't think one can set an arbitrary age for a teenager to begin to date. The maturity of the teenager must be taken into account, along with the social customs of the community. Parents worry primarily about daughters and their first dating experiences, presumably because boys take out younger girls and because fathers remember what their expectations and aspirations were when they were teenagers—and mothers remember, too. Unfortunately, the double standard is still with us. Though parents certainly may put restrictions on their children by insisting on curfews and on being told how an evening will be spent and with whom, your teenager's common sense and the values you have instilled in your child must be respected. The first-date dilemma was solved for one set of anxious parents when the boy whom their daughter had a special crush on asked her, for her first date, to have dinner with his family. Possibly the boy's parents were a bit anxious, too, and wanted to meet the girl their son had talked so much about.

INTRODUCING PARENTS TO DATES

When a boy calls for a girl at her home for a date he comes to the door. She invites him inside, and if he hasn't met her parents she introduces him. This does not give the parent the right to cross-examine the boy about the evening. Terms of discipline should be worked out exclusively within the family. If you want your daughter home at a specific hour or you want to know where she'll be and with whom, ask her beforehand. She herself may then ask the boy for that information. It may be embarrassing to a girl to have to stand quietly by while a boy she may not know well is grilled by her parents. You are patronizing your daughter if you ask her date to be sure she's home at a certain hour and are therefore implying that he will be taking care of her. I hope you think she can take care of herself.

WHO PAYS

Who pays for the entertainment when a boy and girl go out together depends again on the social customs in the community. Even in communities where adults still subscribe to the traditional roles and the man therefore pays for himself and the woman he is with, those customs are changing among the young. It's perfectly acceptable for a couple to "go Dutch," especially if they go out together frequently. Because prices are so high today, teenagers can afford more extravagant evenings if each pays his or her share. A girl need no longer confine her menu reading to the right-hand price column in order to select a meal which would fit a boy's limited budget. Paying her own way allows a girl to be an equal partner. She may shoulder part of the responsibility of planning the evening. I've spoken with teenage girls who take it for granted

—as do the boys they go out with—that expenses will be shared. If the custom is not a matter of course, a girl may want to suggest to the boy she is with that she will be happy to pay for her own movie ticket. If the boy refuses her offer, she should not insist. She may, however, treat him to an evening at the theater or to a sports event or some other special entertainment.

MAY GIRLS ASK OUT BOYS?

A friend recounted the following lesson she learned as a pre-teen in dancing school when dance cards were still in fashion. When dance cards were issued she eagerly asked the boys of her choice for the various dances. They were all happy to be asked, and her card was effortlessly filled. Only then did she pause to look around her and see the strained, hopeful expressions on the other girls' faces as they waited quietly to be asked by the boys for the dances. She realized she had committed a social sin, and from then on she joined the ranks of the silent, waiting women. Thankfully, the law of the male as the pursuer and the female as the pursued has been altered somewhat; however, it has not been erased. What was once a felony is now a misdemeanor. Girls do ask out boys they know well. They do not, as yet, make the first date, nor do they phone a new boy friend just to chat—not without an excuse for the call. Their fear of rejection, something the boys have had to overcome while the girls sat holding their breath by the phone, forbids it. The teenage girls I've spoken with have not been able to rise above the sensible notion that if the boy wants to get to know her better he will not hesitate to phone, since that has always been his prerogative.

I do encourage teenagers—and their parents—to replace some of their old social behavior with a new outlook on the male–female relationships which may lead us closer to peace and equality in the war between the sexes. (For more on male–female relationships, see Chapter 1, "Everyday Manners in Public Places.")

Curfew

A youngster's curfew is negotiated with parents and is usually a compromise between the parents' wants and the customary curfew for a certain age in the community. Curfews should be negotiated as a compromise between parents and children so that children

will abide by them. Parents, of course, want to know with whom
their children will be spending the evening and what their plans
for the evening are. A curfew is sometimes bent to fit the evening's
plans. Curfews are usually stopped after high school. At eighteen
a young adult may vote, get married or join the Navy. If your
young adult is living at home after high-school graduation, he is in
the eyes of the world old enough to make rational and responsible
decisions, even in the dark of night—or the light of dawn.

Smoking

As cigarette smoking is no longer considered a grown-up or very
wise thing to do, some teenagers are beginning to put no-smoking
pressure on their peers, and even on their parents. If your child
does smoke, and you abhor it, you might try to curtail the habit by
forbidding your child to smoke at home, though I've been told by
teenagers who are forbidden to smoke at home that they do so
when they are away from the house. I see no sense in forbidding
something over which you have no control; still, parents make
their own rules in the house. When your teenager has a party, your
own preference notwithstanding, put out plenty of large ashtrays
so that cigarettes won't be forgotten on furniture or dropped on
carpets.

Many nonsmoking teenagers and children much younger have
been enlisted to help adults stop smoking. I think this children's
crusade is a worthwhile one, and a child may certainly voice disapproval if an adult is smoking. However, a child may say just
once, "Smoking is so bad for you." Some children are like a dog
worrying a bone on the subject of smoking: they finally have a
chance to point out an adult's mistake. A nagging child, or a nagging adult for that matter, may be quieted if you explain, "I realize
what a bad habit smoking is, you must know how difficult a habit is
to break, so please be less strict with me."

Liquor

Liquor may not be served at teenage parties until the teenagers
are old enough to drink legally in the state. Even then, just because
liquor is legal, it doesn't mean it's a necessity. I wouldn't serve hard

liquor at a high-school party. Parties unleash excessive behavior in all of us, and liquor should not be made available to teenagers in such circumstances.

If beer is offered, an adult or two must be present to keep a check on how much is served, and to make sure that certain over-enthusiastic guests don't get more than their share. The teen years are a time for experimentation, and if the beer party your teenager planned results in a few staggering or swaggering guests, be sure that a sober guest drives home a less than sober one, or surrender the living room or the family room as a dormitory for the night and insist that those who you think have had too much to drink don't drive. The adult host's next responsibility is to contact the parents of the teenager who has had too much to drink and to explain that he will be spending the night. Perhaps a weak wine punch of limited supply would serve to circumvent teenage drunkenness and would also eliminate guest's trips to their cars to take a swallow or two from liquor they may have brought for them-selves. Always offer soft drinks. It's best for guests to have the opportunity to quench their thirst with ginger ale, no matter how weak the punch.

Marijuana

Although many teenagers today disapprove of smoking because of health reasons, they are referring to cigarettes only. Some of those teenagers do not disapprove of smoking marijuana, stating that there has been no conclusive evidence that it too is unhealthy. Marijuana is, however, illegal, even if in certain places its posses-sion is only a misdemeanor. Therefore, a teenage host should not offer marijuana to guests. If there is marijuana being smoked, the host may ask those who are smoking either to leave or to stop smoking. An adult should be present to intervene, as a teenage host cannot be expected to discipline his peers.

For Parents Who Smoke Marijuana

Just as the statistics show a higher incidence among teenage cigarette smokers if their parents smoke, teenagers of parents who smoke marijuana are more likely to smoke it, too. In many states today marijuana laws are becoming less stringent. In New York, for instance, smoking marijuana is illegal only if it's done in a public place. Even if you live in New York or a state with a similar law, the marijuana issue is such an emotionally and morally charged one that a parent who allows his or her child to smoke marijuana should still not encourage or permit someone else's teenager to do so.

Sex Education

There has been a long-standing controversy among parents whether to let their children learn the facts of life "on the street" or at home. With sex education instituted in the schools in many parts of the country, this issue has more or less been decided. If your child's school does offer sex-education classes, you may want to inquire about the school's program.

Parents who believe that the place for their children's sex education is on the street should remember that what is passed along as fact is very often the fabrication of the teenage grapevine, and we all know that rumor, though titillating, is often incorrect information.

The best time to have a talk with your child about sex is when the child shows curiosity about the subject. Educators and psychologists suggest that answers be kept short and direct for young children.

Volunteering more information to children than they ask for will only confuse them. One fairly well-known anecdote illustrates my point: When Freddy asked, "Where do I come from?" his mother took a deep breath and went into a lengthy elaboration of the process of conception and birth. "That's funny," the child puzzled after his mother had finished, "Gerry comes from Omaha." Giving a detailed lecture on human sexuality to a young child is giving the child much more than he bargained for and much more than the child can understand. There are many books on the market which explain reproduction to children. Perhaps after you have given your child such a book you may then answer any questions the child may have.

There is no set age when a child becomes interested in the facts of life. If your pre-teen has not already broached the subject with you, don't presume he already knows all. Even in families where no subject is considered taboo your child may be shy when it comes to specific questions regarding his or her sexuality. You might help by initiating the discussion with an explanation of puberty and the changes boys and girls can expect their bodies to undergo within the next few years. Mothers talk with daughters, and fathers with sons, so questions can be answered with accuracy and with as little embarrassment as possible. Single fathers raising daughters and single mothers bringing up sons might ask a friend of the same sex as their child to talk to the child.

Advice Regarding Birth Control

With birth control so readily available, parents of teenage daughters are often concerned—some that their daughters are using birth control, others that their daughters aren't. Parents' concern stems from their desire to protect their children from the emotional upheavals that early sexual experiences may cause and from unwanted pregnancy. Information on birth control should be accessible to teens of both sexes. If a teenage girl is dating regularly and then begins seeing one boy exclusively, her mother may want to be sure that her daughter is aware of birth control information. Bringing up the subject, however, may be viewed by her daughter as an invasion of privacy; whether or not she is sleeping with her boy friend is only her business. An open discussion of birth control initiated by her mother may seem as though her mother is prying into her very private life. One teenager I spoke with said that if she planned to sleep with a boy she would take responsibility for her actions and would not want her mother involved. This, I think, is an attitude parents should respect.

If your daughter brings up the subject of birth control, or if you want to initiate the discussion yourself, the best advice is to suggest that she make an appointment with a gynecologist. The doctor will be able to give her more specific information, and she may be able to ask questions with greater openness. (Naturally, if a parent's religious views do not permit the use of birth control, a parent wouldn't advocate it for a child.)

Those mothers who are opposed to their teenage daughters having sexual intercourse should say so. However, I do think they have a responsibility to their children to provide them with information if they are asked.

CHILDREN

On the other hand, some mothers take the initiative and see to it that their daughters have some kind of birth control, regardless of their daughters' feelings. Birth control should not be treated as a teenage rite of passage. Such invasive action on the part of a parent is inappropriate. A mother has no business making that kind of decision for her daughter. A mother who insists on birth control for her daughter may also be pushing a young girl into having sexual intercourse because she assumes that it's what her mother wants her to do.

When a Grown Child Brings Home a Friend of the Opposite Sex

Years ago, when the grandmother of a friend invited two unmarried couples to spend the weekend, she circumvented the problem by putting all four in the same bedroom. She reasoned that if she split them up, according to sex, into two separate bedrooms, they could switch during the night. I must bow to Grandmother's logic. If all four didn't sleep too peacefully in their dormitory setup, I'm sure Grandmother did.

When children have graduated from high school and leave home for college or to go to work and live on their own, parents have little control over their lives. Children home for a visit must remember that it is their parents' house and that therefore parents are entitled to make the rules. Some parents are casual and accepting of their children's contemporary life style and will put an unmarried couple in the same bedroom. Others, however, vary in degrees from being ill at ease to being utterly appalled with this type of arrangement. If there are younger children in the house, parents may feel that an unmarried couple sharing a room sets a bad example or creates a situation which needs explaining. If your child suggests you are being hypocritical by refusing to accept his or her situation, you may explain that while in your house your child must abide by your rules, and that you would be the hypocrite if, on your turf, you agreed to do something you disapproved of only to appease your child.

This problem doesn't occur only among young adults and their parents. Sometimes the child/parent roles are reversed. Many older people are deciding against marriage, and sometimes their children do not approve. If you are one of those adult children and don't want your parent and his or her friend of the opposite sex to share a bed under your roof, because you wouldn't know how to explain the situation to your friends and would never sanction a similar arrangement in your house for your own children, talk to your parent before he or she arrives and discuss the possibilities of making reservations for the parent and friend in a nearby hotel or motel. Your parent will no doubt understand your feelings. After all, he or she most likely brought you up to believe strongly in the morality of marriage, and should therefore be pleased that the values taught to you as a child still prevail in your house.

HIGH-SCHOOL PROMS

Even the most casual and untraditional-minded teenagers transmogrify into sophisticated and perfectly groomed young adults for a prom. Teenagers who do not subscribe to adult traditions do, however, have traditions of their own, and the prom is one of them. A high-school prom is a graduating celebration and is therefore not taken lightly by its participants.

An Invitation

Proms today may be formal, semiformal or informal. For a formal prom the invitations might read:

The Senior Class
of John Jay High School
requests the pleasure of your company
at the Senior Prom
on Saturday, the eighth of June
at nine o'clock
at the Waccabuc Country Club
105 River Road

R.S.V.P.   *Black Tie*

A semiformal or informal invitation may be left to the prom committee's own devices.

At a coeducational school, boys customarily ask girls, though girls may of course invite a boy from another town or another school. The person who issues the invitation is, of course, responsible for paying for the tickets. If it is customary in the community for a girl to wear flowers, the boy will generally ask the girl what color dress she will be wearing, or he may ask what color or kind of flower she would like. A girl might also suggest the kind of flower she would prefer, since she may have something specific in mind, possibly a flower for her hair, which would compliment what she will be wearing. She should not, however, suggest an orchid or anything equally extravagant.

Flowers are sent the day of the prom, or the boy may bring them when he calls for his date in the evening. Flowers may be arranged in a corsage, which can be the type that ties around the wrist. The arrangement may also be one which is carried or fastened in the hair.

THE COLLEGE WEEKEND

Today so many colleges are coeducational that the official college weekend with all its pomp and ritual is becoming an anachronism. Now that men and women see each other all week, the weekends aren't so special. Of course, men and women attending different colleges still visit one another, but their visits are more relaxed and flexible. Some vestigial customs still apply to today's college visit. The visitor generally pays his or her own transportation. Traditionally a man paid for all expenses during the weekend other than tickets for a dance or concert which, if he were visiting the woman, she would have reserved in advance. Today, a couple may want to work out their financial arrangements for the weekend in a way which would best suit both their budgets and independently of past customs.

DEBUTS

It used to be that a young girl was sheltered at home among close family and relatives. When she was about eighteen she was then "presented" to society at a formal ball. Since most parents today lead more sheltered lives than their teenage children, debut parties are now only symbolic of a young woman entering adult society. A debut may be a private dinner dance or late dance, or a debut may take the form of a late-afternoon reception to which are invited mainly parents' friends and acquaintances. The party is given by the young woman's parents or sometimes her grandparents. At a dance, the young woman wears a long white dress or a dress of a pastel color. At an afternoon reception she would wear a short white or light-colored dress. At a debut the mother, or whoever is presenting the young woman, stands first to receive beside the debutante. If the mother is presenting her daughter, the father may stand last to receive or he may prefer to circulate among the guests. (For invitations to a debut, see Chapter 6, "Correspondence.")

Today the cotillion or formal group debut has by and large taken the place of the private dance. At a cotillion a group of young women make their debut together at a dinner dance or a late dance. The cotillion is generally sponsored by an organization and may be a charity function planned by a committee. The young women pay for the tickets of their escorts (usually each has two escorts), and their families are allotted an equal number of invitations for which the families also pay.

At the cotillion the young women may walk in a procession with their fathers and stand with their parents in a receiving line. Sometimes at large cotillions only the young women make up the receiving line.

Friends and escorts send flowers which are banked together in back of the receiving line of the area where the procession will take place. Committee members may have dinners for the young women and their escorts before the dance, or friends may give dinner parties. The debutante wears a long dress in white or a pastel. Her first dance is with her father, and then she dances with her escorts. Her father then dances with whoever is presenting his daughter.

11 DIVORCE

TELLING PEOPLE: WHOM TO TELL AND WHAT TO TELL THEM

In the midst of a divorce, your concerns will naturally revolve around yourself; but you must also be aware that your divorce affects other people in your social and business worlds. There will be people who want to know, people you want to know, people who need to know. While the last thing you may want to do at this time is make a public announcement, a divorce is news, and your only alternative is to try to keep secret what is essentially public. Most friends and interested acquaintances will make it their business to find out about your divorce in any case, so why not tell them yourself? The attempted cover-up, deliberate or not, is more difficult to carry off and brings with it many more problems than the truth. By "truth," I mean very simply the *fact* of your divorce, not the whys.

Telling people, especially strangers, about your divorce may be one of the hardest things you'll have to do. It makes real what has been until that moment an abstract decision. When strangers see you as "divorced" you'll begin to see yourself in their reflection. Their identification of you is your conformation that the outside world sees you—and therefore you must begin to see yourself—in a new and unfamiliar light. Although telling people won't be easy, there are some people you must tell to make it easier on them—and yourself as well.

Your Children's School

It will benefit your children to tell the school about your divorce. Make an appointment with your children's teachers, one at a time, so that they won't be left in the dark if your children demonstrate any difficulties in adjusting to the divorce. You may also wish to tell the school administration, but this is of secondary importance. Although the administration could be the one to tell the teachers, the story would be clearer if the teacher heard it firsthand. Also, it might be helpful and comforting to learn how your children are doing in school from someone who sees them regularly. But don't go to see the teachers behind your children's backs. Be sure to tell them what you are planning.

Whom You Don't Have to Tell

If it's very hard for you to announce your new status—one woman told me it was two years before she told anyone she was divorced—take heart in knowing that there are a lot of people you won't have to tell at all.

In the first category let's put everyone who will read the simple signs—the household worker, the doormen and so on. They'll find out in their own way, without your help.

The second category includes casual friends and acquaintances whom you see only occasionally. They may or may not have heard —you yourself need tell them only when you are meeting face to face and they unwittingly ask after your spouse. Don't expect them to have heard. Contrary to your fantasy, not everyone is talking about you. One divorced woman I know ran into a couple she hadn't seen in years and was startled when they innocently asked where her husband was. She expected everyone to have heard of her circumstances. But divorces these days are so numerous that most of us give them (other people's, that is) little more than a cursory nod of acknowledgment. Your divorce is endlessly fascinating only to you. Others neither need nor expect an explanation.

So, I repeat, you need tell casual acquaintances only when the situation calls for it. And whenever you tell anyone, be careful not to overexplain and say too much. One woman said she told all her friends the sexual problems which led to her divorce as an indirect plea to them to "please like me and understand me and be *my* friend (it wasn't my fault)." Try to remember that the only information you are called upon to give is legal: you are divorced or separated. Which friends you tell more and how much you tell them is up to you.

How Not to Tell People You've Just Met

One insightful divorced man has noticed that all divorced people refer to their ex-husband or ex-wife—never specifically to their divorce—somewhere in the first five minutes of conversation with someone new. Just like someone who has gone to Harvard, they'll let you know, no matter how long ago it was.

If you feel you must get this information across, by all means do. But stop and think the next time the compulsion overtakes you— the pressure to tell all is coming from you. Unless your divorce is relevant to the conversation, there's no need to remark on it. A divorce decree, unlike a Harvard diploma, is not an accomplishment worthy of dropping into conversation. One woman says that if she tells people about her divorce immediately upon meeting them, she knows she's having a bad day—she's being defensive. Another divorced person says he realizes he's apologizing when he mentions his divorce right away. In order to curtail his divorce information, he now plays a game when he meets new people. For the first fifteen minutes of conversation, he tries to give them as little personal information as he can. By the end of that time the urge to tell has usually passed, and if and when the subject of his divorce does come up it does so in the natural flow of conversation.

Telling Those at Your Place of Work

One woman I know cheerfully poked her head into her boss's office one afternoon and asked if she could leave a bit early to "go and see my lawyer, I'm getting a divorce." Luckily, the incipient divorcée had not been distracted or depressed at work and had managed, in an office where personal problems are often shared, to maintain silence until her divorce was more or less officially proceeding. She was correct to bring up her circumstances when she did, when the divorce was becoming a reality, and how she did, with a short statement of fact.

Although you may be doubtful about introducing a personal problem into your place of work, it's only fair to tell your boss and co-workers—again, with a short statement of fact at an appropriate time. It's more embarrassing for them to ask about your spouse and then have the news sprung on them. A short statement of fact will also cut down on rumors. For most people, a separation or divorce takes a heavy emotional toll—and it shows. People will know that something is wrong, so tell them, when the time is right. But don't expect the support you get from family and friends. Business is still business. One man I know was so overwhelmed by his divorce that he walked through the day zombielike, getting only a minimum amount of his work done and silently beseeching his associates for support. Of course, you can't always hide your emotional problems, and giving them the stiff upper lip can be just as unrealistic as pretending they don't exist. Wallow in your self-pity if you must (we all do upon occasion), but seek professional help if you suspect that you're not healing properly (most likely you'll sense when you've gone too far). At best, you can alienate those at your place of work; at worst, you can get fired—at a time when you probably need your job the most—if you persist in publicizing your unhappiness or are unable to do your work.

If you are very friendly with the people in your office, or some of them, and want to tell them more than the cold, hard facts, do so. But wait until after business hours.

Separation Announcements

Written announcements are generally reserved for special occasions, occasions which are usually festive. A divorce or separation announcement is hardly festive and is turning a private decision into a public matter. We can all say how appalled we are at such an idea, but it is, in fact, a perfectly reasonable idea if you are having difficulties letting people know or if you want to let people know who live far from you, without having to write a letter (and, therefore, an explanation). And let's face it, a simple statement of fact coming from you instead of rumors from the neighbors could save you a lot of explaining and cut down on others prying into your life.

In order to blunt the edges of such an announcement, you may put something as useful as a change-of-address card to a dual purpose. It may read:

> *Sigrid, Tommy and Kim Newell*
> *are now living at*
> *105 North Street*
> *New London, Connecticut [zip code]*

I once received a card which took this idea one step further. It was a New Year's greeting, change-of-address and separation card all in one! I think it's worth reprinting here for those who can still maintain the holiday mood even though they may be getting divorced at Christmas.

> *Andrea, Freddie and Joe Lanier*
> *send you the best for 1980*
> *from their new home at*
> *117 Earle Drive*
> *Santa Monica, California [zip code]*

A name-change announcement can serve the same purpose.

Telling Friends

Divorced people, after the initial trauma of their separation, generally want to put their marriage behind them. This is difficult to do when friends insist upon bringing it up. But since friends *will* bring up the subject, in the beginning, at least, and even if you're careful not to, you'll have to answer some of their questions, however cursorily. It may also be difficult for you not to gush forth with the entire story at first prodding. The problem is to find the line between telling nothing, which might hurt your friends' feelings, and telling all, which might hurt you. If you've just separated, listing for all who ask all your grievances, some of which are private matters to be shared only between husband and wife, will certainly hurt your chances, if there are any, for a reconciliation. The more you talk about the evils of your marriage, the more difficult it will be for you to reconcile those differences. And those who tell friends more than they had intended find themselves resenting those friends for being such good listeners.

There's also the chance that friends who were indeed curious about your circumstances will soon tire of your constant complaints. Those who ask for the whole story are not necessarily promising their support. More often than not, what they want to hear is "all the dirt," *not* all the details, *not* all your pain. Some friends (not those one or two close friends with whom you'd naturally talk about it personally) may rise to the occasion and supply comfort and sympathy, but there's a good chance that the form their comfort and sympathy will take will not soothe your rage but supply you with fresh ammunition—and fresh pain.

Don't demand of anyone that he or she take your side against your spouse. One of the most valued attributes in friends is loyalty. Over the years, you have probably depended upon their loyalty to your spouse as well as to yourself. Don't ask them to suddenly betray that trust.

YOUR DIVORCE AND YOUR MARRIED FRIENDS

There's no such thing as a perfect marriage, and divorce brings out that fact all too clearly. To expect solace from all your married friends may be wishful thinking; your divorce may have them concerned about their own marriages. I know of two women who were friends for twenty-five years; they stopped talking during the time one of them was getting divorced. After the second woman separated from her husband a few months later, she called her old friend to patch up their relationship and confessed to her that she had been jealous of her courage in getting a divorce.

Even those with a marriage in good condition may step back during a friend's divorce. As one man I know said, "It's always interesting when someone is having an affair; but when a couple separates, it's just too scary."

FRIENDS TAKING SIDES

While you and your spouse may have had great times with the couple next door, you'll find it impossible for both of you to maintain a friendship of equal intensity after the separation. First, they'll see you one evening and your soon-to-be-ex the next. Soon, without actually taking sides, they'll begin to favor one of you over the other, and you'll begin to notice. They'll see you on Sunday afternoon with the children—but they saw your almost-ex on Saturday night with a date. That they've chosen one of you over the other should not be seen as a betrayal. To continue to see both of you is a variety of acute voyeurism. One divorced man finally had to be the one to put a stop to such a situation. He said he felt as though his dearest friends were now taking a secret kind of excitement in studying both him and his ex, weighing two sets of stories, watching to see what developed in each newly divorced person's life. There's no point in setting yourself and your ex up in competition for the favors of old friends. Who keeps which friends cannot be turned into a game. You'll continue to see those friends with whom you have the most in common. The lives of divorced people do change, sometimes fairly drastically, but often for the better. You'll soon make a new life for yourself which can accommodate some of your old friends, but certainly not all of them.

It's a nice thought to think that the surviving couple, your close friends, will split their friendship with you. Though the two women and the two men may have had what seemed at one time to be an unbreakable bond, you'll find it surprisingly breakable under the weight of a broken marriage. Your friends may feel too vulnerable to each keep one of you as a friend. Couples tend to present themselves as such, especially during times of trouble. Your split can be extremely threatening to married people close to you.

One divorced friend is emphatic on the subject of your involvement with friends in the period following your divorce. She feels strongly that the mourning period for your family and good friends, which she describes as a kind of homesickness, should not be prolonged. Specifically, my friend suggests, get away from people who remind you of your ex. Of course, there will be a time in your life when you can't make any new friends, can't get a job, can't travel—all the things your psychiatrist is telling you to do—because you can't even get out of bed. But when you do get out of bed, you'll soon realize that trying to keep afloat old friendships which are fast fading is one way of prolonging your period of mourning.

HANDLING GOSSIP

Gossip during divorce is inevitable. Generally, it dies down quickly; no one wants to be absorbed in another's misery for any longer than the quick dip it takes to feel refreshed. Sometimes gossip becomes outrageous, of course. I heard of one instance where the husband was told—and given what appeared to be substantial proof—that his wife was a lesbian. The husband was ready to believe any and all bad news, although the "proof" was fabricated. His wife demanded, rightly, that he tell her where he had heard the rumors. She then called each person—there were two or three—and confronted them. She said, "I understand you've told Peter that I am a lesbian. Do you know this to be true about me? You must call my husband and tell him you do not know that I'm a lesbian and that your story was mere gossip." All those concerned corrected their story. (Ironically, the woman was in fact having an affair with a younger man and kept her secret so well because she was afraid her husband would use it against her in the divorce.)

It is rare, but frightening and possibly damaging as well, to watch rumors about you mature and take the place of fact. If this does happen to you, confront the gossipers and insist that they retract their stories and that they do so personally to whomever they told.

There's another kind of gossip that you must avoid—retroactive gossip, usually told to you by people who are hiding behind the guise of well-meaning and supportive friendship. They'll begin right after the two of you have split up, with such choice nuggets as "Lorraine flirted with every man at the office, and didn't you see her last spring at the Andersons' party with Paul Shapiro? We were all sure you'd noticed. We felt terrible." You may be horrified when friends go on in this vein, but probably also fascinated—like a moth with a flame. Don't allow yourself to listen; change the subject or make an excuse to leave. Whether the information they're feeding you is true or not is no longer of any importance. Listening can only make you feel terrible and will be beneficial only in that you have now seen your friends if not in their true colors, then surely in their worst ones. Stay away.

GOSSIPING ABOUT YOUR EX

Don't you be tempted into a similar transgression—gossiping about your ex. You'll feel guilty, sooner or later, about giving away the secrets of a marriage; although the marriage may no longer exist, the secrets will. If there is any chance for a reconciliation, sharing intimate details of your life together with outsiders can end that chance. Even if your separation is final, when you gossip about an ex-spouse you also breed gossip about yourself: after all, what kind of person could *you* be to put up with such a person for so many years? What did you do to provoke such awful behavior?

WHEN YOU AND YOUR EX ARE INVITED TO THE SAME PARTY

Often, at the beginning of a separation, friends will find it hard to accept the separation, almost as hard as you do. If friends have a large party, they'll probably ask you both. If they have any sensitivity—or just plain sense—they'll also inform you both of your plans. The two of you can decide together which one will accept the invitation; if you aren't on such cooperative terms, at least you'll each know beforehand that the other one will be there.

I advise caution in both of you going to the same party. I remember all too vividly what happened to my friend Helena. Helena was perfectly blasé about attending a party to which her ex had been invited—until she saw him, sitting at the feet of a woman, gazing into her eyes, clasping her hands in a soulful gesture. What made it even worse was that Helena's own escort was the one to point him out—he didn't know who he was, he just thought he looked silly. Helena, flustered, blurted out, "That's my husband," and fled the room.

I'm not claiming that seeing your ex at a party will prove acutely embarrassing for you, but it certainly won't be as easy as you might think. I think it's wisest for only one of you to choose to go, unless a lot of time has passed and you're finally healed. After all, you're going to a party to have a good time, not to worry about how you'll appear to your ex or how the both of you will appear to other people. As Marina put it when asked if she'd mind going to the same party as her recently separated husband, "If we wanted to go to parties together, we'd still be married."

DECLINING AN INVITATION

Although your reasons for not wanting to go to a party when you know your ex will be a guest may be as sensible as the one Marina articulated, you can be so blunt only with close friends; an invitation to a party is not an invitation for confidences. To an acquaintance you can simply decline with regrets, explaining briefly that you're busy that night but you appreciate her thinking of you.

There will, of course, come a time when your divorce is far behind you and you can accept any invitation you choose even though you know your ex has also accepted.

FOR FRIENDS, WHEN YOU WANT TO INVITE BOTH SIDES OF A SEPARATED COUPLE

If you're having a large party, you certainly may invite both sides of a divorcing couple, but do tell each in advance that the other has been invited; it's only fair to let them decide if they both want to go and, if not, which one will stay home. I think it's best to give each one the option to say no. Don't make the decision for them by inviting only one of them, unless you've taken sides and are already divorcing one of them, too. Their situation is new to their friends as well as to them; let them come to terms with it. As time goes on, you'll most likely be seeing only one half of the couple, but in the early stages of friends' divorces no one is quick to divide up the friendships.

Not asking either member of the couple is also not satisfactory. You'll want your friends at your party, and newly separated or divorced people need all the invitations their friends can muster.

Smaller parties call for different rules. If you're having a fairly small dinner party, invite either one half of the couple or the other, not both. There are enough dinner parties to go around. One separated couple invited to the same small party realized too late that they were there to provide an evening of titillation for the other guests. Hire musicians if you want entertainment. Never rely on the possible animosity of your guests toward one another to ignite the party. The best hosts expend considerable energy devising guest-list formulas to circumvent the spark which they know can just as easily burst into a forest fire. Guests with diverse opinions and points of view make for an exciting evening. Inviting people who are emotionally incompatible, as divorcing couples always are, will, at the very least, be embarrassing for you and your other guests and can result in destroying your party and your friendships. Examine your motives. Are you thinking of effecting a reconciliation? Do you think their confrontation at your party will be entertaining? In the first case, you're leaning toward being a busybody; in the second, your good sense seems to have been clouded by malice. Only Shakespeare could entertain a Montague and a Capulet at the same party with any success.

MAKING THE TRANSITION FROM MARRIED TO UNMARRIED

Religious Rituals for the Divorcing Couple

Since divorce is, in essence, the death of a marriage, some people are recognizing that such an event should be acknowledged and shared among the family and close friends. Since the church pays such a significant part in the initiation of a relationship—the marriage—it too should play a part in its termination. Some churches today offer a religious ceremony as a part of the divorce. The minister or rabbi performing the service may talk about the reasons for the end of the marriage, the good that came out of the union, children, for instance, and the feelings of individual members of the family. Both spouses can also participate, and their children as well.

If you are getting divorced you might ask your minister or rabbi about holding such a service if you think it will help you. Following is an example of a divorce ritual taken from the United Methodist Church's booklet *Ritual in a New Day: An Invitation*.

A RITUAL IN WHICH BOTH SPOUSES PARTICIPATE

(This ritual was developed for use by a particular couple who "approached their divorce and met certain of its problems, especially in the light of their commitment and of their desire that the dissolution of their twelve-year marriage, like its institution, should be solemnized with a religious ceremony.")

OFFICIANT: Let us stand in a circle.

ALL: O Lord, our Lord, how excellent is thy Name in all the earth.

OFFICIANT: Dearly beloved, we have gathered here to solemnize the end of one time in Matthew's and Anne's lives, and the beginning of another. We are so made that we cannot live in isolation from our fellow men, but neither can we live too closely joined with them. We are social beings, but also individual selves, and it is the rhythm of union and separation that enables us to live in the communion which sustains our selves, and in the solitude which nourishes our community. As it is written: [*Here he read Ecclesiastes 3:1–8, 11–14.*]

Thirteen years ago, the time was right for Matthew and Anne to be joined in holy matrimony. Then they needed for their growth in grace and truth the visible bond of marriage. Now the time has come when that bond is hampering both their growth as individual persons and their common life. They have resolved, therefore, to sever the ties of their marriage, though not of their mutual love and honor, and have asked us, their friends, to witness that affirmation of their new lives, and to uphold them in their new undertakings.

Matthew Surrey, do you now relinquish your status as husband of Anne, freeing her from all claims upon and responsibilities to you except those you willingly give to all other children of God?

MATTHEW: I do.

OFFICIANT: Do you forgive her any sins she has committed against you, and do you accept her forgiveness, thus freeing her from the burdens of guilt and sterile remorse?

MATTHEW: I do.

OFFICIANT: Do you release her with your love and blessing, in gratitude for the part she has played in your life, in knowledge that her part in you will never be forgotten or despised, and in faith that in separation as in union, you both are held in the grace and unity of God?

MATTHEW: I do.

[*The same questions were asked of Anne, and she replied in the same way.*]

OFFICIANT: Matthew, what sign do you give to Anne as a token of your forgiveness and your release of her?

MATTHEW: Her wedding ring reconsecrated to her freedom.

   [*He placed it on the third finger of her right hand.*]

   [*The same questions were asked of Anne, and she replied in the same way.*]

OFFICIANT: Let us pray. Almighty and loving God, who has ordered that all seasons shall change and that human lives shall proceed by change, we ask thy blessing upon thy children who now, in their commitment to thee, have severed their commitment to each other. Send them forth in the bond of peace. When they meet, sustain them in their liberty. Keep them both reminded that thy love flows upon and through them both. Sanctify them in their lives, deaths, and resurrections, by the power of thy Holy Spirit, and for the sake of thy Son, Jesus Christ our Lord.

ALL: Amen.

OFFICIANT: The peace of God which passes all understanding keep your hearts and minds in the knowledge and love of God, and the blessing of God Almighty, the Father, the Son, and the Holy Spirit be among you and remain with you always. Go in peace.

ALL: In the name of the Lord. Amen.

Taking Off Your Wedding Ring

Most people remove their wedding rings after their separation or after their divorce. You may continue to wear your ring on your right hand, if you'd like. If you want to take off the ring but being ringless makes you feel naked, wear another ring on that finger. One newly separated woman took off her wedding ring only to expose a white line where the ring had been. She said it was as if she couldn't get unmarried. She covered up with another, unweddinglike ring.

For many women, the last thing they need to linger in their new lives is an old engagement, though some women have the emotional stamina to continue to wear their engagement rings on their right hand or on another finger of their left hand. Changing the setting is a good idea if you find you cannot wear the ring in its present style. Or you can save the ring for your children, return it to your ex (so that he can present it to his next victim) or put it away for a year or so. It may start looking good to you again, once some of the association has worn off.

If your ring is of the Elizabeth Taylor variety, or—and here is where the most trouble occurs—if it is an heirloom from his family, remember this: the ring was a present to you. Whether you return the ring to him or not depends solely upon your benevolence.

Changing Your Name

One recently divorced woman said that, for her, being single was something like ceasing to exist: without her husband to help identify her, she wondered who she was. She found herself taking out her credit cards to look for her reflection—the name stamped on the card gave her reassurance.

For some women, returning to their maiden name helps to reestablish themselves as persons separate from their ex-husbands. If you wish to change your name, check with your lawyer. The law differs in individual states: you may have to petition the court for a name change.

Again, if you wish to change your name you may also wish to send name-change announcements. These can read simply:

Sandra Meyer announces
that she will be known as
Sandra Klausner
as of August 1, 1980

Or:

Sharon Strassberg
announces that by permission of the court
Suffolk County, New York
July 28, 1980
she has resumed her former name of
Sharon Detweiler

Or:

Iris Iacono
wishes to announce
that she will be returning to her birth given name
Iris Roland
for all legal and social purposes.

Even if you do send out announcements, you may have a problem convincing friends and acquaintances to stop calling you by your ex-husband's surname. Although it's rude and insensitive for someone to address you by any other name than that which you prefer, unless you're as big as Muhammad Ali or Kareem Abdul-Jabbar or as verbally convincing as Imamu Baraka, you'll have to take the trouble to continually correct people until your new identity becomes firmly fixed in their minds.

You must comply with the procedures required for a name change by credit-card companies, employer policies, school registration, voter registration, etc. If your divorce is a long time coming, there is no reason to wait until it's final to change your name.

Using Both Your Married Name and Your Maiden Name

Women with children who use their maiden names professionally may want to continue to use their married name after divorce. It may be more convenient to have the same name as your children in many instances. Conversely, when one divorced woman resumed using her maiden name, her daughter asked if she could change her name similarly. She wanted the same surname as her mother.

If your children are from a previous marriage, it may be more convenient for you to use that name once again.

Once divorced, never use your husband's first name—"Mrs. Henry Meyer"; "Mrs. Sandra Meyer" is used today. Not so long ago the only accepted name for a divorced woman was her married name preceded by her maiden name: "Mrs. Stutz Meyer." This is not only confusing but, I think, a bit formal and overbearing in our age of directness and simplicity. I can't think of any instance today where this old-fashioned custom would be necessary or would seem appropriate.

Appearances

I spoke with one divorced woman who told me that with her separation came a steady stream of comments about her appearance. Friends and near-strangers alike studied the way she looked as a guide to her emotional ups and downs as one might study a barometer for a weather forecast. Comments—sanctimonious, condescending, and some straightforward and honest ones, too— were so numerous that when someone failed to mention how she looked, the omission stood out as a condemnation. While her ex- husband would pick up the children wearing baggy pants and a weekend beard (no one commented on his looks; my friend asked him), she didn't dare pick up her cleaning without her makeup on. She was dressing out of insecurity, not vanity.

Regardless of makeup and fashion, your feelings inside will often show on the outside. You can't really change the way you look, but you can make the best of it. When you're feeling good, a radiance shines through which no makeup can duplicate. Rouge may be a poor substitute, but use it if that's all you have to rely on for the moment. As for dressing up, the best rules to follow are the same ones you have always followed. There's no reason to begin putting on the dog just to walk the dog. Please don't go in the other direc- tion, either. You have to face the fact that for a little while your separation will be news and people will be watching you with extra care. For your own sake, cast yourself in the best and most natural light you can muster.

For Those Who Are Tempted to Comment

Telling someone that he or she looks marvelous (if it is true) is usually a morale booster. Sometimes people do look wonderful when they're on the brink of catastrophe—summoning all one's energy to cope can bring a flush to one's cheeks—and you should feel free to respond. But even a compliment can be misconstrued as a critical judgment by someone who is aware of being overscru- tinized.

To show that you mean it in the sincerest way possible, don't give a blanket rave; compliment a specific quality instead: "Your hair looks wonderful," or "Green looks terrific on you." Avoid com- ments related to the separation. "You look terrific since you've left Don" implies that you are approving of or condemning personal business which is none of your own.

THE COLD REALITIES

Choosing a Lawyer

Going through a divorce is difficult enough without having to contend with an unsympathetic or unhelpful lawyer. Lawyers, unlike most of the rest of us, seem to be able to bypass decent manners and get away with it. In fact, their brusqueness and their general combativeness carried outside the courtroom is often looked upon as an asset. If your lawyer is difficult to reach, if he or she doesn't return your phone calls or acknowledge your letters, don't be fooled into thinking the lawyer is too important for your meager demands. An unattainable lawyer is reason to look for another.

Some lawyers, possibly because they're so completely immersed in the case, behave as if they were the ones getting divorced. I've heard of one lawyer hanging up on another lawyer because the second lawyer refused to agree to what she considered unreasonable alimony payments for her client. The reason you are retaining a lawyer is that you and your spouse, if left to your own devices, are more likely to make war than to arbitrate a peace settlement. Irrational lawyers won't help your case any more than you yourself in your own mid-divorce irrationality would.

All lawyers who handle divorce cases are used to giving a certain amount of psychological advice. How useful their advice will be is something only you can judge. But do be clear about your expectations: remember, your lawyer has been trained to help you with legal matters; he or she can't be expected to double as a psychiatrist.

Alimony

Alimony is a loaded subject, to say the least. A discussion about alimony can become immensely heated even when none of the participants has a vested interest. The issue of alimony reflects the confusion inherent in the changes our society is making in terms of the roles men and women play. Some people feel that women are entitled to alimony as a form of reparation for a failed marriage into which they poured their career-training or income-earning years. Others feel that the demand for alimony undermines and contradicts the demand for autonomy.

Philosophy aside, many people shudder at the mention of alimony because of their direct experience with it: men who have had to pay "through the nose" to angry and bitter wives; women who have had to deal with late or missing alimony checks withheld by ex-husbands using this as a way of expressing *their* anger. (Using alimony as revenge has, I think, more to do with human nature than with the differences between men and women. Alimony laws have always favored women. It is unfortunate, but perhaps only human, that some women do exploit the laws for emotional reasons.)

If alimony is an issue in your divorce, you will probably have strong feelings about it, whether you are on the paying or the receiving end. When may you discuss your alimony? I'm afraid the answer is "Never."

Never with someone of the opposite sex. For those who seek public sympathy and outrage, these hopes may backfire. One divorced woman finds it very difficult to remain neutral when a man vents his bitterness about his ex, which almost always includes a tirade on alimony payments. She remembers her own divorce and finds herself taking the woman's side. Someone of the opposite sex is likely to side with your ex, especially if he or she is divorced and has been through a similar struggle. But even if they have not been divorced, men and women tend to sympathize with the problems of their own sex.

Never at an all-women or all-men gathering. The topic will only increase its corollary text of self-pity and indignation. You'll end up as part of a Greek chorus.

Never anywhere else. Alimony involves much more than dollars and cents. It pulls too many emotional strings. I know one seemingly reasonable alimony payer who stopped speaking to a seemingly reasonable alimony receiver—both old friends not paying and receiving from each other—after she confided to him how much money she was actually getting. He gave no thought to *why* she might be getting as much alimony as she was: her age, her previous work experience, the financial status of her ex-husband, whether child support was included in alimony. He became so blind with rage and righteous indignation because of his own alimony battle that he passed judgment on a friend whose financial and emotional concerns had nothing to do with his own or his ex-wife's.

Always with your lawyer, the person who can do something about it. Solace will come in the form of practical application toward getting what you want.

Never inquire about someone else's alimony, even if you travel in a social circle where it's expected that you reveal the cost of your house and your yacht. Alimony has little to do with the actual cost of things.

If you're asked about the amount of alimony you receive, simply reply that you would rather not answer such a personal question.

Presenting Yourself to a Prospective Employer

Returning to work or looking for work for the first time now that you're newly divorced or separated can be frightening. While I don't think it's a good idea to accentuate your divorce at an interview—it sounds too much like an apology—I do think you must mention it.

One friend, self-conscious about her recent divorce, thinks that prospective employers put too much emphasis on what she considers personal and privileged information. "They want to know if you're divorced—and your criminal record," she complains. This turns out to be less a matter of etiquette than one of legality. In New York State, for instance, it is illegal to ask those questions. How much of a fuss you make about it, if you are asked, depends on how strongly you feel about the issue or how strongly you feel about getting the job. I, personally, don't think it's appropriate for a personnel form to include a question on marital status. Your divorce or your marriage, for that matter, has overtones only for you.

What I do think is important is how you present yourself as a divorced person. A prospective employer may look at a divorced applicant in two ways: as someone devastated by a failed marriage who needs help or as someone newly committed to a new life and career. To help create the second impression, say as little as possible about your divorce. Whether or not you are paying or receiving alimony is not an employer's business. You may be broke, you may be rich; don't make the mistake of thinking anybody hires out of sympathy. If your chief selling point is Poor Pitiful Pearl, you're presenting yourself as more of a liability than anything else. And for women who think that is the only role available to them, let me point out that in our changing times a divorced woman is more and more often seen as someone who is serious about a job.

LIVING ALONE AGAIN—OR FOR THE FIRST TIME

Asking for Help

A divorced woman has, in the past, assumed mythological proportions in the eyes of others. Either she is Circe, ravenously eying all the husbands on the block, as supposed by their wives, or she is an utterly defenseless woman, as supposed by the husbands. To ward off trouble which can accrue from a certain amount of lingering prejudice toward the divorcée, a woman who is newly single must take some precautions. For instance, when a neighborhood husband has offered to put up your bookshelves or to take a look at the boiler, invite his wife in for coffee at the same time. No one will be able to accuse you of having designs on the husband, and the husband himself will be discouraged from making a pass at you if that was indeed his intention.

You don't have to be coy or hesitant about asking for help. If you never learned how to operate the electric drill, it's perfectly all right to ask a neighbor to help you or, more accurately, to show you. Now is the time to watch what he is doing and to ask questions so you'll be able to solo the next time—or the time after.

Do remember to reciprocate a kindness—with a bottle of wine, or a loaf of home-baked bread or cookies if you're a cook—or your cries for help will be looked upon as taking advantage.

You may wish to combine a request for help with a dinner invitation. But make your intentions clear; don't bring people into your house under false pretenses and then put a hammer in their hands as they walk through the front door. You can invite friends with "Please come for dinner tomorrow. And would you mind helping me hang a couple of pictures [it had better be only a couple] before we sit down to eat? I promise not to work you too hard." Obviously, everyone doesn't enjoy this kind of an evening. Hand-pick friends for this event.

Entertaining

Newly divorced men have a very different problem than women. Once single, a man is much sought after, while a single woman is often considered a burden. This may be changing now for the better, since men are losing their lofty position of being the only thing of any real importance in a woman's life—a woman is no longer considered a failure if she doesn't have one. But I've still heard complaints that newly divorced men are hurriedly pushed into one social situation after another—the extra man at dinner parties, the poor helpless father invited for Sunday dinner with the children—while newly divorced women are forgotten. One woman said that at first she sat home feeling hurt that she wasn't invited anywhere. Finally, because no one was entertaining her, she began to entertain on a small and casual basis by herself—four or six for dinner—and never worried about equal numbers of the sexes. More than once, there were two men to four or five women. Nobody minded. In fact, everyone seemed to have a good time, including the host. And once she began entertaining, invitations were reciprocated by old friends and new ones. She no longer sat home feeling insulted that people didn't seek her out first.

You may be reluctant to invite some of your friends because you're afraid they would not enjoy the entertaining it is possible for you to do. You may return the hospitality of friends with flowers or gifts on special occasions, but I still don't think that is really an adequate gesture. If people have invited you into their home (and you've had a good time), you respond by inviting them into yours. The decision to come or not is up to them. I doubt they'll turn you down, no matter how grandly they live compared to what you think of as your meager existence.

When I was a teenager, my friends were over at our house all the time. Part of the allure was a swimming pool, a pool table and a household staff at our disposal. I was never invited to their houses —and I was hurt. I know their houses weren't as big as ours and they didn't have maids popping out of every room. I didn't care, but they apparently did. Don't let your self-consciousness elicit bad manners.

Once you've gotten over your initial hesitancy about entertaining alone, you'll find that people are delighted to be asked. They'll also realize that it's more difficult to organize and orchestrate a party on your own. You can use their sensitivity to your situation as an excuse (if you need one) to make your party informal and, therefore, easy to handle. Hosting on your own also means you can ask for your guests' help, something you may never have done when you were married, even though your party could have used the steady hand of an experienced and willing vegetable chopper or gravy maker in the kitchen. You no longer have to pretend you can float through an evening coordinating dinner, drinks, conversation, introductions and general party angst.

Co-Hosting

If you're not entertaining because you're afraid to host alone, the solution is simple: give a small *joint* party with a friend—man or woman. In your invitations, be sure to include the information that you and Helen or Jake or whoever are having a small party, so that your guests will know there are two hosts. This also gives you a second choice for your party location in case you think your new home is not big enough or luxurious enough or whatever your rationalization is for not inviting people into it. If it's easier for you to co-host your party at your co-host's, by all means do. The one simple rule to follow here is that you and your co-host must agree beforehand on all arrangements, from the guest list to how much to spend on food to who does what.

(For more on entertaining, see Chapter 2, "Entertaining.")

Your New Style of Entertaining

The important thing is that you do some entertaining, however light. You'll soon realize that people who like you don't care how big your living room is or whether or not your furniture is newly reupholstered, and you'll begin to be less self-conscious of your new image and your new life style, if it has changed.

Two friends of mine lend themselves perfectly as examples of what I mean. Cornelia had for fifteen years been married to an aluminum executive who brought home baubles from Tiffany's along with the bacon. When she decided on divorce, Cornelia packed up both her children and herself and rented a house almost big enough for the three of them. Since she was breaking up the marriage, she felt that it would be unfair to ask for the house, which her husband loved. In any case, she knew she herself couldn't afford to keep the house in the long run.

After her initial move and readjustment, Cornelia began her new life with enthusiasm. She entertained old friends and new ones whom she had met when she began taking classes at the local college, but on a scale much reduced from her past entertaining. In her married days, when she had a party, she hired someone to serve (she loved to cook and so elected to do that herself). Her table was set with the most fragile china and crystal. Both Cornelia and her guests expected a certain level of opulence—after all, she could afford it. Cornelia often makes reference to her "other" life, which she has dubbed her "life of parsley and roses." She remembers one party when she decorated the table with small bud vases; into each vase she placed primroses surrounded by fresh parsley. She now considers such a beautiful touch pretentious. Her new life is the only thing now "real" to her. (Actually, her flower arrangement sounded like such a perfect and elegant touch that I've done it myself with great success.)

When Cornelia invites people today, the food is delicious—she is a terrific cook—but her guests don't expect to sit in Queen Anne chairs or to be pampered and spoiled by a bartender or a maid at the table. Everyone pitches in. The atmosphere is much more informal, which, Cornelia claims, helps to put both herself and her guests at ease.

Although she has abandoned her ideas of parsley and roses, Cornelia does love beautiful things. When she invites people, she occasionally borrows a casserole or a beautiful vase from friends. Once, for a wine-and-cheese party, she borrowed a huge copper pan and filled it with ice and bottles of white wine—a pretty way to put out wine bottles. Fresh fruit served in a neighbor's Delft bowl may brighten up what you think is an unexciting table in comparison to the way you used to live. The only drawback might be that you have to invite the neighbor.

While Cornelia accepted her new surroundings, making do with what she had and using it to its fullest potential, Laura sat in a house big enough for the old woman in the shoe. Entertaining was impossible for her because she was afraid to try it alone. The formality of the house forbade the casualness of informal entertaining, and she could no longer afford outside help. She was afraid to show her vulnerability and ask a friend to pitch in and help. Laura was so worried about her image and possible whispers behind her back about how the mighty have fallen that she was afraid to make any move that she wouldn't have made when she was married. She worried about what she called a "step down" in her style of living. Her fear obscured the fact that no one—certainly, not her friends —cared about the level of her life style. She was keeping up pretenses only for herself.

Obviously, we'd all rather be like Cornelia, enjoying herself with her friends, than like Laura, sitting home alone. This means that you will have to entertain—so make the commitment and do it.

Tips on Entertaining Alone

When you first begin to become accustomed to entertaining alone, take advantage of the obvious. This is one case where you can ask close friends to help; they know you had help when you entertained in the past—at least the emotional sort of help a spouse gives as co-host—so when you're first beginning to entertain alone you may ask one or two guests who are close friends to give you a hand in clearing the table, making drinks, whatever small chores you'd like help with. Don't avoid asking for help because you think friends will view such a request as a demonstration of your inability to cope, or because you think they'll be offended that you put them to work. You'll find that a bit of group effort lends itself to a relaxed time for everybody, rather than guests being at the mercy of an overly anxious host, if that's what you become when you're entertaining alone. A group effort has the added benefit of being an excellent ice-breaker, when mixing old friends and new ones.

Many women newly single find themselves stymied by a function once relegated to husbands—tending bar. The simplest bar setup for you is the self-service one. Put out the makings for a variety of drinks. You needn't mix cocktails in advance; if anybody wants one he can mix his own. Your only job is to see that ice, mixers, glasses and, of course, liquor are replenished. (If your budget forbids spending recklessly on liquor, think about cutting down your guest list instead of cutting down on their liquor consumption, especially if they are hardy drinkers.) For more on tending bar, see "The Cocktail Hour," in Chapter 2, "Entertaining."

After you've greeted your guests and introduced them to one or two other people, point out the bar. Self-service bars can also be a helpful device for your guests. If conversation isn't going well, a guest can break away to the bar and will have a chance to meet more amicable people there. The self-service atmosphere helps bring about a feeling of camaraderie.

When dinner is ready, you, as host, lead the way to the dining room and direct the guests to their places.

DATING

Going Out During Your Divorce

Being in the middle of a divorce poses legal problems as well as social ones. Although it's important for you to begin to meet new people, if papers have yet to be signed you had better ask your lawyer to explain the divorce laws in your state and how they apply to your situation.

Since you're paying a lawyer a good deal for his or her advice, you had better take it. If you'd like to see someone before your divorce is final and your lawyer suggests that doing so will hurt your case, tell that person just what your lawyer has said. (The person who must wait for you until the worst is over is, I think, being spared countless hours of listening to your complaints. If things are going to work out between you, they'll work out better if you begin your relationship with as few ghosts as possible.)

If you are out with someone and unexpectedly meet friends who are not yet acquainted with your circumstances, don't shuffle and hide. Before their heads begin to swivel in search of your spouse and before they have a chance to concoct a story, make your introductions and add that the person you're with is a friend. If your simple statement will not suffice—either to explain the circumstances or to satisfy your friends' curiosity—say, "I'm in the middle of a divorce" or "Jan and I are getting divorced."

Fix-ups

Couples see the world pass by in couples. A newly single friend is not considered whole until he or she is re-paired. After a separation or divorce, friends will inevitably demonstrate their encouragement and support by introducing you to any and every single friend of the opposite sex in the hopes of parlaying "just a quiet dinner at home" into a romance. Most newly divorced people go along with being fixed up for the first few times, though even the most outgoing begin refusing such invitations after a while. The main problem with this process for meeting new people is not that you're likely to come across a series of untouchables (always a possibility), but rather that the situation is usually contrived in such a way as to make everyone, hosts and hopeful guests alike, as uncomfortable as possible. I think introducing divorced friends to other friends is an important contribution. There's no reason to stop the practice, but the format needs changing. There are ways to make the situation more relaxed for everyone.

To cut down on everybody's self-consciousness, invite one or two other people along with your "prospects" so that your party is just a party and not a mating ritual. Don't "warn" the two central characters. They'll surely find it easier to enjoy themselves and each other if they haven't been told in advance that they have a job to do.

If, as a newly single person, you find these dinners of your friends too uncomfortable, or if after a number of them you've come to realize that you manage your social life well enough on your own—much better than your friends are managing it, anyway—tell a host proffering an invitation which you suspect has ulterior motives that you'd love to come for dinner but, as one divorced person has said, "I'll just come as me."

How to "Come as Me"

Anybody's identity is complex—there are a lot of different sides to all of us. Unfortunately, during crisis times we tend to confuse our identities with our crises. Divorced people often present themselves as divorced people, nothing more. There's a good reason for this. Divorced people need to talk about their divorces with others who have had or are having similar problems and are, therefore, often more empathetic, or at least more interested (in comparing notes) than married or never-married people. Although the less you say about your personal problems the better your chances are for a truly enjoyable evening, I've never met a person with such self-control in the early stages of separation and divorce.

I suppose it's perfectly all right to tell a stranger whatever you'd like, but try to concentrate on the here and now and on the other person as a person and not as an inanimate sounding board who will echo your words in similar waves of discontent.

Conversation between a man from one divorce and a woman from another divorce who meet for the first time often follows a pattern. So much so that one divorced man who has done more than his share of talking to other people in the same position insists that he can predict the behavior of any man or woman in the early stages of separation: The man is the lost child; he has sublet a furnished apartment in which he spends as little time as possible; he doesn't cook any meals for himself but goes out instead every night to a friendly neighborhood bar or restaurant. The woman? She isn't seen outside the house much, because she's home with the children trying to stop the boat from rocking. Whether these broadly sketched character studies fully suit or not, certainly what both men and women have in common at this stage is an enormous resentment about their marriage.

Sympathy is well and good, but do try to put your most positive side forward. There's more to you than your divorce—and you'll have a better time if you show it.

To Men Who Pinch

Popular male mythology revels in the presumed sexual availability of the divorced woman: she is inclined to accept and even welcome behavior more aggressive than mere verbal suggestion, because she is divorced and, therefore, must be starving for sex. Don't believe it. If a divorced woman was starving for sex, it was probably when she was still married. It is certainly not now when she has her freedom.

Men: Every person is flattered if another person finds her attractive and lets her know it in a pleasant and nonintrusive way. It is not flattering to be found attractive by someone whose style is unattractive, and by "unattractive" I mean broadly suggestive or downright ugly.

Who Pays for What

There is no point in a divorced woman being "modern" if she is using her grocery money to subsidize an evening she can't afford.

A woman planning on paying her own way should ask her date how he wants to spend the evening. If his plans sound too expensive for her pocketbook, she should tell him. Either he will offer to pay for whatever she can't or he will change his plans.

The divorced woman with children has an added problem. Even if the man offers to pay for an evening out, is he expected to pay the baby-sitter? If you aren't able to go out unless he does, tell him so. There's no point in being coolly sophisticated and enigmatic if it will only cloud your needs. Although it will be very difficult for him to say no, especially if he hardly knows you, it's more unfair to the man for you to turn him down without telling him the reason. So that your confession doesn't turn into an exhortation, offer to make dinner for the two of you, or ask him for a drink before you both go out, to cut down on his expenses.

CHILDREN

On Your Own with Your Children

One divorced woman told me that one of the hardest adjustments she had to make during her separation was restructuring her weekends. What had previously been a time for the family to which she had always looked forward was now a barren space she had to fill up for her children. Finally, in her desperation, she called an old acquaintance, a divorced man who spent a lot of time with his own children. He was delighted to hear from her, and the two of them began to share weekend afternoons: ice skating, bowling, the movies, etc. If you know a separated or divorced person—of either sex—with children, why not share your children and some of your time?

Introducing Your Dates to Your Children

If you go out with someone more than once or twice, it's important that they meet your children at one point or another. Some people think introducing their children to their dates will precipitate too many questions afterward or will give the impression (to children and date alike) that the relationship is more serious than it actually is.

On the contrary, I think keeping children and date apart causes more speculation—on both sides—than bringing them together. Just as your children do when they make new friends, bring your new friends home to meet your family. Keeping someone away from your children will turn each of your evenings out into a mystery to them. Their meeting does not have to be a planned or a tension-provoking moment; you needn't stage an event. A new friend of yours can just say a simple hello or can stay to dinner, whatever fits in naturally with the time you had planned.

If your children behave badly when they're introduced to your friend of the opposite sex—if they're hostile or withdrawn—these problems won't disappear just because you don't confront them. For severe problems, professional help may be the only answer. Hiding your children from your friends and vice versa is definitely not an answer.

I do think it's important for your children *not* to meet your friends at the breakfast table. Unless the children are very young, there's nothing casual about such a scene. A divorced person has every right to do whatever he or she wants to do, but until you're pretty secure in a relationship I think it's best to keep the children out of it. Don't fool yourself into thinking that it's good for the children to have a man or a woman around, unless one person is around on a fairly regular basis. If you know you will be seeing the person only temporarily, remember that love in the afternoon (when the children are on the beach or at the movies) was good enough for Gary Cooper and Audrey Hepburn. On the other hand, if you are sharing a large part of your life with one person, you can begin to explain your ongoing relationship to a young child by saying, "He is my boy friend" or "She is my girl friend." The expression is a part of every child's language, beginning as early as kindergarten. And your child will understand the special significance of your relationship.

There is no formula to solve all the problems and hurt feelings that have been known to arise. Jealousy can occur on both sides; you must be equally sensitive to your children and your new friend. And be sure to plan private time with each.

For Women in Relationships with Men Who Have Children

Women always seem to take the responsibility for the children present, whether the children belong to them or not. When a woman is single, with children of her own, she may be unquestioningly tagged as the one who should look after the children of the men she sees. Deirdre, when she became involved with Jake about a year after her divorce, noticed that the two of them fell easily into operating along traditional lines of responsibilities: she ran the house, whether it was her house with her children or Jake's house with his child. They didn't do everything outside the house together—if Jake went to the zoo with his child, Deirdre was not expected to accompany them; but when the two returned home, Deirdre *was* expected to have dinner ready.

Deirdre, full-time mother to her own children, had automatically assumed the care and feeding of Jake's child. Although she was now unmarried, Deirdre found herself involved with some of the toughest and least rewarding aspects of marriage.

Possibly you'll enjoy taking care of a family again. If you don't, there's no reason for you to have to do it all. Don't take on the role of even a weekend mother to someone else's children because you think it's expected. Your new and possibly temporary family can be structured along more modern lines. Divide the chores and the responsibilities. Why conform to traditional roles in a decidedly untraditional situation? Because there is no prerequisite behavior for this new style of family living, you'll have to experiment to see what works best for you.

Consider Your Children

When you are redefining for yourself and the man you are seeing a structure that accommodates your needs, don't forget the needs of your children. One divorced woman who spends considerable time with a divorced man and his child makes sure the time is spent at her house, because "I want my children and myself on my turf so my kids will feel comfortable and retain their sense of belonging. Whether I'm seeing a man regularly or not, a relationship doesn't disrupt my household. We suffered such drastic changes after the divorce that I want my children's lives to be as stable and regular as possible."

I think my friend is basically right, although she may have to be a bit more flexible if someone else's child becomes involved. Don't drag children from one house to another just because you need to put them someplace.

When two sets of children are living with one parent from each set, there's a danger that if the children fight, the parents will line up behind their own children. I think it's best to divide along very traditional lines: adults and children, not Family A versus Family B.

(One divorced parent sharing weekends with another divorced parent noticed that whether or not the two sets of children got along was a fairly accurate reflection of how well they themselves were getting along.)

YOUR OLD LIFE AND YOUR NEW LIFE: BRIDGING THE GAP

A divorce does not mean that your ex-spouse or ex-family ties disappear from your life, although most divorced people I know would sometimes prefer it that way. In ways, it is not building a new life that presents a problem so much as dealing with the old one. The main difficulty lies in the confusion of feelings you all will have: anger and resentment, yes, but also a sense of loss for each other and for the family.

Doing Things Together as a Family

Many newly separated or divorced people find that one of the hardest things to adjust to is the death of the family. During this vulnerable time, most separated families need only slight provocation—a holiday, a graduation—as an excuse to reunite and celebrate together. Although this tends to make parents anxious and give the children temporary false hopes, it is unavoidable in the beginning of a separation and it helps to make the transition of living without a parent or without each other a little easier.

To sidestep disagreements which might so easily bubble to the surface, it's best to have all the arrangements worked out beforehand. When the restaurant bill came to one separated family celebrating a birthday, the husband suggested through partially clenched teeth that he and his wife split it. There ensued a lengthy discussion about alimony which ended with the children siding with their father, and their mother paying the bill out of humiliation.

I repeat, work out all details such as paying the bill beforehand. You cannot expect the goodwill which motivated the reunion to extend to and resolve all of the difficulties which led to the two of you getting divorced in the first place.

Sharing a Vacation House

A bad idea from the start. If you have one, you'll probably try it anyway, despite my pronouncement, since you both want the house and neither of you can afford to maintain it alone. Try sharing, and continue for as long as you can put up with it. Who knows, you may be the first couple who can make such an arrangement work over a long period of time. In all likelihood, however, one of you will end up taking the responsibility for it and either rent it out for part of the year or put it and its memories, both good and bad, up for sale.

While the two of you are sharing your house, here are a few suggestions which will help to keep the arrangement running at least fairly smoothly, until it has outlasted its usefulness: alternate months, if you can, not weeks or weekends; the less you are confronted with a sink choking with your ex's hair, or possibly with hair of questionable origins, or with flowers cut from your cherished garden, the longer your bihabitation will last.

Telling Your Ex When You Begin to Live with Somebody

One divorced man who dropped his children off at their mother's after a weekend visit made the mistake of bending down to kiss one of them goodbye. Their mother saw an unfamiliar name written on the inside of her ex-husband's shirt collar. She realized that someone else was taking his shirts to the laundry, a sign of some permanence, she surmised.

If you start living with someone, even on a fairly part-time basis, you may not want to tell your ex. Unless the two of you have severed all contact (in which case there is no need for you to tell your ex), he or she will find out soon enough, if not from your shirt collars, then somewhere else. It may, however, be easier on both of you if you are the one to do the telling. That two people who are divorced should lead their own lives unencumbered by the past is a nice theory, but for many a legal decision doesn't obliterate an attachment as strong as marriage.

To make it an easier time for everyone, tell your ex when you've formed a serious relationship with someone new. (For telling your ex when you remarry, see Chapter 7, "Weddings.")

When You're Living with One Man and Receiving Alimony from Another

When you live with someone, you make no legal commitment, nor do you necessarily make even a public commitment, depending on the living arrangements the two of you establish. Though the man you live with is not expected to support you, the two of you are sharing many expenses you would otherwise have to meet alone. Your ex-husband, if he is paying you alimony, is legally bound to support you or to supplement your income. Is he, however, expected to support another household?

If there is a possibility that your new life style may warrant a change in your alimony, you have a responsibility to make your ex aware of it. It's foolish to hide the fact that you're living with someone and dishonest as well if you're afraid your ex will try to renegotiate your alimony settlement on those grounds. He'll be embarrassed when he finds out from someone else and angry that he had to learn of such a serious change in your life from a third party. Although you may think your life is now your own concern and no concern of his, alimony binds the two of you with a common interest.

Of course, I do not suggest that you tell your ex if your living arrangement is only temporary. He needs to know only when you have made a serious long-term living-together commitment.

Getting Along with Your Current Spouse's Ex-Spouse

One woman has complained about her husband's divorce agreement. His ex-wife can ask to see his tax returns, which includes seeing his present wife's tax returns as well, since they file jointly.

As this illustrates, a past divorce often involves a current spouse. I've heard one friend (a new wife) announce that under different circumstances she and her husband's former wife would no doubt be the best of friends. We'll never know, but even best friends don't share their tax returns. I do know that two wives or two husbands, one past and one present, need not be enemies. In fact, most can afford to be enemies only if there are no children involved, and even then most people find it hard to go on being enemies after everyone has settled into a new life and starts letting go of all his or her resentments about the past.

Of course, when children, alimony and child support are concerned, past resentments are often reactivated. Present spouses who aren't susceptible to taking on the emotional burdens of a spouse's past can become mediators and problem solvers of the best kind.

A Group Conference

If there are problems with alimony, children or child support, trying to solve these problems with the person with whom you obviously could not solve them in the past will most likely fail to be productive. I know two couples, related by divorce, who all got together to try to work things out among themselves. They reasoned, quite accurately, as it turned out, that two fairly impartial observer/participants, i.e., current spouses, helped toward sane and workable negotiations.

A Conference Between a Current Spouse and an Ex-Spouse

The woman I mentioned who thought she might be good friends with her new husband's ex-wife took advantage of the sentiment and arranged a meeting with her. Realizing that she could argue on her husband's behalf and perhaps eliminate the existing antagonism between a divorced couple (and the subsequent toll such a meeting would take on both ex-spouses' emotions), she convinced her husband to let her speak with his ex alone. The existing problem was settled more easily than previous ones.

Under no circumstances can participants in such a meeting be surprised. If your relationship to your current spouse and your ex-spouse allows for such a meeting, make sure that you are in agreement in your wish for one. Antagonizing the antagonist won't help your case.

Another possible solution is a telephone "meeting," which saves those involved from a face-to-face confrontation.

It may turn out that, for you, a judge is the only person who can solve your differences. However, don't rule out all other possibilities only because friends or family are horrified at suggestions similar to mine which you may have made yourself. The people involved directly with a problem—not impartial Solomons—are often the ones best qualified to solve it.

HOW YOU CAN HELP DIVORCING FRIENDS

Maintaining Your Friendships

Pre-divorce friends who are used to getting your prime-time hours will be hurt if as post-divorce acquaintances you give them the scrap ends of your time. A pre-divorce friend of one woman I know has had little contact with my friend since her divorce. The pre-divorce friend believes in inviting matched sets to her dinner parties and now squeezes her divorced friend in for coffee around the corner from the school where they both pick up their children.

We all have different friends for different occasions; you may not invite your afternoon bridge partner to your ski house for the weekend, for instance. But if a friend plummets in status from dinner to diner just because she's divorced, you had better reevaluate the friendship. If you saw her because you liked her husband, it's better to break off your friendship with her now—instead of letting your guilt hold her in the wings—and establish a friendship with the half of the couple you liked best. If you think your switching allegiance to her ex would be too painful for her (this is something I hope you have the sensitivity to consider), let the friendship lie dormant for a period of time. Maybe in a few months, or even a few years, the time will be right to be friends again.

One recently divorced woman realized her pariah status when she picked up her child who had spent the afternoon playing with the child of a friend of hers. Her friend poked her head out the front door to announce, "I'm too busy to chat now. I'm having a dinner party for twenty this evening and I'm way behind. See you soon!" Did the woman giving the party expect her friend—whom she used to invite to all her parties—to understand that she was no longer acceptable now that she didn't have a man in tow? Divorce should not bring on such an attack of tactlessness or unfriendliness. I can't say this often enough: your parties will be more lively if you invite *people* whom you enjoy, not just couples for the sake of appearances. The divorce of a friend should not make a difference in the quality of your entertaining friendship. Dr. Jekylls don't turn into Mr. Hydes by the dim light of a divorce agreement.

Extending Invitations

When you invite a divorced person to dinner or to a party, you may want to give him or her the option of bringing someone along. Although for certain occasions this is a thoughtful gesture, it is not a hard and fast rule. If you *always* suggest that they bring someone, they'll begin to assume, and probably quite rightly, that you'd *prefer* that they did. A nice way to take the pressure off a single person who may feel that he or she is expected to bring a "date" is to show that you would like your friend to visit you in the way he or she feels most comfortable. You may suggest, "If you'd like to bring someone, please let me know a day in advance."

I know one woman who tells her single friends specifically *not* to bring dates to her house. She doesn't like the nuisance of strangers who may possibly not get along with or fit in with the rest of her guests. I think she is being a bit too inflexible. When you can, make allowances in your guest list for single friends who may be seeing someone fairly regularly and would be happier bringing that person along (we all know how hard it is to walk into a party alone and fend for ourselves all evening) and also to accommodate those who may rather come alone.

Considering Your Own Needs

Perhaps the people who need the most amount of coaching during the disconcerting back-and-forth togetherness of a separating couple are friends and family who, too often, find they've been taken along on a trip where nobody knows where he's going—the

couple's confusion about their lives and each other, their unwill-
ingness to let go of what is now past.

What are you supposed to do when you visit one half of a couple
and find that the other half is also visiting? Or when the two con-
trive to have dinner together—with you as a captive audience? Too
often, this means that you have been cast in the role of the approving third party who reflects the part of their marriage which, at this
moment, is still intact. Your presence validates, if only briefly, that
they are still a couple. With you present, they can play out the best
parts (or remaining parts) of their marriage, parts reserved for an
audience.

When you're together with a separating couple, you're probably
having a crisis of your own just trying to stop relating to them as a
couple in the way you always have done. Your own ambivalence is
just a hint of what they're experiencing. In these situations, and I
hope there are few of them for all concerned, you can't expect
much from your hosts in the way of helping you to feel comfortable. You must do that on your own. It may help to remember that
there's nothing untoward you can do in such a situation. If you can
tolerate the electricity in the air, you can stay and act more or less
as a shock absorber. Or you can tell them clearly that you are too
uncomfortable to stay, and go home.

Offering Help

Don't be afraid to offer help to someone who's going through a
divorce. Sometimes friends stop calling when a separation becomes public knowledge. Friends sometimes disappear just when
they're needed most, because the change in someone's life makes
them uncomfortable. They're afraid they'll have difficulty assuming the proper attitude, or afraid that the newly separated person
might ask them for something. The proper attitude to assume, of
course, is the one you really feel. Any posturing on your part will
make a difficult situation more difficult. As for being asked for
something, friendships are built on mutual needs. A true friend
offers help to a friend when he or she thinks it might be needed.

12 THE SINGLE MOTHER

TELLING FRIENDS AND FAMILY

Although it has not disappeared, the taboo against the single mother is decreasing as more and more single women are deciding to raise children on their own. A single woman about to have a baby may find that some family and friends are not immediately accepting of her choice. Though she may run into opposition, I think it best for her to tell close friends and family about her decision as soon as possible. It's better for her to deal with reactions openly than to withhold information which might set up barriers between herself and her family and friends. One single woman who was pregnant thought her parents would be hurt by her choice, and to protect them she wrote and told them that she had just gotten married. She delivered prematurely, and her hospital bills came to much more than she could afford. The truth came out when she had to go to them for money. They were supportive in every way. She then realized that she could have depended on them for emotional support all along. A woman who has an open relationship with her parents should by all means share the joy and confidence she feels in having made this most important decision, particularly with parents who have always been loving. Give your parents the chance to form their own opinions. Many pregnant women have found their joy to be contagious.

If your parents do turn their backs at first, take heart in the fact that the joy the birth of a baby brings will almost surely override their misgivings, and their antagonism to your situation will be a part of the past. The parents of one woman refused to see her or even speak with her while she was pregnant. Once the child was born, however, they were so delighted with being grandparents that they gladly welcomed their daughter back into the family.

(For birth announcements and religious ceremonies for the newborn, see Chapter 10, "Children.")

TELLING THE PEOPLE IN YOUR CHILD'S LIFE

When your child is still an infant, the decision as to whom you tell about your being a single mother is left to your own discretion. Once your child is of school age, you'll most likely be familiar enough in dealing with the circumstances to tell people as simply as possible just as much as they ask to be told. When filling out school and medical forms, check off the appropriate boxes; detailed information won't be requested. Tell your child's school, doctor and dentist and, if the question arises, the parents of your child's friends just what you tell your child—I hope it will be the truth.

EXPLAINING TO YOUR CHILD

When a child begins nursery school is probably when she'll come home with questions about Daddy. The simplest answer would be "You do have a father, but he doesn't live with us." A bit later your child will no doubt bring up the question of your marriage. You might reply, "We were never married," although your answer will not actually become clear to the child until she is ten or eleven. Small children perceive marriage as simply a man and a woman living together and then having a baby; a more complex realization of what marriage is will become clear only when children begin to look at the social structure of the family.

A single mother who at first may have been unsure of her role will, as the child grows older, begin to grow more comfortable being a single parent. One woman told me that at first, self-conscious, she had told people she was divorced. As her child grew older and she saw how well she was managing to raise and support a child with little or no outside help, she felt better and better. She felt she deserved to pat herself on the back for doing such a good job and doing it alone. Now when she tells people she is single and has a child, she thinks they will respect her situation and will consider it an achievement, as she herself does.

YOUR CHILD'S LAST NAME

A single mother generally gives her baby her surname. If she later marries, her new husband may adopt her child and they would share a new surname. Or, if the mother retains her surname after marriage, the child may also keep the name he or she is used to.

WHAT TO TELL THE MEN IN YOUR LIFE

One woman whose child is now in grade school went through a series of explanations she suspects are a natural consequence of the self-vindicating posture held by many new single mothers. When her child was a baby, she told men she was divorced. The next step was to overcompensate and tell them her life story. Now, secure in her role, she doesn't mention her child. If the subject comes up naturally, then she tells the truth, a short version of what once was a long story. "Yes, I have a child. No, I'm not divorced. I was never married."

She realizes full well that because of her past she is not always looked upon as the ideal candidate to take home to mother. When she does meet the parents of a man she is seeing, she prefers to tell them about herself rather than have them "warned" ahead of time. Parents, she enlightens us, do not categorically look upon her circumstances as a deficit. One potential father-in-law, a successful businessman, admired her struggle as an analogue of his own Horatio Alger accomplishment of pulling himself up by his bootstraps.

13 HOUSEHOLD HELP

We are living in a society that is striving to be class-less. Since the word "servant" conjures up a class-oriented society, today even the word is outmoded. Terms such as "sanitation workers" and "custodial engineers" are giving respect and stature to jobs whose old names, "garbage men" and "janitors," conjure up another era, another set of values. Although we have adopted progressive names for those who provide certain services, the titles don't always help us over the self-consciousness and ambivalence we may feel in the presence of those who do personal work for us.

Those who work for you in your home should be treated with the same respect and courtesy you would wish from your own employers. Class distinctions are no longer as pronounced as they once were—in fact, the person who cleans your house may be a teenage neighbor—and the personal nature of a household worker's job shouldn't stand in the way of mutual consideration. In this chapter I'll try to solve some of the conflicts which arise between employer and employee because of this unique situation. How do you tell someone what you would like done in your house or the way you would like something done without sounding as though you're giving an order? How do you comfortably share your home, even one day a week, with a part-time household helper? What part does a live-in mother's helper play in your family when you've heard she is supposed to be part of the family but obviously she is not? How can you and your family maintain your privacy? How can you talk above a whisper when you have someone who is essentially an outsider living in? Having someone help you with household chores can become more of a hell than a blessing if it brings an atmosphere of tension to your household.

FINDING A HOUSEHOLD WORKER

The simplest and most reliable path to a competent household worker is a recommendation by a friend. Since such a fortuitous circumstance is not always possible, there are ways to find someone dependable and compatible on your own.

Employment Agencies

When you first contact an agency ask how long it has been established. An agency can run successfully only if it is helped by word of mouth. If an agency has been in business for a few years, that is an indication that their ethics can be counted on.

Advertise

When placing an ad for a household worker in your local paper, specify the kind of help you need, and the days and hours required. You'll get many more replies if you include a phone number in the advertisement than if you request only written replies. When advertising for part-time household help, it's best to leave out the salary unless it's a fixed one not open to negotiation, because the exact type of work to be done differs slightly according to prospective employees. One may like to iron, another to wax the floors monthly.

THE INTERVIEW

Someone being interviewed obviously tends to be anxious about the results of an interview—the nervousness of the interviewer is not always acknowledged. Unless you are in a position in business which requires interviewing on a fairly regular basis, you're apt to be a little nervous. After all, it's your job to take the lead and guide the interview. Unless you know where the interview is going, how can you give it structure? Before the interview, make a list of the work you'll want done so that the job can be discussed point by point.

If you plan to share the work load, find out which chores the applicant enjoys or does best so that you both won't be counting on doing the same things. Let the applicant know how much time you spend at home; one person may like to work more or less in private, another may expect you to be available to talk over what is to be done this afternoon or tomorrow.

It's best to present the job in the clearest—not the brightest—light possible. It's tempting, if you strike an immediate rapport with the person whom you are interviewing, to make the work appear easier than it really is. There's no harm in pointing out the good aspects of a job, but not before you've outlined the work itself in a down-to-earth, unadorned manner. You're not doing your prospective employee or yourself justice if you misrepresent the job. It will only bring rancor into the household, and in all probability you'll soon be interviewing again.

On the other hand, painting the picture a bit bleaker than it really is will not help to secure a satisfied and hard-working employee. No one likes to be misled. Your inconsistency will cause confusion which consequently will make an employee unsure of his or her duties in the house and apprehensive as to your apparent whims. Honesty and forthrightness regarding the job are the best approach and the one which will lead to the most satisfactory results.

Of course it's important to be sure that the person you hire will do a good job, but equally important is how you feel about that person. Are you at ease? Is she? Choose someone whose personal qualities you respond to positively. Whether you are to be sharing your house one morning a week or six full days a week, it's necessary that the person you hire fits pleasantly into your household.

If you and the prospective employee are getting along during the interview it won't hurt to reveal a little about yourself in terms of the running of your household—the amount of time you spend at home, some of the likes and dislikes of your children. To a household worker who will be cleaning out your refrigerator and straightening out your closets, such revelations can hardly be classified as too personal to divulge. The relationship of an employer and a household worker is a complex one today. There was a time not so long ago when a household worker, even though he or she was often privy to the most private part of an employer's life, was considered only a servant, by definition almost a nonperson. Today a household worker is an employee; as in any business relationship, dignity and respect are important. In fact, in an employee–employer relationship of this personal nature, dignity and respect are even more important than in other work situations which are by their nature less personal.

The interview should take place wherever you feel most comfortable: living room, family room, kitchen. Greet the applicant in the same way you would greet someone in any business meeting. Since you are the boss, stand up, offer your hand and introduce yourself: "You must be Marilyn Cullen. I'm Janine Turner." (Introductions include both first and last names, unless you're introducing a child.) I must make a special point here to suggest that you do not address the person you're interviewing by his or her first name during the interview. Since you've just met, you should begin on the professional basis of calling the person Mr., Mrs., Ms. or Miss. After you've hired someone for the job, ask that person how she would prefer to be addressed and what she wishes her title to be. Household workers wish to be called housekeepers, household technicians or household workers, or they may create their own title which fits their work, such as "housemother." The Code of Standards of the National Committee on Household Employment suggests that certain phrases should be dropped: "maid," "my girl," "the servant" and "the master." If yours is an informal household and you'd rather be on a first-name basis with your employee, say so when you first hire the person. "I'd like you to call me Janine," or "Please call me Janine." In such an informal house I'd assume that the person you choose to hire would be someone without a formal air which would demand that employer and employee address each other as Mrs., Miss, Ms. or Mr.

REFERENCES

Whether you're hiring a full-time person or a once-a-week housecleaner, always ask for a reference. During the interview ask the prospective employee to substantiate his references. Early on in the interview you might ask, "Why did you leave your last job?" If you're given a vague answer, say you don't understand and ask that the reason be explained more clearly. After the interview speak directly to the people who have given the references. Checking references by telephone is the simplest method and also possibly the most effective. People tend to be more candid over the phone than they will be in a letter.

Letters of Reference

A letter of reference includes the employee's name, length of employment, the kind of works he did, a mention of the employee's honesty, competence, disposition and any other qualities which made the person a desirable employee. Since the letter is for a future employer to read, it's not necessary to write an introduction or a closing. Do sign the letter and include your phone number.

An enthusiastic letter of reference might read:

> To Whom It May Concern:
> I'm happy to have the opportunity to give Suzanne McConnell a reference.
> Ms. McConnell has worked for me doing general housework for the past two years. She has done all the work which we originally discussed she would do. In addition, she has used her own initiative and, when she has had time, has surprised me on countless occasions by doing much more than I ever asked. She is an honest and cheerful person.
> We're moving to Denver in January and the children and I will miss Ms. McConnell.
> Please do call me if you have any further questions.
> Sincerely,

Of course a letter of reference is meant to help an employee find a job. I do think, however, that if you fire an employee because you think she was incompetent, it's better to write a letter which may sound a bit flat and unenthusiastic than to write no letter at all. To refuse to write any kind of reference may deprive that person of his or her livelihood. Yet you do have a responsibility to the next employer; if someone calls to check on your recommendation, you mustn't lie or omit the facts.

A tepid letter of reference might read:

To Whom It May Concern:

Annette Thompson has looked after my children and done light housework for me for two years.

Ms. Thompson is a hard worker and is cheerful and considerate as well. However, in all honesty I must tell you that she is only fairly reliable. On several occasions she neither arrived at work nor telephoned to give me advance warning. As I must leave for the office before the children get off to school and I return in the evening after the children's dinner time, it is important that I have a reliable person to look after the children.

If you time is more flexible than mine and your life less structured, I hope you'll sit down and talk with Ms. Thompson about this problem, and I hope you'll take her on with the understanding that she will be more reliable in the future. I certainly think she is worth the chance.

The children and I will miss her. Please do call me if I can be of further help.

Sincerely,

If an employee has behaved in a way which you can't condone —if he proves to be an alcoholic or is dishonest—writing a letter of recommendation would be irresponsible. Instead, you might try to direct the person toward getting help.

FIRING

Though firing is almost always unpleasant, there's no reason it can't be done with grace. Naturally there is a temptation to avoid an unpleasant confrontation by doing the firing by telephone or by letter. However, this is a temptation that must be resisted. You must discharge an employee in person. In the process of firing, truth is both a shield and a weapon. Explain accurately the situation that has brought about this meeting. Avoid adding to the hurt of the firing by careless or cruel words. Lies, no matter how well phrased, may make your task easier, but they will leave you with a residue of guilt and leave your employee feeling resentful.

EXPLAINING THE WORK

Before the household worker begins, explain in detail the work you would like to have done and mention how often you'd like certain chores completed—for instance, how often you want the living-room windowsills dusted and the floors waxed. There are chores you'll want done every week (or every day if you have someone working for you that often) and other chores which have to be taken care of only occasionally.

Make certain that the chores you want done can be completed within the time your household worker will be in your home, allowing ample time for lunch and an occasional coffee break.

Write down a daily or weekly cleaning schedule. Tell the household worker that this schedule has worked for you in the past. The two of you can go over it in a week or two to iron out problems should they arise. Then if you want certain things done differently or you are dissatisfied, revising the work schedule won't sound like criticism. In turn, your household worker will be able to bring changes to your schedule without worrying about your reaction to her self-assertion. Also ask what the household worker will need in the way of cleaning equipment. Let the person who is doing the job decide on the products she likes best. After all, she's the professional.

It's also important to tell the household worker what you *don't* want her to do (cleaning breakables, for instance). And remember to ask if there is anything she will not do. Once the job begins, it's unfair to ask someone who is now at least partially dependent on you for her income to move heavy furniture or to paint the kitchen. If you're not home when your household worker cleans for you, write down what you'd like to have done but isn't getting done. Outlining the entire job on paper often works if you hire someone who doesn't speak English well. If necessary she can have the note translated by a friend.

For those meticulous types (I'm one, I must confess) the surest way to have someone do just what you want the way you want it is to spend a couple of days or at least a couple of hours explaining what is to be done and demonstrating how to do it.

Don't be the wicked stepmother who demands perfection. Mistakes, unless they are excessive, or they aren't mistakes, need only to be acknowledged, not dwelt upon. The smart boss, in the office or at home, will accentuate the positive before trying to eliminate the negative. Give the good news first, by giving a compliment: "You keep the silver so beautifully shined. Thank you!" Then mention what you'd like done differently: "Could you start to dust the windowsills twice a week? It seems as if the air is getting more and more polluted and the dirt is ending up inside."

A NOTE TO A HOUSEHOLD WORKER

When writing a note to a household employee, address it as though you were speaking to each other: "Dear Kate [Dear Mrs. Bridges]: Please iron the shirts I left on the drier. Thank you. Judith [or Mrs. Ferguson or Judith Ferguson]."

SPEAKING YOUR MIND

If there are things that aren't getting done, or you are in some way dissatisfied with an employee, it's best to speak your mind. If you want something done, say so. If you resist mentioning that the flat silver hasn't been polished you'll feel resentful, a feeling your household worker is likely to pick up; consequently she'll feel resentful. A frank talk will bring the feelings on either side out into the open, and the employer–employee relationship will run more smoothly. I once hired a full-time household worker who agreed at the initial hiring that she was to work on occasional weekends and evenings. She was a marvelous worker, so when she began complaining about weekend and evening hours at first I tried to reschedule my time to appease her. After a few weeks of unsuccessfully juggling her time and mine, I told her that if she was going to continue to work for me I would need her to work sometimes on weekends and in the evenings. If this wasn't the kind of job she wanted she should try to find another one. She resigned —and the next morning withdrew her resignation. She said she liked working for me too much. Now if either of us has any problems we discuss them.

SAYING "THANK YOU"

To know what to expect from an employee does not mean to take the fulfillment of those expectations for granted. I always say "please" and I always say "thank you." When the mail is brought to me in the morning or a telephone message is given to me when I'm working at my desk, I say, "Thank you." When my full-time household worker goes home in the evening, I say, "Thank you," and she understands I'm thanking her for what she has done for me during the day.

EMPLOYER–EMPLOYEE RELATIONSHIPS

A question which often arises in a discussion of household workers is, how personal should your relationship with your employee be? I think the best tone to adopt is the one *you* are most comfortable with.

I run a relatively formal household. I don't carry on long chatty conversations with the people who work in the house, but I do take an interest in them and in their families. For instance, if I know that my household helper Margaret's cousin, with whom she lives, is sick I'll offer her an extra day off or ask what I can do to help.

I have friends who, characteristically, do chat with those who work for them and have a much more personal and informal relationship with their household help than I do. The relationship you develop with someone who works in your house depends on your own personal style and on the style you set in your household. I've heard of one instance where a household employee was invited to share Thanksgiving dinner as a guest with her employer's family and friends. I think this is still a rare occurrence.

Some people are purposely aloof with their household employees because they fear that if they become too friendly they will be asked for favors. If you are going to say no—or feel bullied into saying yes—when asked a personal favor, it is wise not to become involved in your employee's personal life in the first place. Treat the person who works for you in your home just as you would treat someone who worked for you in an office—or how you would like to be treated by your own employer. An employer has no trouble asking an assistant to make a phone call, type a letter, or retype a letter to correct a mistake. At the same time, she treats her assistant with the same respect given to anyone who does his job well.

SALARY

Before the household worker begins to work for you, the two of you should have agreed on salary and on when and how it is to be paid. Pay no less than the minimum wage. Pay overtime compensation of at least 150 percent of the employee's hourly rate for hours worked in excess of forty hours per week.

The salary for household workers varies depending on where you live. If you're not sure how much to pay, ask an agency what the usual rate is for the kind of work you want done. You may be able to get away with paying less. Don't. If you don't have the money for a car or a cake you have to make do without. That's the way it should be with household workers.

SOCIAL SECURITY

Legally, it is an employer's responsibility to send Social Security payments to the Internal Revenue Service every three months. The employer and the employee pay an equal percentage of the employee's annual earnings to Social Security. It is often assumed that a household worker doesn't want Social Security because then she will have to pay income tax on the earnings. The tax, because the income isn't high, isn't very much, and if she doesn't have Social Security she won't have protection in case of illness and will receive no money after retirement and no insurance for dependants after her death.

If the employee's quarterly pay is $1,000 or more, participate in the State Unemployment Compensation Fund and provide Worker's Compensation benefits. Check with your state office for their required plans of payment.

VACATION PAY

An employee working in a house is given the same kind of consideration as someone working elsewhere. Full-time employees should receive a minimum of two weeks paid vacation a year, according to the National Committee on Household Employment, an organization of ten thousand household workers which has developed a Code of Standards to help create a reasonable business relationship between employee and employer. Of course someone who has been with you for years would receive a longer vacation. A household worker who works one day a week should receive one day paid vacation for each six-month work period. If you go to the country every summer or you spend a month on vacation, tell your employee of your plans when she is hired or as soon as you make them. If you do go away for an extended period (any time over two weeks), possibly your household worker can come in that extra week or so that you're away to attend to those chores which you're always meaning to do but which never get done—say cleaning out the kitchen cabinets or the closets.

Ideally, you would have enough for your household help to do when you're gone on vacation and you should therefore let the employee decide when she would like to take her own—which may be at a different time than yours. It's irresponsible to go away a week here and a week there and expect an employee to vacation whenever you're away. She cannot hope to support herself on your whim.

After Christmas or after a hectic period of entertainment it is thoughtful for an employer to give a household worker one or two long weekends or a couple of extra days off. Don't let an employee's willingness to work especially hard and for long hours go by without being especially acknowledged; the fact that the employee was paid for her extra time goes without saying.

SICK LEAVE

According to the Code of Standards of the National Committee on Household Employment, the number of days allotted for sick leave per year should equal the number of days the employee works in a week.

LEGAL HOLIDAYS

The Code of Standards suggests that day workers should receive a minimum of one legal holiday with pay per year; full-time employees, six holidays per year; live-in workers, eight legal holidays per year.

CHRISTMAS

An employee who works for you one day a week would get an extra one week's salary at Christmas. Since we all need extra money for the holidays, it's thoughtful, if you're giving money for a present, to give it a week or two in advance. You may also wish to give a small present: a pretty Lucite picture frame, a canvas carryall, perfume if you know what scent your employee likes. Though clothes which you don't wear and which are in good condition are welcomed by employees and often by friends, they are not suitable for Christmas presents.

PAID HOLIDAYS

Just as an employee in an office or a factory receives paid holidays, so does yours. What you decide are holidays may vary a bit from the usual legal holidays. If your daily help comes every Thanksgiving, for instance, to help out with an enormous family gathering, you may decide on time and a half for payment or you may substitute her birthday as a holiday in lieu of Thanksgiving.

LOANING MONEY

Loaning money to an employee is a personal decision which cannot be based on outside rules. Each situation must stand by itself. Concern yourself with the realities of the situation and not with abstract rules about borrowing and lending money.

Before making a loan, ask yourself, Am I resentful about making the loan? Do I feel forced in any way to make it? If you answer yes to either question, don't loan the money. If you'd rate yourself a potential, if insecure, lender, arrange at the time of the loan the terms by which it will be repaid. The two of you decide what would be a realistic figure to take out of weekly or monthly paychecks.

If you're the kind of person who is prepared when you loan money not to get it back and you realize full well it's not because people don't want to pay you but rather because they *can't* pay you

—after all, if they had enough money they wouldn't need to borrow any in the first place—don't think that just because *you* haven't thought about the loan since the day you made it the lender has also forgotten. The burden of owing can be much greater than that of lending. An employee who owes you money can think that *you* are thinking all kinds of terrible things about her for not repaying. Best to circumvent such illusory quarrels and make an agreement satisfactory to both for paying back the money.

A fair question to all: How can I seem so selfish as to say, "No I won't loan the money," to someone who by the very nature of our relationship has less money than I? Unless you really don't have the extra money to loan, I wouldn't use that as an excuse. Tell the truth, "I'm very uncomfortable about loaning money," or, if that much straightforwardness sticks in your throat, "Yes, but we should talk about how the loan will be paid back."

THE HOUSEHOLD WORKER'S POSITION IN YOUR HOUSEHOLD

Introductions

A household worker is introduced to each member of the family, and the family is, in turn, introduced to her. "Doug, this is Carol Housman. Carol, this is my husband, Doug Berger." In all introductions first and last names are used, unless you are introducing children, in which case you may use only the child's first name. (See also "Greetings," in Chapter 1, "Everyday Manners in Public Places.")

A host introduces household help to visitors when it would be awkward not to. Overnight guests are introduced to make it easier for the help and the guests during their stay. Dinner or cocktail guests wouldn't be introduced to a household worker unless you wanted a special friend to meet someone who works for you of whom you are very fond.

If a friend visits during the day and you two enter a room where a household helper is working, do make introductions (introduce the help to the visitor first, and then the visitor to the help) if it would make you more comfortable.

In households in which a household worker may come in, say, one day a week, the employer–employee relationship is not so well defined as it is in houses with full-time or live-in help. It's more usual for the employer to introduce a visitor and an employee as a matter of course, just as you would introduce any two strangers who found themselves together under your roof.

(For information regarding guests' tips to a full-time or live-in household worker, see Chapter 4, "Overnight Guests.")

Household Formalities

A household worker answers the phone with "Fergusons' residence," "Mrs. Ferguson's residence," or simply "Hello." What you would prefer depends on the style of your household. Discuss your preference with your employee in advance.

Announcing a meal: "Lunch [dinner] is served."

Offering a guest something to drink: "May I bring you something to drink?" or "Will you have something to drink?"

Answering the door: "Good morning, may I take your coat?" or "Will you leave your coat upstairs?"

THE CHILDREN'S NURSE

Traditionally, a children's nurse is called by title and last name —Miss Francis; she may also be called Nanny or a pet name the children have for her. If the nurse is French she may wish to be called Mademoiselle; if she's German, Fräulein. The name the children call their nurse is the name the whole family uses. Nanny is Nanny to all. Instead of a uniform she might wear a simple dress in a neutral color.

The nurse eats meals with the children. When the children are no longer toddlers and they begin to eat dinner with the parents, the nurse joins the family—unless the parents are entertaining. In this case the nurse may eat her dinner early or she may be served a tray in her room. On these evenings, tell her simply, "Company is coming for dinner tonight. The children knew Michael and Trudy when we lived in Toledo, so they will be eating with us at seven-thirty. Would it be convenient for you to eat earlier?"

WHAT TO SERVE LIVE-IN HOUSEHOLD WORKERS

If a household worker eats alone, don't give her hamburger when the family will be dining on duck *à l'orange*. In the home of a friend of mine, the cook plans a separate menu for the staff. The food, though it isn't served with elaborate garnishes, is as good as the family menu.

MOTHER'S HELPER

Households today with young children and working parents may have a mother's helper, or part-time housekeeper. The informality of a relationship with a mother's helper is much easier to adjust to than the strict correctness of a nurse—for parents as well as for children.

If a mother's helper is to do more than take care of the children —if she is to be responsible for such jobs as cleaning, cooking, shopping, laundry or the washing up—each chore must be specified and agreed to before she is hired. Avoid the resentment of a competent mother's helper who finds herself taking on additional chores as time goes on. If your mother's helper is doing more than she was hired to do, her work should be acknowledged; she should be considered for a raise, or you should again review her responsibilities.

BABY-SITTERS

The most important consideration when hiring a baby-sitter is not whether he can get the children to bed on time or heat up the macaroni without mishap, but rather can the sitter cope in an emergency; is he reliable and sensible?

Age is not always the final consideration. The baby-sitters who take to the responsibilities of the job most naturally are those who have taken care of children before. A twelve- or thirteen-year-old with younger brothers or sisters may often be more desirable than a seventeen-year-old who has not spent time around children.

If someone is sitting for your child, write down specific instructions for care and feeding. If your children are older, put down on paper any instructions which are important to you or your children or any information that you're afraid the sitter may forget. Always, of course, leave a number where you can be reached. If you are on the town, call in during the evening.

Your responsibility to the sitter is to tell him approximately when you'll be home and to abide by your estimated time of arrival. If the sitter is at your home at mealtime, a meal must be provided. Snacks and something to drink should be left for the sitter for nonmeal times.

Pay your sitter the rate standard in your community. Don't underpay. People who are underpaid often take their frustration and anger out on their work. In this case, the money you save would possibly be at your child's expense. If you want your sitter to do more than attend to the needs of your child—to straighten up the living room or wash dishes—this must be agreed upon beforehand, and the rate of pay must compensate for the extra work.

Should Teenage Sitters Be Allowed to Entertain?

It depends on the judgment and maturity of the sitter. Few parents would have reservations if a girl asked a girl friend to keep her company. If a boy is going to keep her company, don't be surprised to see lights snap on as your car pulls into the driveway. Whether or not you allow members of the opposite sex to accompany your sitter is up to you—a house never burned down around necking teenagers, and a child's cries can certainly be heard above heavy breathing probably more clearly than above the sound of the television—but you may not, as I do not, approve of this sort of behavior during someone's working hours, in your house.

THE REGISTERED NURSE

A registered nurse is called by title and last name. She eats her meals with the family or, if she'd rather, has them served to her on a tray in a sitting room. When on duty she wears a uniform which she provides. The nurse takes care of her own room and her laundry.

14 FUNERALS

Years ago, old people lived at home with their families and died at home, generation after generation. Death was part of the everyday. Today, in our society old people are exiled to retirement villages, and death generally occurs in a hospital and is an impersonal event. Medical science keeps us alive longer and longer, increasing our hopes for eternal life and, consequently, adding to our denial of death.

Our unresolved anxiety about death and loss can stand in the way of our helping the bereaved. Death and mourning are treated with prudery—a defense against the pain of someone else's loss— which increases the isolation of the bereaved. We tend to formalize our own distress in clichés, worrying about the proper form to express our sympathy, worrying about what should be said instead of saying and doing what comes from the heart.

Death is the one fact of life about which we should all prefer to remain ignorant. But ignorance about death is no different from ignorance about anything else: it gives rise to unfounded prejudices, fears, myths and painful blunders.

Although no one is comfortable in the face of death, Anne Rosberger, M.S.W., and Henry Rosberger, M.D., directors of the Bereavement and Loss Center in New York City, which provides counseling for the bereaved, believe that, for the benefit of all of us, the subject of death should be brought out in the open. Death would possibly then be less frightening and we would not have to push aside those who symbolize death (widows, for instance, are avoided by many of us as a symbol of death and, therefore, of our own vulnerability). If you look in the dictionary, you'll find the word "widow" also defined as a term for card players; it means an additional hand dealt to the table. As a printing term, "widow" is defined as an incomplete line of type. A widow not only feels this kind of separateness but is also treated as an incomplete person, as an extra.

People should discuss death, so that when it does occur at least some of the external, concrete matters—bills, insurance, etc.—will be known and understood. Although it won't ease your grief —you can't prepare for the way you'll feel if someone you love dies —if certain factors related to death are discussed, your life will be simplified should death occur.

MAKING ARRANGEMENTS

In the face of some opposition, the Superior Court of Los Angeles ruled that Mrs. Sandra Ilene West, widow of a Texas oil millionaire, should be buried as she requested, "next to my husband in my lace nightgown . . . in my Ferrari, with the seat slanted comfortably." A Superior Court commissioner said the request was "unusual but not illegal," and said the costs of the funeral and shipping the car to Texas, about $17,000, should be paid by Mrs. West's estate, which had been unofficially valued at between $3 million and $6 million.

Few of us have the money or, I am sure, the inclination to be buried in the style of Mrs. West. Nevertheless, most of us, I am also sure, do have preferences regarding burial, cremation, donating organs to science, and type of funeral or memorial services. These are preferences which should be expressed now; you won't have a chance when the subject is pertinent.

Even if you don't have strong preferences, funeral arrangements should be made during one's lifetime in order to remove the burden from one's family. It can be very distressing for a spouse or a close member of the family to have to make the arrangements after your death. Last-minute decisions at such a time may not be exercised with the best judgment, and they may turn out to be unsatisfactory and very expensive as well.

You might also prepare lists of information surviving family members will need, such as the names of the family lawyer and accountant, the numbers of bank accounts and insurance policies, the location of safe-deposit boxes, and lists of real-estate holdings, stocks and bonds and other pertinent estate data.

WHAT THE FUNERAL REPRESENTS

The funeral defines the abstract conception of death in very real terms. The ritual gives reality to an otherwise unreal situation; it stands as testimony that the death is true. The funeral also serves as a reaffirmation of life, as it gives meaning and scope to a life recently lived which has so suddenly become only a memory.

Funerals are for the dead as well as for the living and should, therefore, be a reflection of the way a person lived and the way friends, family and community felt about the person who died. There was a time when the elaborateness of the funeral was an accurate measure of greatness—funeral monuments ranged from the flaming barges of the Viking warlords to the Pyramids at Giza. Today, however, we acknowledge simplicity as the best way to honor someone who has died. Don't determine the value of a funeral in terms of dollars and cents. Sometimes the simplest funeral, with the simplest casket, can be the most moving.

NOTICE OF DEATH

Death notices are sent to the morning paper in large cities or the local paper in the country. They contain the date of death, the names of the immediate family and the place and time of the funeral. Sometimes the notice contains requests that a contribution be given to charity in place of sending flowers. If the funeral is private, the notice will say so and neither the time nor the place of the funeral will be given.

A death notice might read as follows:

> SNODEN, JONATHAN, [beloved] husband of Eleanor Knowles Snoden and father of Jeremy and Peter Snoden. Services Sunday, April 10, at 10:30 A.M. at St. Thomas the Apostle Church (1958 Woodhaven Boulevard, Manhasset).

VISITING THE FUNERAL HOME

When my Grandmother Ford was dying, she made arrangements to be laid out in her own home, with white roses in every room. Today, the laying out of the dead almost always takes place in a funeral home. Members of the family receive friends there rather than at home. The laying out of the dead, the Catholic wake, was originally a vigil of waiting for the funeral itself. Wakes used to be held at home. The body was laid out after embalming, and friends and family would sit in an all-night vigil. Now wakes are reduced to defined hours and are for the most part held in a funeral home.

When friends call at the funeral chapel, they sign their names in the register in order that the family will have a record of those who called. One doesn't stay more than the few minutes it takes to offer sympathy to members of the family. And one needn't pass by an open coffin if one doesn't want to. A friend may visit during a time when no immediate member of the family is present, and the family may wish to send a note to those they didn't greet in person (although callers need not be thanked by letter). Similarly, the caller who only signs the register and doesn't speak with a member of the family may wish to send a condolence note also.

FUNERAL SERVICES

A Protestant service can be a brief one or one that runs the length of a regular church service. The Catholic funeral Mass includes readings from the Bible by relatives and friends. The priest delivers a homily and refers to the person who has just died, although there is no actual eulogy. At a Jewish funeral, the rabbi will recite prayers in memory of the person who has died. A eulogy is part of the service. At Jewish and Catholic funeral services, the coffin remains closed. Protestants may have an open or closed casket; it's a matter of the family's choice.

Honorary Pallbearers

At a church funeral, the person in charge of arrangements will ask six or eight men, close friends and/or relatives of the person who has died, to be honorary pallbearers, who walk in front of the coffin as it leaves the church; they do not carry the coffin—that is left to the trained assistants of the funeral director.

There are rarely pallbearers at the funeral of a Christian woman, though at Jewish funerals both men and women may have pall-bearers.

Ushers

In a large church service, ushers—male relatives and close friends of the person who has died—escort people attending the funeral to their seats. Unlike a wedding, the ushers do not offer their arms, except to someone who needs help in walking. At a funeral home, the men on the staff generally act as ushers.

The Funeral

My Grandmother Ford had designated that at her funeral the church was to be filled with only white roses. I'll never forget how beautiful the church looked. I think that every funeral should have a touch of white roses. In other words, the funeral should reflect the beauty in the life of the person for whom it is being held. A funeral should be everything that the person who has died would have wanted it to be.

Bennett Cerf's funeral was, I think, just that sort. All the people with whom Bennett Cerf had surrounded himself in his life were there—friends of authors, publishers and entertainers. Scripture which he had particularly liked was read. The service opened with a medley of some of his favorite songs and closed with Phyllis Newman singing "You Can't Take That Away from Me." The funeral, while unorthodox, had great warmth in a style which was very much Bennett Cerf the television personality and Bennett Cerf the distinguished book publisher, proving that protocol is not important if it in any way depersonalizes the service and obscures the true identity of the person to whom the tribute is being paid.

Offering a Word of Sympathy at the Funeral

Unless the funeral is a very large one, offer a word of sympathy to the family after the service. If you've already seen the family before the funeral, say a word or two about the service. You can just say, "It was a lovely service." If the service wasn't lovely and you don't feel comfortable saying it was, choose something specific about it which you can fairly praise: "I appreciated the minister's reference to Ben's influence on young people."

Those who attend the interment or the short ceremony before the cremation are asked specifically by the family. Generally, only a few people, family and very close friends, are present.

AFTER THE FUNERAL

Generally, after a funeral, there is a reception, with friends and family getting together at the house of one of the immediate family. Close friends and family supply the food. Often a funeral brings together friends and relatives who rarely see one another. This kind of reception after the funeral is a binding together, a reaffirmation and a show of support for the bereaved.

DIVORCED FAMILIES

Funerals, just as weddings, are extraordinary events. At such times, divorced families should call a truce and both sides should be able to attend. A divorced spouse who was close to an in-law who has died or the ex-spouse of a person who has died should be given the opportunity to grieve openly and should be invited to the funeral. Whether or not he or she desires to attend is, of course, a personal decision. A death eclipses family feuds; friends and family must consider this and make the necessary allowances.

SENDING FLOWERS

Flowers are sent to the church or to the funeral home. They are addressed: "The funeral of Jonathan Snowden, Parkhurst Funeral Home, 115 Main Street, Charleston." Always include a plain white card from the florist or your own visiting card. The brief message on the card can read: "Please accept my sympathy at this time," or "My prayers are with you and your family."

You may wish to send flowers to the family in the weeks after the funeral. Your enclosed card might read: "Love to you and your family," or "Thinking of you and your family."

ACKNOWLEDGMENTS FOR FLOWERS

A member of the family or someone from the funeral home should be delegated to collect the cards sent with the flowers and to note a description of the flowers on the back of the card. This is done in order that when thank-you notes are written the kind of flowers or the arrangement of the bouquet can be mentioned.

The thank-you letter need be only a few words. A member of the family or a close friend may write on behalf of the person who has suffered the greatest loss; in this case, they would sign their own name.

A similar acknowledgment is sent when a donation to charity has been made.

If the funeral is a very large one and there are hundreds of acknowledgments to be made, printed cards are usually sent. The card might read: "Your expression of sympathy is greatly appreciated."

If the request to omit flowers is overlooked by a few, a note is still sent to thank these people for their kindness. Friends may not have seen the notice or they simply may have forgotten the request. Whatever the reason, the gesture of concern and sympathy is appropriately acknowledged.

DONATIONS TO CHARITY

When you send a donation, include a note. You can say: "This donation is sent in the memory of Jonathan Snowden, 117 North Avenue, Charleston." Be sure to write your name and address on the note so that the charity can send a notice of your contribution to the family and can send you an acknowledgment that the donation has been received. The acknowledgment from the charity does not take the place of a thank-you note from the family.

CONDOLENCE LETTERS

Here is a time when eloquence won't be enough; in fact, it won't even be noticed. Letters of condolence must come from the heart if they are to serve their purpose—to supply comfort.

Lynn Caine, in her very moving and helpful book *Widow*, in which she writes about her own experiences when her husband died, makes a number of firm suggestions concerning the condolence letter.

The letter should not dwell on how *you* feel. Ms. Caine says that most of the letters she received were expressions of personal awkwardness and discomfort, addressing themselves more to the writer's distress than to the widow's sorrow. Don't tell the bereaved how badly you feel; Ms. Caine says, quite rightly, that they can one-up you in spades.

A good condolence letter offers comfort. The comfort can be in the form of a specific remembrance of the person who has died, something the person once said or did which touched you. You can be specific about characteristics that were special. You can also offer more concrete comfort: your letter may include an invitation for a weekend, in which case you must demonstrate your sincerity by following up with a definite invitation in the near future; you can offer to help. When you do offer help, you may wish to be specific—baby-sitting, car pooling, grocery shopping—or you may just send a general message that you can be counted on to help with whatever is most needed. The offer of help, like the invitation, must be followed up with a phone call to show that it was really meant.

Although the telephone is not a substitute for a condolence letter, if you think making a call will make it easier for you to write, then by all means do so.

It is a thoughtful gesture to include in your letter a line or two to the effect that you understand how burdened the person is at this time and, though you would love to hear from her, she should not feel that your letter requires an answer.

Commercial sympathy cards are, I think, impersonal and superficial. They're the easy way out. If you must send one, please include your own message on the card.

If you're writing to someone whom you don't know well, write your own personal message just the same. Though your friendship may not be a deep one, the reason for your writing is. A note to someone you know only slightly might read:

> *Dear Matthew:*
> *Please accept my sincerest sympathy at this time. I know your mother meant a great deal to you, as she did to*

many people. She was a very fine woman and my prayers are with you and your family.

A condolence letter to the family of an old friend might read:

Dear Mrs. Granger:
I was shocked and saddened to hear of Andrew's death. Although I hadn't seen Andrew in a long while, I have thought of him often and with deep affection. I can now only offer my sympathy and my dearest love.

A letter to a friend in the community might read:

Dear Alice:
How saddened I was to hear of Henry's death. I want you to know that you are often in my thoughts. The early-morning runs the three of us enjoyed on the beach and the fits of giggles we had when we were too exhausted to run anymore will always be precious to me. If I can be of help to you in any way, please let me know.

REPLIES TO CONDOLENCE LETTERS

Your reply can be brief, and it need not be written immediately upon receiving a condolence letter. If you receive hundreds of letters, it is appropriate to send a printed card (either on plain white paper or on the traditional mourning paper with the black border) in return to those whom you know only slightly.

You may wish to reply personally to many people who wrote to you. After my Grandmother Ford died, my father chose two hundred people to whom he wanted to write, although it took him several months to complete the list. Printed cards were sent out to the hundreds of others who sent flowers and letters.

A printed card might read:

The family of Ms. [or Mrs.] Joan Smith deeply appreciates [thanks you for] your thoughtfulness.

CONDOLENCE CALLS

Traditionally, condolence calls were drop-in calls. Today, unless dropping in is a regular custom in your community, it is best to call first.

There is no absolute time to call. If you are close to the family, you would, of course, call immediately upon hearing of the death. If there is a question about when to visit, ask someone within the immediate family. If no one has indicated an appropriate time, it is better to make a call and stay a short time than not to call at all.

You can stay just ten or fifteen minutes, if you like. Remember, you can always come back again.

Because a Jewish burial takes place a day or two after the death, one wouldn't call before the funeral services, unless one is a very good friend. The Jewish period of mourning, called shiva, takes place after the funeral and lasts for seven days. Flowers are rarely sent. Bring food with you when you pay your call. This custom makes it possible for the family to offer food to all callers and to have enough food for the family so that they won't have the extra burden of cooking and planning meals.

Don't worry about what to say when you make your call. Your presence is all that's really required. It is, in fact, better to remain silent than to say something which sounds false.

UNDERSTANDING THE EXPERIENCE OF BEREAVEMENT

After the preparation and confusion surrounding the first few days after the funeral is the time when friends are needed most. In order for friends, relatives and acquaintances to lend their support, it is helpful for them to understand a bit about what the bereaved is experiencing. Anne Rosberger, co-director of the Bereavement and Loss Center in New York City, outlines here the four stages of bereavement:

The State of Shock

In this first stage, the bereaved feels a numbness equivalent to a state of shock. Because the bereaved does not fully relate to what has happened, she or he is detached from the reality and is therefore able to move along fairly smoothly, to make funeral arrangements and to take care of business arrangements. This is also the period when friends and relatives rally around to give the most comfort and support.

The Stage of Pining and Searching

Slowly, the bereaved begins to form a clearer picture of reality, although she or he is as yet unable to fully accept the death. For instance, a woman whose husband has recently died will continue to search for him. She may see someone on the street who, from the back, looks very much like her husband. She'll run to catch up, only to be confronted with a stranger. She may feel her husband's presence in the house, may actually think she sees him sitting in his favorite chair. There are dreams of rejection and abandonment during this period. The widow may dream her husband is leaving her, asking for a divorce, or that she is searching for him but can't find him.

The Period of Depression

Following the period of search comes the full impact of the loss and, with it, depression. The bereaved recognizes that with all the searching, all the pleading and bargaining with God, the person she or he has lost will not return. Often, people close to the bereaved are upset by this emotional state. Remembering how remarkably well she or he held up in the beginning, they wonder how this same person can now be doing so badly.

We all remember Jackie Kennedy's great composure and self-control just after President Kennedy's assassination. Ms. Onassis was, at that time, in the first period of shock and numbness. Unfortunately, her public face did a disservice to widows who didn't see her after she had passed through that shock. Before the full impact has taken hold, it is usual for the bereaved to maintain a great deal of control. However, we expect people to continue to adopt the Jackie Kennedy façade at a time when to remain in control would be abnormal.

During the phase of depression, the bereaved may be anxious, jittery, always on the go; or she could behave in just the opposite manner, sleeping an inordinate amount of time and rarely leaving the house. The bereaved may also be extremely irritable. What she used to hear as words of comfort may now sound annoying. A friend may be unable to discuss with the bereaved what used to be part of their pattern of chitchat. A show the friend has seen, a thought the friend wants to share are totally unimportant to the bereaved in the face of her loss. Friends find themselves constantly walking on conversational eggshells.

The Resolution

The final stage of mourning is the resolution. In this stage, the bereaved begins to make adjustments to a different life, begins to find some satisfaction in events and people outside himself and the life he has had in the past, and begins to explore new situations, new people and new forms of self-expression. The resolution has taken place when there is an obvious movement outward rather than a retreat inward and toward the past.

GIVING THE BEREAVED SUPPORT AND COMFORT

Anne Rosberger suggests some avenues open to friends and relatives which will help the bereaved. She also warns us of some dead-end streets to avoid.

Give (Almost) No Advice

Friends and relatives may feel they ought to provide something to fill up at least part of the emptiness caused by the loss of the bereaved. They may give unsolicited advice about money, funeral arrangements or business arrangements, not because they have special knowledge to offer but because they think *anything* is better than *nothing*. Nothing, however, is by far better than giving poor advice.

Also, stay away from advice regarding the social life of the bereaved: "You ought to date," "You ought to get out and meet people," etc. The bereaved will make up his own mind about when it is indeed time to meet new people. If the bereaved isn't interested, then it isn't time yet. Advice given to coax the bereaved out of mourning, such as "It's time you forget this; other people have been through it before, you're not the only one," is not only worse than useless but insensitive as well.

The only advice a friend might give the bereaved is to suggest that no major decisions be made during the first year. Wait before deciding to sell the house, moving to a new place, having a companion move in. During the first, unsteady year, almost any major decision will be a rash one.

Listen

Unfortunately, there are no words a friend can say which will make the situation better. Friends may walk away after visiting the bereaved, feeling they have offered nothing. It's an empty feeling, one you may want to shake away by offering advice and solutions for something for which you have no advice or solutions. What the bereaved needs most is for you to simply be there, to allow him to express feelings, fears and concerns openly. The most helpful part you can play, in most cases, is to be a good listener.

During the period of search, the bereaved may feel a need to tell the story of the death, the story of his despair and loneliness and guilt over and over again. This almost compulsive need for repetition is to try, through retelling, to make sense out of what seems to make no sense and also to try to make what happened unhappen. If the bereaved continues to explain and reexamine the entire process of what took place, to look for something which perhaps he could have done a little differently, the fantasy is that the bereaved may find the magic key which would unlock the door to life as it was. It's important to have friends who listen at this time.

Don't give in to the urge to share grief stories. You're there to show your sympathy, not swap experiences. That you too had a loss cannot now be expected to be understood or appreciated by the bereaved.

Don't speak of feeling better with time, it would seem gratuitous. The future you're describing offers no consolation now.

Be Encouraging and Giving

You needn't try to distract the bereaved. While distraction may work for a short time, the thoughts of the bereaved are bound to return to his loss, and your distractions will go unnoticed. The bereaved must be allowed to go through the process of grief; only then will he arrive at a state of restitution.

Instead of distraction, your encouragement—not to be confused with arm-twisting insistence—is needed. Encourage the bereaved to do what he might not do alone: take a walk, go out for a meal. Help the bereaved move out of aloneness by your accompanying him.

Don't Expect Thank-You's

Although you may be trying hard to encourage your bereaved friend to begin enjoying life once more, your acts of kindness may be repaid by nothing more than depression and, possibly, tears. Know that anything you do will be helpful in the long-term pull, even if, at the moment, your good deed has gone unnoticed. Don't expect immediate thank-you's and rewards at a time when the enormity of the loss eclipses small favors.

Be Accepting

During the period of depression, the bereaved may be angry at himself, guilt-ridden with feelings of not having been the best husband or wife and, at the same time, angry at the person who has died.

The bereaved may also direct anger at friends for not being able to provide something more comforting than a few soothing words and because friends' lives go on as usual while their own seems to have ended. The bereaved who experience the anger should not feel guilty about it; nor should friends, the recipients of the anger, take the situation to heart and feel they have been betrayed. If you're tempted to retaliate and reject the bereaved because you think a true friend would never behave toward you in this way, try to remember that the anger is not directed specifically against you, but rather that the bereaved is flailing out at life itself. Don't walk away from the person who is now so in need of your friendship.

Continue Your Support Throughout the Mourning Period

The circle of friends and relatives of the bereaved begins to collapse little by little as mourning progresses. Paradoxically, the collapse of the supportive network comes during the depressed time, when the bereaved needs people the most. During this time, friends may become upset just by talking to the bereaved. In order to protect themselves, they rationalize that, since they are obviously of no help, they may as well stop calling. Little by little, the bereaved may be left almost entirely alone.

Continue your contact with the bereaved throughout the entire phase of mourning. The times which are hardest for you, remember, are the times which are the hardest for the bereaved and the times when he needs friends the most.

Don't Foster Dependency on the Part of the Bereaved

When the bereaved is depressed and confused, it can happen that a friend offers so much support that the support becomes controlling, creating a highly dependent relationship with the bereaved. Then, when the bereaved is again able to move out on his or her own, the friend may become resentful: "I was there when you needed me. How come you don't need me now?"

Fostering a dependent relationship is fairly simple when the bereaved is confused. A friend who points in one direction—any direction—may be taken for a port in a storm. After the storm is over, however, what was once support can weigh as heavily as an anchor.

ENTERTAINING THE BEREAVED

In the early stages of mourning, invitations to friends' homes for very small gatherings are helpful. However, don't expect a bereaved person to function well at a dinner party where she is supposed to be a stimulating conversationalist and an exuberant and peppy guest. A larger party may come in quite handy much later on when the bereaved would be happy to meet new people.

BEREAVED CHILDREN

The grief process for a child is the same as for an adult. Therefore, a child can be helped through bereavement in the same way. Those close to the child should be supportive, encouraging and good listeners; children should be included in the discussions and feelings about the death of the loved one.

Anne Rosberger has made note of some of the reactions which can be expected from a bereaved child:

School work may deteriorate. The school should be told, of course, if the child has suffered a loss.

Many children don't mention the death. They are embarrassed by it; they feel it puts them on the outside, makes them different. They know, just as adults do, that they may be rejected because their close relationship to death is so frightening.

Some children, just like some adults, don't seem to react at all. A lack of reaction can be as much of a telling sign as overreaction. If you discuss with your child's teacher what he might expect and if the teacher understands a little about a child's reaction to death, then the teacher can be of help to the child and can also be alert to behavior that may be necessary to bring to a parent's attention.

Children, especially young ones, should be encouraged to take part in extracurricular activities and social life, if they so desire. Older children should be allowed to decide for themselves if they want to participate in their usual social life.

THE BEREAVED OFFICE WORKER OR ACQUAINTANCE

If someone in your office has had a loss, you may want to make yourself available to help in whatever way you can. However, don't be overly solicitous to the point of intruding on the bereaved by constantly bringing up the death. Don't repeatedly ask how she is feeling or if everything is all right, and don't disconcert the bereaved by constant concerned looks.

Again, be a good listener. Be sensitive enough to take your cue from the bereaved. We can't be of much help if we are too busy speaking or too busy trying to do something. Instead, try not to intrude when no intrusion is necessary, and be there to give when your giving is needed.

If you meet an acquaintance who has had a loss and you've already spoken or written to that person, ask how she is getting along and if there is any way you can be of help. If you haven't spoken since the death, offer your sympathy: "I was so sorry to hear about Jonathan."

FOR THE BEREAVED: RESUMING A NORMAL SOCIAL LIFE

The kind of society in which we are now living is so mobile and transient that few of us enjoy the kind of support from relatives and friends that grew out of smaller, more cohesive communities. I think the outward signs of mourning, like mourning clothes, for instance, reflected the cohesive consciousness of the community and, I think, served a purpose. During the mourning period, people rallied around the bereaved and helped them get through a certain portion of the terribly unhappy time.

Today, of course, we have no such guidelines. The closest we come to traditional mourning dress is to wear dark clothes to the funeral. Most widows do not wear black for months or a year. Men usually don't wear the black armband. We reject the idea of outwardly expressing our grief. Black is not even necessarily worn at the funeral, although dark clothes are still required dress. As for the mourning period, most people today come to the funeral and then spend only a short period of time with the bereaved. There isn't a continuous supportive network following the very brief ritual at the ceremony or the chapel.

Since a prescribed period of mourning is no longer acknowledged by most, the bereaved must decide for himself what the mourning observance will be. We all have busy and demanding lives and therefore can't allow ourselves the protection and insulation which a period of mourning once offered. But even when there was a designated period of mourning, each person still had his own way of grieving and resolving the grief. And although mourning no longer takes place within an outward social structure —there's no longer a timetable or set rules—each person, of course, will grieve in his own way.

In our relatively impersonal society you do what makes you the most comfortable, what eases your pain and moves you forward. You do whatever does the most for you to help yourself through a critical time. You needn't stay home, as in the old days of mourning, and cloak yourself in unnecessary or purposeless formalities. You needn't overevaluate the reaction of friends, relatives and neighbors to your chosen mode of mourning. Though it's improbable that you'll feel like attending cocktail parties and the like, readjust your life to your own needs and values.

We all need time to mourn, more time than modern society gives us. Some of us need more time than others. We each have to decide for ourselves.

15 IN THE COMMUNITY: NEIGHBORS

MOVING DAY

Years ago, a newcomer in the community waited patiently for the neighbors to come and call. Today, it's more than likely that the person who is in the process of moving in will be at her new neighbors' door with a haggard smile and some urgent questions regarding the whereabouts of the hardware store or some other store dealing in life-support systems.

If you come through your moving day with all your extension cords intact and in the very boxes you remember packing them in, then you probably haven't yet met your neighbors. Neighbors are often hesitant to appear at a newcomer's door on moving day. They remember how difficult it was in the throes of moving day to meet new people.

It's a thoughtful gesture for an established neighbor to stop in for a moment on moving day with a jar of instant coffee, plus mugs, milk, spoons, etc. Taking your new neighbors' children on a run to McDonald's or bringing back lunch for the family might be more appreciated and more appropriate to the occasion than a homemade pastry from your kitchen.

You may prefer to meet your new neighbors under more ideal circumstances. You won't feel as though you are an unwanted spectator in the midst of a stranger's Sturm und Drang if you wait a day or two before presenting yourself. You can arrive with only a greeting; a gift is not necessary, though a loaf of bread and some salt, traditional welcoming gifts since Joseph moved in with Potiphar and his wife, is a simple and warm symbol of welcome.

GETTING ACQUAINTED

Young children are natural explorers. If you have any children, they'll most likely meet the neighbors before you and will help you to get acquainted. But you don't need children to act as forward observers in a new neighborhood, nor need you arm yourself with questions regarding shopping or school information as an excuse to introduce yourself. You can extend a purely social invitation to your neighbor for late morning or afternoon coffee. (These first meetings are best kept short so that both parties can slowly feel their way into the new relationship.) Even though you may already have met briefly, reintroduce yourself when you phone or even if you drop by; this will save your neighbor from the embarrassing blank moment. If you find it difficult to talk on the phone to someone you barely know, it's fine to make a call in person. Just drop in; if the time is obviously not right to stay and chat, issue your invitation and leave—don't linger.

When Marsha moved to the suburbs, her real-estate agent was thoughtful enough to supply her with the names of families in the neighborhood who had children the same age as her pre-schooler. Marsha took a deep breath and marched her little boy to the house across the street. Her neighbor was very friendly and a little embarrassed that she had allowed Marsha to make the first move. The children ended up spending the afternoon together, and Marsha, as yet without appliances in her new house, jumped at her neighbor's offer to use the washing machine.

MAKING YOURSELF KNOWN IN THE COMMUNITY

Marsha joined her college alumni club—something she had never done when she lived in the city. The club president had a tea to announce the arrival of a new member. To find out about clubs and organizations, ask neighbors, inquire at the Y, if you have one, and scan the local paper.

GOOD FENCES MAKE GOOD NEIGHBORS

Ties formed along the lines of neighborly interdependence can lead to successful friendships. On the other hand, many neighbors are good neighbors, not good friends. From the start, it's important to set up the type of relationship you want to maintain. You can hurt and confuse neighbors if, after an initial period of courting on your part—possibly because you were so glad to see a friendly face —you then decide you don't want your friendship to go beyond chatting over the hedge. While you're getting the feel of new territory, it's safer to escalate friendships slowly. Don't make friendly overtures to overcompensate for favors you are asking. If you are feeling guilty about asking too often for favors or borrowing too often, borrow less. If you don't want to raise your relationship to the status of friends, don't jump the boundaries which readily identify neighbors. Stick to the conversational topics you have in common: the goings on in the community. Be ready for your neighbor to consider you a friend if you bring up personal subjects.

Martha's relationship with her neighbor is a good example of a mutually helpful but not personal friendship. When Martha was new in the community, her neighbor gave a lunch for her and made curtains for her kitchen. The two women regularly share driving, baby-sitting and wholesale buying in quantity. They divide their cooking chores during the holidays; on Thanksgiving, Martha makes enough stuffing for two families, while her neighbor makes a double order of creamed onions. Their friendship, by silent agreement, stops at sundown. The husbands have their own friendship, centered around weekend gardening and household maintenance.

BORROWING

A good relationship with your neighbors can be somewhat symbiotic—it's comforting to have someone to whom you can turn for occasional small favors and, if you're really stuck, for a big one. Abusing mutual borrowing privileges can lead to unneighborly relations, a most unhappy state of affairs. When you borrow expendable items, replace them. Failing to do so may start your relationship on a downhill plunge that no amount of "I'm sorrys" can alter. Your neighbor probably won't even think about it if you forget to return that stick of butter she lent you; but after the butter, the last of her cornstarch, a handful of nails and a gallon of paint remover, she's apt to be angry and resentful.

Susan's unlimited borrowing managed to undo her relationship with more than one neighbor. Susan tried to keep her New York City apartment clean with just a broom and a dust cloth. When the dust began to pile up in drifts, she borrowed a vacuum cleaner from her upstairs neighbor. The next time, she borrowed from her downstairs neighbor. After a slight mishap with the downstairs vacuum (it cost her eight dollars to have a toy removed from the hose), Susan, by now with some trepidation, borrowed again from upstairs. Well aware of the trouble she was causing, she was careful and didn't even vacuum the children's room. Susan returned the vacuum as soon as she'd finished using it; even sooner, as it turned out. As the elevator door closed, she realized the machine she was carrying was still plugged into her living-room outlet. Susan had an instant of panic, inspired by guilt, and thought the cord would wrap itself around her like a boa constrictor. Instead, she was left to explain to her annoyed neighbor why the vacuum was now cordless. Once again, she had to have the machine repaired. Moral: Borrowing can, in the long run, be more expensive than buying what you need in the first place. Or its price may be measured out in pain and suffering—Susan's neighbor didn't speak to her for weeks and has never again progressed beyond the nodding stage, due, no doubt, to her instinct for self-preservation.

CANVASSING THE NEIGHBORHOOD

Another good-neighbor rule to follow: don't make your neighbors feel guilty or resentful. If you're selling raffle tickets for a community organization, or cars, or encyclopedias, a neighbor can be an easy target for the hard sell. Resist the temptation to parlay into a major sale your neighbor's guilt about the time she chipped your Great-Aunt Emma's crystal punch bowl. You have to see your neighbor on a fairly regular basis, and layers of underlying resentment won't help your relationship.

On the other hand, if you are a terrible salesman and dread the thought of canvassing the neighborhood, either by phone or door to door, don't let yourself be bullied into it. Tell your tormentor the truth: you'd be a liability to the organization as a fund raiser of any kind. If you think the organization in question is a worthwhile one and you feel guilty for saying no, offer to donate some of your time in another capacity. It's best to pick a specific activity, such as typing or sitting on the dance committee—whatever you'd feel most comfortable with.

CHRISTMAS CARDS

If you like to spread your good cheer during the holidays by sending Christmas or New Year's cards to both friends and distant acquaintances, you're aware by now that you won't receive a corresponding card for every one you send. Many people don't send cards at all. If you don't send cards, you needn't dash one off to someone just because you're included on her list.

HOW TO SAY NO TO A FRIENDSHIP

Just because you are unwilling to embark on a friendship with some of your neighbors doesn't mean they won't make overtures. You may find yourself in the position of continually declining a neighbor's invitations. If a couple of excuses aren't enough of a hint, don't let your reticence become rudeness, but continue to excuse yourself politely. Don't let yourself be hounded into an invitation you don't want and aren't planning to reciprocate. A few white lies which will prohibit a relationship at the outset will save you later from the unpleasantness of having to extricate yourself from a deeper involvement.

Sandy met a new neighbor at her child's kindergarten registration. After one brief get-together, Sandy realized she had very little in common with the woman. But Sandy's neighbor persisted, and occasionally Sandy felt guilty enough to accept her invitations. The last straw broke one evening around six, while Sandy was busy in the kitchen. Her neighbor, little boy in tow, rang the bell. Sandy, instead of saying she was frantically busy, which was true, invited them in—but for the last time. From then on, Sandy refused every invitation. Her neighbor was first hurt and confused and finally backed off completely. Now, when the two women bump into each other, Sandy gets a cursory nod.

Sandy had assumed, wrongly, that by not reciprocating she was sending out negative signals strong enough for her neighbor to catch. By being agreeable on one hand, and not reciprocating on the other, you are, in fact, sending a double message which is impossible to interpret.

Some feel it is appropriate to reciprocate once, even though they have no intention of building a friendship. If friends you know slightly invite you for dinner and during the course of the evening you realize this is not a friendship you want to continue, don't return the invitation. In inviting them back, you're doing just what you don't want to do. When you cast yourself in the part of unwilling host, you're being hard on yourself and doubly hard on your guests. How are they to know that you're only trying to do the "nice" thing?

WHEN YOUR CHILD AND YOUR FRIEND'S CHILD DON'T GET ALONG

An afternoon visit with a neighbor or friend which disintegrates into a referee match between the children is no fun, but it need not be embarrassing. Acknowledge the problem. Suggest that the two of you continue to see each other without the children for a while. Since small children change their minds hourly, in a few weeks they may drop their weapons and become the best of friends. Otherwise, keep your friendship and your children separate.

WHEN YOU'RE HAVING A PARTY

Let neighbors know in advance when you're having a large party. Your party may become noisy or the people next door may have to get their car out of or into a temporarily impassable driveway; it's less likely the neighbors will harbor a grievance if forewarned.

Proffer a party invitation to neighbors if you like; but don't be offended if they decline. Sometimes the best of neighbors have divergent interests and life styles. Ellen and Bob, who live in harmony with the people next door, don't consider one of their (always large) parties a success unless the liquor consumption is extraordinary. Their neighbors' idea of a good party is to have two or three friends in, listen to music and have a quiet dinner. Both couples realized a long time ago that their good-neighbor policies didn't include sharing each other's entertainments.

APARTMENT DWELLERS

Neighbors in apartment houses often retain strictly "Is it cold enough for you?" friendships. They usually don't become friendly unless they've bumped into each other repeatedly in the laundry room or walking their dogs, and even then their friendliness revolves around discussions concerning soap powders or the problems of curbing. Apartment houses are generally in an area where the community (schools, shopping, business)—the basis for country and, to a lesser degree, suburban life—is diffuse. Shared interests may go no further than the common front door. When so many people live so close together, the obviousness of elbow-to-elbow intimacy is glaring—your dreams and expectations are crimped on all sides by their dreams. Neighbors are hesitant and doubly careful about crossing boundaries of privacy and invading someone else's limited space.

These days, however, our self-imposed isolationist apartment politics are breaking down. Condominiums and cooperative apartment houses have brought about a community born of mutual interests. In landlord-owned apartment houses, where building maintenance or security is wanting, rent strikes or how-to-make-things-run-smoother meetings have brought otherwise insular and self-sufficient people together.

When You Find That Your Home Has Become a Commune

Reserved distance is sometimes exchanged for an almost communal style of living in apartment buildings. As in college dormitories, apartment communities generally run from floor to floor. One young couple were pleased to find their neighbors so friendly. However, they couldn't entertain without their neighbors, who would stop in to chat or borrow and, at the sight of new faces, felt encouraged to stay. The couple began hanging out a "Do Not Disturb" sign. Although this stopped the traffic, neighbors were offended by such an uncharacteristically abrupt and impersonal message. If you're in a similar situation, hold a meeting to set up community rules. Be specific. Complaints aired openly cut down on misunderstandings and hurt feelings.

How and When to Complain

Some of us have neighbors who make things go bump in the night—or worse. The art of complaining is a ticklish one. You don't want to be so belligerent as to make a declaration of war; but you must stand your ground to make your grievance known if you want to get results. If the television next door is turned to an ear-splitting decibel level late at night, resist the temptation to bang on the wall. This kind of retaliation could be misconstrued as a challenge. Instead, put on a bathrobe, leave your hair uncombed, and knock on your neighbor's door—let him see for himself the state he has reduced you to. But stay calm. An angry tone will put him on the defensive, in which case it's doubtful he'll pay much attention to your feelings.

If your neighbor is a chronic offender, reread your lease to see if a tenant can be evicted for the kind of disturbance he is creating. Write your landlord and, if possible, have other tenants cosign your letter.

An even more unsettling problem is how to deal with the couple who fight. One friend tried to stop a fighting couple by outshouting them. This tactic antagonized the couple so that the two of them joined forces in a temporary truce and turned their voices in unison against my friend until she relented. Once she relented, the couple began again to shout at each other. Another neighbor of habitual fighters goes downstairs and rings their buzzer until they stop. Although she has reported success with this method, I don't recommend it. Such retaliation is as unpleasant and rude as the behavior of fighters themselves. Also, you can't predict what people in an irrational state will do to stop you. If a fight sounds dangerous—and some do—call the police. Let them investigate your worst suspicions. If no one is being murdered, the additional commotion caused by the police may be embarrassing enough so that the next fight will at least be quieter.

If you are the ones the neighbors are complaining about, you might want to take a suggestion from another fighting couple. When they moved into a two-family house, they advised the people living below them of their habits. This saved the fighting couple from the embarrassment of an unwanted and, in this case, unnecessary intrusion. The neighbors, though they objected to the noise, knew at least that no one was in danger. While you can't as easily stop fighters from fighting as you can stop someone from playing the stereo at three in the morning, complaints aired at a time other than in the heat of battle can have a sobering effect. The couple in the two-family house perfected a quieter, less strenuous method of arguing after several encounters with the downstairs neighbors who took the opportunity when meeting them casually in the driveway or taking out the garbage to ask them to please keep their voices down.

One final and most important consideration: you know a lot about your neighbors if you live in an apartment building. You may have heard them fight. You may even have heard them make up. Be discreet. Don't forget, they know a lot about you, too. Don't abuse neighbor's privilege and gossip to others about those things which decency and common sense tell you are private.

DROPPING IN

You may have heard an elderly person reminisce about childhood trips when they accompanied their mothers and went "calling." Calling was a social convention with its own rules. A servant screened all callers, and it was not unusual for a maid or a butler to announce that Madame was not at home when, in fact, she might be seen peeking out at the visitor from behind a curtained window in the parlor. Technology has put a stop to what was once a pleasant and leisurely social pastime. Today, few people have the household help to screen unexpected visitors. Dropping in has become something to be reckoned with.

Unless you live in a community where dropping in is part of the accepted social scene, a rule of thumb to follow when you're thinking about surprising a friend or neighbor is: Call first. Even if your host isn't busy when you appear, greeting guests in a bathrobe can make one self-conscious. Company with no warning puts extra stress on the host because the traditional social situation—the host makes the rules and has control—has been reversed.

If you've been interrupted by unexpected visitors and feel in the mood to oblige, ask your guests to please make themselves comfortable in the living room or kitchen (it's fine to treat a drop-in very informally) and finish up whatever you're doing if it can't be postponed. You won't have a very good time and neither will your guests if unfinished business is nudging at the back of your mind.

What to Serve

You are certainly not expected to invite friends who have dropped in at mealtime to sit down with you. Don't feel pressured to pretend you're not about to eat and then go without a meal. If a set table and the smell of food don't deter your guests, tell them firmly you are sorry to cut their visit short, but you're about to sit down to dinner. Mention that you'd love to see them again soon. You can suggest that next time it would be better to make plans in advance so that you can spend more time together.

Jane, who runs her house in an informal and easy manner which suggests an atmosphere favorable to dropping in, admits she used to think she had to feed whoever stopped by. She felt imposed upon and then realized she was imposing upon herself—no one expected to be served a meal or even a doughnut when they just came by for a few minutes to chat. Jane stopped her extra marketing and cooking, and her friends still kept on coming over. She even got an extra dividend: some of her friends started dropping in with a snack for *her*. Jane learned that the quality of her friendships was not determined by her expertise as a short-order cook. Now, when friends stop in, she offers them something to eat only if she has something on hand. If they arrive at lunch or dinner, Jane advises them of her schedule, and her friends feel free to return at another time.

It's All Right to Say No

If a friend drops by at a bad time it's best to tell them so. You can say that you're terribly busy just now, that you don't feel very well, that you're tired; any simple and easily understood excuse will do. It's difficult to say no, but you'll probably find it more difficult to play the role of host when you don't feel like it.

16 FASHION

Fashion in America is as diverse and has as many faces of expression as the country itself. The place in which you live, the life you lead, the way you look and the way you feel about the world and about yourself all help to create a framework of what fashion is for you. The most important part of being fashionable and the part that is the most fun and the most personally involving is finding and dressing for your own style within your framework.

Remember that fashion is *not* a set of arbitrary rules and concepts to which you must subscribe whether it suits you or not; fashion is an expression of your personal taste. Fashion is *not* high-priced designer clothes in which the way you look is subordinate to the price and the label; a Dior gown that does not enhance your own personal style is less fashionable than a simpler, well-cut dress which becomes you.

In his book *Superchic*, author James Brady says that Coco Chanel used to tell him that fashion worked when it caused you to notice the woman, that it failed when you noticed what she was wearing.

HOW TO FIND YOUR OWN PERSONAL STYLE

Your personal style is much more than the clothes you wear, although your clothes help to bring out your spirit, help to communicate an unspoken message about who you are. Your personal style must begin with your own personal insights about yourself; this is the framework into which you will incorporate current fashion ideas; but your figure and the kind of life you lead are the basis for what will be your look, not the fashion magazines' pronouncement of their Spring Look or their New Look. Be aware of fashion; but, more importantly, be aware of yourself. Fashion is there to be exploited to your best advantage, to help you to bring out the best in yourself.

A large part of what is fashionable in terms of your personal style is based on what is practical. Wide, full sleeves, no matter how lovely, would be impractical for an active business woman. On the other hand, a writer I know spends much of her day wearing loose, flowing at-home caftans, comfortable and easy for her to work in. She selects clothes which fit in with her life style and, she says, with her sensibility. Your clothes can be pretty and functional as well. I'm not suggesting a strictly utilitarian basis for fashion; we can each find a look which is suitable as well as becoming.

And I'm not suggesting that a well-dressed woman can't be adventurous. Quite the contrary. But her personal innovations in style must be adapted to her needs and likes, not solely to those of the fashion industry. To be well dressed means, in part, to dress as an expression of your own personality, to dress the way you feel. For instance, I dress conservatively, which is very much an expression of who I am. My sister, Anne, dresses in a much more avant-garde style, an accurate expression of who she is.

Fashion decides for us what shape our bodies will take: sometimes the clothes we wear give us a rectangular shape, sometimes an hourglass shape. Fashion also tells us what parts of our bodies should be covered up or what parts we should show; it has created rotating erogenous zones. Backs, breasts, legs, arms are each given exposure for a time. Instead of relying on our own good sense, we let fashion tell us what is sexy.

Bare as much as you want of whatever you want, as long as you feel comfortable in doing so. If wearing décolletage, a low back or a sleeveless dress makes you self-conscious, if your every move is an attempt to cover up what you've left uncovered, you have let fashion override your common sense. You won't look terrific if you don't feel comfortable.

Fashion changes every few months, causing confusion in us all. When and if you get confused, take that as a welcome sign to stop and rethink your buying plans. Don't let indecision push you over the edge into buying something which looks wonderful on the hanger or on the person in the next dressing room but not so wonderful on you. Be honest with yourself. I know one very tall woman who yearns to wear ruffles and bows and frills. When she goes shopping, she succumbs to the temptation and tries on the ruffles, but when it comes to the actual buying she restricts herself to the simple clothes she knows suit her best.

Most of us in adolescence—more especially in college—went through a period of borrowing friends' clothes. Much of the fun was in playing out a different you—wearing something you yourself wouldn't buy (or your mother wouldn't have bought for you). Testing yourself out in this way not only was fun but could help you to find what was *really* you. Didn't you find that if you actually went out and bought a copy of something you had loved to borrow, it wasn't quite right? Allow yourself the same freedom to play when you're shopping; but when it comes to a purchase, let your sense of reality take over.

You can learn a lot about clothes and fashion from analyzing someone else's style, but admiration shouldn't turn you into a copycat. Wearing a dress which would look wonderful on a friend whose looks and style you admire won't help you to look like your friend. One woman I know realized that the beautiful sweater she had just bought—a heavy wool knit with a collar—was not really so becoming to her as to a well-dressed friend she was striving to emulate. Fortunately it was around Christmas time, and my friend reluctantly wrapped the sweater and gave it to her friend.

When you shop, try to put your other self aside—the self which is a composite of media propaganda, the part of you which yearns to be somebody else, and the part of you which is still bound to your mother's taste and approval. We were dressed by our mothers for so many years that most of us never fully leave behind our mothers' taste in clothes. Haven't we all heard friends say, half jokingly, "My mother would like that," as a rationale for a new purchase? While your mother may have excellent taste, and spending the rest of your life rebelling against it is not the wisest course, do keep in mind that developing an independent and individual style means developing the ability to make independent and individual choices.

BARGAINS

Is there such a thing as a bargain? Is there hidden treasure in unlikely places—at unlikely prices? Definitely, if you know how to choose. I wouldn't necessarily count on building a basic wardrobe from sales, but once you have your basics, sales can be used successfully to provide you with additions to complete your wardrobe. I think we have all learned the hard way that impulse buying at sales can cost you more than shopping without attention to sales at all.

I know one or two women who take care to appear only in designer clothes. They will even go so far as to wear only their French clothes in New York and their clothes purchased from New York designers in Paris. Other women take their own patience, persistence and fashion knowledge on their travels and unearth bargain clothes to fool their public and impress it as well.

One acquaintance of mine whose fashion sense is publicly admired bragged her secret to me in whispers when I complimented her on a jacket she was wearing. The jacket, she was thrilled to confide, was from a bargain basement! She couldn't resist letting me know that her eye for value is as sharp as her eye for fashion. She admitted an addiction to shopping in bargain stores. And I think, in any case, all women with a sense of fashion share the same secret: a piece of clothing that fits well and is becoming is a bargain no matter where or how it is found.

SALESPEOPLE

Some salespeople are disinterested and are of no help whatsoever, which is at least neutral. We all know the hard-sell types to stay away from. They'll insist you look marvelous in whatever you try on and will even attempt to intimidate you if they think it will make them a sale. Stick up for yourself if a salesperson is rude or disagreeable or unhelpful. I don't let bad manners overwhelm me. If I've just walked into a store and am not getting the help I'd like, I walk out just as quickly.

Of course, indulging a fit of pique which takes you out of the store is a luxury you can afford only if you went in to browse. A serious shopping expedition calls for more drastic measures. If you don't deal with the problem immediately, you'll be caught in the dressing room, the helpless victim of a bully or a Houdini who does a disappearing act just when you need her to find that green blouse in a smaller size.

Confront your salesperson nicely at the first hint of misbehavior, before you lose your temper and your back-and-forth parry turns into a brawl. Say, "We seem to be rubbing each other the wrong way. I'd like to have someone else help me." Or, if the argument has progressed further, "You're not being helpful to me at all. Possibly someone else can be."

Finding a Good Salesperson

I don't mean to imply that all salespeople need to be dealt with. There are some who can turn any shopping trip into a triumph. They have the ability to put together a perfect ensemble for you or to pull out the perfect coat or skirt which, until you try it on, seems indistinguishable from the dozens hanging on the racks. They have the unique ability to envision what something will look like on you even before it is off the hanger, while for most of us there is a sameness about rows and rows of clothes hanging side by side. I know that if I see a shapeless piece on a hanger, I'll be ready to pass it by; whereas if I see a dress with definite lines and cut which stand out even when it is hanging, I'll be already half persuaded that that's the dress for me.

If you find a salesperson with a knack, she'll teach you more in twenty minutes than you'd learn from a careful study of a year's supply of *Vogue*. Remember to ask her name so that the next time you're in the store you'll be able to find her again. If you're lucky, she'll still be on the sales floor. Spectacular salespeople are usually discovered early and promoted, which, in the long run, though you lose their personal attention, is even better for you. Their exuberance and talent will now be directed toward buying clothes for the store, and therefore what you have to choose from will initially have been selected by someone whose taste is in your favor.

Being a Good Customer

Part of good manners is acknowledging that all relationships, no matter how transitory, are two-way relationships. The treatment you receive from a salesperson depends, in part, on the consideration you show toward her. A salesperson is there to help you; she is not your personal maid; she is not there to pick up after you or to fetch and carry at your whim. Put clothes you have tried on back on the hanger. Refrain from issuing orders like a general. Don't take your troubles out on her; it's not her fault if the store doesn't carry something in your size. If you act contemptuously toward a salesperson or treat her badly, she'll repay you in kind— or unkind.

It works the other way also. If a salesperson goes out of her way for me, I go out of my way for her. I make it a point to write a complimentary letter about a remarkable salesperson to the head of the department. I think it's just as necessary to show your appreciation when someone is especially polite and helpful as it is to show your displeasure when she isn't.

THE LARGE AND THE SMALL

A friend confides that when she walks into certain stores she is really looking, like Alice, for a bottle that says, "Drink me." Then, magically smaller, she will be able to enter the Wonderland of size sevens.

I do think the larger woman is very much neglected. Clothes for larger women need to be in a style which is simple and tailored. A big woman would stay away from heavy fabrics and large prints which will only make her look heavier. Certain refined vertical stripes, not bold ones, can work very well.

One of the reasons a larger woman may dress simply is that her size works against a flamboyant style. One friend complained that small women can get away with busyness and fussiness not only in their clothing style but also in the way they move through life. My friend says that her size prohibits great physical gestures and posturing, something which she has noticed small women rely on to make a lasting impression and to get a point across. Big women, she thinks, are so self-conscious of their size that instead of using it they try to minimize it in their movements as well as in their style of dress.

I've seen big women carry off a flamboyant style wonderfully— enviably, in fact. In general, I'd say to let your self-consciousness be your guide. The moment you feel uncomfortable is the moment to rethink your style.

The small woman has more leeway in her style of dressing. She has more space around her to fill out. Some small women are conscious of the possibility that clothes with exaggerated lines, such as large collars or sleeves, may overpower them. Like the larger woman, the small woman may also tend toward a tailored, simple look. This is a perfect example of individual style. The small woman who dresses in frills and fuss—the busy look—will not necessarily emphasize her smallness. It may, in fact, work in her favor, and look just as marvelous as tailored, simple clothes look on another small woman.

Whether you're small or large, you must follow the same basic rule of fashion that everyone else does: let your self-awareness determine your style of dress. If your style is an outward expression of the way in which you see yourself, it's bound to work for you. But do try to see yourself as you really are. When we stand in front of a mirror, we may tend to construct our own interpretation of the image which is being reflected. It's important to take a step back to see yourself clearly. Only then can you determine what will look right on you and what you can do to bring out your best points. Don't give in to a mirror which promises to transform you, like some Snow White, with the help of this year's fashion.

WHAT TO WEAR WHEN YOU DON'T KNOW WHAT TO WEAR IN A NEW COMMUNITY

Moving into a new community may mean a new orientation in dress. A careful transition is not made without astute observation and possibly a little research. Take note of what people are wearing in your new community at restaurants, at the movies, even at the A&P. You can drive by the country club to see how people dress up for an evening out. Once you're tuned in to the general and acceptable manner of dress in your group, you can add a bit of your own style and flair to what's fashionable. Individuality is appreciated—but let it flourish within established custom.

Any effort to fit in is an important part of making friends in a new community. New friends and neighbors will be flattered by your attempt to conform to their dress and manners. If you're invited out and are still not sure of the style in which your new community dresses, your safest bet—for those who like to play it safe—would be something conservative. A long dress, perhaps, but one which is wool and in a neutral color, might do, or you can fall back on black and pearls, something understated so as not to compete with your host and others with whom you hope to form friendships. If you have a basic wardrobe, a simple dress or a pretty skirt and blouse will probably insure that you'll be dressed correctly.

Of course, a basic wardrobe will vary from one part of the country to another. Discover the mode in which to dress. You wouldn't want to appear in shorts at a picnic when all the other women were in pretty summer dresses. If you aren't sure what to wear for an occasion, simply ask: "Are you wearing a long dress or a short dress to dinner?" "Will jeans be all right for a barbecue?" Everyone is flattered to be asked for an opinion. The answer will probably be a complete report on what the other guests are likely to turn up in.

If you're going to shop for new clothes to go with your new move, you might ask a new friend to accompany you. One woman I know who had moved physically but not psychologically from New York to California invited a new friend to accompany her on a shopping expedition. Without the friend, who rejected all her initial choices as "too drab," she would, she claims, have ended up with another closetful of clothes smashing by New York standards but inappropriate to the California sunshine.

Going Out: Your Host Has the Answer

When I've been invited out and am not sure what to wear, I call my host and ask her what she'll be wearing. True, a host can wear anything, but her own choice will give me a guideline for how she expects her guests to dress. A general rule of thumb: if my host will be wearing a long at-home dress, then I know I can wear a short cocktail dress or a long skirt or long dress which is rather simple. If my host plans on wearing a silk evening dress, I know I can pull out all the stops.

If you're invited to a situation that's new for you, and you're anxious about what to wear, my advice is the same as in any other situation when you're anxious about your appearance: downplay your costume. Play it safe with conservative dress.

I remember one small dinner party to which I invited a young up-and-coming man in our office and his wife. She arrived dressed most appropriately in a long simple dress, with tiny gold earrings her only jewelry. Her husband, however, appeared rather too casual in a turtleneck sweater and a sports coat in a roomful of dark-suited men. This was a very small faux pas indeed, but since he was coming to the boss's house for dinner, he'd probably have felt more at ease if he'd blended in with the other male guests. (For more on what to wear to a party, see Chapter 2, "Entertaining.")

This particular man may not have called because he didn't think men should do so, or because he was nervous about asking the host when the host was his boss. Both reasons are silly. Men should follow the same basic rule as women, and that rule is simply: when in doubt, ask. As a host, I welcome such phone calls. I want my guests to be comfortable and I know that will happen only if they're comfortable in what they're wearing.

On the other hand, my guests know they needn't check with me for fear of offending me by showing up in something unsuitable. I appreciate a bit of difference and don't expect everyone to appear in uniform, especially when they aren't all members of the same regiment. Someone who is in the arts or in the designing end of the fashion industry won't dress like someone on Wall Street. Since my guest list mixes life styles, I expect a diversity of dress. Again, as long as my guests are comfortable, I'm comfortable.

WHAT THE HOST WEARS

You, as host, can dress completely differently from your guests if you wish, and much more elaborately. An exception is daytime entertaining, when the host generally dresses in the same mode as her guests. In the evening, a host can wear an at-home long skirt or dress or a silk at-home pajama pants outfit while her guests may be wearing street-length dresses or dressy slacks. You're the star of the evening, after all, so why not dress the part?

Men can also take advantage of our age of individuality and, if hosting, wear whatever pleases them without undue regard to what the male guests will be wearing. I remember a recent party in which the male host looked particularly distinguished as well as festive in a white peasant shirt with big, loose sleeves.

However, only some men feel unself-conscious enough about fashion and how they look to be able to appear gracefully in a costume. The idea that men have a place in the changing world of fashion and that men's fashion is any more intricate than a choice between black and brown shoes may still inhibit some men. Only those who feel at ease being ultrafashionable should attempt it.

While a woman who has taken the time to dress up is complimented, a man may run into friendly fire. "What did you have to
do to get that suit," I overheard one gray-flanneled man ask a
flamboyantly dressed business associate, "shoot Oscar Wilde?"

EVENING DRESS

I attend many formal occasions, and I've learned from observation that dressing up formally is probably the acid test of self-confidence. One recent premiere at the Metropolitan Opera, graced
with the most fashionable and elegant of women, stands out in my
mind. The orchestra seats rustled in waves of taffeta, silk and chiffon. The women making the waves were wearing clothes which
seemed to require constant adjustments. They were busy throughout the evening, pulling and straightening and tucking at their
clothes. I don't mean playing absent-mindedly with a necklace or
a collar, which, if done unself-consciously, reminds me of an elegant jungle cat's self-assured and imperious grooming; these
women obviously felt—and looked—awkward.

If you're not completely relaxed and comfortable with what
you're wearing, no matter how beautiful it looks when you're standing stock still in front of the mirror, the beautiful dress can be a
hindrance to your appearance instead of an enhancement.

Actors never appear in a costume until they have worn it
through several rehearsals so that they can move naturally and
easily; otherwise, the audience would never believe them. Avail
yourself of the same preparation. If you look marvelous in a new
but unfamiliar style, why not try wearing it at home a few times?
Of course, you can't wear it to Sunday-morning breakfast, you'll
have to create a setting worthy of costume, such as a party, but the
effort is worth it. Getting used to the dress in familiar surroundings
will help you overcome the urge to tuck or straighten once you're
out in public. Don't decide against buying a dress which might feel
a bit strange at first. The dress may require a little bit of getting
used to, but why not give it a try? An adventurous nature is part of
being well dressed. If you succeed, you'll have jumped a fashion
hurdle and will have conquered self-consciousness as well. And if
you don't, take heart that you've learned a little more about who
you are. The more you experiment, the more you'll learn and the
more fashion sense you'll have.

Wearing the Same Evening Gown

Ever since Rosalynn Carter wore the same dress to the Presidential Inauguration that she had worn to the gubernatorial inauguration four years earlier, no one has to worry about being seen in the same evening dress more than once. Good evening dresses stay in fashion for a very long time. I may not wear one dress for two or three years and find, when I try it on again, that it looks just as fashionable as when I bought it.

You can also spruce up an old evening dress with accessories. A sash or a shawl can alter your look significantly. I once borrowed a beautiful embroidered shawl from a friend to wear with a black evening dress. The shawl elicited more compliments than the dress did.

Black Tie

For men, black tie always means a dinner jacket or a tuxedo worn with a black bow tie. Dinner jackets change with the fashion. Some men may want to stick with the traditional dark-blue or black fine worsted. Others may opt for a plaid dinner jacket, or even a brocade. In summer, white is popular.

What a woman wears to a black-tie occasion depends on the custom in her community. It may be anything from a short dinner dress to a long, lavish gown. The elaborateness of your dress will follow the local pattern. If I'm going to a party which will be fairly dressy but not formal and I feel in a dressing-up mood, I might wear a dressy long dress, even if the men will be wearing suits. Dressing up is a compliment to your hosts.

Certainly, you can't dress below the level set by the invitation. So if the invitation reads black tie, honor it. In other words, gentlemen, don't try to get away with your charcoal-gray suit—and don't stay home either. If you don't own a dinner jacket, rent one. It's more economical and more convenient to rent than to buy if you don't have regular occasion to attend formal functions.

White Tie

If an invitation reads white tie, the men must wear a tailcoat and a white piqué tie. Women wear the most formal kind of dress in fashion at the moment. Although an occasional New York charity event may call for white tie, with the exception of old Fred Astaire movies white tie is almost never worn anymore.

HATS

Traditionally, a covered head was an expression of reverence; today a private audience with the Pope requires you to cover your head, as does a visit to Ascot. Almost every other function allows you freedom of choice in this regard. Since Vatican II, a hat is no longer required even in a Catholic church, so you can appropriately attend church, weddings and funerals unhatted. For those of us who don't look so ravishing in hats, this is good news. These days I wear a hat only to protect me from the cold, and, of course, only mad dogs and Englishmen would go out in the tropical noonday sun without a hat.

Women once resorted to hats to cover up hair that needed a wash and a set. But with today's simple haircuts and hair styles, coupled with the fact that women can now bring the paraphernalia of the beauty parlor into their homes and do their own professional styling, hats are fun—but not necessary. Hair is the thing—and no wonder. If a cover-up is needed, we can cover with hairpieces or wigs, which are sometimes more in fashion than our own hair. Hairpieces and wigs, which today look so natural, are not only fashionable but a lifesaver for the woman with thin hair, damaged hair or just too busy a schedule to fuss.

If you're wedded to hats and/or can't get the hang of a hairpiece or a wig, consider the turban. I like the kind you can wrap yourself. The already wrapped versions have a staid, off-the-counter feeling about them. Turbans and creatively wrapped scarves also need agility, but once you have the knack you'll use them often when your hair needs help and you're in a hurry.

TOUPEES FOR MEN

A man doesn't wear a toupee as a nobleman might have worn his powdered wig—because it is fashionable. Toupees are neither fashionable nor unfashionable. They are Biblical. A man who disguises his baldness is not so much demonstrating his vanity, a pardonable sin, as he is demonstrating his strength, à la Samson. This is a touchy topic, when so publicly acknowledged, and it is always public, because toupees are always noticeable. A toupee, more obvious than a balding head, takes away from a man's character. It makes him suspect. Why is he attempting to disguise the obvious? A woman, I think, can go in any direction of luxury, if she wants. Historically, she has that privilege. A man doesn't.

JEWELRY

One or two pieces of good jewelry—a pin, a necklace, a bracelet, a ring—can add to almost anything you're wearing. But, please, wear jewelry with discretion. Don't lose yourself behind too many bangles and baubles. For a black-tie dinner, I wear my good jewelry, diamond and emerald earrings and a ring. I don't try to dazzle the company with too much of a good thing, although I do know some women who do. They can't resist wearing everything at once. Even women with a decidedly large complement of precious jewelry may consider their jewelry more of a nuisance than an adornment. Because of high insurance rates and the possibility of theft, they lock away their real jewelry—the kind worth stealing— and wear fabulous costume jewelry in its stead.

Today's excellent costume jewelry gives every woman the opportunity to dress up in the evening. Although I don't suggest an Elizabeth Taylor impression, no one has to limit herself to a simple strand of pearls, considered good taste in the days when all jewelry was the real thing. Today you can wear costume jewelry *with* the real thing—and I doubt that many people could tell which was which. But wear both in moderation or you'll look like a Christmas tree.

If you have a matching set of jewelry: a necklace, earrings, bracelet or a ring, don't wear the set all at once. Break it up and wear the necklace with the ring and, perhaps the bracelet with the earrings.

GLOVES

Just as with hats, gloves play a small part in today's casual world. Gloves, which used to complete any costume worn for a social occasion and were removed only for eating, drinking and smoking, are rarely seen today. Brides are getting married without gloves, though the mother of the bride will probably be wearing them— old customs die hard.

I recently discovered that it's not just Americans—always the front-runners of casualness—who have discarded their gloves. I was invited to the Philippines to stay with President and Mrs. Marcos. On my one-day stopover in Los Angeles, I remembered to buy a pair of gloves, thinking I'd surely need them for evenings at the Presidential Palace. I needn't have bothered. Although dinners there were always in evening dress, only the footmen wore gloves.

If, like the mother of the bride, you do wish to wear gloves, you needn't prescribe to the once fashionable code of length: gloves to midarm or to elbow with dresses which have short sleeves or no sleeves. Nowadays, you can wear short gloves with any sleeve length. Older women can wear a longer glove if they'd like. Consider how your arms look and what length harmonizes best with the lines of the dress you're wearing.

Although it is perfectly appropriate to receive without gloves, it can be a sticky business shaking dozens and dozens of hands without them.

Gloves are no longer worn to most formal balls.

FURS

Furs can be worn anytime from November through April. Fur stoles are generally worn only in the evening. However, if you're attending a special lunch, a wedding, a reception or a similar day-time function, of course you can wear a fur stole or jacket.

Fake furs are a practical substitute for the real thing. Even people who have real furs also wear fake ones. People who are conservation-minded wear only fake fur, even though they might have owned or can afford to buy real fur. Although fake fur is fun, it's a sporty look and cannot compete with a really great-looking cloth coat for elegance.

A coat made from the fur of an animal which is in danger of becoming extinct is definitely not elegant.

17 SPORTS AND GAMES

Sporting events, some of mankind's oldest rituals, have been a part of every culture and every age, and today as in times past they present to us a microcosm of our social fabric. Sports are a pleasant way to stay fit, relax and have fun, but they also allow us a common ground on which to meet and communicate with others. Among many men and increasingly among women, a discussion of sports provides a way for us to come into close contact even with strangers. "Oh, do you play tennis, too?" or "Did you hear what happened today in the World Series?" can provide the opening to change a casual seatmate on an airplane or a stranger at a cocktail party into an enthusiastic conversationalist.

At one time it was fashionable for so-called intellectuals and women to pretend that sports didn't exist, but these days its almost impossible for us to come into contact with anyone who isn't a devotee of some kind of sport, either as a participant or as a spectator. From jogging and tennis to professional basketball and the Olympics, sports and sporting activities have become a common topic for discussion—and activity—for most Americans.

SPORTSMANSHIP

To fully appreciate any sporting activity, both participant and spectator should have a working knowledge of the game. But while each activity has its own rules, the general codes of common sense and common courtesy are always in effect. For instance, the unwritten rule that no player should talk or create any kind of disturbance when a golfer is readying himself for a swing (especially true on the putting green) is really a simple observance of common-sense courtesy—interrupting someone's concentration is impolite whatever the situation. The same is true in watching or playing tennis, or bridge or backgammon. The rules of courtesy apply in the same way they would in any other situation, and they are a reassuring guideline when a person finds himself suddenly in new and unfamiliar territory.

The essential factor in good sports manners is simply good sportsmanship. Sportsmanship, like courage, is merely grace under pressure. Though the anger of the loser is understandable, a transparent anger, such as throwing your tennis racquet, destroys not only the pleasure for the winner but also the pleasure for both participants in the game itself. Conversely, the exultant, gloating winner turns the joy of the game sour. The best sportsmen are those who compliment their opponent on his good play and let their own failures go undiscussed.

Another essential factor in sportsmanship is being on time. Particularly in cases where you have reserved court or tee-off time, you owe it to your opponents to be prompt.

Rules of sportsmanship—such as paying debts, playing straight, obeying the rules and not cheating—are never to be taken lightly. Even a bet placed casually may result in a debt; be prepared to pay immediately. And as for cheating, even the most honest are sometimes tempted, over a match point or a final putt, so make fun your top priority.

If you practice a sleight of hand it would be unwise to think that your opponent hasn't noticed. Though it may not be mentioned to your face, such untoward behavior will be acknowledged privately and perhaps talked about; it will certainly not be forgotten.

Interrupting the play to mention unsportsmanlike conduct to your opponent is not a good idea in that at best it will be embarrassing for both of you and at worst the discussion will disintegrate into a "You did," "I did not" argument. However, I do think an acknowledgment by the sportsman at the end of the game is not inappropriate, to let the other person know he hasn't gotten away with something. There are ways of letting your opponent know you did not miss his dishonesty. A simple "I thought that ball was in on that serve" will usually be enough. Your point cannot be recovered, but peace of mind will prevail.

To be a good opponent, you must first learn the rules of your game. To learn the rules of specific games you'll have to turn to books devoted to the subject. There are, however, some ground rules for both spectators and participants which fall into the common-sense-courtesy category.

SPECTATOR SPORTS

The subject of spectator behavior at sporting events has become a major topic in the sports pages of newspapers and magazines. Pictures of spectators tearing up the baseball field and carrying pieces of the sod home after a World Series victory, or bombarding a losing team—even a home team—with beer bottles and Cracker Jack boxes, have become common. For some reason, many Americans (not that this trend is confined to the United States; riots at soccer matches in Europe and South America have frequently resulted in injuries and even deaths) feel that the purchase of a ticket to a sporting event entitles them to take an active part in what happens on the field—or at times to take the field itself. Buying a ticket to watch the game doesn't give the purchaser the license to support mob rule and leave rational conduct at home.

Apart from such extreme behavior, there are still a few guidelines to follow so that you, and those seated near you, will thoroughly enjoy the occasion. If you must enter or leave your seat during the play, do so during a lull, so that you won't block your neighbors' vision. Similarly, don't rise every time a play gets exciting or exasperating; those behind you may not choose to follow suit. Many people hold their children up so that they can see better, which is also frustrating to others trying to concentrate on the game. This, again, is unfair and inconsiderate.

Observe the usual rules about smoking, if smoking. If you are permitted to smoke, ask the people seated near you if they would mind if you had a cigarette—but never a cigar. And if you do mind if someone smokes, it is perfectly acceptable to say so. Smokers are getting used to this.

There will be noise enough at the event, so don't play your transistor radio for company. (If you must, use an earplug, so that only you will hear.) If there is another event being aired and you are eager to hear the progression, do check with your neighbors. They may be interested in hearing as well, but you should not force your diversified interests upon them.

In a large stadium, it is more important to be comfortable, and warm or cool enough, than to look like a fashion plate. Dress accordingly. Sporting events are for informal fun. Other events, formal tennis matches or dinner in a racetrack clubhouse, may require dressier attire. Check on this in advance.

I think it's important to say a word about noise. Do cheer, by all means, in a large stadium and over an exciting play. A crowd roaring is part of the exhilaration of spectator events. Obscenities, however, aimed at your favored team, their opponents or even the referee, are always inappropriate. But save your shouts to cheer your team and not to jeer the opposition.

CHILDREN, PARENTS AND SPORTS

I've heard more than a few instances and I've been witness to a few more in which parents lose sight of the part which sports and healthy competition play in their children's lives. I once overheard, at a riding competition, a father berating his son by shouting that the boy had ridden much better that very morning at practice than he had during the event itself. This threw a shadow over the entire competition for all within hearing distance. Some parents behave as though their child's success at sports is related directly to their own success as parents. Sports are important for children for body building and for coordination, social skills and a healthy sense of competition. Winning is not the only thing to emphasize. If winning is the only thing, those who develop slowly will be sitting on the sidelines. As parents, instead of pushing your child to win, you should be teaching her that the fun is in the playing, and in cases where a child is bested a parent should encourage him to jump the net graciously. To all those frustrated parents who live out their victories and defeats through their children, may I suggest you organize a game of your own. The joys of the game as well as the disappointments are best experienced first hand.

TENNIS

Tennis Dress

Though tennis whites were until not so long ago the only acceptable attire on the court, today one may play tennis wearing colorful clothes. Men generally wear white or off-white shorts and a colored or white short-sleeved cotton-knit shirt. Women wear white or light-colored tennis dresses, skirts or shorts and shirt. White tennis clothes now are often trimmed with another brighter color, as are white tennis socks and sneakers or tennis shoes. At some clubs the all-white rule is still in force, so if you are visiting tennis-playing friends it is wise to check with them about court rules on attire. Actually, there is an aesthetic reason for tennis to be played in white clothes, particularly on hot summer afternoons. Colored shirts, particularly dark shades, show perspiration, and the player is apt to look more frazzled than he is even in the midst of a difficult match and ninety-degree heat. Wearing white, or white with colored trim, always looks neater and cooler. And don't try to look like a pro team player. Sequins and such are for show-business tennis.

Tennis Tips

In addition to the proper clothes, here are a few tips on court diplomacy and fair play:

A guest at a private court should offer to help maintain the court both before the game and after. A court takes a lot of raking, rolling, lining and weeding to keep it in top playing condition.

Remember to bring at least three new balls to each tennis date.

Keep your side of the court clear of balls at all times, and return them to the server after a point has been scored.

Return balls which have appeared from neighboring courts as soon as there is a pause in your, and their, game.

When serving, announce the score before you serve. Miscalculations can then be ironed out immediately.

Don't argue about a call you think is inaccurate. The person closest to the line where the ball went out of bounds (or stayed in) is responsible for the call.

Weekends are busy times on most courts. At especially crowded times when weekend rules do not prevail, responsibility is with those on the courts. Singles players should finish their game and invite a pair of waiting players to play doubles, or they may play three sets of singles at most before playing doubles or leaving the courts to let those waiting have a chance. For those who are waiting to play: It's up to the players already occupying the court to invite you to play, so don't ask to join. It's up to you to accept or decline. And since you've watched your prospective hosts play, don't say yes if your game is much weaker or stronger than theirs.

Tennis is a quiet game for players and spectators alike. There's little chatter on the court even in the most casual of circumstances, since the game is so strenuous and playing takes every ounce of energy and concentration. Spectators are equally silent so as not to distract the players.

Doubles Diplomacy

If you've never played with your partner, decide before the game which area each of you will cover.

Don't complain about your partner's playing.

If you're the better player, it's better to be asked advice than to simply volunteer it.

If your playing isn't up to your partner's, ask for pointers. You owe it to your partner to play the best game you can, and here's your chance to improve.

Don't poach. Let your partner take the shots which are his, even if you know you'll win the point if you step in.

GOLF

There are three things which are almost unbearably irritating to golfers: golfers who fail to take good care of the course, golfers who dawdle along, golfers who pretend that the rules don't exist. There are few rules governing the golfer's attire. Just be comfortable, and allow plenty of room in your clothing to swing properly. Do bring the proper equipment with you on the course (even if you have to rent). Caddies are usually tipped after the eighteenth hole is finished and the foursome is on the way to the clubhouse. However, if you've forgotten to bring money onto the course, you can give the tip to the caddiemaster later; just be sure to specify which caddie served you. (Adding a good word about the caddie if appropriate will be appreciated.) If you're a guest, pay the greens fee and your caddie's fee, unless you are also a member of a golf club, in which case you need only repay your host by inviting him as your guest. At a club where members sign for the greens fee, a guest pays both caddies' fees. If in either case your host makes a point of stopping you, it is your duty to stand firm and pay. Be sure to discuss any bet you may place well in advance of teeing off. A polite bet is almost a custom in the game of golf, and even if you're not a hard-core bettor do not be surprised or offended when the subject arises. Your handicap, and your opponents', will start you off on even ground—but you never have to agree to betting more than you care to.

SAILING AND BOATING

If you're asked for an afternoon or weekend on a sailboat or a motor yacht, the degree of formality of dress will be set by your host, but no matter what you'll be wearing, you'll always need soft-soled shoes so that you don't slip and fall. A boat, regardless of size or type, is designed with economy of space as the prime concern. Accommodations are cramped on a boat, which makes it doubly difficult and doubly important that nonsailors stay out of the way when the crew is working. Those who don't know the first thing about sailing are not expected to pitch in with the work (although the nonsailor is certainly welcome in the galley and should certainly offer to help with the cleanup chores). The need for precision and alacrity in the tasks involved is apt to turn the most mild-mannered on-shore captain into a martinet on the water.

Even though you're not a sailor, if your hosts take their sailing seriously it's advisable for you to learn the specialized vocabulary of boating. Spend an evening with a good book on sailing or motorboating. Your hosts will appreciate your interest and you'll have more fun if you can understand the mechanics of the sport.

The cramped quarters on a boat make it essential that you as a guest put the comfort of the other boaters ahead of your own. Tempers flare easily on a boat, and remember, you're a long way from shore. If you think you may get seasick, bring along appropriate medication (available without prescription in a drugstore) and bear it as best you can. Your host is not expected to head for shore at the first sign of your squeamishness. Expect that sleeping arrangements and personal facilities will be a bit crowded. You may even be bunking with a total stranger. Be courteous about monopolizing the facilities—now is not the time to try to achieve a new hair style with your blow-dryer. Another good idea is to bring along plenty of reading material, as during an extended sail everyone needs a chance for quiet time. (I like to also bring a surprise—a magnetic game, or a book of crossword puzzles for everyone to share—which comes in especially handy during a storm, when the group is gathered in the cabin.) And just one more caution: the sun is much stronger when it is reflected off the water. Do bring plenty of sunscreen lotion.

SKIING

Though I've skiied with several young skiers who wear their blue jeans onto the slopes, I think if you're over twenty-five you might prefer clothes made with skiing in mind. With the new synthetic fibers has come a revolution in ski clothes. The clothes are lightweight and very warm as well as extremely flattering. I do have one word of warning for beginners: though you should take special care to equip yourself with the proper clothes, calling attention to oneself in the perfect chocolate-brown one-piece jumpsuit before you've learned to ski is looked upon with derision by others gliding effortlessly down the slopes and is generally considered a breach of good fashion sense. So don't go high fashion until you've mastered the christie. What to pack for après-ski? Informality predominates in ski resorts; sweaters and slacks or long skirts are always appropriate.

Those just learning to ski must keep in mind that there are a number of rules which are in practice to insure the safety of all. Beginners may not immediately recognize certain precautions:

On a ski tow or lift don't jump off in such an abrupt manner as to cause the lift to swing back and injure a fellow skier.

After a fall, smooth out the indentations your fall made in the snow. Irregularities in the snow can cause accidents.

For your safety, and that of others, ski the trails which are your speed. Don't wear a long scarf. It could get caught on the lift and you'll end up like Isadora Duncan.

Skiing is both a solitary and a social activity. If you are skiing with friends who are more experienced skiers, insist that they have some time to ski on their own on the more advanced slopes. No skier likes to spend the entire day on the bunny hill, no matter how much he likes his friend. By the same token, if the experienced skier is acting as host, do feel free to leave your beginner friend to practice the snowplow turn—and don't feel any guilt about it.

Another word to the ski host. You are not expected to entertain elaborately. Make it clear to your guests that the fun will be informal. Just have plenty of good hot food—and good ski conditions —and your guests will be wonderfully contented. The host may also want to have an extra pair of ski mittens and a few pairs of extra socks on hand; your guest may not have anticipated how cold it gets on the slopes. And even if you're not a big breakfast eater, plan ahead to serve something hot (or to have the guests make it themselves), since for most skiers the start of a good long skiing day is a good breakfast.

CROSS-COUNTRY SKIING

Just as skiing is growing in popularity, so cross-country skiing is drawing new enthusiasts every winter. This is a sport that requires more strength than skill. It's slower than downhill skiing, and more strenuous: the cross-country skier propels herself without the aid of those sloping hills. Devotees will talk of the different kind of exhilaration that comes not from speed but from feeling the body in motion and being able to stop and observe the untouched wintertime landscape.

Cross-country skiing can be done by anyone, anywhere. Even in New York, along Park Avenue and in Central Park, I have seen cross-country (or cross-city) skiers making the most of a snowfall. Dress is more casual and less codified for this type of skiing. Wear layers of clothing which can be removed as the sun gets higher or your work more difficult; the quilted vest you shed at noon may be a godsend at four o'clock. In a cross-country tour, one member of the party (this may be the most proficient member) will bring along a backpack of some sort. This can hold hot drinks, simple first-aid supplies, a flashlight, and a map or a compass if you are headed into territory that is unmarked.

Listen carefully to the weather reports, and plan accordingly. Bear in mind, when charting your course, that long distance will be difficult to traverse for the less experienced. If you are out to break last year's record, do so with skiers whose abilities match yours. If your route will run across private property, make sure that you check in advance to see that you will be welcome as guests and not blocked by fences or no-trespassing signs.

HORSEBACK RIDING

Riding is one of the most tradition-bound of all participant sports. Here is one of the few remaining areas of modern life where clothing—proper clothing—is vital to social acceptance as well as to safety and comfort. A proper costume for a beginner would include breeches or jodhpurs, boots, a black or tweed riding coat and perhaps a riding vest, a shirt or turtleneck sweater and gloves. A hard hat is essential for safety and is also correct riding wear. The dress for riding in a Western saddle is informal: boots, well-washed jeans (not stiff new ones) and a hat.

There are certain basic points of good manners. Always treat a horse with care, consideration and common sense. It is your responsibility to make sure its tack is clean, comfortable and properly fitted, and you should take the time to acquaint yourself with the animal before mounting. Do not gallop a horse or jump it unless the owner says you can (and only then if you know how). Don't let the horse get too hot or take it over rough or stony ground at a fast pace. If the horse ever gets hot, walk it back to the stable slowly until it's cool and dry, and don't let it drink. When out riding, always pass another rider by asking permission first, then going past slowly. When riding with others, warn your companions if you are going to trot or canter. Keep to the same side of a bridle path or trail as you would if driving a car, and give other riders plenty of room in case your horse shies or kicks. Before riding at a strange stable or riding establishment, ask what the rules are. Don't ride over other people's land without permission, and if you can't control your horse, walk it home before you hurt yourself. Tip grooms, and usually tip riding instructors, unless they own the stable. It you want to tip the horse, give it a carrot broken into bite-size pieces, not sugar.

JOGGING

A recent poll shows that some twenty-four million Americans are jogging, making this our fastest-growing sport today. What's appealing about the sport is that it can be done anywhere, at any time, and that in time and cost its requirements are minimal. Wear whatever is most comfortable (unless, of course, you are racing and a special T-shirt is required), but all runners do agree that to cushion the feet and legs, and to prevent shin splints, the purchase of proper running shoes is essential. Shoes are also a psychological boost, as once you have a fancy pair of jogging shoes in your closet you will feel compelled to use them!

Most joggers prefer to go it alone, to set their own pace and keep their own time, but if you're running with a friend don't feel awkward about running ahead—or lagging behind—if you're not in the same shape as your companion. Runners don't talk much as they run (on crowded tracks, even a hello is rare); you'll have plenty of time to converse after you've finished.

Joggers should be considerate and give the right of way to pedestrians, unless a track has been set up specifically for joggers, in which case the courtesy is reversed. Similarly, don't, as a jogger, run down the middle of a bicycle path or a road—stick to the curb and obey all pertaining laws, for safety as well as courtesy's sake. Pedestrians and passengers in cars passing by should accord the same courtesies to joggers—no catcalls or jeers, please. Runners have become an attractive part of our landscape, and if you'd like to greet them a friendly wave is all that is necessary.

CARDS

The rules of card games must of course be thoroughly learned by beginners. I will impart some general information on card playing:

Find out about the stakes before you accept an invitation to play. Don't play when you can't afford to. Instead, offer a forthright "The stakes are too rich for my blood."

Settle up your debt immediately. Just because it hasn't been mentioned, don't think the winner hasn't noticed that you've neglected to pay. It's not the winner's responsibility to ask.

Don't pit yourself against experts if you're a novice. To those putting together players for a card game: ask about the ability of each new player. All those playing together should have roughly the same level of expertise. To new players: tell the truth about your ability. It's as bad to mask your ability behind a Sergeant Bilko façade as it is to let on that you're a better player than you really are. In either case, you'll be found out as soon as you sit down to play.

A card player as great as Ely Culbertson feels that the cards have a life of their own, and a winning (and mannered) player will never abuse them. That means don't slam them down, crimp the corners, bend the edges or the like. Not only is it bad manners, but the cards may end up getting back at you.

If you're losing, do so quietly. Don't try to amend each loss with an excuse.

Refrain from telling others what they did wrong in the last hand just as you'll refrain from criticizing your partner or apologizing for your own play. In other words, let the cards come and go, and don't try to bring a dead hand to life.

Don't keep up a running monologue throughout the game. Serious players don't want their concentration interrupted—or their tempers tried. Additionally, avoid all mannerisms that might be irritating to other players. Exaggerated facial expressions, gasps and other signs of disapproval are always unwelcome. Drumming on the table, clanging bracelets and unnecessary fidgeting are also distracting to others at the table.

Bridge

There are two kinds of bridge players: the casual, or afternoon, player, and the serious player whose game always comes before any of the social amenities the casual player enjoys. Hosting a bridge party of either kind is relatively simple. Be sure to have two (preferably new) packs of cards, four score pads and the most up-to-date rule book you can find. Play in an open, well-lighted area, providing comfortable seating, ashtrays if necessary, coasters for the glasses and, if you'd like, a bowl of candy or nuts for munching. Don't ever try to serve your dessert during the game—the table is for playing, not for eating.

It's very important in bridge to set up the games so that players are of equal ability; this is not the time to repay social obligations. If a game is organized at the spur of the moment, each player appropriated for the game should be honest about her level of play. If these levels are not equal, and you decide to play anyway (serious players may consider this a bad idea), then no one should be criticized or made to feel that an apology is necessary; just make sure that the game takes on a social tone.

Play quickly; plan your strategy at the outset of the hand and don't deliberate over each play. Such grave thinking is for tournament play only. And don't monopolize the bidding, even if your partner is much the weaker player. Remember, you have agreed to play, so play graciously. Even the dummy hand in bridge is a participating one, and the dummy shouldn't leave the table to wander around. The dummy has duties, primarily to watch the play to protect her partner against revoking. You may organize the dummy hand or place it closer to your partner, but don't ease individual cards closer to his hand. Never play out of turn or act as if you're intending to. It is also frowned upon by good players to assume too much by throwing down your remaining hand too early. But if you must, lay the cards down so that they are all visible in order that the other players may see your cards or challenge your conclusions. Finally, always give at least one rubber's warning when you want to call it quits, whether it's a money game or not. This is considered fair, even if you are the big winner.

BACKGAMMON

Backgammon has been around for centuries, and today it's more popular than ever. Travel sets and magnetic boards make it possible to play anywhere—and its alluring combination of luck and skill makes it possible for even a top player to enjoy a game with someone who has just mastered the fundamentals. Do, from the start, memorize the opening moves. These are for the most part standard and will get you off to a fair start when you're playing with a stronger player. And know the board; don't count out each move—this simply isn't done.

Backgammon games are played quickly—another reason to avoid counting each bar as you go—and, because of this, games are played in relative silence, as strict concentration is required. Each player rolls her dice on one side of the board only, so that the dice never intermingle. Cocked dice, dice that land somewhere other than flat on the player's side of the board, require that the player roll again. Each move is made with one hand, so that the other player and any spectators can fully view the exact play. A play is never over until the player picks up his dice, and the opponent should never roll (or shake her dice cup to indicate such an intent) until the first player has done so. It is customary for the loser to concede before the end of the game, but he should never do so if the possibility of a gammon or a backgammon is still in question. Players may agree to a draw, but only if they adjust the value shown on the doubling cube to what they both agree will be the probable outcome of the game.

18 TRAVEL

BY SHIP

Bon Voyage

Some ships no longer permit visitors on board, because of security reasons. If you're sailing on a ship which does allow bon-voyage parties, the party may be held either in the voyager's stateroom or in one of the lounges or bars on the ship. If you expect a crowd to see you off, make arrangements after boarding with the bar steward or your cabin steward for hors d'oeuvres, ice and glasses to be sent in. Liquor can be bought by the bottle from the bar.

What to Wear

When on board ship, dress as you would at an elegant resort hotel. Some shipping lines are dressier than others; short cruises are by and large less formal than long ones—a cruise around the world, for instance, is a gala event—and cruise ships are more informal than transatlantic liners. You can contact the steamship line after you make your reservations or ask your travel agent what clothes would be appropriate. In cabin class, evening dress is optional; in tourist class, evening dress is not required. Many ships are classless today, and you may dress formally on special evenings if you wish.

A first-class transatlantic crossing used to mean evening clothes at night, as it was the posh way to travel. In fact, the word "posh" derived from first-class steamship travel. It is said to be an acronym standing for "port out, starboard home." Shipboard dress today, even in first class, is not so formal as it used to be. While those in first class may still wear evening clothes (with the exception of the first night out, Sunday evening and the last night out), business suits for men and dresses or evening pantsuits for women are also appropriate. The night of the captain's party one does wear evening clothes.

In the public rooms aboard ship, wear informal clothes, but never a bathing suit. When you're not sure what to wear for certain occasions, ask the purser. He is essentially the ship's manager, and his office will help you with any questions or complaints.

Meals

After you come on board, see the chief steward in the dining room to make arrangements for your meals. There are two seatings for meals. The first seating is generally for families; the second seating is more companionable and leisurely. You may be assigned to a table with strangers, in which case the table becomes one social group during meals. However, unless you're sitting at the captain's table or an officer's table you need not wait for everyone to arrive before you order. If you are seated at an officer's table, arrive promptly—he will—and order only after the officer has arrived. If you're unhappy with your table there is a possibility that the steward can reassign you to another. Do not suggest a transfer if you're at the captain's table, as such an assignment is considered an honor.

Deck Chairs

The deck steward will assign you a deck chair. If you find that the person in the neighboring chair is unsociable or too sociable, ask the steward to assign another chair to you.

What to Call the Officers

The captain is addressed as "Captain Blye." Officers are addressed as "Mr. Christian."

A Caveat Regarding Fellow Passengers

Part of the fun of ship travel is making new friends on board. However, don't be overexuberant about making fast friends immediately. You may find that first impressions aren't always accurate after your friends have stuck fast.

Tipping

Your cabin steward and your dining-room steward are tipped at the end of the voyage. The total amount of the tip should be based on a tip of two dollars or two-fifty a day for each.

When you tip, keep your accommodations in mind. If you have a suite you'll tip your steward more than if you're sharing a room.

Bar and lounge stewards are tipped fifteen to twenty percent of each bill.

Ship's officers are professionals and are therefore never tipped.

Cruise ships generally have a list of tipping suggestions which may be obtained at the purser's office.

The porters who take your luggage aboard are employed by the steamship line; however, they expect a tip from you. Since you're traveling by ship, you'll probably have quite a bit of luggage. So you should tip approximately five dollars. If you travel like a maharaja, you'll have to tip like one.

AMERICAN TRAIN TRAVEL

If you travel overnight by train in the United States you'll almost surely be traveling by Amtrak. Today's typical Pullman car has six bedrooms, each sleeping two people. (The word "Pullman" is still used for sleeping cars. A man named Pullman invented the concept of the sleeping car, and the Pullman Standard Company at one time built them all.) Each bedroom has a bathroom and a closet. You may also travel in a roomette, which is a single bedroom equipped with a seat and a fold-down bed, or a slumbercoach, which is the most economical sleeping accommodation. When you travel long distances by train, take only as much luggage as will comfortably fit in your bedroom. The rest of your baggage can be checked through to the baggage car.

Ask the sleeping-car attendant to make up your bed no later than eleven, as he can't be expected to be a night owl if you are. A sleeping-car attendant is tipped a minimum of one dollar for each person on an overnight trip. If he has been especially attentive he should be tipped accordingly.

To begin an overnight journey, report to the car you've reserved and to the sleeping-car attendant who will be stationed there. Assistance with baggage is available from redcap attendants at most major stations. Though redcap attendants are employees of the railroad, they are tipped approximately twenty-five cents for each bag, and take into consideration how long a walk it was to the train. Don't give your baggage to anyone who offers to help except to a redcap. He knows how and where to locate your train and your car. A well-meaning free-lance porter may help you begin your Florida vacation on the way to Chicago. More to the point, a redcap won't walk (or run) off with your luggage.

The Dining Car

When sitting with strangers or new traveling companions in the dining car, each person receives a separate check. Dining-car waiters and bar stewards are tipped fifteen to twenty percent of your check.

Smoking

Smoking is permitted in club, café, lounge and sleeping cars and in other areas specifically identified as smoking areas on all Amtrak trains. Pipe and cigar smoking is permitted only when the entire car is designated as a smoking area. Smoking is not permitted in any other car, including full-service dining cars.

EUROPEAN TRAIN TRAVEL

The espionage films of the 1940s made European overnight train travel as renowned as it was notorious. Today, the slouch hats and the trench coats have gone with the era, and accommodations are up to date. European trains offer two types of sleeping accommodations: couchettes and sleepers. The couchette is a second-class accommodation. There are six people in each compartment. At night, the seats are converted into bunks and the conductor makes up each bunk with a pillow, a sheet and a blanket. Because men and women share the couchette, you should wear wrinkle-free clothes when you travel, as you'll be sleeping in them. In France and Italy one may also reserve a first-class couchette. The only difference between first and second class is that in first class there are only four bunks to a compartment. The sleeper, a private cabin with one or two beds, is the more expensive overnight way to travel. A tourist-class sleeper offers a double or triple bedroom. The toilet in all European trains is at the end of the car. Sinks are installed in every sleeping compartment.

Tip the man who makes up your bed the equivalent of one dollar per person a night.

The Dining Car

The dining car on a European train has two seatings. Make arrangements for your meals with the maître d' after you board the train; he'll assign you to a table. The dining car is open to all traveling classes on the train.

TRAVELING BY PLANE

When entering the airport, tip your porter fifty cents for each bag. In developing countries you'll often find an addition to the usual airport cost: a man who takes the baggage from the porter and puts it on the scales for the airport attendant. He receive a tip of about fifty cents.

As plane travel is by necessity light and extras at the last moment will cause more problems than delight, bring good cheer and wishes to an airport bon voyage, but don't bring gifts. If you want to give a friends a special sendoff you may have a bottle of champagne or other wine delivered to the plane in care of the passengers' name, and the flight attendant will surprise your friend in flight by serving your gift. Don't forget to include with the present a card bearing your name.

While on Board

If you find yourself with a loquacious seat mate and you're not in the mood for a chat, just say, "I'm sorry, but I've a lot of work (sleep, reading) to catch up on." Or for you aerophobes, "I'm a white-knuckle flyer and my concentration can't be broken, as it's keeping the plane in the air."

If you do feel like talking, test out the responsiveness of your traveling companion with a general opener such as "Are you traveling for business or pleasure?" If you're answered in a monosyllable, take the hint and don't persevere.

Other considerations to adhere to while in flight:

Never smoke in the nonsmoking section of the airplane.

Always look in back of you before reclining your chair, as it can score a direct hit to the knees of the person sitting directly behind you. Similarly, don't recline your seat just after a meal, as the passenger behind you may still be eating and your seat shooting back may cause his Jell-O to end up in his lap.

Children on Planes

The flight attendant will warm a bottle or baby food for you and should have disposable diapers on hand should you run out of them. Though parents change diapers without a second thought, think twice when traveling. Don't change diapers at your seat (unless the ride is bumpy) while others are eating; go to the bathroom to do so. Never hand the flight attendant a dirty diaper or dispose of one by putting it into the seat pocket. (For more on traveling with children, see Chapter 10, "Children.")

Consideration Regarding Arrivals and Departures

When visiting friends, plan your arrival and departure times to fit in with your host's schedule. If your flight does arrive at midnight, offer to take the limousine service, a bus or a taxi from the airport.

DRIVING

Driving is one instance where consideration and goodwill have a sizably larger impact than promulgating your charm and likability would have in less practical, more social situations. Failing to be courteous behind the wheel is a liability to your safety and the safety of others—your lack of courtesy may have lethal consequences. Your consideration will serve to keep you calm in times of stress when those not so well-mannered may otherwise goad you to near-apoplexy. Your cool head will make you a careful and therefore a better and safer driver.

A Hired Car and Driver

Drivers of hired limousines are tipped about ten percent of the cost of the car rental. Drivers of airline limousines aren't tipped at all.

European travelers may decide to hire a car and a driver to tour the countryside. The cost will include the driver's meals and accommodations. Some drivers make excellent guides, and you may find their expertise invaluable even in restaurants ordering dishes indigenous to the region. If you get on well together, you may wish to share meals with your driver. At the conclusion of your tour, tip the driver ten percent of the rental.

HOTELS

Hotels offer various types of accommodations. Under the American plan your room plus all three meals are included; a modified American plan includes your room and two meals a day, generally breakfast and dinner; the Continental plan includes your room and breakfast, either a European breakfast of rolls, butter, jam and coffee or tea or an American breakfast. In a European plan, prices quoted are only for your accommodations; meals aren't included.

If you're making hotel reservations yourself, do so by letter or cable as far in advance as possible. Include the number of rooms you'd like, the number of people in your party (many hotels have family rates whereby children can share a room with an adult at a sizable discount), your time of arrival and approximately how long you will stay. If you're not sure how long your stay will be, give the maximum number of days you're likely to stay, as it may be difficult to extend your reservations during a busy season. When telephoning for reservations, ask for a written confirmation. For reservations abroad, specify whether you'd like a private bath and whether you'd prefer air-conditioning. Write in English unless you are fluent in another language; otherwise your linguistic mistakes may cause havoc with your reservations. Always bring your confirmation with you to safeguard yourself against possible hotel error. If you do have a confirmation and the hotel has no record of your reservation and no available rooms, the desk clerk will try to find you a room in a hotel of similar quality.

If you are unhappy with your room, don't complain to the man who has accompanied you to the room with your luggage, as he hasn't the authority to help you. Rather, call the manager to register your complaint firmly but politely. Unless you have arrived at the peak of the season or in the midst of a large convention, he should be able to assign you to another room directly.

Checking In

Sign your name to the register, Geraldine Smithers or Gerald Smithers. If you're traveling with your spouse, Mr. and Mrs. or both names if you prefer. In Europe sign Mr. and Mrs., since Ms. is unheard of. If you'd like to blaze the trail, sign Ms., though it may go unnoticed; you'll be doing your bit to change the custom. When traveling with children, write "and family" after your name. Register separately by name others who are traveling with you. Older children may also be registered separately so that they will be listed at the desk and therefore will be able to receive mail and messages.

Pilfering

It seems axiomatic that a guest in a hotel or restaurant does not leave with ashtrays, towels or silverware. However, stealing is so prevalent in some hotels and restaurants that people seem to think

just because some do it, the hotel expects it. The hotel abhors it.
One superhotel in Las Vegas has resorted to only plain glass ashtrays in all its public and private rooms, which has solved its problem of theft.

Particulars Regarding European Hotels

THE CONCIERGE

In European hotels the concierge provides innumerable services. He handles mail, sightseeing, travel reservations and car
rentals. He'll also recommend restaurants and shops and even arrange for a baby-sitter. The concierge presents his own bill at the
end of your stay. However, one tips him for each service he provides. For instance, if he obtains theater tickets for you or makes
travel arrangements, your tip would be from fifty cents to a dollar.
Though most services he provides are chargeable ones—getting
stamps, for instance—many are not. When he makes a dinner
reservation for you at a charming restaurant you never would have
found in the guidebooks, that is not a chargeable service and he
should be tipped about a dollar for his trouble. If your stay is more
than just a day or two and your contact with the concierge is
considerable enough for him to greet you by name as you pass in
and out, tip him a few dollars at the end of your stay, especially if
you plan to return and will desire his help in the future.

THE SERVICE CHARGE

The service charge in European hotels and restaurants is generally about ten percent of the bill but may be as high as twenty
percent. The service charge is distributed among employees.
When the service charge is ten percent you're still expected to tip
about five percent to bring the tipping total up to the usual fifteen
percent. When you arrive in a hotel, find out if there is a service
charge so that you won't undertip or overtip during your stay.

THE BATH

When your bath is separate from your room, reserve a time with
the maid for your bath. She'll run the bath and give you a towel
and the key to the bathroom. You may be charged extra for each
bath.

TIPPING

In Hotels (in Addition to the Service Charge, if Any)

Bellboys take your bags at the desk when you check in and accompany you to your room. Tip the bellboy about fifty cents for each bag and an extra fifty cents for turning on lights in the room and opening the window—essentially for showing you hotel hospitality.

The chambermaid is not a personal maid, so remember to take care of your own things—hang up clothes and put away your toilet articles and makeup. Tip the chambermaid from twenty-five to fifty cents for each small service she performs for you, or you may give her about two dollars per person per week. When you check out you may give her the money in person or leave it in a marked envelope in the room or, safer yet, at the desk.

The doorman at the hotel should be tipped fifty cents for each bag if he takes your luggage into the hotel and twenty-five cents if he calls a taxi for you.

The headwaiter in your hotel is tipped about five dollars when you take your first meal there if you expect to use the dining room often and if you want a special table or other special service. A headwaiter should be tipped approximately five dollars a week if you've asked for lots of extras, and two or three dollars a week if you have required little service.

The waiter receives five percent of the check when there's a service charge and fifteen to twenty percent when there isn't.

The room-service waiter also receives fifteen to twenty percent of your bill. Your tip is in addition to the room-service charge.

Miscellaneous Tipping

Theater ushers in France and England are tipped the equivalent of twenty-five cents when they show you to your seat.

On a bus tour one should always tip the guide, about seventy-five cents for a half-day tour. However, what often happens is that as the passengers file out of the bus the first passenger doesn't tip and those in line tend to follow the leader's example. Therefore this is one service which is sorely undertipped. As you leave the bus, remember to leave your tip, and at least those in back of you will probably fall into step.

WHAT TO WEAR WHEN TRAVELING

When traveling it's best to wear basically what you wear at home. Your style is your own and travels with you. You're apt to feel uncomfortable in a brand-new "travel wardrobe" bought with only drip-dry and wrinkle-free in mind. Today's fiber blends are surprisingly easy to care for, even when you're on the road. And you don't need to travel with trunks of clothes. Even on a tour, when the same people in the same clothes see each other every day, you're all in the same boat, so don't worry about it. Traveling means clothes economy. You might try accessorizing a much-worn outfit with a new belt or scarf or a new pair of dangling attention-diverting earrings.

Do pack some traditional clothes, especially if you're planning to visit developing countries. Friends of mine traveling in Africa were most surprised when they reached the Malawi border and were told that women were not allowed to wear slacks and that their dresses must cover their knees and men were not to wear bell-bottomed trousers. Conversely, situations and places which you'd think would adhere to the most traditional forms of dress may surprise you. A traveler in Russia had taken great pains to shop for an elegant dinner dress to wear to the Bolshoi Ballet, only to discover when she arrived at the ballet that people come to the Bolshoi directly from their work; the audience was composed of many in suits and dresses coming from the office and just as many in overalls coming from the factory.

TRAVELING WITH A FRIEND OR A LOVER

Traveling with another person—friend or lover—is one of the supreme tests of a relationship. Your trip may be a most joyful and exciting experience which draws you closer to each other, or so much togetherness in a strange land with no familiar places or faces to act as buffers may turn out to be the deciding factor in an unworkable relationship. Michelle and Robert spent months planning what was to be a one-year trip through Africa. They began their excursion in North Africa. A seclusive ten-day drive through the Sahara turned out to be a revelation, after which Michelle and Robert divided their laundry and Michelle was on the first plane home. The setting was an apocalypse for Michelle. I'm retelling this story to illustrate that even the best-laid plans may go awry. In order to be as cautious as possible, if you will be traveling with someone whom you don't know very well, it's best to discuss thoroughly your plans and your likes and dislikes before you set off. To circumnavigate some unpleasant surprises, decide who will pay for what beforehand. Don't forget to include tipping. Is your friend a big tipper while you're watching your every lira? Discuss whether or not you plan to do *everything* together—take every meal and every sightseeing trip *à deux*. Traveling intensifies any relationship, as your friendship is the one constant in a sea of unfamiliarity and it can become cloying. It may be best to spend at least an occasional morning sightseeing on your own. Before you buy your tickets, ask yourself do you have similar interests—in other words, do you have the same vacation in mind? If you're mainly interested in the night life of the big city and your friend has plans for daily excursions to little fishing villages, you'd better find out before you get there or you'll soon be going in different directions.

Be sure the type of vacation you plan is to *your* liking. Fred and Paula used to take skiing vacations in the Alps, until Paula realized she was spending her hard-earned money and hard-earned vacation time only to please Fred. He loved to ski. She began by trying to like it and ended by loathing it. Before their relationship schussed downhill, Paula confessed her feelings to Fred. For their last vacation they spent one week skiing and another week prowling museums and restaurants in Paris—a compromise which pleased them both.

AN UNMARRIED COUPLE SHARING A HOTEL ROOM IN A FOREIGN COUNTRY

In many countries it is no longer required that guests surrender their passports at the hotel desk. Whether or not the hotel clerk asks for your passports, it's best to sign the register, Count Vronsky and Anna Karenina (Ingrid Bergman and Roberto Rossellini); register as two people with different names who will be sharing a room. In any cosmopolitan area you'll almost surely be given a room together. In Eastern Europe, in Africa and in rural areas in Europe or South America you may be asked to take separate rooms. In Malawi friends witnessed an unmarried couple turned away at the border. To avoid a drama, make at least some of your reservations in advance and check beforehand to learn whether an unmarried couple may share a room.

A WOMAN TRAVELING ALONE

Penny, a veteran traveler, says her search for high adventure brings with it her love of traveling alone. She likes the freedom of going where she wants when she wants and doing what she wants when she gets there. Penny didn't begin gradually with solitary weekend trips. On her first trip alone she traveled through Africa. Her words of advice and encouragement: If you want to do something, do it. Don't let self-consciousness and the inhibitions imposed by society stop you. Penny is specific about the kind of trip and adventures a woman traveling by herself generally finds. Pick a place which offers sights and a way of life you are excited about, and plan your adventures for the daytime. If you're chiefly interested in night life, she suggests you travel with a friend, as a woman alone is socially restrained from sampling night life to any great degree and she can't be sure that in her travels she'll meet a congenial group who will share evenings out.

When traveling alone, don't be afraid to talk to people. They are generally delighted to be of help to a stranger in their city, and you may even make a new friend. One traveler stopped a man on the street in Boston to ask directions, and when he discovered she was a first-time visitor to his city he spent the afternoon showing her the town. You needn't restrict your friendly forays to single people. Couples who are traveling are interested in meeting new people just as much as single travelers are.

If you have just met a man or a couple at a restaurant or café it's best to pay for your own cocktail or dinner. Travelers are generally on a fairly tight budget, and it's unfair to take advantage of your status as a single woman. Liberation may cost you a bit more, but you'll find it's worth it to keep on an equal footing.

Dining Alone

A woman may always eat in a restaurant at one of the better hotels in a city or town. When picking out a restaurant in a smaller town, keep to the ones on the main streets, unless one has been specially recommended. A rule of thumb: the better the restaurant, the better you'll be treated. Make a reservation beforehand. If you're refused or discouraged—one woman was told when phoning one of San Francisco's most famous restaurants that they would honor a single reservation for six o'clock or eleven o'clock only—ask to speak with the maître d' or the owner and call them on their discriminatory practices. If, unhappily, they won't be budged, you'll at least have time to make other plans. A woman may eat lunch almost anywhere and, if she'd like to meet fellow travelers, take tea in an outdoor café.

(For more on eating in a restaurant alone, see Chapter 1, "Everyday Manners in Public Places.")

Bars

If a woman alone would like a cocktail before dinner, she should pick a bar which offers tables. Sitting at a bar alone is still, I'm afraid, a man's prerogative, unless you choose a "singles" bar at which all customers may sit alone at the bar. You may also sit at a bar on board ship or in the club car of a train.

MONEY ABROAD

When traveling abroad, don't treat the money of the country you are visiting as though it is a joke. To you it may seem like play money: it isn't, though its value and look are different from your own. It is insulting to your host country to denigrate their monetary system. In doing so you are implying that their economy is worthless.

TAKING PHOTOGRAPHS ABROAD

Ask before you take a photograph of someone. Though it's easy to just snap the shutter, in doing so you may offend people who don't want to be characterized as "colorful locals." Asking permission demonstrates that you are a gracious and considerate guest. In the Mideast it's best not to take pictures of the women, since many Muslim women are in purdah, which means they are to be secluded from public observation. For instance in Saudi Arabia women aren't even allowed to drive, and Saudi justice for women is Biblical: the penalty for adultery for women is death by stoning.

THE LANGUAGE

Try to learn at least a few words of the language of the country you're visiting. Even when many people you meet speak English almost as fluently as you do, your attempt at their language demonstrates your interest and willingness to learn about your host country.

SMOKING ABROAD

When at the table with people from another country, refrain from smoking until after the last course has been finished. In most countries smoking between courses is certainly frowned upon, if not unthinkable. In Muslim countries you may have to get along without smoking at all at meals. The Koran forbids smoking and drinking, and while some Muslim countries do not abide strictly by this rule, others, such as Saudi Arabia and other countries in the Arabian Peninsula, follow it to the letter.

BARGAINING

Bargaining in flea markets and bazaars abroad is an art. For those to whom bargaining does not come easily there are a few general rules to help you get started and to make sure you end up with a fair deal. Don't opt out of the bargaining and accept the first price offered; that's not playing by the rules. You'll only confuse the seller, and you won't end up with a bargain, which is why you're shopping in the bazaar in the first place. To begin with: when the seller gives you a price, counter with about thirty percent of his offer. The outcome, after a few more rounds of bids, should be somewhere near the middle of the original asking price, about sixty percent of what the seller suggested in the first place. If in a certain instance you're not sure whether bargaining is appropriate, say, "It's beautiful, but I really can't spend more than twenty-five dollars." Either you'll be shown something less expensive or the game is on.

ADAPTING TO NEW CUSTOMS ABROAD

When you travel, you are essentially the guest in a foreign country. You are the one with the curious customs. Don't be offended if your openness is not returned in kind, as it is an almost singularly American characteristic, which is appreciated, if silently. When you're in doubt as to what to do in certain circumstances, ask. Your questions indicate your courtesy and your attempts to be a considerate guest. In a country whose customs are considerably different from those you are used to, put your self-consciousness aside. If you're feasting with Bedouins, follow their lead and go ahead and eat with your (right) hand. Don't just observe but let your travels broaden your experience.

Shaking Hands

In Europe, shaking hands is the universal greeting. Men on occasion still gallantly kiss a woman's hand, but don't count on it. A woman should extend her hand in the usual manner and not offer up limp fingers waiting to be kissed. A man faced with such an offering will do better to shake the hand lightly rather than attempt a kiss if he isn't used to the gesture.

Confoundingly, what is considered acceptable behavior in one part of the world is rude in another. For example, in Belgium friends shake hands each time they meet and take leave of one another even though they may meet several times in one day. In India people do not shake hands, as touching another person is considered rude; however, it is a sign of good manners to take a personal interest in another, so don't be surprised if you're asked about your family, your job or other personal matters.

Forms of Address

First names are used rarely at first, second or even third meetings. In northern Europe even the title of Mr., Mrs., or Miss often isn't formal enough. In Germany I once overheard a man receiving change on a bus address the conductor as "Mr. Chief Conductor," as apparently "Conductor" or even "Mr. Conductor" would not have been enough. By the same token, lawyers are addressed as "the honorable lawyer" and doctors as "Mr. Doctor" or "Mrs." or "Miss Doctor." Though you won't be expected to know the fine points, this gives you some indication of the formality expected. It may seem stodgy to us, but to northern Europeans to forgo the titles would be a breach in formality and would seem peculiarly out of place.

Conversation

The people of your host country set the style of the conversation and the level of formality regarding forms of address and topics of discussion. Wait and listen before you jump in with a personal story when others are still talking small talk. Temper your conversation with sensitivity to your surroundings and location; don't air your feelings about international oil politics in the Mideast, though the subject need not necessarily be taboo. You may ask questions regarding a topic as long as they aren't designed to put anybody on the defensive. Questions must be asked out of genuine curiosity and not out of attempts at one-upmanship.

Toasts

Toasting people's health, wealth and well-being, and almost anything else for that matter, is very European. In Eastern Europe there is an inordinate amount of toasting at meals, so wait before you take the first sip of your drink. In Western Europe toasts are given only at fairly formal functions. At a friendly, informal gathering you may drink without hesitation—unless, of course, you'd like to offer a toast.

Being Entertained in a Private Home

Europeans by and large don't invite casual friends into their homes as Americans do. A European's house is the family sanctuary, though the farther north you travel the less this rule applies. In Scandinavia and Germany you are more likely to be entertained in private homes than you are in southern Europe, where your host is apt to entertain you in a restaurant.

European at-home entertaining is not as casual as it is in the United States. If you are invited to dinner at home, as a rule you should bring flowers or send them the next day. If you present flowers to your host when you arrive, they should make a simple arrangement. A host has no time to create an elaborate decoration with guests already present. A thoughtful gesture is to send flowers the day of the party to save your host the trouble of arranging them when guests have begun to arrive, yet affording your host flowers to add to the party atmosphere.

A European house does offer the same informality as an American home in that you may speak with anyone at the party whom you would like to. Strangers do not need an introduction when under the same roof.

(For letters of introduction, see Chapter 6, "Correspondence.")

Think Twice Before You Say No

Whether you're invited to a private house or a coffeehouse, it may be considered an insult if you refuse. In Finland, for instance, you're being complimented if you're asked to a sauna, and refusing the invitation would be insulting to your host. Similarly, in Greece, if you're asked to drink coffee in a café, a refusal is taken as an affront. Refusing an offered drink may also be viewed with disfavor. A friend who visited Saudi Arabia reported that he almost drowned in coffee—tiny cups were filled and refilled, no-thank-you's weren't acknowledged—until a kind soul took pity on him and explained that to say no convincingly one must almost imperceptibly jiggle one's cup as the coffee is offered. My friend was also warned never to sit with one ankle resting on the other knee, as to put forth the bottom of your shoe for all to see is considered to be an extreme insult.

Punctuality

An American traveler must learn to be patient abroad. In America promptness is taken for granted, as it is in Europe as well; eight o'clock means just that. (In Germany eight o'clock means 7:55.) In many other countries, however, time is not of the essence, and an agreement to meet at eight o'clock could very well mean nine or nine-thirty. In Latin America, in Eastern Europe and in the Mideast you may try to clarify exactly what time your appointment will take place by stating, "I'll be there punctually at eight o'clock." Your new acquaintance will probably nod and say, "So will I," but don't count on it. The exchange may have been nothing more than a formality. Since you can't be sure, as the guest you must arrive promptly and be prepared to wait.

Patience

Americans are always in a hurry. In other countries getting things done may seem to you to take an inordinate amount of time. In many parts of the world people take the small disturbances of life in their stride and in their good time. Your patience and politeness are important in such times of strain, since you're the guest and essentially must do things your host's way, possibly delivering a polite and hesitant American push to keep things moving, but nothing more drastic or obvious than that.

TRAVELING IN EASTERN EUROPE

Those small disturbances of life, from mailing a letter to making a phone call, will be about ten times more disturbing, complicated and time-consuming than you are used to. Be patient and persevere. When you ask for help with a small task, the answer to your question will invariably be no. Insist politely. After several nos and several more maybes (a couple of packs of chewing gum or a pack of cigarettes has been known to decrease the maybes) you'll eventually receive a yes, so don't despair, patience is rewarded. One encouraging hint: the more Western the country, Rumania for instance, the less red tape you'll run into.

19 PETS

HOSTS AND THEIR PETS

The basic rules for a dog are few: no jumping up, no begging at the table, and learning to walk on a leash. A polite dog in our crowded cities and small apartments is a must. Though you may love little Pepper no matter what he does, other people won't. He must be taught to behave so that he'll be popular with those in his world—visitors and neighbors.

When you are entertaining a visitor who is allergic to animals or who doesn't like them, as eccentric as that might seem to you, even a polite pet is better shut in another room or left outside for the time being. The visitor who is allergic or averse to pets should tell her host; otherwise, a visit spent with a feared animal present will be unpleasant indeed for both host and guests.

Cats, especially, seem to jump into the laps of those who like them least. And cats, to those who don't know them and love them as you do, may appear unpredictable and startling. Put the cat in another room during the visit; otherwise your guest will be anxiously glancing over her shoulder in search of the enemy.

TO VISITORS

Don't encourage the bad habits of a pet. Don't feed a pet when you're at the table, or slap your thigh to encourage a dog to jump up. Refrain from inviting a dog to share the cushion on the couch with you until you ask your host if such behavior is allowed.

TO OVERNIGHT GUESTS

Even if your host and your dog are already great pals, don't ask to bring him. Remember, their friendship is based on your turf. Your pet should accompany you on an overnight visit only if he has been specifically invited, or if you're the proud owner of a dog as impeccably trained as Rin Tin Tin. Animals in strange houses may act strangely. Sweet gentle Spot may take a nip at your host's Queen Anne chair, sweep the Dresden figurines off the coffee table with one wag of his tail, or just generally harass your host with his doglike behavior.

WHEN A GUEST ASKS TO BRING A PET

If a guest asks to bring a pet and you would prefer the guest did not, say simply, "I'd rather you didn't bring Bijou. I'm not used to having dogs in the house. Although I love him on his own territory he'd make me uneasy if he invaded mine."

PETS AND NEIGHBORS

A dog must also be well-behaved in the neighborhood. If Goldie's fondest wish is to dig in Mr. Small's newly planted garden every spring—or all summer—keep her on a leash or fenced in at home. The owner of a dog who is destructive in any way to neighbors' property or to neighbors themselves should apologize in person or by letter, offer to repair (or replant) the damage if possible, and, most important, take every precaution not to let the transgression happen again.

Neighbors can be driven to distraction by incessant barking. The hour-after-hour barking can transform the most mild-mannered neighbor into a red-eyed vigilante, fists clenched and threatening. If yours is a watchdog who warns you about each passing car or moth on the back-door screen, reassurance can be the cure. A puppy who thinks he hears a noise in the basement should be taken and shown that there is nothing there. An older dog who barks often and at nothing should be scolded. A dog who barks when he is alone might be cured if you leave on the radio or the TV for company; it's worth a try.

Your dog is your responsibility. You can't expect others to make allowances for his behavior if it isn't within the limits of the norm. (By norm I mean nondestructive play and low-decible and infrequent vocalization.) Just as children are often seen as the mirror of their parents, pets, it's often remarked upon, seem to take on the characteristics of their owners.

CITY DOGS

In New York City a law passed in August 1978 insists that dog owners clean up after their pets, which I think is the only satisfactory solution in a city crowded with dogs and people.

In other urban areas which have not passed specific laws the dog lovers and the dog nonlovers are engaged in an ongoing struggle. One side is represented by dog owners who neither curb their dogs (this euphemism means simply that dogs should relieve themselves only off the curb, in the gutter) nor put them on a leash—they just love them. On the other side are advocates who won't rest until they see a legally dog-free city. While I think those who choose to keep a dog in the city should be allowed to do so, they should not be permitted to abdicate the attendant responsibility. Dogs on the street in the city should be kept on a leash at all times. People have the right to go unmolested by a hostile (or overly friendly) dog; other dogs have that right, too. (In New York City it's also against the law for a dog *not* to be on a leash.) City dog owners must also curb their dogs. I've witnessed an incident in a large American city when a pedestrian took it upon himself to reprimand a dog owner who had not bothered to curb his pet. The dog owner accused his assailant of being rude and a meddler. At this point I chimed in in defense of the pedestrian. Any dog owner who is so frivolous or lazy as to assume that personal convenience takes priority over public cleanliness must be corrected by the public—you and me —if necessary.

LEAVING YOUR PET IN THE CARE OF FRIENDS

To you, your dog may be the most perfect and adorable snookums, without flaw. Before you arrange to have a friend or an acquaintance look after Snookums for you, it's time for an honest appraisal of your pet's behavior and his reaction to strangers. To leave friends with a less than fairly well-behaved pet is selfish and most thoughtless. Kennel fees are a lower price to pay than the loss of a friendship, which is just what happened to Imogene and her husband, Ivan. Buttons, Imogene's friend assured her, was the most warmhearted and amiable of English bull terriers. Since Imogene's friends were going on a winter cruise, they would be delighted to have Imogene, Ivan and the baby spend Christmas week in their house in the Caribbean. All Imogene and Ivan had to do was look after Buttons, who they were afraid could never adjust to the rigors of kennel life. Ivan and Imogene's airport taxi pulled up to the beautiful house overlooking a tropical sea on Christmas Day. The first thing which caught their eye was a six-foot-high chain-link fence surrounding the yard, which should also have been their first clue. Imogene stepped from the car and sat the baby down on the front steps while she helped carry luggage to the house. Their first sight of Buttons was a white blur in the yard hurling itself against the fence in the direction of the front steps and the baby. Close up, they saw that Buttons' teeth, set in an overshot jaw, were sharp as wire cutters. He was pacified only by the disappearance of the baby and the appearance of his second-favorite thing to eat: kidney and horsemeat stew, carefully chopped and simmered. (The care and feeding of Buttons were explained in a lengthy note left by the absentee owner/hosts.) Imogene, Ivan and the baby spent their Christmas week in a hotel, keeping vigil on Buttons and his meals and his general well-being. They kept their word. (I would have sent him to a kennel.) A friendship and what could have been a glorious vacation were spoiled by a pet owner's blind love.

20 OFFICIAL PROTOCOL

THE MEANING OF OFFICIAL PROTOCOL

The Office of the Chief of Protocol of the U.S. Department of State has described protocol as the body of accepted practices which has grown up among the nations in the course of their contacts with one another; it is the recognized system of international courtesy. The need for an international standard of behavior has been made evident in the course of history. In the eighteenth century at a court ball in London, the French and Russian ambassadors quarreled violently over their respective places at the table. They were then obliged to resolve their quarrel with swords, and the Russian ambassador was wounded in the duel. Though disagreement over places at the table today would be improbable cause for an international incident, common procedures and practices have developed which reflect the mutual respect and consideration one nation shows another.

Though the style of the White House depends on the President who is living there—Jefferson and Lincoln were noted for their unpretentiousness and simplicity, and John Kennedy for his elegance and international style—protocol remains the same.

Washington hosts pay close attention to precedence and the formality often required by official protocol. Who sits above the salt or below the salt is determined by a set of unbendable rules. When entertaining officials, it's important to observe the distinctions if you don't want to offend your guests who are used to having their position acknowledged.

PRECEDENCE

Title and position are given precedence; age has no bearing on rank. The wife of an official takes her husband's rank if he is present, and the husband of an official similarly takes his wife's rank. A woman who holds her own official rank would be seated according to her own position, if invited by herself. If invited with her husband, she is seated according to his rank. Many disagree with this solution and believe that any woman holding an official position should outrank women who are wives of ranking men; however, the above rules still stand.

Protocol does not recognize as a couple the man and woman who live together but aren't married. A man or a woman living with an official is not accorded the official's rank. If the partner of the official is invited, each is seated as though they were single.

At Dinner

Those present who are of higher rank than the guest of honor are given precedence at the table and take the place of honor to the right of the guest.

In American homes, foreign guests have precedence over Americans of comparable rank, with the exception of an American ambassador. It's a good idea in each situation to let any guests who are not seated according to precedence know in advance in order to avoid any misunderstanding.

INTRODUCTIONS

Always introduce officials by using the correct form of address. The President and the Vice President are always addressed as "Mr. President" and "Mr. Vice President." In a conversation of any length, the address may be varied with "sir." The wife of the President is addressed by her husband's surname, i.e., as "Mrs. Roosevelt." A governor is "Governor Clinton" or "Governor." An ambassador is "Mr. Ambassador" or "Madame Ambassador." Members of the Cabinet, "Mr. Secretary." A male official is announced before his wife and may even precede her into the room, though generally he will step aside to let her go first.

(For forms of address to be used in correspondence as well as introductions, see the "Forms of Address" table in Chapter 6, "Correspondence.")

TITLES AND PLACE CARDS

Use formal introduction forms on place cards. When only one person holds a title you need not include the surname, for instance "The President," "The Chief Justice," "The Secretary of the Interior." However, you may write instead "Chief Justice Burger," which sounds less starched. When more than one person holds the title, write "Mr. Justice Marshall," "Governor Clinton." Place cards for royalty may be written to include the title or the name, "The Duchess of Leicester" or "Lady Elizabeth Crouch."

SMOKING AT THE TABLE

Though Americans do sometimes smoke in between courses, this is not the case in many other countries. At an official diplomatic function, even if cigarettes and ashtrays are on the table, wait for some signal from your host before you begin smoking before the meal is finished.

AFTER DINNER

At many official functions the sexes are still separated after dinner. This I think is an old-fashioned and today unworkable practice. What of the woman ambassador and other women in official positions, plus the countless women today who are extremely knowledgeable about politics, economics and world problems and contribute meaningfully to the conversation?

At private parties the guest of honor is expected to stay until all the other guests have gone. At official parties the rule is reversed: no one leaves before the guest of honor, if he or she is also the ranking official.

Questions regarding official protocol will be answered by the

Office of the Chief of Protocol, Ceremonial Division, U.S. Department of State, 2201 C Street, Washington, D.C. 20520.

AN INVITATION TO THE WHITE HOUSE

Formal Invitations, Acceptances and Regrets

A formal invitation from the White House is answered by hand on plain or engraved personal stationery. An engraved invitation means black tie, unless white tie is specified. The answer should be sent within a day of receiving the invitation.

A formal acceptance:

> *Mr. and Mrs. Karl Langsam*
> *have the honor of accepting*
> *the kind invitation of*
> *the President and Mrs. Roosevelt*
> *to dinner*
> *on Thursday, the twenty-fifth of September,*
> *at eight o'clock.*

There are only four reasons for not accepting a White House invitation: illness, travel, a death in the family or a family wedding. When you regret a White House invitation, include the reason:

> *Mr. and Mrs. Karl Langsam*
> *regret that owing to the illness*
> *of Mr. Langsam*
> *they will be unable to accept*
> *the very kind invitation of the President and Mrs. Roosevelt*
> *to dinner*
> *on Thursday, the twenty-fifth of September,*
> *at eight o'clock.*

Or:

> *. . . regret*
> *that owing to the recent death*
> *of Mrs. Langsam's mother . . .*

Or:

> *. . . regret*
> *that owing to the wedding*
> *of their son . . .*

Or:

> *. . . regret*
> *that owing to the absence in Berlin*
> *of Mr. Langsam . . .*

Informal Invitations, Acceptances and Regrets

The social secretary of the President or the First Lady will write, telephone or cable an informal invitation. When you answer, follow the same form as the invitation. If your answer is written it could be on personal writing paper. Reply yourself, don't have your secretary reply for you, and answer within a day of receiving the invitation.

An invitation to lunch will read:

> *Dear Mrs. Langsam:*
> *Mrs. Roosevelt hopes you'll be able to lunch with her at the White House on Tuesday, September twenty-third, at one o'clock.*
>
> > *Yours truly,*
> > *[Signature]*
> > *Secretary to Mrs. Roosevelt*

Your acceptance:

> *Dear Mrs. ____:*
> *Would you be kind enough to tell Mrs. Roosevelt that I would be happy to lunch at the White House on Tuesday, September twenty-third, at one o'clock.*
> *With many thanks,*
>
> > *Sincerely,*

An informal invitation to dinner:

> *Dear Mrs. Langsam:*
> *The President and Mrs. Roosevelt have asked me to invite you and Mr. Langsam to dinner at the White House on Thursday, the twenty-fifth of September, at eight o'clock, black tie.*
>
>
>
> *Yours truly,*
> *[Signature]*
> *Secretary to the President*
>
>

Your acceptance (the wife traditionally handles all social correspondence, and this is a most traditional event):

> *Dear Mrs. Roosevelt:*
> *My husband and I shall be delighted to accept the kind invitation of the President and Mrs. Roosevelt to dinner at the White House on Thursday, the twenty-fifth of September, at eight o'clock.*
> *With many thanks,*
>
>
>
> *Sincerely,*
>
>

Your regrets to an informal White House invitation:

> *Dear Mrs. Roosevelt:*
> *I regret that I will be unable to accept [or: that my husband and I will be unable to accept] the kind invitation of the President and Mrs. Roosevelt to lunch at the White House on the twenty-fifth of September, as I will be in London at that time.*
> *With many thanks,*
>
>
>
> *Sincerely,*
>
>

What to Wear to the White House

At formal receptions or dinners, guests wear evening clothes—black tie—unless white tie is specified. (See Chapter 16, "Fashion," for distinctions between white tie and black tie.) Gloves are no longer obligatory for women; however, if the invitation states "white tie" and a woman's evening dress is sleeveless she wears long elbow-length gloves. Gloves are not removed when going through the receiving line, but one never eats or drinks with gloves on.

At a formal afternoon reception men wear dark suits and women wear afternoon dresses.

At formal and informal lunches men wear dark suits amd women wear dresses with sleeves, or suits.

At the White House Gate

Arrive at the gate about fifteen minutes early. Your name will have been given to the guard and will be checked. At the door of the White House you will be directed to the room in which guests are gathering.

The Receiving Line

The President and the First Lady aren't present while guests assemble. Just before the President comes in, aides will have arranged guests in the order they will be received. The President, the First Lady and the guests of honor will then enter and form a receiving line. In an official receiving line the husband precedes his wife in the line, gives his name and then presents his wife, "This is my wife." When being presented, just say "How do you do" or "Good evening, Mr. President" as you shake hands, and nothing more. Guests go directly into the dining room after the receiving line. If the dinner is a fairly small one, there will not be a receiving line. The President and his wife will walk around the room shaking hands with each guest.

After Dinner at the White House

After dinner, the President, the First Lady and the guests of honor rise and, followed by the other guests, enter the reception room. Guests remain standing until the President and his wife are seated. When the President and the First Lady leave the gathering to escort the guests of honor to the front door of the White House, perhaps saying good night to a few of the other guests on their way out, this is the signal for other guests to depart. Guests do not leave before the President.

Thank-You Notes

Write a thank-you note to the First Lady after your visit. You needn't write if your visit was to a large reception or a similar gathering.

Large Receptions at the White House

If you're invited to a large reception you may send your regrets with no explanation. At such a large gathering there is sometimes a receiving line and sometimes not. The President and the First Lady may be present or someone else may be designated as the official host. If the President is there don't leave before he does. If, however, he stays only briefly you may leave whenever you'd like. At a large reception you may talk with anyone who seems approachable, just as you would at any large party.

PRESENTS TO THE WHITE HOUSE

If you'd like to give a present to the President you must first clear it with an aide. Don't bring any surprises, since this is against security regulations. If you want to send something, again, clear it with an aide or the President may never receive your gift.

A BUSINESS MEETING WITH THE PRESIDENT

Request to see the President through a presidential aide or through your congressman. Arrive a few minutes ahead of time. Before your meeting begins, you'll be told by an aide how much time you'll have.

When the President or a member of his family is leaving or entering the White House, you'll hear a buzzer sounding. If you're in the corridor you'll be asked to step behind a closed door. This is a White House security measure.

THE AMERICAN FLAG

Below are listed the existing rules and customs pertaining to the display and use of the American flag.

The flag may be flown every day from sunrise to sunset. It may also be displayed at night on special occasions. The flag should be hoisted briskly to the top of the mast and lowered ceremoniously.

The flag should be displayed on all days when the weather permits, especially on New Year's Day, January 1; Inauguration Day, January 20; Lincoln's Birthday, February 12; Washington's Birthday, February 22; Army Day, April 6; Easter Sunday (variable); Mother's Day, second Sunday in May; Memorial Day (half staff until noon), May 30; Flag Day, June 14; Independence Day, July 4; Labor Day, first Monday in September; Constitution Day, September 17; Columbus Day, October 12; Navy Day, October 27; Veterans' Day, November 11; Thanksgiving Day, fourth Thursday in November; Christmas Day, December 25; such other days as may be proclaimed by the President of the United States; the birthdays of states (dates of admission); on state holidays.

When other national flags are flown with the American flag, they should be flown to the left of the American flag. The American flag is always flown farthest to its own right (the observer's left). All the flags should be flown at the same height and be approximately the same size. When flown with other flags, the American flag should be hoisted first and lowered last.

When flown with flags of cities, states or associations, the American flag should be the center and on a larger staff than the others.

When flown on crossed staffs with another flag, the American flag is on the right, staff in front.

When flown on the same halyard with other flags, the American flag is always at the peak.

When flown in a street, the flag should be hung with the blue field to the north in an east–west street or to the east in a north–south street.

When the flag is displayed from a staff projecting horizontally or at an angle from the windowsill or balcony or front of a building, the blue field should be placed at the peak of the staff, unless the flag is at half staff.

On parades, the flag is carried at marchers' right when other flags are carried, too, or it may be carried in the center out in front.

On a speaking platform the flag is hung flat above and behind the speaker or it may be flown from a staff to the speaker's right on the platform. The flag is never used to cover a table or a desk.

When used to cover a casket, the blue field should be at the head and over the left shoulder. The flag is not lowered into the grave.

When flown at half mast, first hoist the flag to the top and then immediately lower it to half-mast position. The flag should be again raised to the peak before it is lowered for the day.

When the flag is displayed on a car, the staff should be fixed to the chassis or clamped to the radiator cap.

On Memorial Day the flag is flown at half mast until noon and is then hoisted to the top of the mast until sunset.

A flag is flown upside down only as a distress signal.

The flag should not touch the ground or water.

When a salute to the flag is given, men and women stand with hands over their hearts or at their sides.

During the Pledge of Allegiance one stands and may repeat the words or just stand quietly.

THE NATIONAL ANTHEM

One stands during the playing of "The Star-Spangled Banner" or the national anthem of a foreign country. If you're on your way to your seat at, say, a sports event, stop and wait until the national anthem is finished.

INDEX